In our culture, the practice of apologetics has moved from being a "boutique" topic for specialists to being a requirement for even having a conversation with one's neighbor. Joshua Chatraw and Mark Allen have produced the most comprehensive, accessible, and up-to-date manual on Christian apologetics that I know of. Despite how full its treatment of the subject, it is eminently readable. The authors present all the various approaches to apologetics respectfully, proposing their own pathway that incorporates a large range of insights from many disciplines and thinkers. Highly recommended.

TIM KELLER, pastor emeritus, the Redeemer Presbyterian Churches of New York City

One of the best books about apologetics I've read. It offers a compelling vision for the place of apologetics in the life of individual believers and the church, drawing on the rich wisdom of the Christian past and the best recent approaches to the apologetic task. This book will both enrich the lives of Christians and help them defend and commend their faith in today's complex world.

ALISTER E. MCGRATH, professor of science and religion, University of Oxford, and director, Ian Ramsey Centre for Science and Religion

Just when you think this book is the comprehensive apologetics textbook you've been looking for—covering Scripture, history, philosophy, and culture—you realize it's also something more: a creative, original proposal for an "inside-out" apologetic that is precisely what we need in our secular age. If you're skittish about "apologetics," like I am, this book will show you another way.

JAMES K. A. SMITH, professor of philosophy, Calvin College, and author of *You Are What You Love* and *How (Not) to Be Secular*

This is a welcome addition to the library of books on apologetics. It is also a rare book: most defenses of the faith do not make the gospel their lodestar and template. This one breaks new ground in letting the reason for the Christian hope—Jesus crucified and risen—guide and govern the forms and methods of faith's defense. *Apologetics at the Cross* incorporates biblical materials, the history of apologetics, and theology to make a cumulative case for the church as a socially embodied cruciform argument whose members are alert to how different people may need to be shown various different paths (i.e., kinds of arguments) that lead to, and into, the reality of the gospel. This is a book brim full of apologetic wisdom—most notably, the wisdom of the cross.

KEVIN J. VANHOOZER, research professor of systematic theology, Trinity Evangelical Divinity School

Imagine a book on apologetics that not only deals with content, but discusses tone and heart, is gentle and wise, and overviews method and approach with care and balance. That is *Apologetics at the Cross*. Not only does it walk through the common questions; it orients one to the different ways people think and relate to those issues. Here is a book that does apologetics with depth, not just of the mind, but of the soul.

DARRELL BOCK, executive director for cultural engagement, Center for Christian Leadership and Cultural Engagement, Dallas Theological Seminary

Drawing on key biblical themes and the best of the Christian tradition, Josh Chatraw and Mark Allen have provided readers with a much-needed work for those looking to think more deeply about the Christian faith and the importance of Christian apologetics for our post-Christian world. This creatively written volume offers an unapologetic commitment to the gospel message, skillful analysis of a wide-ranging survey of the field of apologetics, and a helpful introduction to contextualization through the lens of the cross. *Apologetics at the Cross* not only informs and educates, but also points toward authentic witness and faithful living. Students, pastors, and church leaders will be strengthened by this outstanding resource, which serves as a trusted compass that people will not only read, but to which they will likely turn again and again for guidance. Highly recommended!

DAVID S. DOCKERY, president, Trinity International University/
Trinity Evangelical Divinity School

For many Christians, if we're going to be honest, to picture ourselves "defending the faith" is almost like imagining perpetrating an act of mental abuse on the unsuspecting. But more often than not, we feel this way because we've inherited outdated, culturally insensitive models for apologetics. I love this book by Joshua Chatraw and Mark Allen, not because it says, "This is exactly how you do apologetics," but, much more helpfully, because it provides a map for applying key principles within a culturally sensitive framework. If this is an area you struggle with, read it—and learn!

NICHOLAS PERRIN, chair of biblical studies, Wheaton Graduate School

This book lives up to its title and then delivers even more. It shows us in a general way what a cross-shaped way of defending the faith looks like and then gets specific with relevant and engaging cultural analysis to help us understand the moment in which we are called to be faithful. This is a book with wisdom to ponder and suggestions to practice, one to return to again and again for insight and clarity.

TREVIN WAX, Bible and reference publisher, Broadman and Holman,
and author of *Eschatological Discipleship* and *This Is Our Time*

Apologetics at the Cross offers a compelling Christ-centered vision for what a Christian apologetic ought to be—rooted in the humility of the cross and born out of the endurance of a suffering church. Joshua Chatraw and Mark Allen have a gift for making complex ideas clear and ancient ideas accessible as they situate contemporary apologetic approaches in the light of their biblical and historical antecedents. They demonstrate the rich and diverse tradition of apologetics we have to draw from and how relevant that tradition remains today. With a balanced and insightful treatment of apologetic methodologies and much practical wisdom for treating those who are skeptical as persons rather than projects, *Apologetics at the Cross* is an ideal resource for anyone seeking to winsomely and compassionately engage today's culture with the gospel of Jesus Christ.

JO VITALE, dean of studies, Zacharias Institute, and apologist, RZIM

textbook*plus*⁺

Equipping Instructors and Students with
FREE RESOURCES *for Core Zondervan Textbooks*

Available Resources for Apologetics at the Cross

Teaching Resources

- Instructor's manual
- Presentation slides
- Chapter quizzes
- Midterm and final exams
- Sample syllabus

Study Resources

- Quizzes
- Flashcards
- Exam study guides

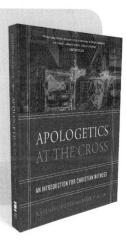

*How To Access Resources

- Go to www.ZondervanAcademic.com
- Click "Sign Up" button and complete registration process
- Find books using search field or browse using discipline categories
- Click "Teaching Resources" or "Study Resources" tab once you get to book page to access resources

⋯⋯⋯⋯⋯⋯⋯⋯⋯➤ *www.ZondervanAcademic.com*

APOLOGETICS AT THE CROSS

AN INTRODUCTION FOR CHRISTIAN WITNESS

JOSHUA D. CHATRAW

MARK D. ALLEN

ZONDERVAN
ACADEMIC

ZONDERVAN ACADEMIC

Apologetics at the Cross
Copyright © 2018 by Joshua D. Chatraw and Mark D. Allen

ISBN 978-0-310-52472-4 (ebook)

ISBN 978-0-310-56628-1 (audio)

Requests for information should be addressed to:
Zondervan, *3900 Sparks Dr. SE, Grand Rapids, Michigan 49546*

Library of Congress Cataloging-in-Publication Data

Names: Chatraw, Josh, author. | Allen, Mark D. (Mark Dwayne), 1961- author.
Title: Apologetics at the cross : an introduction for Christian witness in late modernism /
    Joshua D. Chatraw, Mark D. Allen.
Description: Grand Rapids, MI : Zondervan, [2018] | Includes bibliographical references.
Identifiers: LCCN 2017043825 | ISBN 9780310524687 (hardcover)
Subjects: LCSH: Apologetics. | Witness bearing (Christianity)
Classification: LCC BT1103 C.463 2018 | DDC LC record available at https://lccn.loc.gov/2017043825

Cover design: Brian Bobel
Cover photo: Shutterstock
Interior design: Kait Lamphere

Printed in the United States of America

19 20 21 22 23 24 25 26 27 28 29 /LSCC/ 21 20 19 18 17 16 15 14 13 12 11 10 9 8 7 6 5 4

For my first gospel mentors,
Mom and Dad.

JOSH

For Karen, with heartfelt appreciation.
Your cruciform life witnesses every day
to the gospel's reality.

MARK

CONTENTS

PART 3:
The Practice of Apologetics at the Cross

ABBREVIATIONS

BIBLE BOOKS

Gen	Genesis	Amos	Amos
Exod	Exodus	Obad	Obadiah
Lev	Leviticus	Jonah	Jonah
Num	Numbers	Mic	Micah
Deut	Deuteronomy	Nah	Nahum
Josh	Joshua	Hab	Habakkuk
Judg	Judges	Zeph	Zephaniah
Ruth	Ruth	Hag	Haggai
1–2 Sam	1–2 Samuel	Zech	Zechariah
1–2 Kgs	1–2 Kings	Mal	Malachi
1–2 Chr	1–2 Chronicles	Matt	Matthew
Ezra	Ezra	Mark	Mark
Neh	Nehemiah	Luke	Luke
Esth	Esther	John	John
Job	Job	Acts	Acts
Ps/Pss	Psalm/Psalms	Rom	Romans
Prov	Proverbs	1–2 Cor	1–2 Corinthians
Eccl	Ecclesiastes	Gal	Galatians
Song	Song of Songs	Eph	Ephesians
Isa	Isaiah	Phil	Philippians
Jer	Jeremiah	Col	Colossians
Lam	Lamentations	1–2 Thess	1–2 Thessalonians
Ezek	Ezekiel	1–2 Tim	1–2 Timothy
Dan	Daniel	Titus	Titus
Hos	Hosea	Phlm	Philemon
Joel	Joel	Heb	Hebrews

Jas . . . . . . James
1–2 Pet . . . 1–2 Peter
1–2–3 John 1–2–3 John

Jude . . . . . . Jude
Rev . . . . . . Revelation

GENERAL

AD . . . . . . *anno Domini* (in the year of [our] Lord)

ca. . . . . *circa*, around, about, approximately

cf. . . . . *confer*, compare

ch(s). . . . . . chapter(s)

diss. . . . . . . dissertation

ed(s). . . . . . editor(s), edited by, edition

e.g. . . . . . . *exempli gratia*, for example

et al. . . . . . *et alii*, and others

i.e. . . . . *id est*, that is

n(n). . . . . . note(s)

n.d. . . . . . . no date

n.p. . . . . . . no place; no publisher

p(p). . . . . . page(s)

repr. . . . . . reprinted

rev. . . . . . . revised

trans. . . . . translator, translated by

v(v). . . . . . verse(s)

vol(s). . . . . volume(s)

PREFACE

The idea for this book started several years ago as we met for coffee. We were lamenting that many of our students weren't being equipped to integrate various knowledge streams together to be effective apologists in our current cultural context. They were learning different pockets of information, but they were unable to integrate the disciplines for effective witness. If they were efficient in one area, they seemed deficient in another.

We also sensed a disconnect between apologetics and the local church. Pastors and professors understandably speak to and within their own social location, but sometimes we simply talk past each other—and at other times we just don't listen well. The conversation eventually shifted to what we might do about these problems.

Since that initial meeting, we've met together for breakfast once a week. While this project was on the forefront of our conversations, our weekly meetings also consisted of a variety of topics, including the Lord and his work in our lives, our relationships, and our work. In other words, we came together for this book because we have a mutual concern for the church's witness and a shared vision for teaching Christians to engage the world, but it has also served as a touchstone to go on mission as friends. We are convinced that this project is all the better for the friendship that has spurred it on.

A community of people provided input and support as we wrote. A special thanks to our wives and kids for their encouragement; you finally get to see what we were working on during all those late nights and early mornings. Thanks to Madison Trammel, our editor at Zondervan, for his professionalism and keen editorial eye. Thanks to our Sunday school class at Forest Baptist Church and our classes at Liberty University for your interaction as we presented much of this material to you before it reached print. We also greatly appreciate Trevin Wax, Nathan Rittenhouse, and James Spiegel, who read early copies of the manuscript and offered suggestions. Finally, a big thanks to our students who helped out in various ways: Micailyn Geyer, Jack Carson, Kevin Richard, Megan Gentleman, Joshua Erb, Doug Taylor, Maria Kometer, Isaiah Griffith, and Dickson Ngama.

AN INVITATION TO APOLOGETICS AT THE CROSS

> I grew up in a Christian culture in which "defending the faith" was carried out by using the Bible as a weapon. Anyone who challenged my faith was treated as an enemy.
>
> *Eugene Peterson, on back cover of Dallas Willard's*
> The Allure of Gentleness

If ever there were one proof-text for apologetics, 1 Peter 3:15 would be it:

> But in your hearts revere Christ as Lord. Always be prepared to give an answer to everyone who asks you to give the reason for the hope that you have. But do this with gentleness and respect.

The apostle Peter commands that we as Christians be able to give an answer for our hope. The word translated "answer" or "defense" in our English versions is the Greek word *apologia*. As you have probably guessed, this is where we get our English word *apologetics*. We are to be prepared to give an *apologia* or an *apologetic* for our hope in Jesus Christ. Yet many books on apologetics stop at this verse and don't explain the surrounding context deeply enough.

Roughly two thousand years ago, the apostle Peter composed a letter to a Christian community to encourage them not to give up (cf. 1 Pet 5:9, 12). These believers were experiencing not only physical and psychological pressures to conform to the surrounding culture, as well as social antagonism from nonbelievers, but also temptation to return to their former lifestyles, tensions within the Christian community itself, and their own spiritual doubts. Peter's audience, weary of the trials they were facing, seems to have been teetering on the brink of giving up. As one New Testament scholar has observed, "When one's Christian faith is criticized and even mocked, it is natural that one may begin to doubt the truth of the gospel of Jesus Christ."[1]

What would Peter's words be to this community on the edge of giving up?

Peter seems to have had some fight in him. It was Peter who cut off the right ear of the high priest's servant when the crowd came to arrest Jesus (how about that for a culture warrior!). Considering Peter's disposition, it seems plausible he would have offered persecuted Christians a William Wallace-like battle speech and called them into war—at least a war of words. He could have led this weary community to respond with hostile tactics—to fight fire with fire. He could have encouraged them to demand respect. He could have launched what we will later describe as an "apologetic of glory." But he didn't.

Perhaps Peter could still hear Jesus' admonishment: "Put your sword away! Shall I not drink the cup the Father has given me?" (John 18:11). For years, Peter must have had his Savior's words ringing in his ears: "Whoever wants to be my disciple must deny themselves and take up their cross and follow me. For whoever wants to save their life will lose it, but whoever loses their life for me and for the gospel will save it" (Mark 8:34–35).

The cross was far from a comforting thought in those times. No one wore a cross around their neck—torture devices don't make nice symbols for jewelry. And how could Peter forget the time Jesus had reminded the disciples, "'A servant is not greater than his master.' If they persecuted me, they will persecute you also" (John 15:20).

By the time Peter wrote this letter, he could have replayed the final week of Jesus' life repeatedly in his mind. It had all happened just as Jesus had predicted: He had come and given his life as a ransom (Mark 10:45). The way of Jesus, the way he conquered evil and sin by laying down his life, must have left an indelible mark on Peter. It was this way, the way of the cross, that shaped Peter's advice to this community surrounded by a hostile culture.

With Jesus as his model, Peter writes the beleaguered community and instructs them not to retaliate, but rather to rejoice in suffering, trusting in the reward secured by the resurrection of Christ (1 Pet 1:6; 4:12–14). In the midst of their suffering and trials, Peter reminds them that God has called them as a *community*, not simply as individuals, to declare his praises to the world (2:9). Peter instructs them to live lives characterized by compassion, respect, and humility (2:11–12, 15–17; 3:8–9)—lives so noble they would positively impact hostile nonbelievers. For Peter, the way of the cross set the pattern for how believers should interact with nonbelievers and, in particular, hostile nonbelievers (2:22–24).

---

1. Karen H. Jobes, *1 Peter*, Baker Exegetical Commentary on the New Testament (Grand Rapids, Baker Academic, 2005), 42.

It is in this context that 1 Peter 3:14–15 must be read: "But even if you should suffer for what is right, you are blessed. 'Do not fear their threats; do not be frightened.' But in your hearts revere Christ as Lord." Notice that in verse 15, "in your heart revere Christ as Lord," Peter puts positively what he just wrote negatively in verse 14: "Do not fear their threats; do not be frightened." This contrast reveals the choice these believers had to make: either to succumb to fear or revere Christ as Lord, trusting that he is ultimately in control (v. 17). The second option, trusting Christ and revering him as Lord, meant responding with an *apologia*.

This study of the context of 1 Peter 3:15 reveals that even though Peter believes the gospel can and should be defended, he is not setting the course for a war of words; he is not pitting Christians against unbelievers. Instead, Peter sets the tone for apologetic conversations by giving a persecuted community hope and by encouraging them to endure with joy.[2] Peter gave downtrodden Christians not a triumphalist call to throw intellectual knockout punches for Jesus, but rather level-headed instructions using words and phrases like "gentleness," "respect," "a clear conscience," and "good behavior."[3] As theologian Kevin Vanhoozer notes, "Peter's focus is not on what to say but on how to say it."[4] In the face of the gauntlet laid down by the gospel's opponents, Peter called the Christian community to reasoned answers, a humble spirit, and joy. We call this approach "apologetics at the cross."[5]

A WORKING DEFINITION

Apologetics, in its most basic form, is *the practice of offering an appeal and a defense for the Christian faith*. In other words, apologetics, through word and deed, answers both why a person *can* believe (defense) and why a person *should* believe (appeal). The goal of apologetics is to clear away the debris of doubt and skepticism in order to make a path for the gospel to be heard.

For some of you, this sounds attractive. For others, an invitation to *the practice of making an appeal and a defense for the Christian faith* doesn't sound

---

2. The apostle Paul also emphasizes joyful suffering as bringing assurance of and witness to salvation. For example, see 1 Thessalonians 1:4–10.

3. See Miroslav Volf, "Soft Difference: Theological Reflections on the Relation Between Church and Culture in 1 Peter," *Ex Auditu* 10, no. 4 (1994): 21, www.pas.rochester.edu/~tim/study/Miroslav%20 Volf%201%20Peter.pdf.

4. Kevin J. Vanhoozer, *Pictures at a Theological Exhibition: Scenes of the Church's Worship, Witness and Wisdom* (Downers Grove, IL: InterVarsity, 2016), 218.

5. As Paul often did (e.g., 1 Cor 1:16–27; Eph 2:16; Phil 3:18), throughout this book we're using the word *cross* as basically a synonym for the word *gospel*. Though at times we will simply use the word *gospel*, as we will explain in chapter 1, we are following Paul in adopting the word *cross* for certain strategic reasons.

welcoming at all. If you are in the latter group, we can empathize. As you will see below in our stories, both of us were at one time on the fence about apologetics, at least as we understood it. Yet we came to appreciate it. We hope you find points of contact in one or both of our journeys.

OUR STORIES

Apologetics is irrelevant. At least, that's what I (Josh) used to think. During college and into graduate school, I was passionate about sharing my faith and trying to walk with God, but I wasn't concerned with apologetics. This may seem like a strange dichotomy for some of you, but for others it will resonate. As I look back on my apathy toward, and sometimes outright dismissal of, apologetics, two reasons come to mind.

First, apologetics didn't resonate with me because I was committed to the gospel, not arguments. I knew there were many things I didn't understand well, but understanding the gospel seemed the only *necessary* thing. People around me were hurting, and what they needed was the gospel. However, as I later discovered, being committed to the gospel should include ways of breaking down the barriers between people and the gospel. My definition of "gospel-centered" was too narrow.

Second, the guys I knew who were into apologetics (and for whatever reason, they were mostly guys!) *were not good at interacting with others in general—let alone with those who did not share their beliefs.* The problem was that my friends in college who loved apologetics were pretty good at winning *arguments*, but not at winning over *people*.

My experiences serving as a pastor, evangelizing neighbors, and teaching students have taught me that it is rarely effective to simply force standard arguments onto others—arguments that, while perhaps well-reasoned, don't pay proper attention to context and the uniqueness of the other person. Measured arguments are not unimportant; in fact, they are vital. However, winning an argument against someone is not the same thing as persuading them. Those victories can actually be losses.

Neither of these objections offer a fair assessment of apologetics, and that's part of the point! I share these impressions because they may be the same impressions you have. However, they do not fit what apologetics *could* and *should* be.

Over the years my uneasiness about apologetics gave way to a practical need for it in my own life, and that practical need gave way to an enthusiastic appreciation as I entered pastoral ministry.

The first shift began to occur when I took an undergraduate religion class at the state college I attended. During the first day of class, the professor said he knew many of us had signed up for the class because our interest in the Bible was rooted in personal devotion or faith traditions. He informed us, in what felt like a condescending tone, that in his class we would be talking about history and what the vast majority of scholars had known about the New Testament for some time: "the sure results of historical-critical scholarship."

The professor viewed it as obvious that students needed to be baptized in the conclusions of critical scholarship. The Enlightenment had happened centuries ago, so if you wanted a devotional life, that was fine—but in his class, we were going to deal with historical matters, not matters of faith. I now know Christian philosophers would have had a field day with this false dichotomy between history and faith, but I was no philosopher, and it all sounded intimidating.

Not only was I anxious about the questions raised, but I was also frustrated. Why had I not heard of these issues in my local church? All my life I had been taught the "whats" of Christianity, that is, the content of Christianity. Now I was desperately searching for what Timothy Keller calls the "whys" of Christianity, the answers to the question, "Why should I believe this?"

The church too often leaves "why" questions out of preaching and discipleship. I remember becoming disillusioned, thinking, *I've grown up in the church all my life, and this is the first time I've heard these questions. Why am I unequipped to answer them? Are there reasonable answers?*

Later, when I began pastoral ministry, I saw that others were asking the "why" questions too or needing help to answer the "why" questions their friends asked of them. Apologetics became indispensable. I realized I needed it to aid those I was interacting with daily, both inside and outside the church.

―――――

"Apologetics is where it's at." When a distinguished colleague made that assertion, I (Mark) remember thinking, *Are you serious?* Observing the professors and administrators around me nodding their heads in agreement, I quickly realized there was a disconnect between the way they saw apologetics and the way I saw it. While they embraced it, I held it at arm's length. I had serious questions about its relevance, such as: "Isn't apologetics a failed experiment of modernism? Isn't it passé—a relic of old-school fundamentalism that is no longer helpful, respectable, or sustainable? In this late modern world, haven't we seen the end of apologetics' usefulness?"

Perhaps I perceived apologetics as a relic of the past because I had never considered that the apologetics I learned as a college and seminary student could be reimagined and recontextualized. During the most formative years of my life, when I was in college and seminary, the apologists of that generation had been helpful to me. They enabled me to establish the reasonableness of my faith. They convinced me I did not have to commit intellectual suicide to believe the Bible was true and Jesus Christ was the Savior of the world. When I later began to view apologetics negatively, I had to ask myself, *How did I get to this point?*

First, apologetics seemed only to answer questions no one in my orbit was asking. For several years, I pastored a church in suburban Virginia. Our congregation was mostly made up of young, up-and-coming, middle- and upper-middle class families. They were not asking for philosophical arguments about God. What they wanted to know was how to make their marriages work, raise healthy and high-achieving kids, succeed in their careers, reduce stress, deal with their feelings of loneliness, overcome addictions, recover from loss and pain, and know that God was real and working in their lives. It seemed that if God existed, we would be convinced of his existence not by arguments, but rather by experiencing him in our daily lives.

A few years later, I pastored a small church made up of mostly elderly folks, located in the county seat of a farming community. Early in my tenure, we advertised a Sunday evening series based on David T. Lamb's book, *God Behaving Badly*.[6] A layperson had recently taught a popular Sunday evening series on end-time events, so it seemed reasonable to expect this series would also be well attended. Yet when the time came, no one from the community was there. The congregation seemed to enjoy the series, but I'm not sure many of them understood its relevance. It seemed for that community, *apocalyptics* were more intriguing than *apologetics*.

Second, apologetics seemed so cerebral that it was intimidating. Being an apologist seemed to require not only quick-wittedness and a great memory but also precise skills in logic. The apologists who helped me most had an incredible ability to think quickly on their feet, to draw instantly from an impeccable memory and a vast storehouse of knowledge, and to spot a logical fallacy in a split second. They did it all with complete calm and almost no emotion, Spock-like. As a pastor, whenever I preached on proofs of the resurrection or led a small group on defending the Christian faith, I felt like I was wearing an ill-fitting suit, trying to be someone I was not. My greatest fear was that someone would ask a question beyond what I had studied and I would look like—well, what I would look like if I were ever a contestant on the game show *Jeopardy*. It seemed that apologetics required me to speak from the brain more than the heart.

Although a certain brand of apologetics had shaped my faith during my

---

6. David T. Lamb, *God Behaving Badly: Is the God of the Old Testament Angry, Sexist, and Racist?* (Downers Grove, IL: InterVarsity, 2011).

twenties, as circumstances changed, I couldn't see how those same approaches were relevant anymore. My academic interests during my doctoral studies at the University of Notre Dame led me to focus on other issues raised by historical-critical scholarship—that is, until the practicality and relevance of present-day apologetics hit close to home.

My twenty-year-old son hit a crisis of faith. At first, all was well. Colton's first year of college was life-changing, and I had never seen him so happy. But then at the beginning of his second semester, Colton crashed. It was like he had lost his way. He didn't know what he wanted to do. School was no longer interesting to him. He dropped out of college and began hanging out with friends who were intelligent, but unambitious and atheistic. Colton spiraled into a morass of doubt and depression. I hoped he would benefit from reading apologetic books. The material initiated fruitful discussions between him and me. While not leaving all of his doubts behind, he began to grow in his faith again.

Through these books and the conversations we had, God sparked something in Colton. He matriculated in a different university and majored in biblical studies. He was like a sponge, soaking in all the school had to offer: Bible, theology, philosophy, and, of course, apologetics. His faith awakened his curiosity; his sincere doubts only pushed him deeper into faith. By God's grace, this experience affected me as well, sparking my own imagination concerning the past, present, and future of apologetics.

After I became chair of the Bible and theology department at a university, another experience revealed the relevance of apologetics in today's world. I received an email from a former church member. She and her husband had been model Christian parents at our church, deeply involved in serving others, homeschooling their children, and living in vibrant Christian community. They were the kind of family that gives strength and stability to a young congregation, which is why I was surprised by the contents of her email.

Her husband had become an agnostic. He came to this decision by reading works that espouse other worldviews and intentionally undermine Christianity—in particular, the writings of Bart Ehrman.[7] He wanted to voice his doubts about Christianity to their children and teach them the truth of what he had discovered. She looked to me for help: What should she do? Though a capable and intelligent person, she felt overwhelmed in this situation. In her own words:

---

7. For a response to Bart Ehrman at a popular level, see Andreas Köstenberger, Darrell Bock, and Josh Chatraw, *Truth Matters: Confident Faith in a Confusing World* (Nashville: B&H, 2014); see also Andreas J. Köstenberger, Darrell L. Bock, and Josh D. Chatraw, *Truth in a Culture of Doubt: Engaging Skeptical Challenges to the Bible* (Nashville: B&H, 2014).

To be honest, I am really trying to stay calm and not worry about him sharing with the kids and what that could mean for their futures. Due to that, I don't want to be ignorant and not be able to counter some of the issues. But as I start to reluctantly step my toes into the water, all I see is a bunch of scholars who don't agree, debate (and attack) each other's arguments, and think that they have the answer and the other side is ignorant/blind.

This is a snapshot of the world we live in. Her words reminded me that many issues formerly left to academia were now being introduced to the masses, often by skeptics. No longer can apologetics be left to scholars. Current and future Christian leaders, whether working inside or outside the academy, must be prepared and able to teach others.

Maybe, after all, apologetics *is* where it's at . . .

THE CHANGE IN CULTURE

Our world has changed not only on the street and in the halls of the academy, but also in the pews of the church. Philosopher James K. A. Smith describes the fragility of faith in our present age:

> We live in the twilight of both gods and idols. But their ghosts have refused to depart, and every once in a while we might be surprised to find ourselves tempted by belief . . . On the other hand, even as faith endures in our secular age, believing doesn't come easy. Faith is fraught; confession is haunted by an inescapable sense of its contestability. We don't believe instead of doubting; we believe *while* doubting. We're all Thomas now.[8]

Smith describes well the Western world many of us live in. Christians today must not only fight against lust and for purity, against greed and for contentment, against pride and for humility; we must also fight against doubt and for faith. We must cry out to Jesus as the man in Mark 9 did, "I do believe; help me overcome my unbelief!" (v. 24). Our battles for faith today may be different from the battles of the past.

---

8. James K. A. Smith, *How (Not) to Be Secular: Reading Charles Taylor* (Grand Rapids: Eerdmans, 2014), 3–4. Smith is offering commentary on Charles Taylor's magisterial *A Secular Age* (Cambridge, MA: Harvard University Press, 2007), which serves as an important resource for this book (especially chs. 11–12). Taylor stresses how for the majority of Western civilization it seemed implausible for most to disbelieve in God. Today the environment in the West is different; the default cultural assumptions in many places (especially intellectual centers) make belief in God implausible or, at the least, one possibility among many options (e.g., see pp. 590, 595 in *A Secular Age*).

At the same time, Christians have long understood that doubt is part of life. About five hundred years ago, John Calvin wrote that it is possible for Christians to have a "perpetual conflict" with doubt and unbelief.[9] Even this great Protestant Reformer recognized the fragility of faith, and he lived in a context considerably different from our own.

As Smith points out above, though, the situation in the West has changed drastically since the days of Calvin. The doubt of that day existed within a societal framework of belief. The overarching framework of Christendom was not called into question so much as the sincerity of the individual's faith. In the past, doubt could be summed up with the question, "Am I a true believer?" In our late modern age, the question has become, "Is Christianity true?"

It is not just philosophers and theologians who have noticed this cultural shift; scholars from other disciplines are making similar observations. Sociologist James Hunter notes that social conditions have made what was once an inevitable belief in God dispensable: "The presumption of God and of his active presence in the world cannot be easily sustained because the most important symbols of social, economic, political, and aesthetic life no longer point to him. God is simply less obvious than he once was, and for most no longer obvious at all—quite the opposite."[10]

We may not want to admit it, but faith is contested around every corner. Looking the other way is not an option. Most people today—believers and unbelievers alike—live in the space between absolute faith and absolute doubt. When we understand our context, we realize that reflecting deeply on and practicing apologetics remains important. Apologetics is as vital as ever.

A VISION FOR APOLOGETICS

In the chapters that follow, we will present what we call *apologetics at the cross*—a biblical, historical, philosophical, theological, and practical vision for offering an appeal for Christianity in our contemporary context. While a number of helpful books have been written on the philosophy and methodology of apologetics, on the history of apologetics, and on evangelism or practical apologetics—many of which we are indebted to—this book takes a different approach. Through years of service in the church and ministry training institutions, we have seen that effective apologetics today needs to be shaped by a robust vision that integrates a variety of disciplines.

---

9. John T. McNeill, ed., *Calvin: Institutes of the Christian Religion*, vol. 1, III.ii.17 (Philadelphia: Westminster, 1960), 562.

10. James Davison Hunter, *To Change the World: The Irony, Tragedy, and Possibility of Christianity in the Late Modern World* (New York: Oxford University Press, 2010), 203.

In the rest of the book, we will build an apologetics house. When building a house, one begins with the foundation and then proceeds with walls, the roof, and the interior. In chapters 1 and 2, we'll lay a biblical foundation for apologetics. Chapters 3 and 4 will complete the foundation with a brief sketch of the historical development of apologetics since the early church.

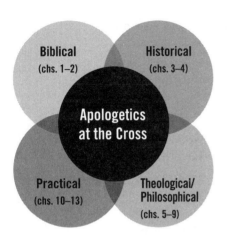

Chapters 5–9 will provide the walls and exterior for our apologetics house. In these chapters, we discuss contemporary methods (ch. 5) and outline a theological vision for apologetics (chs. 6–9). Chapters 10–13 move to the interior of our house, exploring the practical outworking of *apologetics at the cross*. In these chapters, we address the items people immediately notice: paint, everyday décor, and furniture. Chapters 10 and 11 focus on particular challenges in today's culture and offer an "inside-out" approach for apologetic conversations. Chapter 12 addresses the critiques, or "defeaters," often leveled against Christianity. Finally in chapter 13, we conclude with guidance on how to make a case for Christianity.

In a study of evangelism in the early church, theologian Michael Green writes that leaders applied deep learning alongside practical witness in order to win hearts and minds.[11] He suggests that the modern church would do well to imitate these early Christian leaders, since one of the greatest needs of the church today is "for those who are theologically competent to come out of the ivory tower and evangelize."[12] Our prayer is that the chapters that follow will faithfully retrieve this vision for apologetics—one that combines a commitment to the life of the mind with a steadfast allegiance to Jesus Christ and his gospel.

---

11. See Michael Green, *Evangelism in the Early Church*, rev. ed. (Grand Rapids: Eerdmans, 2004), 18. For a charge to pastors, see Josh Chatraw, "The Pastor Theologian as Apologist," in *Becoming a Pastor Theologian*, ed. Todd Wilson and Gerald Hiestand (Downers Grove, IL: IVP Academic, 2016), 173–83.

12. Green, *Evangelism in the Early Church*, 19.

PART 1

THE FOUNDATION
FOR APOLOGETICS
AT THE CROSS

CHAPTER ONE

APOLOGETICS IN THE BIBLE: PART 1

True to the cross of Jesus, Christian persuasion has to be cross-shaped
in its manner just as it is cross-centered in its message.

Os Guinness, Fool's Talk

1 CORINTHIANS 2:1–5: The Cross and Apologetics

We saw in the introduction that if ever there was a proof-text for apologetics,
it is 1 Peter 3:15. On the other hand, if ever there has been a proof-text *against*
apologetics, it is surely 1 Corinthians 2:1–5:

> When I came to you, I did not come with eloquence or human wisdom as I
> proclaimed to you the testimony about God. For I resolved to know nothing
> while I was with you except Jesus Christ and him crucified. I came to you
> in weakness with great fear and trembling. My message and my preaching
> were not with wise and persuasive words, but with a demonstration of the
> Spirit's power, so that your faith might not rest on human wisdom, but
> on God's power.

Some critics take these verses to mean that Paul made a mistake in Acts,
realized his error, and is now vowing to preach only the cross. "Apologetics!"
these critics scoff. "Paul swore off all that apologetics nonsense and decided
to preach the gospel alone." Once this passage is read in context, however, it
becomes clear that far from serving as an anti-apologetic proof-text, it actually
has important implications for how apologetics should be done.

Throughout the book of Acts, Paul's ministry is upheld as a model, and
there is no indication that the many instances of persuading and reasoning
with nonbelievers are an exception to that model. Paul demonstrates both in

his own ministry and in his instructions to others that he values various forms of persuasion. In his second letter to the Corinthians, Paul writes, "Since, then, we know what it is to fear the Lord, we try to persuade others" (2 Cor 5:11). It's not persuasion that Paul shuns in 1 Corinthians 2, but rather a certain type of *manipulative* persuasion.

In 1 Corinthians 2, Paul alludes to a movement of his day known as sophism. Sophists were rhetoricians who maintained public careers based on their ability to speak and follow oratorical conventions. It is difficult in our day to grasp what an idol oratory had become in the Mediterranean world. Rhetorical skills were valued to such an extent that "public speakers who either could not meet [the sophists'] standards, or who for any reason chose not to, were viewed as seriously inferior."[1]

It was in this context that Paul spoke against "eloquence" and "human wisdom." He refused to allow the gospel message to be judged by the speaker's rhetorical ability. In Lystra, a city outside of the sophists' influence, Paul was distressed to discover he spoke so persuasively that he was praised as Hermes, the Greek god of communication (Acts 14:12). As New Testament scholar D. A. Carson writes, "What Paul avoided was artificial communication that won plaudits for the speaker but distracted from the message . . . [Paul's words] warn against any method that leads people to say, 'What a marvelous preacher! [or apologist!]' rather than, 'What a marvelous Savior!'"[2]

In this letter to the church in Corinth, we learn an important lesson. In order to win people to the gospel, Paul was willing to be flexible in his persuasive efforts (e.g., 1 Cor 9:19–23). However, his flexibility was not unlimited. Paul vigilantly guarded against anything that might jeopardize the gospel message.

This explains Paul's objection to the use of "eloquence" and "human wisdom." Yet the issue raised by the critics mentioned above is not only *how* Paul spoke, but also *what* he said. Paul appeared to place severe limits on the message Christians are to preach: "For I resolved to know nothing while I was with you except Jesus Christ and him crucified" (1 Cor 2:2). However, common sense reveals that Paul was not prohibiting any message that was not about Jesus' death. In this very letter to the Corinthians, he discussed a wide array of topics, including sexual immorality, marriage, singleness, worship, spiritual gifts, speaking in tongues, and the Lord's Supper.

Paul wasn't saying the cross is all that matters. He meant that everything matters only if viewed through the lens of the cross. Rather than negating apologetics, these verses in 1 Corinthians reveal the proper foundation for

---

1. D. A. Carson, *The Cross and Christian Ministry: Leadership Lessons from 1 Corinthians* (Grand Rapids: Baker, 1993), 34.

2. Carson, *The Cross and Christian Ministry*, 35.

apologetics and should guide its focus. They show that the goal of apologetics cannot simply be intellectual respectability or a defense of theism, as if belief in any deity will do. *The goal of apologetics must be the cross.* Apologetic appeals using historical evidence, logic, desire, story, experience, and imagination are important, but they must not become of first importance (cf. 1 Cor 15:3). They should serve to bring people to what is of first importance—namely, the cross.

The cross, a symbol of humility and suffering, should shape the way we do apologetics. Paul reminded the church in Corinth, "I came to you in weakness with great fear and trembling" (1 Cor 2:3). Instead of masking his weaknesses with triumphalist proclamation or a forceful personality, Paul spoke with transparency, a natural outcome of humility. This point will be developed later, but for now it is enough to observe that Paul did not see his weaknesses as things to hide, but rather as opportunities to boast in the power of God.

We must also remember that our appeals are only made effective "with a demonstration of the Spirit's power, so that your faith might not rest on human wisdom, but on God's power" (1 Cor 2:4–5). Apologetics inevitably goes wrong when it relies on a system, a rhetorical style, or a charismatic personality rather than on the power of the Spirit. When the faith of a new disciple is wrapped up in anything other than the gospel and God himself, danger looms. This is why the implications drawn from 1 Corinthians 2:1–5 and Paul's emphasis on the cross serve as a centerpiece for this entire book.

Throughout the book, we will refer to the cross as a synonym for the gospel, just as Paul often did (see 1 Cor 1:16–27; Eph 2:16; Phil 3:18). Paul seems to have chosen the word strategically, not to exclude Jesus' life and resurrection or to imply they were less important than his death, but to emphasize the scandal of the gospel—to emphasize how the wisdom of God transcends human wisdom. Similarly in our title, *Apologetics at the Cross*, we do not exclude other dimensions of the gospel, but instead we imitate Paul in using the cross as a substitute for the word *gospel*.

Apologetics and the Trinity

Significantly, 1 Corinthians 2:1–5 also points to the Trinity, with each person performing an essential role. Biblical apologetics is not about any god, but about the God revealed in the Old and New Testaments. An emphasis on the Trinity also reveals how God in all three persons is deeply involved in the apologetic enterprise. God the Father reveals himself in creation. Jesus argues for his own identity. The Holy Spirit bears witness to the truth.

Because it is important to consider the full biblical framework and not simply mine the Bible for apologetic nuggets, in the next two chapters we will highlight points that occur throughout the biblical story line. Though the Bible was revealed progressively—meaning the story unfolded over time—today we have the whole biblical narrative from start to finish. Thus, we can understand not only isolated events but also the structure that holds the Bible together. We know the purpose of the story. At the center of this grand narrative, at the heart of its purpose, is God on a cross, God gloriously rising from the dead. Jesus Christ was God himself in human flesh. Crucified. Dead. Buried. Risen. Ascended.

In the next two chapters, we will take an inductive approach to the biblical text, allowing the Bible to speak for itself about how apologetics should be done. As you read these chapters, you will see that the Bible has its own highly contextual approaches to persuasion. We've arranged these approaches into fifteen categories. If the biblical narrative were a play, we might call these categories apologetic "performances" that demonstrate how the Bible *does* apologetics.[3] Because we're convinced that living in the world of the Bible with cross-colored lenses is a vital foundation for apologetics, we will spend more time than many introductory apologetic books do on this biblical background.

1. CREATION, GENERAL REVELATION, AND PROVIDENTIAL CARE

Creation and General Revelation

According to Psalm 19:1–6, the heavens act as an apologist for God! Without saying a word, the sky, and by extrapolation all of creation, declares the majesty of the Creator. Continuously, night after night and day after day, the heavens reveal that God exists and that he is glorious. This phenomenon is what theologians refer to as *general* (or *natural*) *revelation*.

In verses 4b–6, the psalmist poetically describes a day in the life of the sun. When this biblical poet observes the joyful emergence, grand course, and ubiquitous warmth of the sun, he is filled with awe and wonder at what is obviously a revelation of the one true God. But not so fast. The heavens and sun may "prove" God's existence to the Israelite worshiper, but they certainly don't to everyone. Other religions in the ancient Near East looked at the same natural revelation and yet claimed that the sun, rather than pointing to one true God, is itself a manifestation of a god—and one god among many, at that.

---

3. We are borrowing this metaphor from Kevin J. Vanhoozer, *The Drama of Doctrine: A Canonical Linguistic Approach to Christian Theology* (Louisville: Westminster John Knox, 2005), 363–444.

An Egyptian hymn to the sun god uses similar imagery to the poetic description in Psalm 19:

> Hail to you, Re, perfect each day, who rises at dawn without failing . . .
> Fine gold does not match your splendor . . .
> When you cross the sky all faces see you . . .
> In a brief day you race a course . . .[4]

The Mesopotamians also wrote a hymn that sounds very similar to Psalm 19, addressed to Shamash, their sun god: "You cross regularly through the heavens, every day you traverse the vast earth."[5]

Three different people groups looked at the same sun, but interpreted what they saw differently. Two groups saw it as a god, while the other saw it as a creation of the one true God.

This raises a set of perplexing questions. If, as the Bible claims, creation declares the glory of God, why don't all people confess and praise his name? Why do some people worship something quite different? Is creation not an apologist after all?

The apostle Paul answers these questions in Romans 1:18–25. He explains that while God makes his eternal power and divine nature known in creation, humans suppress the knowledge of God available to them. Creation reveals God, but people deny the truth that is right in front of them.

Paul's affirmations about general revelation are consistent with Psalm 19. What may be known about God is plain to humankind through creation. God's divine nature and eternal power are clearly and repeatedly revealed through what God has made and continues to sustain. Therefore, the problem lies not with the revelation of God in nature, but rather with people, who suppress and twist the revelation and end up worshiping, as was the case in Egypt and Mesopotamia, creation rather than the Creator.

In sum, we are given a true knowledge of God through creation. Nature reveals him. The heavens declare his glory. Creation is an apologist. The problem is that humanity suppresses this revelation. Humans deny the truth, twist natural revelation, and bow to created things. We can and should point to natural revelation in apologetic dialogues, but we must remain aware of context and human sinfulness.

---

4. Quoted in John H. Walton, ed., *Zondervan Illustrated Bible Backgrounds Commentary: The Minor Prophets, Job, Psalms, Proverbs, Ecclesiastes, Song of Songs* (Grand Rapids: Zondervan, 2009), 5:335.

5. Quoted in Walton, *Zondervan Illustrated Bible Backgrounds Commentary*, 5:336.

General Revelation and Apologetics

We have seen in this section that, depending on the interpreter, nature can be "read" in different ways. This was true not only in the ancient world but also in more recent history, as seen, for example, in the divergent interpretations of creation offered during the Enlightenment (see chapter 4). We suggest that nature, rather than having value in "proving" or rationally coercing belief in the *true God*, is, as the apologist Alister McGrath has written, "imaginatively compelling and rationally persuasive" when read through the lens of Christian revelation. We might ask others to consider nature through the lens of the Christian imagination and story, in contrast with their own framework, in order to "appreciate the aesthetic power and rational satisfaction" of Christianity.[6]

Of course, there is a long history of arguments for a general theism, which if properly used can serve a valuable role in a larger argument for Christianity. However, keep in mind that Psalm 19 and Romans 1 are referring specifically to the God of Israel (and not simply a general deity), and that interpretive frameworks play a central role in how nature is "read."

Providential Care

God also reveals his existence through his care for the world and the people in it. He didn't create this world and leave it to run on its own; he continues to nurture and care for it. Acts 14:14–18 includes a classic statement about God's care for the world (cf. Acts 17:24–31):

> But when the apostles Barnabas and Paul heard of this, they tore their clothes and rushed out into the crowd, shouting: "Friends, why are you doing this? We too are only human, like you. We are bringing you good news, telling you to turn from these worthless things to the living God, who made the heavens and the earth and the sea and everything in them. In the past, he let all nations go their own way. Yet he has not left himself without testimony: He has shown kindness by giving you rain from heaven and crops in their seasons; he provides you with plenty of food and fills your hearts with joy." Even with these words, they had difficulty keeping the crowd from sacrificing to them.

After Paul performs a miracle in Lystra, much to his and Barnabas's dismay the people identify them as gods and want to sacrifice to them. In their objection, Paul and Barnabas explain God's creative act and providential care for all he has

---

6. Alister E. McGrath, *Re-Imagining Nature: The Promise of a Christian Natural Theology* (West Sussex, UK: Wiley Blackwell, 2017), 131.

created. Rain. Crops. Plentiful food. Hearts filled with joy. All these testify to the existence of one true benevolent Creator God. God's bountiful and extravagant care, both past and present, bears witness to his existence.

There is another apologetic related to God's providential care in Scripture: God's deliverance of his people, the Israelites. In Isaiah 41, for instance, God promises to defeat his people's enemies and bring their plans to nothing. Toward his people, however, God shows gentle care; he takes their right hand and assures them, "Do not fear; I will help you" (v. 13).

God's provision for his people has an apologetic purpose. God cares for Israel "so that [others] may see and know, may consider and understand, that the hand of the LORD has done this, that the Holy One of Israel has created it" (Isa 41:20). It is not uncommon for believers today to witness God's loving, sustaining grace in the way he has provided for and protected them. Many can share instances of God overcoming challenges on their behalf. Testimonies like these strengthen Christians' hope that God is real and there for them.

Yet in ancient times and today, many also lament when God does not seem to rescue them.

Jeremiah wept bitterly over the ruin of his city.

Paul endured verbal and physical beatings for his faith.

Christians today are martyred by the thousands; they die in car wrecks, lose everything in catastrophic events, and suffer through disease.[7]

The Bible unabashedly asserts that God's deliverance of his people is an apologetic for his love. We can know God is real because he cares for his people, but it's also true that sometimes he doesn't protect, heal, provide for, or deliver them. Sometimes their comfort and health, their hopes and dreams, are put on a cross and crucified.

Does this mean God's care for his people is not a useful apologetic? Not entirely. We just have to understand its limits. The Bible is not simplistic. It is clear that in this life, there are few guarantees. Sometimes we suffer for purposes bigger than we can understand. God will forever and completely deliver his people, ushering them into a world of peace and plenty, but that lies in the future. Until then, in our present life, God's temporal acts of providential care are glimpses into who he is and the world to come. It's amazing that God allows his final deliverance to invade our present reality. When he provides for us, our eternal home comes to us now, and we are assured of his reality and his love. God's care for his people *is* an apologetic, if understood rightly.

---

7. For two other examples, see Habakkuk and Hebrews 11.

2. POLEMIC

In the Old Testament world, the primary question was not whether or not a god or gods existed, but which god was true. For this reason, Old Testament prophets often employed polemics against false gods. Much of the Old Testament was written in defense of the true God and against ancient Near Eastern gods.[8]

To maintain a balanced view of the Old Testament, one must remember that the prophets spoke not only *against* the culture of their day but also *with* and *for* it.

With the Culture

First, the prophets spoke *with* their culture. That is, they thought, spoke, lived, and imagined within an ancient Near Eastern context; it was the air they breathed. As Old Testament scholar John Walton writes, the ancient Israelite authors of the biblical text were "resonating" with their own culture.[9] The prophets were a part of their culture, and their culture was a part of them.

Polemic Approach

With Culture
- Think, speak, live within culture
- Speak with pre-understanding of the hearers and culture

For Culture
- Speak for culture
- Reveal the truth

Against Culture
- Speak against culture
- Redefine presuppositions

Against the Culture

Second, Old Testament prophets spoke *against* their culture, challenging it, often in the form of polemics.[10] In his book *Against the Gods*, John Currid explains that in using polemics, Old Testament writers took familiar aspects of their culture—its "thought forms and stories," its "expressions and motifs"—and "[filled] them with radically new meaning"[11] in order to vividly contrast their beliefs and way of life with that of the pagan culture around them—in particular, their worship of the one true God as opposed to the worship of many false gods so prevalent in the ancient Near

---

8. Examples include Exodus 3:19–20; 5:1; 6:1; 7:4–5, 8–13, 17; 10:2; 12:12; 1 Kings 18:22–39; Isaiah 19:1. Also see John D. Currid, *Against the Gods: The Polemical Theology of the Old Testament* (Wheaton, IL: Crossway, 2013).

9. John H. Walton, ed., *Zondervan Illustrated Bible Backgrounds Commentary: Genesis, Exodus, Leviticus, Numbers, Deuteronomy* (Grand Rapids: Zondervan, 2009), 1:ix.

10. See Walton's spectrum of the varieties of ways Old Testament literature interacts with its own cultural and literary milieu (*Zondervan Illustrated Bible Backgrounds Commentary*, 1:x–xii).

11. Currid, *Against the Gods*, 25.

East. In this way, the polemics employed by the Old Testament writers were, above all, characterized by a commitment to monotheism and a fierce critique of polytheism.[12] The Israelites spoke *with* their culture, that is, out of a shared conceptual world, while simultaneously speaking *against* their culture in order to uphold the existence of the one true God.

For the Culture

Third, the Old Testament is *for* the various cultures and peoples of its day. Genesis 1–11 takes a universal perspective: God created the world for the good of all people. Similarly, in Genesis 12, God calls Abraham, the father of Israel, to be a blessing to all people. Old Testament prophets defend the God of Israel against false Egyptian, Canaanite, and Babylonian gods, not because God is against these peoples, but because he is ultimately for the nations. When God chooses Israel to be at the center of his redemptive plan, he does so to bless all people through them.

The Old Testament's apologetic method of being with, for, and against culture is illustrated well in the very first chapters of the Bible, as outlined in the chart below.

COMPARISON OF BIBLICAL AND BABYLONIAN CREATION ACCOUNTS[13]

GENESIS ACCOUNT	ENUMA ELISH
God is seen as ultimate source of power; transcends creation.	Magic incantations are ultimate source of power; the gods are subject to nature (III.101; IV.1–26, 91).[14]
Organized coverage of creation; systematically includes general realms of nature.	Does not include creation of vegetation, animals or light—the existence of these is assumed. Moon and stars created, but not the sun (V.2–22).
Purpose: Praise to God as Lord of creation; acknowledging him as such. A tribute to God's ultimacy and authority.	Purpose: Hymn of praise to Marduk as champion and mightiest of the gods. Creation is incidental (VI.100ff.).
Begins before things as we know them existed (1:1); as God created, he gave names (1:5, 8, 10).	Begins before heaven and earth were *named*; cannot imagine situation before they existed (I.1–2).
Starts with primeval deep. Hebrew: *tehom* (1:2).	Starts with the deep—fresh water (Apsu) and salt water (Tiamat)—cognate of *tehom* (I.3–4).
Creation given time sequence; set in blocks by "days" (1:5, 8, 13, etc.).	No chronological structure of "days."

---

12. See Currid, *Against the Gods*, 25.

13. John H. Walton, *Chronological and Background Charts of the Old Testament* (Grand Rapids: Zondervan, 1994), 80.

14. Enuma Elish references designate tablet number and line.

GENESIS ACCOUNT	ENUMA ELISH
Creation by speech (1:3, 6, 9, 11, 20).	Creation from formerly existing matter (IV.137–140; VI.33).
Waters separated above and below by firmament (1:6–8).	Corpse of Tiamat divided in two and set up as waters above and below (IV.137–140).
Man created to rule creation (1:28).	Man created to do the service of the gods so the gods wouldn't have to work so hard (VI.8, 34).
Man created from the soil (2:7).	Man created from blood of slain hero—Kingu (VI.33).

First, the biblical authors reasoned *with* their culture. If we expect early chapters of Genesis to reflect the prevailing scientific worldview of our day, which is naturalistic and empiricist, we will be disappointed.[15] Ancient Near Eastern cultures, though interested in "how the world works and how it came to work that way," searched for answers in a very different place than we do today, namely, in the supernatural realm.[16] They explained the existence of the universe in terms of how it functioned based on supernatural activity. As we should expect, the biblical text speaks within the conceptual world of its day.

Second, the biblical creation account speaks *against* the surrounding culture, defending its view of creation against the prevailing cosmological narratives. Many differences set the biblical narrative apart, including an insistence that (1) there is one God, not many; (2) God creates the world effortlessly out of his word, not out of a cosmic battle; (3) God is before and above creation, and he creates and assigns names, as contrasted to the preexistence of unnamed matter; and (4) people are created in the image of God to rule creation; people are not created to ease the workload of the gods. While there are similarities between the Bible and other creation stories of the ancient Near East, the dissimilarities are more pronounced. The biblical creation account presents a superior explanation of how the world works and how it came to be. It defends the existence of the one true Creator God, as well as the dignity of humankind assigned by that God.

Third, the text speaks *for* the culture, revealing a powerful and benevolent God who created the world to be well-ordered and saw it as "good." This God shaped all people in his image and gave them a noble purpose. Recall once again the larger narrative of the book of Genesis. Chapters 1–11 take a universal perspective. In Genesis 12, the focus turns toward Abraham and his descendants, but even then, God creates Israel in order to bless all people. God is for the world.

---

15. See Walton, *Zondervan Illustrated Bible Backgrounds Commentary*, 1:9.
16. Walton, *Zondervan Illustrated Bible Backgrounds Commentary*, 1:9.

John's gospel employs a similar approach in describing Jesus, the divine *logos* or Word. "In the beginning was the Word [*logos*], and the Word [*logos*] was with God, and the Word [*logos*] was God" (1:1). Why did John use the culturally weighted term *logos* rather than simply writing that Jesus is the Son of God? Because John chose to communicate in a way that was comprehensible to the Greek worldview. He spoke *with* his audience's culture by using the familiar concept of *logos*, then *against* it by redefining *logos* in terms of the Old Testament conception of the divine Word, and finally *for* it by presenting the *logos* as a person who lovingly gave his life for the world.

In both the Old and New Testaments, polemic is used as a culturally relevant defense of the true Creator and Redeemer against false gods. While revealing the inferiority of other gods or the inadequacies of people's understanding of the one true God, polemic demonstrates the reality and superiority of the God of the Bible and persuades people both to trust in his goodness and power and to align their lives with his purposes.[17]

3. MIRACLES AND ACTS OF POWER

Old Testament Miracles and Acts of Power

In the Old Testament, God's acts of power serve as both a defense against alternative deities and an argument for the reality of the living God. In Exodus, for example, God demonstrates his power over false gods by turning Moses's rod into a serpent and by directing the ten plagues against particular Egyptian gods.

Many such acts of power are recorded in the Old Testament, but perhaps the most famous occurs in 1 Kings 18, when Elijah challenges the prophets of Baal. Elijah sets the terms of competition: the god who ignites the wood under a sacrificial bull on an altar will be recognized as the true God. The 450 prophets of Baal shout loudly, prophesy frantically, dance around the altar, and cut themselves with swords and spears, but they are unable to awaken their god. When they finish, Elijah douses his sacrifice with eight large jars of water and then asks God to ignite it so "these people will know that you, Lord, are God, and that you are turning their hearts back again" (v. 37). The fire of the Lord falls, consuming everything—the sacrifice, the wood, the stones, the soil, and the water. When the people see this miracle, they fall prostrate and cry, "The Lord—he is God! The Lord—he is God!" (v. 39). God, through acts of power, is his own apologist.

---

17. In chapter 10, we will introduce a framework we call "inside out," which is inspired in part by the way the Bible interacts with culture, as displayed in this section.

Sarcasm and Ridicule as Old Testament Apologetic Methods

Sometimes the Old Testament prophets ridicule the absurdity of false beliefs. The polemics of the prophets point out the outcome of false belief structures (e.g., Lam 2:14) or poke fun playfully at the basic illogicalities and absurdities of false hopes and beliefs. For example, in Habakkuk 2:18–19, the prophet ridicules idolatry by pushing the idea of man-made idols to the limits of absurdity. Perhaps, as Os Guinness suggests, this subversive use of sarcasm and irony could be used wisely and carefully today as a "table turning" technique, particularly when standing up against skeptical bullies.[18] However, caution and wisdom must be exercised (and we don't suggest this for those who are just learning to engage with others over matters of faith). As we'll see in chapter 7, we should give careful consideration to the pattern for tone established in the New Testament by Jesus and Paul, as well as the wisdom of the cross, before adopting sarcasm as a rhetorical tool.

The Miracles of Jesus

Jesus likewise performed miracles to validate his message about the kingdom of God and to demonstrate his identity and God's love for all people. Jesus performed so many miracles that John writes, "If every one of them were written down . . . even the whole world would not have room for the books that would be written" (John 21:25). John states the apologetic value of miracles clearly: "But these are written that you may believe that Jesus is the Messiah, the Son of God, and that by believing you may have life in his name" (20:31).

Miracles in the Early Church

Miracles continue in the book of Acts, where the apostles perform them to verify that God is at work. On the Day of Pentecost, the Holy Spirit enables the disciples to speak in foreign languages. Peter connects this miracle to the prophecy of Joel 2 and to the signs and wonders God performed in Jesus' ministry. The fact that some bystanders believed the apostles were babbling drunks shows how God may give a clear apologetic, yet some people will misinterpret it. Further revelation is often needed to understand a divine act.

In 1 Corinthians, Paul identifies miraculous powers (12:10, 28), healing (12:9, 28), tongues (12:10, 28), and interpretation of tongues (12:10) as tangible witnesses to God's reality. Some call these Spirit-given abilities "sign gifts" because they point to the authenticity of the gospel; they could even be called "apologetic gifts." The author of Hebrews further affirms that signs, wonders,

---

18. See Os Guinness, *Fool's Talk: Recovering the Art of Christian Persuasion* (Downers Grove, IL: InterVarsity, 2015), 116–19.

miracles, and spiritual gifts testify to the message of salvation announced by the Lord (Heb 2:3–4).

Throughout Scripture, miracles and acts of God's power are presented as powerful apologetics. Even so, many who witnessed them did not believe. The miracles recorded in the Bible and the occurrence of miracles today can have a powerful apologetic impact, but they have limits. Some will need the cumulative impact of other apologetic methods to be persuaded, and others will not believe at all.

4. HISTORICAL VERIFICATION, EYEWITNESS TESTIMONY, AND EVIDENCE

At the beginning of his gospel, Luke claims access to eyewitness testimony of Jesus Christ's life. He asserts he carefully investigated[19] what eyewitnesses told him before writing down an orderly account; he thoroughly researched his gospel so the reader could have confidence in what he recounted. In Luke's own words:

> Many have undertaken to draw up an account of the things that have been fulfilled among us, just as they were handed down to us by those who from the first were *eyewitnesses* and servants of the word. With this in mind, since I myself have *carefully investigated everything from the beginning*, I too decided to write an orderly account for you, most excellent Theophilus, so that you may know the *certainty* of the things you have been taught.[20]

In Acts 1, Peter stands before 120 believers and urges them to choose a disciple to replace Judas. The primary qualification: the new disciple must "have been with us the whole time the Lord Jesus was living among us, beginning from John's baptism to the time when Jesus was taken up from us" (1:21–22). Significantly, in the early church, some eyewitnesses were able to give testimony, not just to certain episodes of Jesus' life, but to the whole of his story, from his baptism onward.[21] These eyewitnesses did not disappear after Jesus ascended, leaving the retelling of Jesus' story to passionate but ill-informed converts. Quite the opposite. They became leaders in the early church, and many were still alive when the Gospels and New Testament letters were written. These eyewitnesses were living guarantees of the gospel tradition.

In 1 Corinthians 15, Paul asserts that Jesus appeared after his resurrection to "Cephas [Peter], and then to the Twelve. After that, he appeared to more than

---

19. Or "thoroughly understood" (Richard Bauckham, *Jesus and the Eyewitnesses: The Gospels as Eyewitness Testimony*, 2nd ed. [Grand Rapids: Eerdmans, 2017], 123).

20. Luke 1:1–4, emphasis added.

21. John 15:26–27; Acts 10:36–42; see Bauckham, *Jesus and the Eyewitnesses*, 114–16.

five hundred of the brothers and sisters at the same time, most of whom are still living, though some have fallen asleep. Then he appeared to James, then to all the apostles, and last of all he appeared to me also, as to one abnormally born" (15:5–8).

Paul seems to be saying, "The evidence for Jesus' resurrection abounds. Check it out. Ask the eyewitnesses yourself. They are still alive!" It would have been easy to destroy Paul's credibility if the claim were untrue.

John writes that the apostles saw Jesus with their eyes and touched him with their hands: "That which was from the beginning, which we have heard, which we have seen with our eyes, which we have looked at and our hands have touched—this we proclaim concerning the Word of life" (1 John 1:1). John could be alluding to the preexistence of Jesus with the words "from the beginning," but more likely he is referring to the start of Jesus' ministry at his baptism, emphasizing that the apostles were eyewitnesses from day one.[22] They had not casually or occasionally encountered Jesus; they had been with him throughout the entirety of his ministry, including his life after resurrection (John 20:24–29). The apostles could verify Jesus' bodily life among them, and thus that the life-giving message John proclaimed was historical reality.

5. FULFILLED PROPHECY

A favorite apologetic method of New Testament authors and preachers is fulfilled prophecy. Sometimes Old Testament prophecies fulfilled by Christ were employed to convince unbelieving Jews; at other times, they were used to ground the faith of those who already believed.

In general, Jesus fulfills all Old Testament hope. At the beginning of his ministry, Jesus identified himself as the fulfillment of the Old Testament Law and Prophets; he stated that he did not come to destroy the Law or the Prophets, but to fulfill them (Matt 5:17). After his resurrection, Jesus taught two discouraged disciples how the Old Testament witnessed to him (Luke 24:27). Just before his ascension, he grounded the gospel message for his apostles in the Old Testament (Luke 24:44–49).

Jesus does not contradict the Old Testament's story, but brings it to its intended goal. He also fulfilled many specific prophecies, such as the prophecies that the Messiah would be born in Bethlehem and would preach to the poor and brokenhearted.

The primary audience for New Testament authors was religious Jews who accepted the authority of the Old Testament. Teachers spent their time poring over it, interpreting and counterinterpreting it. There was constant dialogue over

---

22. See Raymond E. Brown, *The Epistles of John*, The Anchor Bible (New York: Doubleday, 1982), 154–58.

the meaning and relevance of the Law. Thus, first-century believers demonstrated that their faith in Jesus Christ was in continuity with Old Testament hope, pattern, and prophecy.

Fulfilled Prophecy as an Apologetic Today?

The New Testament authors often used the Old Testament in rich and nuanced ways. Biblical scholars have emphasized how sophisticated the New Testament authors were in their reading of the Old Testament. In our present context, this means we cannot simply use a fulfilled prophecy to make an apologetic point without understanding the apostles' Christological reading of the Old Testament. Otherwise, we might be surprised when an unbeliever who reads the New Testament and Old Testament carefully compares them and claims that the New Testament authors were misreading Jesus into the Old Testament.

Fulfilled prophecies can be used in apologetics, but it must be done with care, wisdom, and insight. Each fulfilled prophecy must be understood in its own right; each New Testament allusion to the Old Testament must be interpreted on its own terms. The apostles were interpreting the Old Testament in ways that would have been more convincing in their first-century world. Today, if we're going to help our friends grasp fulfilled prophecy, we would be wise to develop a better understanding of the various ways the New Testament uses the Old Testament.[23]

---

6. CHRISTIANS AS GOOD CITIZENS WITH EXEMPLARY CHARACTER AND LOVE

The lives of Jesus' followers ought to make an apologetic impact. The way we live is evidence of the living reality of God.

Salt and Light

At the beginning of the Sermon on the Mount, Jesus summarizes the counter-intuitive norms of God's kingdom, pronouncing a blessing on those who are poor in spirit, who mourn, who are meek, who hunger and thirst for righteousness, and who are persecuted (Matt 5:1–12). Ironically, it is those who seek peace and show mercy, people who do not put themselves first, who are blessed—persecuted, but blessed.

The humble, cruciform lives of God's people are meant to be an apologetic for the reality of the kingdom of heaven. Jesus calls us "the salt of the earth" and the "light of the world" (Matt 5:13–14). As the salt of the earth, we preserve the world from moral decay and function as an influence for good. As the light of the world, we do good deeds in such a way that some people will recognize

---

23. An important work on this subject is G. K. Beale and D. A. Carson, eds., *Commentary on the New Testament Use of the Old Testament* (Grand Rapids: Baker Academic, 2007).

us as children of God, and come to praise our Father (Matt 5:16).[24] Through our lives, we add value to the world and give evidence of the heavenly Father.

By This Everyone Will Know

In another well-known teaching often called "the Upper Room Discourse," Jesus prepares his disciples for his crucifixion and for life after his resurrection and ascension.

During a meal before the Passover, Jesus gets up, takes off his outer clothing, wraps himself with a towel, and washes his disciples' feet: "Now that I, your Lord and Teacher, have washed your feet, you also should wash one another's feet. I have set you an example that you should do as I have done for you" (John 13:14–15). Later in the discourse, after predicting Judas's betrayal and Peter's denial, Jesus gives a "new" commandment filled with apologetic power: "Love one another. As I have loved you, so you must love one another. By this everyone will know that you are my disciples, if you love one another" (13:34–35).[25] Love—self-sacrificing, cruciform love—testifies to the reality of Jesus and his mission. Such love is unifying (John 17:23), and it demonstrates that the Father has sent the Son.

Put another way, when Christians sacrifice for one another and live in unity, they make more plausible the theological truth that the Father sent the Son into the world on a mission to create a loving community filled with his Holy Spirit. The love of the church can make our three-in-one God more plausible to the world.

Good Citizens

New Testament authors guard against combative impulses, because Christianity is a transformative faith, not a militant or revolutionary movement.[26] Luke in his gospel and Acts provides an example of this perspective. He takes a nuanced view of the relationship of Jesus and his disciples to the Roman government, noting several factors:

- First, Christians were not a political threat to Rome. In Luke, Pilate initially wanted to free Jesus (Luke 23:16). In Acts, Roman authorities argue that the "new" faith does nothing to demand a response from Rome (Acts 18:12–15; 23:23–30).[27]

---

24. Two helpful works on the Sermon on the Mount are D. A. Carson, *The Sermon on the Mount: An Evangelical Exposition of Matthew 5–7* (Grand Rapids: Baker, 1982), and Jonathan T. Pennington, *The Sermon on the Mount and Human Flourishing: A Theological Commentary* (Grand Rapids: Baker, 2017).

25. See also 1 John 4:7–12, 19–21.

26. See Romans 13:1–7; 1 Timothy 2:2–6.

27. See Darrell L. Bock, *A Theology of Luke and Acts: Biblical Theology of the New Testament* (Grand Rapids: Zondervan, 2012), 340–41.

- Second, the Romans' hands were not entirely clean. It was the Romans who ultimately ordered the crucifixion of Jesus and imprisoned Paul for preaching the gospel.[28]
- Third, in Luke and Acts, the only sense in which the Christian faith might have presented a danger to Roman rule was that it changed people, making them lead lives markedly different than the lives of those in the culture around them.[29]

Overall, it is evident from Luke and Acts that as Christians in the early church began to face the reality that Christ would not return for years to come, they were forced to recognize the need to learn to live life in this present world, which meant learning how to interact with secular authorities. As a dynamic cultural force, Christianity would inevitably come into contact—and conflict—with secular political powers such as the Roman government. Christians needed to learn how to demonstrate not only that the church and state could coexist peacefully, but also that Christians could make good citizens, not in spite of their faith, but because of it.[30]

The New Testament approach to citizenship matured as the early church stretched into the second and third centuries. For its very survival, Christians at times had to demonstrate that they were not a threat to existing political structures and instead sought to be a positive influence in the culture. Good citizenship remains an apologetic witness in any time and place.

STOPPING FOR A BREATHER

We have covered a great deal of material. You may feel like you're drinking out of a fire hydrant. Not to worry; it's time to stop for a breather before continuing to drink from the apologetic waters of the Bible in the next chapter. But first, a reminder: Apologetic methods should not be understood apart from the climatic event of Jesus' life, death, resurrection, and ascension. Jesus himself rebuked the religious leaders of his day for studying Scripture apart from him: "You study the Scriptures diligently because you think that in them you have eternal life. These are the very Scriptures that testify about me" (John 5:39). May we never lose sight of Jesus as we study apologetics.

---

28. See Bock, *Theology of Luke and Acts*, 340–41; see also Avery Cardinal Dulles's analysis in *A History of Apologetics* (San Francisco: Ignatius, 2005), 20–21.

29. See Luke 1:50–53; Acts 4:32–37. The church cared for the poor and powerless; the Roman Empire exalted the wealthy and elite (see Bock, *Theology of Luke and Acts*, 331–32, 341).

30. See Dulles, *History of Apologetics*, 21.

CHAPTER TWO

APOLOGETICS IN THE BIBLE: PART 2

High-order thinking is not so readily forced into preexisting categories.

Marilynne Robinson, "Grace," in The Givenness of Things

A DEFINITIVE BIBLICAL APPROACH TO APOLOGETICS?

When I (Josh) was a student, I remember hearing Christian leaders speak on what they thought was *the* biblical approach to dating. While many of these talks were filled with insightful biblical principles, I realized after some reflection that many of them overreached. There is, after all, no single model given in the Bible for dating—it's not as though you can turn to the seventeenth chapter of Romans to find Paul outline rules for courtship. If one tried to appropriate directly a model for finding a spouse from the Bible, they would get some pretty strange results, especially to our Western eyes: Having an arranged marriage? Lying down at someone's feet while they sleep? Just going to a well and waiting? The Bible clearly has not given us a step-by-step method for finding a spouse. What it does offer, however, are principles that we can apply to our current cultural situation to guide us in relationships and marriages.

In the same way, we should not expect to find a definitive approach to apologetics in the Bible. Various approaches bring helpful insights and practices to Christian persuasion, yet there is no one rigid method in the Bible for doing apologetics. Scripture is a bit messier than that—in a good way! It is messy in the sense that it was written in different contexts involving different situations. In other words, God inspired the authors to adopt different persuasive approaches for a variety of contexts. Does the Bible give a universal, context-free, step-by-step apologetic system we can apply to any and every apologetic situation? No. But it does offer tools and principles we can apply to our current cultural location, enabling us to think biblically about apologetics.

This chapter adds nine more biblical apologetic categories to the six explored in the previous chapter.

7. PERSONAL, ECCLESIAL, AND HOLY SPIRIT TESTIMONY

Three distinct but related apologetic agents in the Bible are the individual person, the church, and the Holy Spirit. An intrapersonal witness testifies to the reality of God; the people of God give evidence of God's existence; and the Holy Spirit functions as a persuader for the presence of the living God.

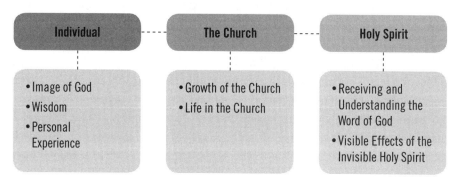

Image of God, Wisdom, and Personal Experience

First, there is an intrapersonal witness to the reality of God.

Image of God. In the creation narrative, humans are made in the image of God (Gen 1:26). The word *image* is significant because in ancient Near Eastern culture it was believed that an image of something contained the essence of whatever it represented. Moreover, it was this essence that enabled the image to carry out the function it was made for.[1] Accordingly, as God's image bearers, we contain his very essence within us, and it is God's essence that enables us to carry out our function, which, according to Genesis 1:26–28, is to rule over the earth. A large part of what being made in the image of God means, then, is a duty we have to represent him on earth by stewarding his creation and, in some sense, extending his rule over it.[2] Because humans are created in the image of God, they have an exalted purpose. This idea of God creating humans in his image stood in direct contrast to other ancient Near Eastern cosmologies, in which people were created to be subservient tools for the gods and cater to their whims.

---

1. See John H. Walton, ed., *Zondervan Illustrated Bible Backgrounds Commentary: Genesis, Exodus, Leviticus, Numbers, Deuteronomy* (Grand Rapids: Zondervan, 2009), 1:20.

2. J. Richard Middleton, *The Liberating Image: The* Imago Dei *in Genesis 1* (Grand Rapids: Brazos, 2005), 60.

In a similar way today, an exalted vision of humans as created in the image of God stands in contrast to the bleak vision of many contemporary worldviews that force people to conclude there is no ultimate purpose to life or to invent their own arbitrary purposes. These contemporary worldviews clash with the intuitive sense we have that we are here for a purpose. In biblical thought, this intuition is the residual effect of being created in God's image.

Wisdom. In the Bible, there is a broad genre referred to as "wisdom literature." This genre serves an apologetic function by showing how everyday life works best with God at the center.[3] One familiar example of wisdom literature is the book of Ecclesiastes, in which the author poses a research question: "Is there any meaning in this world without God?"

Surprisingly, the author's research first leads him to the conclusion that wisdom and knowledge are meaningless. He then explores pleasures and concludes, "Meaningless!" He circles back around, comparing wisdom and folly: "Both meaningless!" His quest continues: "Does our work give us ultimate purpose?" "Meaningless!" "What about advancement?" "Meaningless!" "Do riches give us fulfillment?" "Meaningless!" Finally he arrives at the answer to his research question: There is no meaning in this life *without God*. When someone fears God and keeps God's commands, their life becomes whole. It coheres. Wisdom, knowledge, enjoyments, accomplishments, advancement, and wealth *do* hold meaning and fulfillment when God is at the center.

At this point, we must offer full disclosure: Even those who wisely place God at the center of their lives experience sickness, loss, pain, and suffering. Sometimes all hell breaks loose, and their lives completely fall apart. Yet biblical wisdom literature (Job, Proverbs, Ecclesiastes, and Song of Songs) is very aware of this problem. Job's harrowing trials and his response to them reveal that when life comes unglued, we often see God with new insight, in a more profound way.

The wisdom literature highlights the Christian framework's explanatory power for the whole range of human experiences, such as marriage, suffering, beauty, meaning, and work. The Christian worldview comprises a holistic approach to life that has the power to bring contentment and harmony to our lives. Wisdom literature invites the reader to "try on" biblical prudence in order to see if it makes the most sense of the human condition and results in human flourishing.

Personal experience. In the Scriptures, people often personally testify to an existential encounter they have had with God. After Job encounters God, he

---

3. Ultimately, as the biblical narrative plays out, Jesus Christ is the embodied wisdom of God, and his cross shapes the life of wisdom.

testifies to the new perception he has of God and himself: "My ears had heard of you but now my eyes have seen you. Therefore I despise myself and repent in dust and ashes" (Job 42:5–6).

Isaiah the prophet recounts how when he saw "the LORD, high and exalted, seated on a throne," he cried out, "Woe to me! . . . I am ruined! For I am a man of unclean lips, and I live among a people of unclean lips, and my eyes have seen the King, the LORD Almighty" (Isa 6:1, 5).

Paul's life is radically changed by his encounter with the Lord Jesus Christ (Acts 9:1–9); twice in the book of Acts, he testifies to his life-changing encounter with the resurrected Messiah (22:3–16; 26:9–18).

After her conversation with Jesus at the well, the Samaritan woman goes back into the city and tells everyone about her meeting with Jesus. Many of the Samaritans believe her testimony and go see Jesus for themselves, ultimately acknowledging him as Savior through her testimony (John 4:39–42).

In the Bible, there are many more personal encounters with God such as these—so many that it would take volumes to recount all of them. Today God still uses personal experiences as an apologetic to bring people to himself.

The Church

Second, the people of God give evidence of God's existence.

The three apologetic agents mentioned in the previous section could certainly fit under the category of the church. The difference is that while the preceding section looks primarily at the individual experiences of believers, this section focuses on the church corporately, as a collection of interrelated individuals in community with one another.

Growth of the church. The book of Acts demonstrates that the expansion of the church—from a small gathering of Jews in Jerusalem to a thriving community of both Jews and Gentiles extending to Rome—was the providential work of the God of Israel. In Acts 1:8, forty days after his resurrection and just before his ascension, Jesus foretells that the church will grow through the witness of his disciples. In line with Jesus' prediction, the rest of Acts reports the phenomenal growth of the church: "And the Lord added to their number daily those who were being saved" (Acts 2:47). As we know from observing the contemporary church, the growth of a single church or the universal church at any point in time is not absolute proof that God is at work. Churches can grow for all the wrong reasons. What is actually indicative of the sovereign work of God is the growth of the church throughout history—a growth spanning hundreds of years, pointing to the power of the resurrected Christ and God's Holy Spirit.

Life in the church. The way the church lives together as a corporate witness is an apologetic for the reality of God. For example, through their good works produced by faith, their labor prompted by love, and their endurance inspired by hope in the Lord Jesus Christ, the Thessalonian church witnessed to the vitality of the gospel (1 Thess 1:3). Their faith in God became known everywhere. In the same way, as the members of the modern church love one another, serve one another, forgive one another, care for one another, and pray for one another, the non-Christian community sees an embodied manifestation of the risen Christ.

The Holy Spirit as an Apologist

Third, the Holy Spirit functions as a persuader for the presence of the living God.

Receiving and understanding the Word of God. The Holy Spirit plays an active role in helping us to receive and understand the gospel. In this way, the Holy Spirit is an apologist. He gives us spiritual discernment so that we can understand spiritual truths, enlightening us so that we can understand the wisdom (1 Cor 2:6–16) and the hope of the gospel (Eph 1:15–21).[4] This doesn't mean we can't understand the basic tenets of the gospel or other theological concepts without the Holy Spirit. What it does mean is that we all have a basic resistance to gospel truth, which clouds our spiritual cognition. Our opposition to truth creates a spiritual blindness. The Holy Spirit must open up our affections, enabling us to spiritually discern the validity of the gospel.

In 1 Thessalonians 1:4–5, we see the relationship between Word and Spirit. The reason the Thessalonians received Paul's words as the word of God rather than one man's opinion was that the Holy Spirit was at work within them (2:13):[5] "[the] gospel came to you not simply with words but also with power, with the Holy Spirit and deep conviction" (1:5). The Thessalonians certainly had the mental capacity to understand the gospel message, but it took the power of the Holy Spirit to open their minds to receive the Word and understand it in a spiritually discerning way. It is the Holy Spirit who enables us to see the beauty, goodness, and truth of the gospel.

For believers, the Holy Spirit also testifies to the presence of God in our lives and to our identity as his children. He is an apologist for our adoption into God's family. One manifestation of this reality is that true children of God are to cry out to him in prayer, "*Abba*, Father" (Rom 8:15), "as a child of the Father rather than like a slave addressing a master."[6]

---

4. See Graham A. Cole, *He Who Gives Life: The Doctrine of the Holy Spirit*, Foundations of Evangelical Theology (Wheaton, IL: Crossway, 2007), 265.

5. See Cole, *He Who Gives Life*, 264.

6. Cole, *He Who Gives Life*, 270.

The visible effects of the invisible Holy Spirit. In a conversation with a religious leader, Jesus gives an illustration of the work of the Holy Spirit: "The wind blows wherever it pleases. You hear its sound, but you cannot tell where it comes from or where it is going. So it is with everyone born of the Spirit" (John 3:8). His point is that even though we cannot see the wind or understand where it comes from—remember this was before modern-day meteorology—we can still see and hear its effects. The same is true of the invisible Holy Spirit, who becomes visible as he works in and through believers. In the same way, the personal and ecclesial testimonies mentioned above are visible manifestations of the invisible God and are thus an apologetic for his reality.

Paul encourages Christians to be filled with the Holy Spirit (Eph 5:18). The inevitable result of being filled with the Spirit is worship, which consists of "speaking to one another with psalms, hymns and spiritual songs, singing and making music from your hearts to the Lord, always giving thanks to God the Father for everything, in the name of the Lord Jesus Christ" (Eph 5:19–20, authors' translation). Paul also instructs Christians to walk by the Holy Spirit (Gal 5:16) and keep in step with the Holy Spirit (Gal 5:25), and says that doing so will produce "love, joy, peace, forbearance, kindness, goodness, faithfulness, gentleness and self-control" (Gal 5:22–23). Acts of worship and virtues are visible manifestations of the invisible Holy Spirit. These visible manifestations cause the personal and corporate lives of Christians to testify to the reality of the living God, forming an apologetic and revealing the Holy Spirit to be a powerful apologist.

8. RAISING QUESTIONS WITH AN INTENT TO UNDERMINE OR DISARM FALSE BELIEFS

In the Bible, God often uses a subversive methodology in which he asks insightful questions in order to challenge and undermine false beliefs. Here are few examples:

- In the book of Job, God challenges Job by asking a series of rhetorical questions that compare Job's limited knowledge and management of the created world to God's own infinite knowledge and sovereign, creative power (Job 38–41): "Brace yourself like a man; I will question you, and you shall answer me" (Job 38:3).
- When Jesus' authority is questioned, he replies, "John's baptism—where did it come from? Was it from heaven, or of human origin?" (Matt 21:25).

- When questioned about paying taxes to Caesar, Jesus responds, "Whose image is this? And whose inscription?" (Matt 22:20).
- Jesus asks the Pharisees a series of questions concerning the nature of the Messiah in Matthew 22:41–46:

  "What do you think about the Messiah? Whose son is he?"

  "How is it then that David, speaking by the Spirit, calls him 'Lord'?"

  "If then David calls him 'Lord,' how can he be his son?"

All of these questions are designed to undermine and disarm false beliefs. Questions can both subtly subvert wrong assumptions and directly challenge erroneous dogmas. While questions do not prove anything apologetically, they do cause skeptics settled in false beliefs to stop and think. Intelligent questions point out cracks in a skeptic's assumptions and make them rethink their perspective, creating space for them to consider Christianity. Questions are powerful because they are involving; that is, they engage the person we are speaking to.[7] Questions force people to think for themselves, and in turn they force us to directly listen and respond to their thoughts rather than just talk at them. This enables a richer, much more personal exchange of thoughts and feelings and can set a relational context for persuasion.

9. ANSWERING OBJECTIONS

Sometimes objections to the faith are immediate and present; at other times they are anticipated. Almost all apologetics in the Bible fall under this category in some form. There are two primary ways the Bible responds to anticipated objections: explanations and reframing.

Explanations

Very often in Scripture, the author of a text or a character in a narrative anticipates and responds to an objection with an explanation. We could produce an almost endless list of examples, but one of the most familiar is the way Scripture anticipates objections to faith in Jesus Christ and responds with parables, provocative questions, witty sayings, logical reasoning, Old Testament fulfillment, and enlightening stories. Here are some specific examples of objections and corresponding explanations from the life of Jesus.

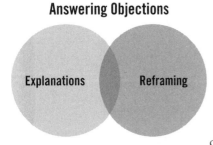

Answering Objections

Explanations   Reframing

---

7. See Os Guinness, *Fool's Talk: Recovering the Art of Christian Persuasion* (Downers Grove, IL: InterVarsity, 2015), 161–64.

OBJECTION EXPLANATION

Objection	Explanation
How could the Messiah be crucified on a cross when everyone crucified on a cross is cursed?	In order to redeem us from the curse of the law, Jesus became a curse for us (Gal 3:13–14).
Wasn't Jesus demon-possessed? Did he not drive out demons by the prince of demons?	Jesus answers in parables and asks, "How can Satan drive out Satan? A kingdom divided against itself cannot stand" (Mark 3:23–24).
Wasn't Jesus' birth a result of sexual immorality?	No, it was a virgin birth in fulfillment of Old Testament prophecy (Matt 1:18–25; Luke 1:26–38).
Why did Jesus not urge his disicples to fast?	Jesus' disciples did not fast while he was with them; they would fast when he was taken from them: "How can the guests of the bridegroom fast while he is with them?" (Mark 2:19).
Why did Jesus not keep the Sabbath?	Jesus again answers with a question about whether it was lawful for King David and his companions to eat from the consecrated bread. Jesus, the Son of Man, is Lord of the Sabbath (Mark 2:23–26; see also 3:1–6).
Why did Jesus not observe the Pharisaic laws of ritual purity?	Observing or disobeying man-made rules does not make people pure or defile them. The evils that come from inside a person are what defile them (Mark 7:1–23).
Why did Jesus associate with sinners?	Jesus says, "It is not the healthy who need a doctor, but the sick. I have not come to call the righteous, but sinners" (Mark 2:17).
How could Jesus claim the authority to forgive sins?	His ability to heal proves his ability to forgive sins, because such power proves that he is the Son of God (Mark 2:1–12).
Didn't the disciples of Jesus steal the body of Jesus and claim that he was resurrected?	The chief priests and elders bribed the soldiers to make this claim (Matt 27:62–66; 28:2–4, 11–15).
If Jesus is the Messiah, why did the Jews not accept him as such?[8]	1. Because of the hardness of human hearts (Matt 13:14; Mark 4:13; Luke 8:10; John 12:40; Acts 28:26–27; Rom 11:1–10, 25). 2. Because of the power that Satan has to blind people (2 Cor 4:4).

It is important to recognize that many of the questions and objections above, which were raised in the first century, are not the questions being asked today. This is one reason that contextualization and wisdom are so necessary for contemporary apologetics.

---

8. See Brian K. Morley, *Mapping Apologetics: Comparing Contemporary Approaches* (Downers Grove, IL: InterVarsity, 2015), 36–37.

Reframing

The Scriptures often redraw our mental maps, rescript our narratives, and reframe our perceptual models. Consider God's response to Habakkuk's complaint in the book of Habakkuk. The prophet is angry at God for letting the kingdom of Judah get away with so much injustice: "How long, LORD, must I call for help, but you do not listen?" (1:2). In so many words, God responds, "You wouldn't even believe what I am going to do if I told you: I will use the Babylonians, that 'ruthless and impetuous people,' to punish my own people, Judah" (1:5–11).

Habakkuk is stunned and confused. He affirms that God's "eyes are too pure to look on evil" and that he "cannot tolerate wrongdoing" (1:13a). But then, in effect, he asks very pointedly, if God is perfectly pure, how can he use the Babylonians to punish his own people? "Why then do you tolerate the treacherous? Why are you silent while the wicked swallow up those more righteous than themselves?" (1:13b).

Instead of answering Habakkuk directly, God gives him a revelation of future judgment, which is to be written on stone tablets as a sign that it will surely happen. Then God pronounces five "woe" judgments on the violent, the unjust, and the lawless. In the end, God will bring justice and peace, and his glory will be ubiquitous: "The earth will be filled with the knowledge of the glory of the LORD as the waters cover the sea" (2:14). God's "woes" close with the command for quietness: "The LORD is in his holy temple; let all the earth be silent before him" (2:20).

God answers Habakkuk's objections. But instead of answering them directly, God reframes Habakkuk's narrative by showing him how things will be set right in the judgment to come. Sometimes God does not directly confront an objection but instead gives people a glimpse of himself and his plans for the future, which in turn reframes the way they see the present. There are distorted mental maps, wrong perceptual models, and invalid interpretive narratives in which God doesn't make any sense. In some cases, rather than defending himself within these false models, maps, and narratives, God simply shatters them. He sets himself within a true map, a proper model, an accurate narrative, that corresponds with reality and in doing so enables us to see life in the proper perspective.

10. REASONS FOR SUFFERING

Lament: Registering a Complaint with God.

The Bible never shies away from the fact that there is suffering in the world. In fact, its pages are filled with expressions of raw emotions that are caused by evil and suffering. There is even a genre called *lament* devoted to the expression of these emotions and an entire book of the Bible titled "Lamentations" (in Hebrew the title is simply "How!"). Thus, one of most common apologetic methods the Bible uses in addressing the problem of suffering is to invite the sufferer to engage God with honest grief and complaint. In biblical laments, the Bible gives verbal, lyrical, and liturgical shape to the messiness of our confusion.

Why Do We Suffer?

Does the Bible give an apologetic for our suffering? Put simply, does the Bible give a reason for our suffering? Yes. Without exhaustively answering every question related to suffering, the following are different ways the Bible addresses the issue:

- Humanity suffers because of sin. Adam and Eve chose to disobey God's one command; as a result, sin entered the world, and suffering followed (Gen 3).
- Israel suffers because they disobeyed the Deuteronomic covenant.
- God's children sometimes suffer from human disregard and abuse in order to accomplish a greater divine good (Gen 50:20).
- Suffering gives the faithful new insight into God (see Job) and his written revelation (Ps 119:67, 71).
- Disciples of Jesus suffer persecution because they follow Christ, who was persecuted himself (Matt 5:10–12).
- Early Christians suffer persecution because of the jealousy and hatred of human leaders (Acts 13:45; 14:2, 19; 17:5, 13; 21:27).[9]
- Christians suffer in order to know Jesus better (Phil 3:10).
- Christians share in Jesus Christ's sufferings in the present in order that they might share in his glory in the future (Rom 8:17).
- God's children suffer because God disciplines his children out of his love for them (Prov 3:11–12; Heb 12:5–6).
- Christians suffer in order to mature spiritually (Jas 1:2–4), grow in righteousness and peace (Heb 12:5–11), and be conformed to the image of Jesus Christ (Rom 8:28–30).
- Christians suffer so that their faith can be proven genuine (1 Pet 1:6–7).

God Suffers

The God of the Bible becomes completely human and hurts in every way that we do—from physical pain to social rejection, misunderstanding, hatred,

---

9. See Morley, *Mapping Apologetics*, 36.

violence, and death. He endures it all. And because he suffers all of this with us, he can empathize with our sorrow and pain. Even more amazingly, Jesus' death on the cross and his resurrection are the avenues through which he overcomes all evil, pain, and misery and is able to offer us the promise that disappointment will give way to joy, brokenness to eternal healing, and evil to good. Because of Christ's agony, death will die and life will live on forever. God's primary biblical apologetic for suffering is grounded in his own anguish on a cross.

Suffering Points to the Existence of God

It may sound odd, but in the Bible, the reality of suffering and evil is actually an argument for the existence of God. As we discussed earlier, the fact that God made man in his image and created the universe to be good is the basis for humanity's primordial sense of right and wrong. We intuitively know that human suffering, pain, and evil are wrong; we perceive that this world is not as it should be. Sometimes a vision of what ought to be moves us to cry out against suffering, to long for the good, and to chase what the Old Testament calls shalom—peace, wholeness, and well-being. The Bible would argue that our distaste for suffering is grounded in the Creator God's own desire for what is good, harmonious, and healing. Our sense that there is a "right" and a "good" has been implanted in us by God. Thus, laments reveal the sufferer not only to be complaining about evil against God, but also to be engaging with the One who is believed—sometimes faintly and other times ferociously—to be the ultimate source of all good. In this way, the Bible reveals that, ironically, suffering and evil actually argue for the existence of God.[10]

11. LOGIC AND REASON

That Sounds Reasonable

Throughout its pages, the Bible employs logic to demonstrate the reasonableness of its theological positions. While Scripture does not present pure rationalism in a vacuum, it does depict biblical authors and characters reasoning within the context of their respective audiences. In general, the Scriptures call for speakers and writers to employ rational arguments that would make sense to those receiving their message.

We have already seen some level of logic used in the earlier sections of chapters 1 and 2. We see this because throughout all of Scripture, biblical

---

10. See Gregory E. Ganssle's more philosophical argument in "Evil as Evidence for Christianity," in *God and Evil: The Case for God in a World Filled with Pain*, ed. Chad Meister and James K. Dew Jr. (Downers Grove, IL: InterVarsity, 2013), 214–23.

authors and characters use logic to persuade people to certain theological beliefs. Again, while the Bible does not use pure rational thought or modal logic to prove systematically the existence of God, it definitely uses reason to bring a particular audience to certain conclusions about who God is and how he works. For example, the Bible does not set out to prove that a greater being created the world. In the context it was written, there was no need to; ancient Near Eastern peoples already believed that the world was created by a god or gods. Instead, the Bible argues that a certain God created the world with a particular purpose in mind.

The Limits of Reason

For the following three reasons, we must keep a balanced perspective about the limits of reason. First, any time we are discussing rationality, we must ask, "Whose rationality?" The Western conception of reason many have become accustomed to—heavily influenced by modern Enlightenment rationalism—is quite different from that of the premodern ancient Near Eastern culture, which reasoned in terms of poetry, narrative, parable, wisdom, etc.

Second, we must recognize that God is far beyond humanity's grasp. We can know him, but not exhaustively. There will always be a mystery to who he is that goes beyond our cognitive ability. He is, after all, God!

Third, people are more than minds. Humans are not merely reasoning and thinking beings; we are also desiring and believing beings. The Bible recognizes this, and while logic is ever present, it is employed within a framework and a shared set of assumptions that take our total humanity into account.

12. APOCALYPTIC APOLOGETIC

In the Bible, apocalyptic literature helps suffering faith communities reconcile a sometimes harsh reality with a seemingly inactive God in regard to their pain. A marginalized people who feel outnumbered and threatened need to know how God intends to right the world. Apocalyptic literature, by explaining why pagans prosper with such power and what awaits those who persecute the faithful, has apologetic value and can be found in both Daniel and Revelation.[11] We will focus particularly on three aspects of these two books that have apologetic value.[12]

---

11. For more information on Jewish apocalyptic literature, see John J. Collins, *The Apocalyptic Imagination: An Introduction to Jewish Apocalyptic Literature*, 2nd ed. (Grand Rapids: Eerdmans, 1998).

12. Other biblical texts that might be considered apocalyptic in nature are Isaiah 24–27; 56–66; Ezekiel 38–39; Joel 3–4; Zechariah 9–14; Matthew 24; Mark 13; Luke 21:15–38; 1 Thessalonians 4:13–18; 2 Thessalonians 2.

Apologetic Aspects of Apocalypticism

Opposing powers (God and Satan).[13] Both Revelation and Daniel pull back the curtain of reality on earth as humans see it to reveal the ongoing cosmic battle between God and Satan, angels and demons, good and evil. There is at this very moment, breaking into the realm of experience and history, both an evil realm that is under the power of the Evil One and an eternal kingdom of God. This dualism can be seen in Daniel when the angel Michael helps a heavenly messenger, perhaps the angel Gabriel (Dan 8:16; 9:21), overcome the resistance from the prince of Persia, probably a demonic power who fights on behalf of the Persian Empire (10:12–14; see also Rev 12:7–9).

Daniel and Revelation reveal something we could not have perceived with our natural senses. They explain, in graphic terms, why marginalized people are suffering and are persecuted: We are caught in the middle of a cosmic battle between good and evil. Satan and his demons are real, and their attacks are ruthless. Apocalyptic as an apologetic assures those who are afflicted because of their faith that evil spiritual forces are behind their sufferings.

However, this apologetic aspect of apocalypticism is not sufficient in itself. Those who suffer for God must also know that their God is not weak and is ultimately victorious.

Sovereignty (God's plan for history and his ultimate victory). Even though this present world is tormented by the Evil One, God has always been moving history according to his preordained plan toward its final destiny: the ultimate victory of good over evil. Satan is real, but God is sovereign. God determines the epochs of history and moves them toward his own triumph over evil. Persecuted and afflicted believers are not persevering in vain, because God has a glorious plan for their future.

In Revelation 5, John weeps because no one in heaven or on earth is worthy to break open the scroll of destiny—that is, until he sees the Lamb "looking as if it had been slain, standing at the center of the throne" (Rev 5:6). Jesus Christ alone is worthy enough to reign over history and determine the destiny of all. This includes the final outcome of all history. In the end, everything will be made new. God will wipe away his people's tears, with the promise that "there will be no more death or mourning or crying or pain" (21:4).

This apologetic explains that marginalized and persecuted Christian communities are suffering for a purpose. Their afflictions are not random; they are a part of the unfolding defeat of evil, victory of the Messiah, and triumph of

---

13. For these three characteristics of apocalypse, see Robert H. Mounce, *The Book of Revelation*, rev. ed. (Grand Rapids: Eerdmans, 1998), 3–4.

the kingdom of God. Jesus Christ is sovereign over his people's sufferings and will assure their victory.

Last things (God's final judgment of evil and establishment of his peaceful and righteous kingdom). In the end, the future will break into the present. God will judge sin and bring peace and righteousness. Enough will be enough. Daniel 12 relates that after a time of distress like no other, some will be raised to shame and everlasting contempt, and some will be resurrected to everlasting life. God's people, whose names are written in the book of life, will be delivered: "Those who are wise will shine like the brightness of the heavens, and those who lead many to righteousness, like the stars for ever and ever" (Dan 12:3; see also Rev 20–21).

Apocalyptic literature provides a suffering community a framework that enables them to make sense of what seems to be the inactivity of God and the ascendancy of evil. It offers them an apologetic, explaining to them that God will put an end to all evil and will establish justice and peace forever, ensuring an eternal reward for those who persevere.

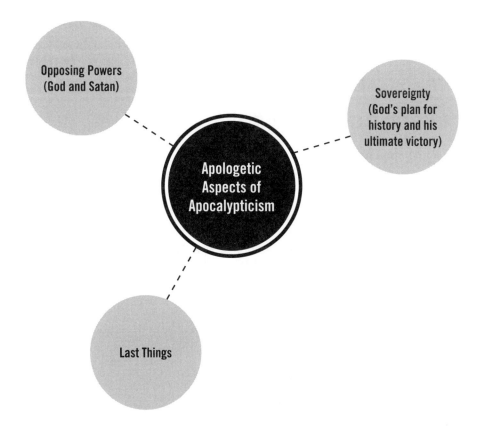

While it may seem strange to think of the apocalyptic and science fiction novels and movies of today as having apologetic value, apocalypses were actually one of the primary means for exiled Jewish communities to make sense out of their suffering between 300 BC and 200 AD. Extrabiblical Jewish apocalypses depicted ancient seers traveling in visions to alternative dimensions to find meaning for their present experiences and foresee where history was headed. It appears that the book of Daniel, a biblical account of actual visions, might have been the catalyst for much of this literature. By the time John wrote his apocalypse, the genre was far more prevalent. Thus, biblical apocalypses combined (1) a culturally relevant way of explaining reality with (2) authentic visions from God to help suffering communities make sense out of their present afflictions.

James K. A. Smith suggests that apocalyptic literature is still a relevant genre for today. Just as the book of Revelation unmasks the real weaknesses of a tyrannical ruling empire by revealing an alternative reality in which the Lamb of God sits on the throne, so too can apocalyptic thinking today unmask the "spin" of hegemonic cultural powers. Smith asserts, "What we need . . . is a kind of contemporary apocalyptic—a language and a genre that sees through the spin and unveils the religious (and idolatrous) character of contemporary institutions that constitute our own milieu."[14] A modern-day apocalyptic apologetic, by setting forth an alternative reality, would counteract the spin of the ruling cultural narratives.

13. ARGUMENTS FROM PAGAN SOURCES

In Paul's speech before Athenian philosophers on Mars Hill, he quotes the pagan poet Aratus (ca. 315–240 BC): "We are [God's] offspring" (Acts 17:28).[15] Paul's argument that springboards from this quote is as follows: "If we are God's offspring, then obviously we should not think of him, as you Athenians do, in terms of gold or silver or stone images. God creates us; we do not create him. He gives life and breath to us; we do not design and make him. God is the Creator, and we are created in his image." In this way, Paul uses a pagan quote to support his own point, but he "contextualizes the citation and presents it in a fresh light, setting up his critique."[16] Ironically, Paul uses a Greek quote originally referring to Zeus as a critique of the Greek philosophers' own idolatry. Paul masterfully

---

14. James K. A. Smith, *You Are What You Love: The Spiritual Power of Habit* (Grand Rapids: Brazos, 2016), 40.

15. For more on this reference to Aratus, see Darrell L. Bock, *Acts*, Baker Exegetical Commentary on the New Testament (Grand Rapids: Baker Academic, 2007), 568; Ben Witherington III, *The Acts of the Apostles: A Socio-Rhetorical Commentary* (Grand Rapids: Eerdmans, 1998), 530.

16. Bock, *Acts*, 568.

argues within the plausibility structure of his audience by quoting their own poet, reimagining the quote in light of biblical truth and then turning it against their pagan beliefs. This demonstrates that the Bible is not against reasoning within secular cultural narratives, because those very narratives can be turned on their heads and used as highly effective apologetic tools.

14. JESUS' UNIQUE AUTHORITY

Jesus' teaching, in both its content and style, has a self-testifying, self-authenticating ring of authority to it that possesses apologetic value. In Scripture, whenever he teaches, people immediately recognize that unlike their own teachers, who based their teachings heavily on the traditions of earlier teachers, his instruction—his words—carry authority.[17] At the end of the Sermon on the Mount, for example, the people are amazed at Jesus' teaching "because he taught as one who had authority, and not as their teachers of the law" (Matt 7:29). Jesus in his teaching has an inherent authority that is palpable. Unfortunately, even though the people are amazed by the authority with which Jesus speaks, not all commit to him and his teaching.[18] The human heart has an amazing ability to suppress what it knows to be true.

Jesus' authoritative teaching continues in the mouths of his followers. At the end of the book of Matthew, Jesus sends his disciples out, with his presence and his authority, to make disciples of all nations by baptizing the people and teaching them to obey his commands (28:19–20).[19] Still today, Jesus' teachings can attract even the most hardened skeptic to the faith.

15. STORY

The Bible is a storied story. That is, it is one big story made up of many smaller stories. The Bible tells one grand narrative by recounting many smaller vignettes. First let's look at few of the smaller stories.

The Smaller Stories

We have already seen many examples of how this works. To begin with, under the heading of Polemic, we learned how the Bible, while speaking within an ancient Near Eastern understanding of creation narratives, counters these

---

17. See Donald A. Hagner, *Matthew 1–13*, Word Biblical Commentary (Dallas, TX: Word, 1993), 33a:193.

18. See Michael L. Wilkins, *Matthew*, NIV Application Commentary (Grand Rapids: Zondervan, 2004), 328–29.

19. Other references to authority in Matthew include 8:7–9; 9:6–8; 10:1; 21:23–27.

narratives by telling a better, truer story of creation. The biblical account of creation is more meaningful and beautiful, revealing a creation that is good, fertile, and productive. It assigns to humankind a higher function: to serve as divine image bearers by ruling over the earth and flourishing with life and creativity. Just as God creates, shapes, names, and rules, so do people receive the divine task of performing life-giving work.

The teacher in Ecclesiastes tells a more meaningful story by articulating that people only find purpose in life—pleasure, knowledge, and work—by fearing God and keeping his commandments (12:13). People who live according to this narrative find deep pleasure, true knowledge, and meaningful work.

Recall how in John 1:1, John, by introducing Jesus as the *logos* (Word), chose to communicate his message in a way that was comprehensible to the Greek worldview. John first spoke *with* the *logos* preunderstanding of his hearers and then *against* that understanding by defining it in terms of the Old Testament's conception of the Word. He does this in order to present the person Jesus as the divine *logos* who gave his life to save the world. John tells a better story than the Greek culture around him.

Finally, as we just saw above, John uses explanatory power to tell a better story in his apocalypse. He explains to a suffering community that, although ruthless powers seem to be winning the day, God will ultimately bring an end to evil, lift up the marginalized, and establish eternal justice.

This apologetic methodology is pervasive in the Bible. Examples abound throughout the pages of Scripture, and some of the most obvious apologetic stories are contained in the Gospels and the book of Acts. In their own way, each of the gospels tells a story that defends and clears the way for faith in Jesus Christ. The book of Acts, though orderly and well researched, is also a story that defends belief in the resurrected Christ, the work of the Spirit, and the growth of the church. These shorter and longer stories blend together into one grand biblical narrative. Let's turn now to the bigger story.

The Big Story

The grand narrative of the Bible plays out in four movements: creation, fall, redemption, and new creation.[20] Apologetically, the Bible claims that this grand narrative is better than any other prevailing cultural narrative. In fact, it isn't just a better story; it's the *best* story. It is a truer story than any other. It is a cross-centered story about a God who became a human himself because of his deep love for all people. This God humbled himself even to the point of death

---

20. See also Kevin Vanhoozer's five-act division of the grand narrative in *The Drama of Doctrine: A Canonical Linguistic Approach to Christian Theology* (Louisville: Westminster John Knox, 2005), 2–3.

on a cross for the sins of humanity. There is no other story quite like this one. It is *the* story. In the chapters to follow, we show how the big story of the Bible leads to the good and beautiful life.

Today, we are living between redemption and the new creation. Yes, that's right; we are a part of the story. Thus, to help skeptics make sense of the Bible's grand narrative, we must live in and live *out* the story. Again, our lives are an apologetic.

CONCLUSION: Contextual and Cross-Centered

The fifteen approaches surveyed in this and the previous chapter have served not only to immerse you in the apologetic world of the Bible but also to display the diversity of the Scriptures. Much in biblical apologetics depends on the historical setting, the nature of the conversation, and the audience in view. So while we have drawn out many specific insights, the one overarching implication of this biblical survey is that the Bible takes a contextual approach to apologetics.

Furthermore, it is essential to recognize the progressive movement of the Bible toward one climactic event: Christ's life, death, and resurrection. An apologetic should be measured by *the degree of clarity with which it points to and functions in light of the most important event in human history.* We invite you to continue with us on our journey in developing an apologetic that is deeply rooted in the Bible, is formed at the foot of the cross, and points to the power of God in the gospel of Jesus Christ. To this end, we now turn to tracing some of the key apologetic turning points in the history of the church.

CHAPTER THREE

APOLOGETICS WITHIN THE GREAT TRADITION: PART 1

Poring over the traditions of Christian practice and reflection is not "an impossible return to the past" but an opportunity to see the present situation of theology for what it is: as a moment in the history of redemption.

John Webster, "Ressourcement Theology and Protestantism," in Ressourcement: A Movement for Renewal in Twentieth-Century Catholic Theology

THE BUILDERS WHO WENT BEFORE US

In chapters 1 and 2, we began to build our "apologetic house" with a biblical foundation. In this chapter and the next, we will complete that foundation with a survey of how apologetics has developed since the early church. In order to cover a span of nearly two thousand years of apologetic history effectively in only two chapters, we will hit the high points, giving an overview of significant people, movements, and apologetic approaches.

In this chapter, we will discover some good news: We do not have to completely rebuild our apologetic house from the ground up. Many bricks in the foundation have already been laid. Just as any modern builder uses the technology handed down through the ages rather than attempting to reinvent it all himself, so too will the best apologists retrieve and use the apologetic resources handed down to them. While many books introducing apologetics give little to no attention to the history of apologetics, we believe that having a panoramic view of the discipline's developments will make you a more effective apologist. Yes, we should fit our apologetic approach to our present context, and, yes, we should be creative and innovative. *But our innovation should be built on the foundation of Scripture and our ancestors in the faith on whose shoulders we stand.* We should always use the apologetic foundation the church has given us. With that said, we are now prepared to finish the foundation of our apologetic house.[1]

THE EARLY CHURCH

The early, formative years of the church, which scholars refer to as the "patristic period," were not easy. The very survival of the church was threatened. As converts joyfully turned to the way of Christ, they found themselves facing serious challenges—especially from heretics, religious Jews, and Greeks. Forced to defend the church from such challenges and to establish the church's viability, the early church fathers carved out a place in the world for the church.

Heretical Challenges

Hoping for a better way, heretics unsuccessfully explore a different path. Throughout the history of the church, a heretic has been defined as "someone who has compromised an essential doctrine and lost sight of who God really is, usually by oversimplification."[2] More often than not, the originator of a heresy did not set out to be heretical, but was actually attempting to share the Christian faith more effectively by making it compatible to the reigning thought forms of a particular culture.[3] Ironically, something that begins with apologetic motivations can go off course and become in need of orthodox apologetics.

The following were some of the most threatening heretical beliefs propagated in the early church:

Gnosticism. Only those with secret, insider knowledge may reach God, and only through a series of lesser gods called Aeons. Jesus is not God; he is merely an Aeon.

Marcionism. Its teachings are as follows:

- Some of the Bible is good; some of it is bad.
- Spirit is good; material is bad.
- Jesus is good, loving, and peaceful; the Creator God of the Old Testament is bad, mean, and angry.
- Gospel is good; law is bad.
- Christians are good; Jews are bad.
- Jesus is not actually human; he is only divine.

---

1. This chapter, as well as chapter 4, is aided by two sources in particular: Avery Cardinal Dulles, *A History of Apologetics* (San Francisco: Ignatius, 2005); William Edgar and K. Scott Oliphant, eds., *Christian Apologetics Past and Present: A Primary Source Reader*, vols. 1–2 (Wheaton, IL: Crossway, 2009, 2011).

2. Justin S. Holcomb, *Know the Heretics* (Grand Rapids: Zondervan, 2014), 11.

3. See Alister McGrath, *Heresy: A History of Defending the Truth* (New York: HarperCollins, 2009), 176.

Gnosticism and Marcionism appealed to those who perceived the actions and regulations of the Old Testament God as harsh compared with the character and teachings of Jesus.

Manicheism. Combines Christianity with other religions to create one great world religion. Jesus was not really born; he did not suffer; and he did not rise from the dead. His sufferings were merely symbolic. Some accepted Manicheism because it explained suffering as a conflict between good and evil; God is good but is impeded by evil forces.

Arianism. There was a time when Christ did not exist; Jesus was created by God the Father before the world began. And although he is like God, he is not of the same substance as the Father. Arianism offered a simple solution for those struggling with how Jesus could be human and divine.

How did the church respond to these heresies?

It's no secret. In the second century, Irenaeus (ca. 140–ca. 198), the bishop of Lyons in Gaul, wrote *Against Heresies.* In it he claims that knowledge of the truth is no secret, because a rule of faith has been handed down publicly to the entire church by the apostles. The rule of faith clearly lays out the entirety of God's plan for all to see, from creation to Christ's earthly ministry, death, and resurrection; to the growth of the church and spread of the gospel; to the return of Christ and the consummation of all things. It is a public confession of the basic tenets of the faith, often recited at worship services and baptisms. Thus, the truth is not hidden; it's public knowledge. Anyone can know the truth.

The Creator is good . . . and just. Tertullian (ca. 160/70–ca. 220), the earliest of the Latin church fathers, wrote *Against Marcion* in direct response to heresy. Like Irenaeus, Tertullian uses Scripture and the rule of faith in order to make his point, demonstrating that the Old and New Testaments testify to one true Creator God, who, while he is perfectly good, is also just and must therefore punish sin. Tertullian also explains that salvation would not be possible without Jesus Christ suffering in an actual human body.

Jesus' suffering is real and necessary. Augustine (354–430), one of the great theologians in church history, practiced Manicheanism for ten years before he converted to Christianity. Augustine titled his response to the heresy he had denounced *Against Faustus the Manichaean.* In it he explains that Christ's physicality is real; Jesus proved it by inviting Thomas to touch him and put his hand in his side. Like Tertullian, Augustine argues that Christ had to suffer physically for our salvation, and, like Irenaeus, he claims that the Old Testament is legitimate because it was written by God and foretells Jesus' coming.

Jesus is God because Jesus is Savior. Athanasius (ca. 296–373), a bishop of Alexandria who encountered many enemies, combated the heretical teaching that Jesus is not fully God with three decisive and enduring arguments:

1. Only God can save humanity. Jesus saves humanity. Therefore, Jesus is God.
2. God himself taking on human flesh and dying for the sins of human-kind is the only way God could satisfy both his justice and his mercy. Thus, Jesus had to be God to be our Savior.
3. In the church's liturgy Jesus is worshiped as God. It is blasphemy to worship a mere creature. Thus, in its worship the church confesses that Jesus is God.

Although the heresies mentioned above have made and still make temporary comebacks in different forms—think Dan Brown's *Da Vinci Code*, which spins a narrative out of the Gnostic gospels—the substantial responses of early church fathers not only successfully combated the forms the heresies took in their day, but they also are still useful for combating contemporary forms of these heresies.

Jewish Religious Challenges

We can imagine the sort of questions a practicing Jew might have had for Christians in the early church: "Why don't Christians practice the Mosaic law?" "Why do Christians believe that Jesus is the Old Testament Messiah?" "Why do Christians worship Jesus as God?"

Many apologists dealt with these questions, but perhaps the most noteworthy is Justin Martyr (ca. 100–ca. 165), a converted pagan philosopher, who responded to them out of his own personal experience. Before converting to Christianity, he had been searching deeply through various philosophies of his day. One day, while on a walk along the seashore, he met an old Christian man who encouraged him to read the Hebrew prophets. After reading the Old Testament Prophets and the Gospels, Justin converted to Christianity. Reflecting on his conversion later, he wrote, "I fell in love with the prophets and these men who had loved Christ; I reflected on all their words and found that this philosophy alone was true and profitable."[4]

Ultimately, Justin ended up in Rome, where he founded a Christian school.

---

4. Quoted in James D. Smith III, "Worship in the Early Church: A Gallery of Wordsmiths of Worship," *Christian History Institute* (1993), www.christianhistoryinstitute.org/magazine/article/worship -gallery-of-wordsmiths.

It was during this time that he wrote *Dialogue with Trypho the Jew*. In a narrated conversation with Trypho, Justin attempts to answer a number of Jewish objections to Christianity. With a respectful tone, Justin argues that (1) Old Testament prophecies affirm that Jesus is divine and that he is the Messiah; (2) since the new covenant replaces the old covenant, Christians are in a better position to interpret the Old Testament; and (3) the Christian church is the new Israel. The *Dialogue* ends, not with Trypho's conversion, but with Justin offering Trypho and his companions these amiable parting words:

> After this they left me, wishing me safety in my voyage, and from every misfortune. And I, praying for them, said, "I can wish no better thing for you, sirs, than this, that, recognizing in this way that intelligence is given to every man, you may be of the same opinion as ourselves, and believe that Jesus is the Christ of God."[5]

We should aim for our modern-day apologetic conversations to conclude with such clarity and love.

Greek and Roman Challenges

The early church faced two types of challenges from the Hellenistic culture: (1) political/cultural and (2) philosophical.

Political and Cultural Challenges

The accusations the Greeks leveled against early church Christians were some of the most damning and encompassed many of the most pressing apologetic issues that existed during the patristic period. These accusations were based mostly on misunderstandings and misperceptions of Christian practice and doctrine. How do you think the following stereotypical allegations might have developed?

- Christians are immoral.
- Christians are incestuous.
- Christians are cannibals.
- Christians practice infanticide.
- Christians are atheists.
- Christianity undermines civic loyalty and national stability.
- Christianity is new.

---

5. Justin Martyr, *Dialogue with Trypho the Jew* 142, www.earlychristianwritings.com/text/justinmartyr-dialoguetrypho.html.

You may find this list surprising. Cannibalism? Infanticide? Atheism? Those aren't exactly the sort of charges made against the Christian faith that we often hear today. But then again, these types of accusations may be more familiar to us than we think. There are certainly many people who misunderstand Christianity and believe its morality is out of step with the mores of our contemporary world. The early church responded to the challenges mentioned above by vindicating the Christian faith, showing how its teachings were actually beneficial for the well-being of society. Now that we are facing similar challenges, it is our task to do the same.

Here are some examples of the most powerful Christian responses to the Roman Empire's objections to the Christian faith:

- **The Christian God is superior, and Christians are virtuous.** *The Apology of Aristides on Behalf of Christians* (ca. 125) was perhaps the first formal Christian apology written after the composition of the New Testament books. The author, Aristides, was probably a philosopher from Athens who converted to Christianity. In his apology, he argues that the Christian God is superior to pagan deities. The Christian God is the Creator of the world and is morally perfect, lacking nothing. In contrast, pagan deities are immoral, are invented by their worshipers, and are often considered a part of nature. He also argues that Christians are virtuous: they are humble, care for one another, show compassion for the poor, love their enemies, and keep themselves sexually pure.

- **Plurality should make room for Christian beliefs.** In his work *Embassy for the Christians* (ca. 177), Athenagoras of Athens eloquently addresses the Roman emperor Marcus Aurelius and his son Commodus in order to counter the charge of atheism being leveled against Christians. Athenagoras argues that the plurality of gods and religious practices in the empire ought to allow for the observance of Christianity. Furthermore, it is not only Christians who deny the existence of the gods of other religions; even pagans who worship a collection of gods don't believe in *all* gods and therefore deny the existence of some.

- **Christianity's roots are ancient.** More than any other apologist of the second century, Theophilus (died ca. 183–185), the Syrian bishop of Antioch, developed the argument for Christianity from its antiquity. In his work *To Autolycus* (ca. 180), he demonstrates that because Christianity has its roots firmly established in the most ancient writings of the Old Testament, far from being a new religion, it is an ancient one.

- ***Christianity is good for the empire.*** Tertullian argues in *Apology* that Rome made its greatest progress and achievements before it turned to the worship of the many false gods of its defeated foes. Worshiping the one true God would not undermine the empire; in fact, Christian prayer and charity would be beneficial to both Rome and its emperor.

Today, just as in the time of the Roman Empire, there is much at stake for Christianity. In both politics and culture, there is much antagonism toward and misunderstanding of the Christian faith. How might we, like the early church, justify Christianity's value and viability in the face of such challenges?

Philosophical Challenges

The list below is representative of the kinds of philosophical challenges that Christians faced from Greek opposition in the patristic period.

- Jesus concocted the story of his virgin birth to avoid the shame of illegitimacy.
- Certain events in the Bible cannot be verified as truly historical.
- Jesus' disciples invented the account of his resurrection.
- The miracles Jesus and his disciples performed are inauthentic.
- Mosaic descriptions of God are immoral and childish.
- God loves only the Jews, not all people.
- Greek philosophers discovered truth without special revelation.
- Christians reject reason and rely on blind faith.
- Pagan religion is necessary for people to flourish.

Sound familiar? We hear similar objections today.

Looking at how the early church responded to opposition provides insight into how to counter current resistance. In the following segments, we will examine how the early Christians both made general appeals for the Christian faith and directly responded to opposition—not only in what they said, but also in how they said it.

Metaphor. Clement of Alexandria (ca. 150–ca. 215), a teacher at the catechetical school in Alexandria, Egypt, took a positive view of Greek philosophy and sought to make Christian appeals based on the aesthetic sensibilities and thought forms of his day. For example, he employed a creative and artistic metaphor to explain the work of the Christian God within the human spirit and the universe. Leveraging Greek culture's high regard for music, he presented Christ as the minstrel who brings harmony to the universe, tames souls, and restores health to troubled minds.[6]

Exposition. Clement explains that the Old and New Testament Scriptures present an exalted view of God, especially in their report of God's transcendent power manifested among us in the person of Jesus Christ. He contrasts this biblical view of God with the Hellenistic idolatry and mythical stories of the gods.[7] Thus, Clement counters objections to the Christian God by clarifying what the Bible actually says about who God is.

Point-by-point refutation. In his work *Contra Celsus*, Origen (ca. 185–254), a radically devoted Christian and enormously influential intellectual, counters an anti-Christian tract titled *True Doctrine*. This tract, written by a zealous supporter of Hellenism named Celsus, attacks Christianity, alleging that it undermines the structure of society. Origen systematically responds to each of Celsus's points with a corresponding counterargument. Here are a few examples:

- In light of Jesus' high moral character, it is very unlikely he would lie about his virgin birth in order to avoid the shame of his accused illegitimacy.
- It is unfair to demand a level of historical verification of particular biblical events that is not expected to prove the reality of certain events in Greek history like the Trojan War.
- Moses's descriptions of God are often anthropomorphic portrayals of God and should not be taken in a slavishly literal way.[8]

Cumulative case. Cumulative case arguments combine several different pieces of evidence to argue for Christianity. There are many important examples of works that use this apologetic approach, but we will mention just one: *The Proof of the Gospel* by Eusebius (ca. 260–339). Eusebius, an early church historian regarded as the father of church history, develops the idea of the antiquity of Christianity by tracing its connection to the faith of the patriarchs in Genesis. He also, like many apologists before him, demonstrates the validity of Christianity by showing how the events of the gospels fulfill Old Testament prophecies. From the New Testament, Eusebius presents several arguments in support of Christianity: (1) the loftier morality of Jesus Christ, (2) the superiority of the gospel to Greek philosophy, (3) the miracles of Jesus, and (4) the credibility of the apostles as witnesses to miracles—in particular, the miraculous resurrection of

---

6. See Dulles, *History of Apologetics*, 39–40.
7. See Dulles, *History of Apologetics*, 40.
8. See Dulles, *History of Apologetics*, 43–47.

Jesus. It is interesting to note that John Chrysostom (ca. 347–407), the bishop of Constantinople who was regarded as the prince of preachers in the early church, did not include miracles in his cumulative case, because pagans in his context did not believe miracles were genuine.[9] Thus, the cumulative case argument varied according to the apologist's cultural context.

Sarcasm. Eusebius made an argument for the historical truthfulness of the apostles' testimony using sarcasm, which Avery Cardinal Dulles summarizes well: "[Eusebius sarcastically] suggests that perhaps one should suppose that [the apostles] entered into an insidious pact to this effect: 'let us manufacture untruths that will profit neither ourselves nor those being deceived, nor indeed Christ Himself. What could be finer . . . than to renounce all things just to deceive and be deceived?"[10]

In other words, Eusebius is using sarcasm to make the point that it would hardly make any sense for the apostles to invent and adhere to a fantastical claim that they knew would inevitably lead to their demise.

Similarly, in *The City of God*, Augustine uses sarcasm to turn the tables against those who deny the existence of miracles when he writes, "Nevertheless, if they do not even believe that those miracles were effected through Christ's apostles, to ensure belief in their proclamation of Christ's resurrection and ascension, then this one overpowering miracle is enough for us—that the whole world has come to believe in it without any miracles at all!"[11]

In effect Augustine is asking, "What would be the greater miracle: God healing people and multiplying food, or thousands of people coming to believe in something with no proof [miracles] at all?"

Dialogue. Marcus Minucius Felix (early third century) was a Roman, likely from Africa, who converted to Christianity and became one of the earliest Latin apologists. His work *Octavius* depicts an imaginary conversation between three people: the pagan Caecilius, the Christian Octavius, and the author himself functioning as a pagan judge. The reason Minucius does not quote Scripture even once in this dialogue is that he is keeping his audience in mind. Minucius wrote *Octavius* for upper-class Romans who were completely unfamiliar with the Bible and therefore needed a basic, inviting introduction to Christianity.[12]

Paradox. To Tertullian, paradox is a strong example of how human reason often must bow the knee to the unfathomable mystery of God. For this reason, he actually sees the absurdity of the crucifixion as an argument for the validity of

---

9. See Edgar and Oliphant, *Christian Apologetics Past and Present*, 1:191.
10. Dulles, *History of Apologetics*, 65.
11. Augustine of Hippo, *City of God*, trans. Henry Bettenson (London: Penguin, 2003), 685–86.
12. See Dulles, *History of Apologetics*, 47–48.

the Christian faith: "The Son of God was crucified; I am not ashamed because man must needs be ashamed of it. And the Son of the God died; *it is by all means to be believed, because it is absurd.*"[13]

Desire. Central to Augustine's apologetic is an appeal to the intrinsic human desire for happiness. According to Augustine, the inescapable drive that all people have to obtain happiness can only be satisfied in God. It is with this in mind that he so famously says to God in his *Confessions*, "Thou hast made us for Thyself and our hearts are restless till they rest in Thee."[14]

Faith and reason. While Augustine's approach to apologetics is often "subjective and psychological,"[15] he also uses rational arguments to establish the existence of God and to clear the way for faith. In fact, Augustine insists that reason is essential: "God forbid that He should hate in us that faculty by which He made us superior to all other living beings. Therefore, we must refuse so to believe as not to receive or seek reason for our belief, since we could not believe at all if we did not have rational souls."[16]

At the same time, Augustine often echoes Isaiah 7:9 in asserting that we cannot truly know until we first have faith.[17] He writes in his *Tractates on the Gospel of John*, "If we wished first to know and then to believe, we should not be able either to know or to believe."[18] In other words, faith gives us the framework within which we can reason accurately.[19]

Christological coherence. In answer to the question, "Why four gospels instead of just one?" Chrysostom explains (1) that the agreement in the essential content of all four gospels establishes the veracity of their witness, and (2) that any disagreement in details proves there was no deceptive collusion involved in writing them. And even though there are differences in details and perspectives within the gospels, there is absolute unity on the main points of Jesus' life and doctrine.

Just as Chrysostom found a basic coherence within the four gospel accounts, others such as Tertullian and Irenaeus earlier had found a christological coherence across the Old and New Testaments. As noted before, Christians in the early

---

13. Tertullian, *On the Flesh of Christ* 5 (emphasis added), www.newadvent.org/fathers/0315.htm.

14. Augustine , *The Confessions of Saint Augustine*, trans. Frank Sheed (London: Sheed and Ward, 1944), 1.

15. Dulles, *History of Apologetics*, 75.

16. Augustine of Hippo, *Letters*, vol. II, trans. Sister Wilfred Parsons (Washington, DC: Catholic University of America Press, 1953), 302.

17. An early Latin translation, based on the Septuagint, of Isaiah 7:9 reads, "Unless you believe, you will not understand it."

18. Quoted in Erich Przywara, ed., *An Augustine Synthesis* (Eugene, OR: Wipf and Stock, 2014), 58.

19. Later apologists, such as Lesslie Newbigin (see ch. 4), emphasize and incorporate Augustine's idea of faith prior to understanding as a kind of believing rationality based not primarily on natural theology but on the rule of faith and the teaching of the church.

church sometimes referred to this basic christological content as the rule of faith. The rule of faith, because it tied the entire content of the Bible together, is what enabled apologists to defend the faith against accusations of contradiction.

The logos. In Greek philosophy, *logos* referred to either the rationality that governs the universe or the principle of intelligence or rationality within the universe. The early church fathers took different positions as to how the *logos* of Greek philosophy related to Christianity—in particular, how it related to the Word (*logos*) of John 1:1.

Some of the patristic apologists ridiculed the word *logos*'s Greek heritage and saw no connection between the Greek concept of *logos* and the divine *logos* of the Bible. Tertullian gives an excellent example of this negative stance, reflected in his famous line:

> What does Jerusalem have to do with Athens, the Church with the Academy, the Christian with the heretic? Our principles come from the Porch of Solomon, who himself taught that the Lord is to be sought in simplicity of heart. I have no use for a Stoic or a Platonic or a dialectic Christianity. After Jesus Christ we have no need of speculation, after the Gospel, no need of research.[20]

Others attempted to claim the *logos* for Christianity by connecting the concept of divine *logos* to Christian revelation. There were basically three views on how philosophers received Christian revelation: either (1) the Greek philosophers borrowed knowledge from Moses, since he predated them; (2) God raised up prophets among the Greek philosophers; or (3) pagan philosophers were enlightened by the divine *logos* (Word).[21] Justin Martyr exemplified this third position when he asserted that Christ was partially known even by Socrates, because Jesus is the Word (*logos*) who is in every person.[22]

Thus, Tertullian argued that Greek philosophy and its *logos* had nothing to do with Christianity, while Justin Martyr proposed that Greek philosophers, enlightened by the divine *logos*, were in some sense Christians without even realizing it.[23] The majority of the early church apologists fell somewhere between these two extremes.

---

20. Tertullian, *Prescriptions Against Heretics*, in *Early Latin Theology*, vol. 5 of *Library of Christian Classics*, ed. S. L. Greenslade (Philadelphia: Westminster, 1956), 7.
21. See Dulles, *History of Apologetics*, 37.
22. See Justin Martyr, *Second Apology* 10, www.newadvent.org/fathers/0127.htm.
23. See Justin Martyr, *First Apology* 46, 55, www.newadvent.org/fathers/0126.htm; *Second Apology* 8–10, www.newadvent.org/fathers/0127.htm.

Back to the Future

Significant connections exist between our present context and the world of the early church, in particular, the degree to which Christians were set apart from the cultures they lived in. The historian Larry Hurtado, who specializes in Christian origins, summarizes this idea well:

> Early Christianity of the first three centuries was a different, even distinctive, kind of religious movement in the cafeteria of religious options of the times. That is not simply my historical judgment; it is what people of the time thought as well. In fact, in the eyes of many in the Roman era, Christianity was very odd, even objectionably so . . . even among those who took the time to acquaint themselves more accurately with Christian beliefs, practices, and text, the response was often intensely negative.[24]

Christians in the early church lived in a pluralistic society, as do we. Their ethics were strange to their neighbors, as are many of ours. They felt like outsiders in their own country, as many Christians today do. Their religious beliefs were not mainstream, as ours are not. They experienced political pressure from the state against their faith, as some believers are currently experiencing.

THE MIDDLE AGES

The Christians in the church of the Middle Ages (476–1500) faced not only some of the same challenges as the patristic period, but also challenges unlike any they had seen before. In particular, among the challenges for Christian theology and apologetics was the need, with the expansion and growing strength of Christianity, to synthesize by uniting, filtering, and categorizing the wide range of existing thought.

Heretical Challenges

While Nestorian and Euytchian heresies originated in the late patristic period and were rejected by the church at the Council of Chalcedon in 451, the battle against them continued into the Middle Ages.[25]

Nestorianism. Nestorius (ca. 386–451), the patriarch of Constantinople, asserted that in the incarnation, Jesus maintained not only two natures but

---

24. Larry W. Hurtado, *Destroyer of the gods: Early Christian Distinctiveness in the Roman World* (Waco, TX: Baylor University Press, 2016), 183.
25. See Dulles, *History of Apologetics,* 93, 95, 117, 126, 138.

also two *persons*. Nestorius split Jesus into a human person and a divine person and insisted that though the human Jesus suffered, the divine Jesus did not.[26]

Eutychianism. Named after Eutyches (ca. 378–456), an elderly monk in Constantinople who was actually, for the most part, a figurehead used by others, Eutychianism is the belief that Christ had only one nature.[27] The divine nature and human nature of Christ were so comingled that they produced a new or third kind of nature—almost in the same way that yellow and blue make green. Thus, in the incarnation, Jesus is one new person with only one nature.[28]

Jewish and Muslim Challenges

During this period, Christians began to feel a greater responsibility to evangelize the Jews, especially since Christians were being asked to take up arms against Muslims. As Islam, which was founded in 610, rapidly grew in power, Christian apologists directed much energy toward engaging its basic tenets. Thus, to the west was the missionary challenge of reaching unconverted Jews, and to the east was the cultural, military, and religious threat of Islam.[29]

Synthesis challenge. During the Middle Ages, Christian theologians and apologists continued to answer questions of synthesis and integration such as, "How do faith and reason relate?" and "What is the connection between theology and philosophy?"

Responses

The following are some of the most significant ways that Christian theologians and apologists responded to the threats and opportunities presented in the Middle Ages. We do not recommend without qualification that you use all of these approaches today, but with discernment, we can learn much from these methodologies employed by the church.

Speak the language; define the terms. Boethius (ca. 480–524), a Roman consul in the administration of Theodoric the Great who was accused of treason, imprisoned, and ultimately executed, courageously tackled the problem of synthesis. Boethuis suggested that the difference between philosophy and theology is found in the difference between their methodologies: philosophy discovers truth through reason alone, while theology discovers truth through the scriptural revelation given to the church. Boethius suggested that the two could be integrated, because philosophy could be used to help theology articulate its truths.

---

26. See Holcomb, *Know the Heretics*, 136.
27. See Holcomb, *Know the Heretics*, 123.
28. See Holcomb, *Know the Heretics*, 121–25.
29. See Dulles, *History of Apologetics*, 91, 98, 105–6, 122–27.

In *A Treatise against Eutyches and Nestorius*, Boethius defends the Christian faith against heretical views regarding the person of Jesus Christ. At stake in the church's conception of Christ was not only the nature of worship, but of salvation itself. In Boethius's defense, he contributed to the precise orthodox terminology we use today to refer to the person of Jesus Christ. He often did not employ terminology directly from the Bible, but instead utilized philosophical nomenclature to describe biblical concepts, defining philosophical terms according to biblical and traditional doctrine.[30] For example, although the term *Trinity* does not appear in the Bible, it is a biblical concept.[31] In this way, Boethius ironically used the philosophical language of his opponents to guard the purity of biblical and theological truth.

Condemn and defend. Some Christian apologists were very direct and pointed in their response to Islam. John Damascene (ca. 675–749), a Syrian monk and priest, took such an approach. In *On Heresies* and *Dialogue between a Christian and a Saracen* (Muslim),[32] he points out the problems with Islamic faith and practice and responds to Islamic criticisms of Christian beliefs. The following are some of his most pointed criticisms of Islam: (1) It denies that Jesus is fully God and is therefore an Arian heresy; (2) Muhammad was misguided; (3) the Qur'an is an empty dream; (4) Islam encourages polygamy and divorce; and (5) it cultivates licentious sentiments toward women.[33] Be careful about using such arguments today without sensitivity and evidence.

Use an allegory. Theodore Abū Qurrah (ca. 740–ca. 820), a disciple of John Damascene, offered an allegory in answer to such questions as, "When there are so many religions—including Judaism, Islam, and Christianity—how can one judge which is true?" Avery Cardinal Dulles summarizes Abū Qurrah's allegory as follows:

> A certain king, he narrates, had a son who had never seen him. In a foreign land the son fell ill and sent to his father for medical advice. Several messages came, one from the father, the others from the latter's enemies. The son, assisted by the advice of a doctor, scrutinized each message from the point of view of what it indicated about the author, the understanding of the disease, and the reasonableness of the proposed remedy, and he accepted the prescription that best satisfied all three criteria. Applying the allegory to the choice of a religion, Abū Qurrah tries to show that Christianity presents the most plausible idea of God, exhibits the fullest

---

30. See Dulles, *History of Apologetics*, 319.

31. See Edgar and Oliphint, *Christian Apologetics Past and Present*, 1:316–17.

32. In its earliest usage, Saracen refers to any of the nomadic tribes on the Syrian borders of the Roman Empire. Later, during the early medieval period, it came to mean an Arab. In the later medieval period, during the times of the Crusades, Saracen became a term used by Christian writers to refer to Muslims.

33. See Dulles, *History of Apologetics*, 92–93.

understanding of humanity's actual religious needs, and prescribes what appear to be the most appropriate remedies.[34]

Thus, applying this allegory to modern-day apologetics, we might respond to the question, "Why should I believe in Christianity when there are so many other religions?" with the assertion that Christianity brings the greatest healing and flourishing to humanity and that Christianity's God, of all the major religions, understands most personally the human condition and need.

Demonstrate the rationality of the Christian faith. Following Augustine's maxim "First believe, then understand," Anselm (1033–1109), an archbishop of Canterbury, stated the relationship between faith and reason in this way: "For I do not seek to understand so that I may believe; but I believe so that I may understand. For I believe this also, that 'unless I believe, I shall not understand.'"[35] To Anselm, true faith is rational; there is a "logic of faith." To enter into and understand this logic of faith, one assumes the truth of Christianity and then uses reason to both affirm and explore more deeply what Scripture and the creeds teach.[36] In this way, Anselm affirmed the inner coherence and rationality of the Christian faith.

Interestingly, Anselm posited that, once believed and then understood rationally, the Christian faith could be explained logically even to unbelievers. Further, one could demonstrate that the faith is reasonable and worthy of belief even without appealing to the authority of the Scriptures or the church or to the illuminating power of grace or prayer.[37] Anselm was convinced that because the Christian faith is so logically consistent and rationally demonstrable, even the fool who denies the authority of revelation must assent to its irrefutable rationality.[38]

Prove that the greatest being must exist. Though Anselm never referred to it as such, the ontological argument is his best-known and most enduring contribution to apologetics. Anselm's basic argument for the existence of a perfect being is as follows:

- God is by definition that than which nothing greater can be conceived.
- It is greater to exist in reality than to exist only in the mind.
- Therefore, God must exist in reality. If he didn't exist, he wouldn't be the greatest possible being.

---

34. Dulles, *History of Apologetics*, 94–95.

35. Brian Davies and G. R. Evans, eds., *Anselm of Canterbury: Major Works* (New York: Oxford University Press, 1998), 87.

36. See Dulles, *History of Apologetics*, 99.

37. See Dulles, *History of Apologetics*, 100–101.

38. See Dulles, *History of Apologetics*, 103.

Although this argument has been criticized, it has been employed by many well-known theologians over the centuries and is still in use today. Philosopher and apologist Alvin Plantinga has dealt extensively with the objections to this argument and is a persuasive contemporary proponent of it.[39]

Reason your way to faith. Peter Abelard (1079–1142), a brilliant French theologian, philosopher, ethicist, and logician, emphasized the value of reason in bringing an unbeliever to an incipient faith. Through an analysis of Christian evidences, a person can attain a rudimentary faith, which then paves the way for a supernatural faith produced by God's grace. Abelard was very much against an impulsive faith that lacked evidence and reason and discussed the rational grounds for faith at length in *A Dialogue between a Philosopher, a Jew, and a Christian*.[40]

Thomas Aquinas (1225–1274), the most famous and influential medieval theologian-apologist, did not begin his apology with scriptural authority. Rather, because of his missionary aim and because some of his adversaries denied the authority of Scripture, he started with reason and natural revelation. In the first three volumes of Aquinas's great apologetic work *Summa Contra Gentiles*, he claims to prove certain theological truths that we can know empirically and rationally without the aid of special revelation—for example, the existence of God and certain of God's attributes.

In volume 4, Aquinas's method changes. He uses Scripture to prove certain theological truths that *cannot* be discovered rationally or empirically apart from Scripture, such as the doctrine of the Trinity, the incarnation of Jesus Christ, and eschatological knowledge. Such theological truths are certainly not irrational or illogical, but they cannot be discovered through reason alone. The special revelation found in Scripture is necessary to discover them.

Aquinas does not bridge the gap between natural revelation and special revelation by simply asserting the authority of Scripture and expecting others to accept it by blind faith. Instead, he reasons his way empirically to scriptural authority. Here is his line of reasoning:

1. The miraculous existence of the church proves the validity of biblical miracles and fulfilled prophecy (recall Augustine's argument for miracles).
2. The biblical signs of miracles and fulfilled prophecies make it credible that the Scriptures as a whole are a revelation from God.

---

39. Alvin Plantinga, *God, Freedom, and Evil*, rev. ed. (Grand Rapids: Eerdmans, 1989), 85–112.
40. See Dulles, *History of Apologetics*, 107–8.

3. As revelation from God, the Scriptures are absolutely authoritative.

4. Therefore, any doctrine taught in Scripture, even if it is not empirically or rationally provable, may be accepted by faith.[41]

So while concepts such as the Trinity and the incarnation cannot be proven, the authority of Scripture can be. As a result, such doctrines, because they are contained within Scripture, may be accepted by faith. Thus, faith for Aquinas is an "essentially intellectual assent to doctrines not provable by reason."[42]

Contrary to the probability arguments we will see in future periods, Aquinas believed that the existence of God could be proved with certainty: "[Aquinas maintained] that we Christians must use only arguments that prove their conclusions with absolute certainty; for if we use mere probability arguments, the insufficiency of those arguments will only serve to confirm the non-Christian in his unbelief."[43]

Aquinas's Five Ways to Demonstrate God's Existence

According to Aquinas, there are five certain ways we can prove God's existence:

1. Movement or change has a mover. Since there is not an infinite regress, an Unmoved Mover is necessary. God is the Unmoved Mover.
2. Nonbeing cannot cause being. Since there cannot be an infinite regress of causal beings, a first cause must exist. God is the First Cause.
3. Beings in this world exist necessarily, but appear contingent. Therefore, a noncontingent necessary being must exist. God is the Necessary Being.
4. Limited beings depend on an unlimited being. God is the Unlimited Being.
5. Design in nature must have a designer. God is the Ultimate Designer.

Respect those you disagree with. Through an allegorical disputation in the *Book of the Gentile and the Three Wise Men*, Raymond Lull (ca. 1232–1316), an intriguing and exceptional individual who had many personal gifts, respectfully acknowledges the humanity of a Gentile philosopher, a Jew, a Christian, and a Saracen (Muslim). At the end of the book, the Gentile devotedly worships

---

41. See William Lane Craig, *Reasonable Faith: Christian Truth and Apologetics*, 3rd ed. (Wheaton, IL: Crossway, 2008), 32–33.

42. Craig, *Reasonable Faith*, 33.

43. Craig, *Reasonable Faith*, 32.

his Creator, and the Jew, the Christian, and the Muslim resolve to continue an amiable dialogue and to honor and serve one another. Thus, Lull does not use weak ad hominem arguments to undermine his opponents. Even in today's social media-driven world, any argument that amounts to nothing more than, "You're stupid and we all know it, so your claim cannot be true" is still generally considered a logical fallacy. The Christian virtues of gentleness, kindness, and compassion more effectively persuade skeptics of the truthfulness of the gospel.

Use an eclectic approach. In *The Triumph of the Cross*, Girolamo Savonarola (1452–1498), a Dominican monk and preacher, demonstrates an eclectic methodology in which he uses art, experience, reason, and argument—all centered around a focus on the cross of Christ. Savonarola's work is divided into four books. In book 1, the wounded and resurrected Christ is depicted on a chariot with a cross and both Testaments, surrounded by the Virgin Mary, apostles, martyrs, Old Testament patriarchs and prophets, doctors of the church, and many others. A throng of men and women from all races, rich and poor, young and old, follow in the procession behind Jesus. This moving picture of Christ's power to unite all people is an effective use of art, which could be even redolent of the great murals painted in Florence during the Renaissance.[44] In book 2, Savonarola offers, as a proof for the Christian faith, the goodness and wisdom of Christ, along with the virtues, peace, and joy produced in those who are attached to Jesus Christ by faith. In book 3, he demonstrates that the moral teachings and doctrines of the Christian faith are compatible with reason. In book 4, Savonarola defends the truth of Christianity by pointing out the error of alternative religions—specifically paganism, Judaism, Christian heresy, and Islam (which he regards as a combination of Judaism and Christian heresy).[45] Savonarola's eclectic combination of art, experience, and reason creates a powerful cumulative argument for the Christian faith, almost as if Michelangelo, Mother Teresa, and Thomas Aquinas had cooperated to produce one great argument for the Christian God.

TURNING TO THE REFORMATION

During the Middle Ages, Christianity was taken for granted by most of Europe. In the general population, Christianity ruled the day. Thus, apologetics focused mainly on Jewish and Muslim challenges, with some apologetic efforts given to residual Nestorian and Eutychian heresies. The secular society that we know today had not yet taken over the Western world.

---

44. See Dulles, *History of Apologetics*, 141.
45. See Dulles, *History of Apologetics*, 142; Edgar and Oliphint, *Christian Apologetics Past and Present*, 1:439.

But as we will see as we turn to the next chapter, the coming of the Reformation ushered in a much more complicated time. The church in the West would split into two camps: Catholic and Protestant. Disputes over church doctrine would occupy much of the apologetic efforts of the church for centuries. And while the church turned inward, wrangling over issues of salvation, church, and authority, the world was moving on toward the Enlightenment and modernity, which would come to present vast philosophical, scientific, and moral challenges to the Christian faith. Sadly, the major figures of the Reformation period hardly addressed the primary task of apologetics at all.[46] Even more significantly, as the church divided and focused inward, the undercurrent of skepticism outside the church would become more and more mainstream.

46. See Dulles, *History of Apologetics*, 145.

CHAPTER FOUR

APOLOGETICS WITHIN THE GREAT TRADITION: PART 2

> The doctrinal heritage of the past is thus both a gift and a task, an inheritance and a responsibility. What our forebears in the Christian faith passed down to us must be appropriated, in order that we may wrestle with it within our own situation, before passing it on to those whose day has yet to dawn.
>
> *Alister McGrath,* The Genesis of Doctrine

KEEPING THE CROSS AT THE CENTER

We now finish our survey of the development of apologetics across church history. But two observations must first be made. First, as we travel through church history, we see that whenever times and locations change, effective apologetics adjust to meet new challenges. Each generation of apologists is forced to think in new ways about apologetics; thus, an apologist in any era must be flexible, innovative, and practical. Specifically, throughout the ages when church apologists have been faced with a new situation, they have responded by . . .

- directly applying an old approach
- slightly altering an old approach
- creating a new approach
- combining old approaches
- combining old and new approaches

Second, we will see that the longevity of any apologetic methodology depends on its grounding in the cross. Throughout church history, there have been apologists and theologians who have so thoroughly conformed the gospel to the assumptions of their day that they lost its most essential tenets. While it's one thing to make the gospel message as accessible as possible, it's quite another to allow the thought forms of a given culture to change the gospel. Be warned: If taken too far, apologetics can negotiate away the very soul of the church, the very heart of Christianity. For this reason, an apologist must be vigilant that the cross *never* be sacrificed in order to make Christianity palatable to the reigning ethos of a certain place or time.

THE PROTESTANT REFORMATION

The Catholic monk Martin Luther (1483–1546) was for many years deeply disturbed by his own spiritual inadequacies and moral failings. But through the study of Scripture, intense spiritual experiences, and time, the Holy Spirit enlightened his troubled mind to the doctrine of justification by faith, and he finally felt relief from his burden of sin and guilt. Knowing that it was faith in Christ that made him righteous soothed his soul and made him feel as if he had been born anew and the gates of paradise had been flung open to him. It was as Luther realized that salvation is by grace through faith that God comforted his heart, causing him to launch a reform that, along with other factors, led to what we now know as the Protestant Reformation.

Just before Luther's time, the church had begun to fall into very, very bad shape. Corruption, greed, and immorality were rampant. A wide chasm existed between the clergy and laity. The clergy took large amounts of revenue from the church but were rarely seen among the people, except when leading them in worship, and even then, the priests were so uneducated that they barely knew how to conduct a service. In such times, the church needs reforming. However, during intense reformation, apologetics turns inward, happening almost exclusively within the church. That said, the thought leaders of the Reformation still had a notable influence on how the church would think about apologetics far into the future.

Philosophy and Reason Must Yield to the Cross

Martin Luther challenged both the value of Aristotelian philosophy—"He who wishes to philosophize by using Aristotle without danger to his soul must first become thoroughly foolish in Christ"[1]—and the use of reason in coming to faith. Essentially, Luther asserted that reason apart from the humility of the cross is no reason at all, and that reason only truly works inside a framework of faith. Thus, while there is an inner, logical coherence within faith, outside of faith, philosophy and reason must yield to the foolishness of the cross.

---

1. Martin Luther, *Heidelberg Disputation (1518)* 31, www.catchpenny.org/heidel.html.

Reason Can Prepare a Person for Faith in the Gospel

Luther's fellow Reformer and systematizer Philipp Melanchthon (1497–1560) completely agreed with Luther's opinions about faith and reason—until he didn't. While at first Melanchthon wholeheartedly rode the anti-philosophy train with Luther, he later disembarked when he realized that reason could actually prepare someone to receive the gospel. He found that reason, without the aid of special or scriptural revelation, could establish many truths, including God's existence, some of his attributes (his mercy, eternality, goodness, wisdom, and truthfulness), his creation of the world, his sustaining power over creation, and the judgment to come. Truths such as these, proved by nature and reason alone, could prepare a person for faith in the gospel.

The Spirit Gives Inner Testimony to the Truthfulness of Scripture

The French Reformer, teacher, pastor, and theologian John Calvin (1509–1564) affirmed that reason enables all human beings to know something about God. Anyone can discern God's existence and much about God's attributes just by contemplating the created world. Yet Calvin was also aware of a serious impediment to this knowledge, namely, that humanity is depraved. People are naturally idolaters—they all too often take what they know about God and twist it into a contorted, false image of him. Calvin asserted that this human limitation is why God must personally reveal himself and his truth to humans through special revelation, which he does primarily through the Scriptures. Thus, though humankind is fallen, there is still hope for them. Not only does all humanity have within them an inner testimony to the truthfulness of Scripture, but they are also capable of discovering and understanding rational arguments for the credibility of the Bible. However, Calvin claimed that these arguments alone would not convince a person without the inner witness of the Spirit and that, conversely, one with the inner witness of the Spirit would not need rational arguments. Calvin's thoughts on this subject still shape apologetics today.[2]

THE CATHOLIC COUNTER-REFORMATION

The Catholic Church did not sit idly by, completely ignoring both the corruption within their own church and the work of Protestant Reformers. Catholics not only led a reformation of their own, but also systematized polemic and apologetic responses to the challenges of the Protestant Reformers. Italian Jesuit Robert Bellarmine (1542–1621) organized the greatest counteraction against

---

2. For an insightful introduction to John Calvin, see Randall C. Zachman, *John Calvin as Teacher, Pastor, and Theologian: The Shape of His Writings and Thought* (Grand Rapids: Baker Academic, 2006).

the Protestant Reformers; in fact, his *Disputations concerning the Controversies of the Christian Faith against the Heretics of This Age* was so popular that in the 150 years after its initial publication, it would go through one hundred editions.

During their Counter-Reformation, the Catholics did not simply turn their focus inward or to the Protestant Reformers. They also continued to produce impactful apologetic works targeting those outside the church. One such example is *On the Truth of the Christian Faith* by Spanish humanist Juan Luis Vives (1493–1540). Vives was not the most original thinker—he borrowed heavily from other apologists like Augustine, Aquinas, and the Italian Dominican monk Ricoldus de Monte Croce—but he did structure his apologetic very effectively. Book 1 centers on God and the human soul. Book 2 presents revealed mysteries of the Christian faith: the incarnation and the life, death, and resurrection of Jesus. Book 3 narrates a dialogue between a Christian and a Jew, primarily over messianic prophecies in the Old Testament. Book 4 relates an interchange between a Muslim and a Christian over Muhammad and the Qur'an. Book 5 argues for the superiority of Christianity over all other faiths.[3]

THE SEVENTEENTH AND EIGHTEENTH CENTURIES

Following on the heels of the Reformation, the seventeenth and eighteenth centuries were a time of apologetic transition. The Enlightenment presented a whole new set of problems to apologists. Immanuel Kant (1724–1804), a key figure of the Enlightenment who attempted to synthesize rationalism and empiricism, defined enlightenment as "man's emergence from his self-incurred immaturity" and then went on to explain, "*Immaturity* is the inability to use one's own understanding without the guidance of another. This immaturity is *self-incurred* if its cause is not lack of understanding, but lack of resolution and courage to use it without the guidance of another. The motto of enlightenment is therefore: *Sapere Aude!* [Dare to be wise!] Have courage to use your *own* understanding!"[4]

The Enlightenment celebrated the goodness of human nature and the value of human progress through science. The following list identifies some of the most notable Enlightenment figures, along with a summary of their thought:

- **René Descartes** (1596–1650)—Humans can progress, as long as they are guided solely by their own rational thoughts and individual freedom.

---

3. See Avery Cardinal Dulles, *A History of Apologetics* (San Francisco: Ignatius, 2005), 153.
4. Immanuel Kant, *An Answer to the Question: "What Is Enlightenment?"* (London: Penguin, 2013), 1, emphasis in original.

- **Benedict de Spinoza** (1632–1677)—Miracles are impossible because they would violate the inviolable laws of nature and contradict reason. Moses did not write the first five books of the Bible.
- **John Locke** (1632–1704)—Individual empirical investigation and reasoned reflection, and not the pressure of an external authority or majority or an innate store of ideas received at birth, are the ultimate sources of true knowledge.
- **François Marie Arouet de Voltaire** (1694–1778)—God exists, but the church and Scriptures are full of tyrannical superstitions, injustices, and immoralities.
- **David Hume** (1711–1776)—Miracles are not empirically verifiable; thus, no testimony would be sufficient to establish a miracle.
- **Immanuel Kant** (1724–1804)—We can know things only as they appear to us, not as they actually are.

In order to understand the Enlightenment, it is first necessary to understand the following terms: *empiricism*, *rationalism*, and *individualism*. *Empiricism* asserts that people must look for truth in demonstrable data discoverable by the five senses rather than in claims to supernatural or miraculous events. *Rationalism* seeks truth with human logic alone, apart from divine revelation. *Individualism* asserts that a person should place ultimate authority in their own thoughts and feelings rather than in an external entity such as the church.

Where's the Trinity?

A cautionary tale from this period is the tendency of some apologists to develop a natural theology for apologetics that gave little to no attention to the doctrine of the Trinity, likely because the "rationality" of their day didn't find it logical. For more on how to defend the doctrine of the Trinity, see chapter 12.

From the seventeenth century until about the middle of the twentieth century, the prevailing cultural environment of the West was modernity. Enlightenment thinking founded the modern age. Alister McGrath explains that because modernity placed such an emphasis on "universal human reason, common to all people and times, capable of gaining access to the deeper structures of the world," rational argument became the ultimate tool of persuasion. Apologists soon realized that learning to craft arguments and present a "rational defense of the Christian faith [was] of paramount importance."[5] Christian thinkers formed the following apologetic approaches in response to the Enlightenment and modernity.

Pascal: Logic of the Heart

Blaise Pascal (1623–1662) was a brilliant French mathematician, scientist, and philosopher who, along with many other extraordinary discoveries, invented the *pascaline*, which is considered the precursor to the computer.[6] On November 23, 1654, after an earlier conversion experience, a divine intervention for his own physical protection, and a miraculous healing of his niece Marguerite, Pascal experienced a mystical illumination. He expressed the intense passion of this experience with two simple expressions: "Joy, joy, joy, tears of joy" and "Fire,"[7] which demonstrate why the heart's affections were essential to his apologetic approach.

Because Pascal's era was infected with deism, skepticism, and indifference, his apologetic approach is best understood with those factors in mind. Another important factor to be aware of is the shaping influence that Augustine had on his thinking. Since Pascal never completed his great apologetic project, *An Apology for the Christian Religion*, today we have only fragments of his thoughts known simply as *Pensées* ("Thoughts"). Here are the highlights of Pascal's apologetic methodology:

Reasons of the heart. Rather than appealing to philosophical proofs or nature to argue for theism, Pascal appealed to experiential, historical, and intuitive attestations to the Christian God. In other words, Pascal's methodology did not aim at purely rationalistic arguments, but instead targeted the intuitive reasons of the heart: "The heart has its reasons of which reason knows nothing: we know this in countless ways."[8] Nevertheless, do not misunderstand Pascal's approach as pitting faith against reason and evidence, especially since he even listed twelve "proofs" for Christianity.

The foolish logic of the cross. Pascal asserted that outside of Jesus Christ, a person cannot understand himself, the meaning of his existence, or even who God is.[9] Commenting on 1 Corinthians 1–2, he added that miraculous signs

---

5. Alister E. McGrath, *Mere Apologetics: How to Help Seekers and Skeptics Find Faith* (Grand Rapids: Baker, 2012), 27.

6. See William Edgar and K. Scott Oliphant, eds., *Christian Apologetics Past and Present: A Primary Source Reader* (Wheaton, IL: Crossway, 2011), 2:174.

7. Edgar and Oliphant, *Christian Apologetics Past and Present*, 2:174.

8. Blaise Pascal, *Pensées* (London: Penguin, 1966), 154.

9. Pascal, *Pensées*, 148; see Peter Kreeft, *Christianity for Modern Pagans: Pascal's* Pensées *Edited, Outlined and Explained* (San Francisco: Ignatius, 1993), 313.

and wisdom can prepare us for faith, but that ultimately we must submit to the folly—the foolish logic—of the cross.

The wager. Perhaps the most familiar of Pascal's apologetic methods is his wager, in which he essentially says to the unbeliever, "You cannot be completely certain that Christianity is or is not true. You have to make a bet either way. On the one hand, if Christianity is true and you reject Christ, then you will be faced with eternal damnation. On the other hand, if Christianity isn't true and you follow Christ's teaching, then you will have lived a good, moral life, and no harm will have been done. Clearly then, it would be wisest to assume and live as though Christianity is true."[10]

The God-shaped vacuum. Although the phrase "God-shaped vacuum" is often attributed to Pascal, he never actually used it. It is, however, an accurate summary of one of his most persuasive arguments for belief in God—an argument that builds on Augustine's famous "restless heart" quote, mentioned in the previous chapter. An emptiness exists in the human heart that only God can fill.

Grotius: In Defense of the New Testament

On the Truth of Christian Religion by Hugo Grotius (1583–1645), written in a popular and readable style, was phenomenally successful and enduring, and it was translated into numerous languages. As Grotius respectfully acknowledges, each of the six books the work comprises were built on the work of his apologetic predecessors and are therefore mostly unoriginal. What is unique to Grotius's work is found in book 3, in which he uses critical methodologies to establish that the New Testament books were actually written by the authors that tradition espouses. In book 3, Grotius also demonstrates the credibility of these authors and argues that the apparent yet minor inconsistencies between their writings actually prove they were not in collusion.

Butler: An Apologetic of Probability

Joseph Butler (1692–1752), sometimes referred to as "the philosopher of Anglicanism,"[11] wrote *The Analogy of Religion* not to prove the existence of God but to counter the deists of his day. At that time in England, deists did not deny that God created the world or even that he actively governed it, but they did deny that special revelation is necessary to know God. According to these deists, all that one needs to know about God can be known through nature and reason. Three words encapsulate Butler's response to these deists: *analogy*, *probability*, and *cumulative*.

---

10. See Pascal, *Pensées*, 149–53; Kreeft, *Christianity for Modern Pagans*, 291–95.
11. See Edgar and Oliphint, *Christian Apologetics Past and Present*, 2:195.

Analogy. By way of analogy, Butler reasons from natural revelation to the existence of special revelation. Observable experiences in the natural realm are analogous to truths in the supernatural realm. For example, in the same way that our childhood and adolescence mature us, preparing us for adulthood, the years we spend on earth are meant to mature us so that we are prepared for the next life.[12]

Probability. Butler reasons that since our knowledge of the physical realm is only partial and therefore merely probable, we should not be shocked by the fact that our knowledge of the supernatural is the same. Thus, we can say that while it is not certain, it is probable that Christianity is true. Butler's probability argument appears much less absolute than Aquinas's sure proofs. (Remember that they lived in very different times.) Yet according to Butler, the probability is very high that Christianity is true. In fact, we might say with tongue in cheek, "Combine Pascal's wager with Butler's probability argument, and any gambler worth his salt would bet that Christianity is true."

Cumulative. Butler masterfully brings different evidence together in order to demonstrate the likelihood of Christian revelation being true. Avery Cardinal Dulles explains that the force of Butler's argument comes not merely from the sum total of evidence he provides, but rather from the way in which each piece of evidence interacts with and is strengthened by all the other pieces, creating a whole greater than the sum of its parts.[13] As Butler himself observes, "Probable proofs, by being added, not only increase evidence but multiply it."[14]

Paley: The Watchmaker

English theologian and philosopher William Paley (1743–1805) wrote two well-known apologetic works: *A View of the Evidences of Christianity* and *Natural Theology*. The first was required reading for entrance into Cambridge University until the twentieth century, and Charles Darwin was "charmed and convinced of the long line of argumentation" in it.[15]

Paley's strongest arguments in this work can be framed in two questions: (1) Why would the apostles propagate lies in order to teach virtue? and (2) Where in the entire course of history can we find anyone who endured such hardships as the apostles were willing to suffer for the veracity of their testimony—all for

---

12. See Edgar and Oliphint, *Christian Apologetics Past and Present*, 2:196.

13. Dulles, *History of Apologetics*, 183–86.

14. Joseph Butler, *Analogy of Religion, Natural and Revealed, to the Constitution and Course of Nature*, ed. G. R. Crooks (New York: Harper, 1860), 300.

15. Frances Darwin, ed., *Autobiography of Charles Darwin: From the Life and Letters of Charles Darwin* (n.p., n.d.), 24; quoted in Edgar and Oliphint, *Christian Apologetics Past and Present*, 2:240.

a lie? Paley reasons that it makes no sense that the eyewitnesses to Jesus' miracles and his resurrection would suffer so many hardships for a lie and would teach integrity founded on a falsehood.

Natural Theology contains Paley's famous teleological argument: the analogy of the watchmaker. Just as the intricate inner workings of a watch—its design—imply a designer, so too do the complexity and order of this world imply a designer. After refuting David Hume's arguments against the watchmaker apologetic, Paley asserts, "Upon the whole; after all the schemes and struggles of a reluctant philosophy, the necessary resort is to a Deity. The marks of *design* are too strong to be got over. Design must have a designer. That designer must have been a person. That person is GOD."[16]

Why Did Paley's Argument Work So Well?

Paley's argument worked, at least in part, because it resonated with his cultural context and the biases of his period. However, the current assumptions of our day present challenges to this argument and make it unconvincing to many. In our present context, many people approach nature in a way that does not lead them to see it as a pointer beyond itself.[17]

Leibniz: The Best of All Possible Worlds

German philosopher and mathematician Gottfried Wilhelm Leibniz (1646–1716) made many advances in apologetics, but today he is perhaps best known for what he termed his "theodicy" (an apologetic for the problem of evil). His theodicy contains three important components. First, he states that God predetermines all things, yet without coercing man's free will. God foreordains free, unforced actions. Second, God could have chosen to create any world, but being perfect, he decided to make the best possible world. Even the evils in this world contribute to a greater good.[18] Third, sin and suffering are the inevitable result of man's finitude. Humanity is necessarily limited by virtue of not being God, and evil results from these limitations.

---

16. William Paley, *Natural Theology; Or, Evidences of the Existence and Attributes of the Deity, Collected from the Appearances of Nature* (New York: Sheldon, Blakeman, 1857), 246.

17. For more on this, see the discussion on the "immanent frame" in chapter 10. For more on this point, see Alister E. McGrath, *Re-Imagining Nature: The Promise of a Christian Natural Theology* (West Sussex, UK: Wiley Blackwell, 2017), 30.

18. Voltaire lampoons the "best of all possible worlds" view with biting satire in *Candide*.

THE NINETEENTH CENTURY

As we move to the nineteenth century, we must note the lasting impact the Enlightenment and modernity had on apologetics. In some cases, the apologetic innovations and emphases of the nineteenth century were a reaction against the very logic of the Enlightenment. In other cases, nineteenth-century Christian apologetics responded to modernity by working within modernity's own logic. Some apologetic methodologies started with revelation and faith; others started with reason as a vehicle to establish revelation and faith.

Schleiermacher and Kierkegaard: Existential Apologetics

Revising Christianity. It is rare in the history of Christianity for anyone to succeed in doing something radically new, but Friedrich Schleiermacher (1768–1843), the father of modern liberalism, innovated apologetics in a way unlike anyone before him. In an attempt to make Christianity acceptable to his intellectual companions, he fundamentally revised the very meaning of traditional Christian concepts like "miracle, revelation, inspiration, prophecy, God, and immortality."[19] Most significantly, Schleiermacher asserted that it is not the historical fact of Jesus' death that produces belief and is the true essence of Christianity, but rather a person's experience of Christ's redeeming power through the work of the Holy Spirit. Further, Jesus Christ is our example in his own God-consciousness. If we will but open ourselves up to love, we too will experience a higher level of God-consciousness.

Sensing and tasting the infinite. In his apologetic, Schleiermacher had no taste for traditional rational proofs or standard empirical evidence. He did not set out to prove the existence of God or revelation; rather, he tapped into the universal human longing for the transcendent. Schleiermacher asserted that religion is not primarily what you know or do, but it is about what you feel or intuit. Religion is a deep, inner feeling of dependence. More than any other world religion, Christianity, because of its spirituality and conduciveness to human freedom, has the greatest potential to bring a person to the sense of the divine. Further, true religion flourishes most within the communal framework of a "church." If a world religion has any usefulness whatsoever, it is found within its social life, since humans are social beings. Thus, Schleiermacher reasoned from the universal human longing for God to the utility of the Christian church as an avenue for experiencing a higher level God-consciousness.

Avery Cardinal Dulles says of Schleiermacher's apologetic, "As he reconstructs

---

19. Dulles, *History of Apologetics*, 210–11; see Edgar and Oliphint, *A History of Apologetics Past and Present*, 2:268.

religion from the inside outward on the basis of inward emotions and disposi-tions, he turns the apologetic sword against traditional orthodoxy."[20] In doing so, he takes apologetics too far, falling into the trap we mentioned at the beginning of this chapter. In an attempt to be relevant, he changed the very essence of Christianity. Schleiermacher exemplifies contextualization taken to such an extreme that the orthodox message of the cross is compromised.

Taking a leap of faith. Søren Kierkegaard (1813–1855), a physically frail and emotionally melancholy Danish philosopher, primarily reacted against two ideas: (1) the concept of "Christendom," which considered anyone a Christian by virtue of what nation they lived in, and (2) Hegelianism, a popular philosophy of his day,[21] which saw all of history and all of reality as a progressive unfolding of an Absolute Mind. In contrast to these two ideas, Kierkegaard emphasized *individual* choice—specifically the "leap of faith" that everyone must choose to make in order to achieve self-actualization. According to Kierkegaard, truth is subjective, and it only becomes objective when an individual makes a decision to become a true disciple and *live it out.* Our existence becomes reality not by assenting to doctrines or attending church but by choosing for ourselves to live out the truth. Orthodox beliefs about the incarnation, suffering, and resurrection of Christ are important, but they must be lived out in order to become true in an individual's life. Thus, in the mouths of some people, the truth can become untruth, if it is not lived. In this way, individual experience is more real than an abstract, universal norm.

Believing in the absurd. Kierkegaard soundly rejected the idea of presenting proofs for the existence of God. Why would you attempt to prove the existence of your roommate when he is sitting on the couch across from you eating a sandwich? Kierkegaard quipped, "to prove the existence of one who is present is the most shameless affront, since it is an attempt to make him ridiculous."[22] To "prove" God's existence is an insult to his existence. In a similar vein, Kierkegaard rejected the use of logical reasoning in coming to faith. He asserted that faith is not accessible through reason, because the core of Christian belief—the incarnation—is absurd. It makes no sense for the Creator and the creature, the infinite and the finite, the eternal and the temporal, the necessary and the contingent, to be united in one being.[23] Yet to Kierkegaard, the absurdity of Christianity is the very thing about it that truly meets the need of humanity.

---

20. Dulles, *History of Apologetics*, 211.

21. Absolute idealism or Hegelianism was developed by the German philosopher Georg Wilhelm Friedrich Hegel (1770–1831).

22. Søren Kierkegaard, *Concluding Unscientific Postscript*, trans. David Swenson (Princeton, NJ: Princeton University Press, 1941), 485.

23. See Dulles, *History of Apologetics*, 219.

The miraculous leap of faith that each individual must make paradoxically brings them one step closer to the reality of their own being.

Chateaubriand: Apologetics of Beauty

Mystery, morality, immortality, art, music, metaphysics, education, and charity—these are all gifts to the world from the church. And all of them can be captured in one word: beauty. François-René de Chateaubriand (1768–1848) in *The Genius of Christianity; or, the Beauties of the Christian Religion* argued that Christianity is true from its effects, that is, from the gifts it has given to civilization. His method was, in his own words, "not to prove that Christian religion is excellent because it comes from God, but that it comes from God because it is excellent."[24] The nineteenth-century Theatine Gioacchino Ventura (1792–1861), after paying tribute to Chateaubriand for having revived apologetics, declared poignantly, "The most effective apologies of the faith and of virtue are not so much those which make it believed as those which make it loved."[25] By showing the beauty that Christianity produces, Chateaubriand hoped to demonstrate its value to civilization in order to move others to sense that God gifted the Christian religion to the world.

Newman: Apologetics of Converging Probabilities

John Henry Newman (1801–1890), a cardinal in the Catholic Church, reasoned that while we cannot use philosophical or historical arguments to prove the truth of our religious convictions absolutely, the convergence of probabilities from such arguments enable us to reach a legitimate level of certitude. In other words, when divergent facts point to the same conclusion, we may attain a practical certainty that cannot be rationally dismissed.[26] (Thus, in Newman, we hear echoes of Joseph Butler's probability argument.) Newman offered an impressive argument based on the convergence of certain historical realities: Israel's monotheism was unique in the face of the rampant and persistent idolatry of its time. And along with their monotheism, Israel developed a growing and relentless hope in a coming Messiah. Christianity was the fulfillment and partial correction of Israel's messianic hopes. Jesus' prediction that the Christian faith would spread all over the earth not through force but by "sanctity and suffering" has proven true.[27] The convergence of all these unique historical realities makes it highly probable that Christianity is true.

---

24. François-René Chateaubriand, *The Genius of Christianity*, trans. Charles E. White (Baltimore: Murphy, 1856), 48.

25. Quoted in Dulles, *History of Apologetics*, 242.

26. See John Warwick Montgomery, "A Short History of Apologetics," in *Christian Apologetics: An Anthology of Primary Sources*, ed. Khaldoun A. Sweis and Chad Meister (Grand Rapids: Zondervan, 2012), 25.

27. See Dulles, *History of Apologetics*, 248–49.

Kuyper and Orr: Worldview Apologetics

Abraham Kuyper (1837–1920), a Dutch Calvinist and politician, had a great disdain for apologetics, reflected in his estimation of its value for the church: "In this struggle [against modernism] apologetics have advanced us not one single step."[28] Yet ironically, Kuyper himself developed an apologetic approach that certainly did advance the church—though he did not call it that, as it did not fit his narrow definition of apologetics. Kuyper did not engage in the apologetic battle, like so many of his contemporaries did, by offering conventional proofs or arguments for the existence of a generic deity. Rather, Kuyper formulated a worldview approach to Christianity, explaining how Christianity is not only a set of beliefs but also an entire system for interpreting the world. In his view, Christianity was the only way of viewing the world that truly makes sense of it.

Kuyper's contemporary James Orr (1844–1913) intentionally developed a worldview approach to apologetics. Orr asserted that Christianity, as a comprehensive system of thought and life, is most effectively defended from the attacks of its antagonists when it is conceptualized as a worldview. A person's worldview—their framework for interpreting the world—shapes the way they see or read evidence, and therefore it must be the starting place for apologetics. Orr believed that the center of the Christian worldview is the incarnation of Jesus Christ. Thus, he believed that apologetics is not about arguing for bare theism, but rather about articulating a coherent, meaningful, and all-encompassing worldview, with Jesus Christ as the starting point and the center.

THE TWENTIETH CENTURY

We will see how apologists in the twentieth century tapped into the approaches of the previous four millennia of biblical and church history. Doubtless you have found yourself identifying with some of the approaches described thus far. You may find more that resonate with you ahead, for the twentieth century includes a wide variety of methodologies: rational, presuppositional, combinational, literary, aesthetic, and revelational. Some continue to claim there is no value to apologetics—or at least very little value. But as we've seen already with Kuyper, most apologetic deniers end up practicing some form of apologetics anyway, even if they avoid the A-word.

Warfield: Rational Proof

In response to ever increasing attacks on the authority and inspiration of the Bible, Benjamin B. Warfield (1851–1921), a professor of theology at Princeton

---

28. Abraham Kuyper, "Calvinism a Life-System," in *Lectures on Calvinism: Six Lectures from the Stone Foundation Lectures Delivered at Princeton University* (Grand Rapids: Eerdmans, 2009), 5.

Seminary, defended its inerrancy by employing an apologetic of evidence and argumentation. Unlike Abraham Kuyper, who emphatically believed that the Spirit, without rational proof, moved people to accept the inspiration and authority of Scripture, Warfield argued that logical arguments and hard evidence could prove the inerrancy of Scripture to non-Christians. Thus, although Warfield was generally an enthusiast for Kuyper's work, he and Kuyper vigorously debated both the usefulness of apologetics and the unregenerate person's ability to be persuaded to believe by evidence and rational argumentation. Warfield placed apologetics first among theological departments, but Kuyper strongly disagreed.[29]

Van Til: Presuppositional Apologetics

Cornelius Van Til (1895–1987), a professor at Westminster Seminary, sought to develop an apologetic approach consistent with his understanding of Reformed theology.[30] He studied under Benjamin Warfield, but he was profoundly influenced by Abraham Kuyper—specifically by Kuyper's understanding of a fallen person's inability to reason correctly and his conception of Christianity as a worldview. Van Til developed presuppositional apologetics (sometimes called transcendental apologetics), which asserts that Christianity is the only worldview that can ground knowledge and rational thought. Because a fallen person's reason cannot function correctly, Christianity cannot be proven to an individual's autonomous reasoning apart from God and then accepted; rather, it must first be accepted and presupposed. Once Christianity is presupposed, the believer can then know that Christianity is true with absolute certainty. Van Til asserted that truth is in the whole or sum of all things and that all things are connected.[31] Thus, one cannot understand any one part of Christianity without accepting the whole.

Van Til's presuppositional apologetics does not function like most apologetic approaches that use traditional positive arguments for Christian theism. Instead, it attempts to convince non-Christians that it is impossible for them to live consistently within their own worldview, since all alternative worldviews to Christian theism are rationally inconsistent. For example, Van Til would point out the hypocrisy and absurdity of a nonbeliever using knowledge and rational thought to argue against Christianity, since knowledge and rational thought are grounded in Christian theism. Van Til did not attempt to prove

---

29. See Dulles, *History of Apologetics*, 321.

30. See Cornelius Van Til, *Christian Apologetics*, ed. William Edgar (Phillipsburg, NJ: P&R, 2003); Cornelius Van Til, *The Defense of the Faith*, ed. K. Scott Oliphint (Phillipsburg, NJ: P&R, 2008).

31. See Brian K. Morley, *Mapping Apologetics: Comparing Contemporary Approaches* (Downers Grove, IL: InterVarsity, 2015), 66.

the superiority of the Christian worldview with traditional positive arguments, because he believed it would be a useless pursuit. As explained above, an unbeliever cannot even understand the Christian worldview unless they already think within it. It is only once the unbeliever accepts the whole of Christianity that they can then begin to understand how all the parts of their lives and reality fit together.

Carnell and Schaeffer: Combinationalism

Combinationalism, a view of apologetics asserting that Christianity is logical, factual, and livable, is so named because it combines several tests to verify that Christianity corresponds to reality.[32] Edward John Carnell (1919–1967), a student of Cornelius Van Til and later the president of Fuller Theological Seminary, is an example of an apologist who used combinationalism. Like Augustine, he believed that humankind is capable of knowledge and rational thought because they are created in the image of God. Rather than asserting that a person must first repent and believe in the Christian worldview, as Van Til did, Carnell posited that a person can accept Christian theism as a working hypothesis and then verify it with three tests: (1) Does the hypothesis contradict itself? (2) Does it fit with the facts? (3) Can it be lived out without hypocrisy?[33] Carnell did not believe that Christianity could be proven with absolute certainty, but he was convinced that Christianity could be demonstrated as highly probable: "A rational man settles for that position which is attended by the fewest difficulties, not one which is unattended by any."[34] It is also worth noting that Carnell's apologetic methodology was contextually aware, often both starting with the felt needs of an individual and taking the current times into account.

For Carnell, apologetics involves three ways of knowing.

- **Experiencing:** Experience is immediate knowledge that is relational and has to do with our acquaintance with the truth.
- **Reasoning:** We can know something is true if it reasonably coheres with reality and is noncontradictory. True knowledge is built on a sufficiency of evidence.
- **Doing:** Knowledge is moral, spiritual, and volitional. It must be acted on. It involves the will. Mere intellectual knowledge is not enough; we only know truly by doing.

---

32. See Morley, *Mapping Apologetics*, 147–84.

33. See Morley, *Mapping Apologetics*, 156.

34. Edward J. Carnell, *Introduction to Christian Apologetics: A Philosophic Defense of the Trinitarian-Theistic Faith* (Grand Rapids: Eerdmans, 1948), 111.

Francis Schaeffer (1912–1984), who founded L'Abri in Switzerland alongside his wife, Edith, was, like Carnell, both a student of Cornelius Van Til and a combinationalist. More of a practitioner than a scholar (though he did give a highly rational defense of the faith), Schaeffer emphasized the importance of Christians loving one another and engaging culture. His basic apologetic method, like that of Carnell, could be called "presuppositional-lite." Positively, he asserted the Christian worldview as a working hypothesis and then verified its fit with reality. Negatively, he demonstrated that non-Christian worldviews fall short of this exact criteria. Non-Christian presuppositions always involve a tension created at points where a worldview contradicts itself, lacks factual support, and proves unlivable. It was at these points of tension that Schaeffer leveraged his apologetic arguments against non-Christian presuppositions.

Chesterton, Lewis, and Sayers: Literary Apologetics

In twentieth-century England, apologists emerged who combined artful flare with profound insight, producing uniquely enduring arguments for Christianity. Three of the most distinguished literary apologists of the twentieth century were G. K. Chesterton, C. S. Lewis, and Dorothy L. Sayers.

G. K. Chesterton (1874–1936), the foremost apologist of the early twentieth century, author of a hundred books, and a successful public debater, came to believe in Christianity, oddly enough, because of its opponents. Chesterton found the arguments of those attacking Christianity implausible and contradictory, for, as Avery Cardinal Dulles explains, it seemed to him that they claimed Christianity was at the same time "too pessimistic, too optimistic, too timid, too aggressive, too particularistic and too similar to other religions, too peaceful and too belligerent, too Puritanical and too corrupt!"[35] To Chesterton, these contradictions were illuminating, and he concluded that the problem was not with Christianity, but rather with its critics. In fact, he reasoned, to warrant such contradictory criticisms the Christian faith must be an extraordinary thing! Chesterton's ironic journey to the Christian faith, in which he was convinced to believe by atheists and skeptics, was not lost on him. He critiqued contemporary culture with a paradoxical literary flare laced with humor, sarcasm, and elegance. Here are a few of his witty and biting sayings from his classic work, *Orthodoxy*, and one from his book, *St. Thomas Aquinas*:

- "Certain new theologians dispute original sin, which is the only part of the Christian theology which can really be proved."[36]

---

35. Dulles, *History of Apologetics*, 293.
36. G. K. Chesterton, *Orthodoxy* (1908; repr., New York: Image, 2001), 9.

- "[Mr. Blatchford] has a strange idea that he will make it easier to forgive sins by saying that there are no sins to forgive."[37]
- "And the more I considered Christianity, the more I found that while it had established a rule and order, the chief aim of that order was to give room for good things to run wild."[38]
- "It is the fact that falsehood is never so false as when it is very nearly true."[39]

It is difficult to overestimate the influence of G. K. Chesterton, but the most profound impact of his work has been felt through his influence on C. S. Lewis (1898–1963).[40] Lewis, chair of medieval and renaissance literature at Cambridge, was an atheist turned theist turned Christian. Even before his conversion from atheism to theism, Lewis recognized that "Chesterton had more sense than all the other moderns put together"[41] and later testified to Chesterton's part in the process of his conversion: "I read Chesterton's *Everlasting Man* and for the first time saw the whole Christian outline of history set out in a form that seemed to me to make sense."[42]

Lewis had not fully converted to Christianity at that point. But he later described his transition from theism to Christianity: "I know very well when, but hardly how, the final step was taken. I was driven to Whipsnade one sunny morning. When we set out I did not believe that Jesus Christ is the Son of God, and when we reached the zoo I did."[43]

After his conversion to Christianity, Lewis began to write the works he is best known for, in which he defends classical Christianity by appealing to human longing, imagination, and reason. The various genres of his literary works illustrate the eclectic nature of his apologetic approach: allegory, satire, dream-vision, mythological space-novels, autobiography, and didactic pieces.[44]

Lewis's logical and persuasive powers are illustrated in this famous quote from *Mere Christianity*: "A man who was merely a man and said the sort of things Jesus said would not be a great moral teacher. He would either be a lunatic—on

---

37. Chesterton, *Orthodoxy*, 26.
38. Chesterton, *Orthodoxy*, 97.
39. G. K. Chesterton, *St. Thomas Aquinas*, in *The Collected Works of G. K. Chesterton* (San Francisco: Ignatius, 1986), 2:473.
40. Among others, Lewis was also influenced by George MacDonald and J. R. R. Tolkien. See C. S. Lewis, *Surprised by Joy* (New York: Harcourt, Brace and World, 1955), 213, 216.
41. Lewis, *Surprised by Joy*, 213.
42. Lewis, *Surprised by Joy*, 223.
43. Lewis, *Surprised by Joy*, 237.
44. See Dulles, *History of Apologetics*, 318–19.

a level with the man who says he is a poached egg—or else he would be the Devil of Hell. You must make your choice."[45]

Lewis's appeal to the imagination and human emotion can be felt in his depiction of Jesus Christ as a kingly lion in *The Lion, the Witch and the Wardrobe*:

> "Aslan a man!" said Mrs. Beaver sternly. "Certainly not . . . Aslan is a lion—*the* Lion, the great Lion."
>
> "Ooh" said Susan. "I'd thought he was a man. Is he—quite safe? I shall feel rather nervous about meeting a lion . . ."
>
> "Safe?" said Mr. Beaver . . . "Who said anything about safe? 'Course he isn't safe. But he's good. He's the King, I tell you."[46]

In these quotes, one can see why C. S. Lewis's influence has been so profound and lasting. As a teacher and apologist, he opens windows, enabling us to see in previously unimaginable ways.

C. S. Lewis and His Apologetic Genres

Avery Dulles illustrates various genres that contain Lewis's apologetics:

Allegory: *The Pilgrim's Regress: An Allegorical Apology for Christianity, Reason, and Romanticism*
Dream-vision: *The Great Divorce*
Mythological space-novel: *Perelandra* and *That Hideous Strength*
Autobiography: *Surprised by Joy*
Didactic: *The Problem of Pain, The Case for Christianity*, and *Miracles*[47]

Before she focused her attention on more overtly Christian apologetics and theological writings, Dorothy Sayers (1883–1957), an acquaintance of C. S. Lewis, translated Dante's *The Divine Comedy* and wrote crime fiction featuring the beloved detective Lord Peter Wimsey. But it would be a mistake to assume that her crime fictions had no apologetic value, for through the adventures of Lord Peter Wimsey, she illustrated the consequences of ignoring humanity's sad state, the joy and value of good work, and the power of good to overcome evil

---

45. C. S. Lewis, *Mere Christianity* (New York: Macmillan, 1952), 56.
46. C. S. Lewis, *The Lion, the Witch and the Wardrobe* (1950: repr., New York: HarperCollins, 1978), 79–80.
47. Dulles, *History of Apologetics*, 318.

in a chaotic world.[48] The following quote from Sayers's *Letters to a Diminished Church* illustrates the punchiness and power of her apologetic voice:

> The people who hanged Christ never, to do them justice, accused him of being a bore—on the contrary, they thought him too dynamic to be safe. It has been left for later generations to muffle up that shattering personality and surround him with an atmosphere of tedium. We have very efficiently pared the claws of the Lion of Judah, certified him "meek and mild," and recommended him as a fitting household pet for pale curates and pious old ladies.[49]

Barth: Nein Apologetics?

"Nein!" ("No!") was Karl Barth's (1886–1968) response to Emil Brunner's implication that natural knowledge of God apart from divine revelation has apologetic value. Brunner, a professor of systematic theology in Zurich, angered Barth with the publication of *Nature and Grace*, in which he accused Barth of six different false conclusions.[50] Barth responded with an article titled, "No! An Answer to Emil Brunner." In it he asserted that we love people by helping them guard the distinctiveness of the Word of God as a special revelation that comes to us through the Holy Spirit and the Scriptures, not by offering them the "useless bridges and crutches" of natural theology.[51] People have no capacity to see the true God or God's law in creation, and no natural point of contact exists between God and people.[52] Nor can we reason our way to God's reality through traditional apologetic argumentation. Thus, apologetics should not exist as a distinct discipline. Instead, the best apologetics is a good dogmatics[53]—in other words, the church's public confession of faith is its own apologetic.

Barth asserted that God must reveal *himself* to us through Jesus Christ, by our faith. But once God has been revealed to us, we are given the capacity to think rationally about him within the revealed knowledge. Once we have had a revelatory encounter with the Word of God through faith, we then have the mental capacity and framework to prove his existence to ourselves. Inversely, "to suppose that human reason, by itself, could demonstrate God's existence is to fall into idolatry."[54]

---

48. See J. E. McDermond, "Sayers, Dorothy L.," in *New Dictionary of Christian Apologetics*, ed. W. C. Campbell-Jack and Gavin McGrath (Downers Grove, IL: InterVarsity, 2014), 636.

49. Dorothy L. Sayers, *Letters to a Diminished Church: Passionate Arguments for the Relevance of Christian Doctrine* (Nashville: W Publishing, 2004), 4.

50. See Emil Brunner and Karl Barth, *Natural Theology* (Eugene, OR: Wipf & Stock, 2002), 19–35.

51. Brunner and Barth, *Natural Theology*, 125.

52. Brunner and Barth, *Natural Theology*, 80–90.

53. Dogmatics is the church's public confession of faith as opposed to private opinion.

54. Barth, quoted in Matthew Levering, *Proofs of God: Classical Arguments from Tertullian to Barth* (Grand Rapids: Baker Academic, 2016), 199.

So why does Barth matter? Barth is one of the most influential theologians, if not *the* most influential theologian, of the twentieth century. His negative attitude toward apologetics caused many to disavow apologetics altogether, and some would even say that Barth caused a crisis for apologetics' legitimacy in the middle of the twentieth century.[55] But Barth might have later softened his views on apologetics just a bit. According to Avery Cardinal Dulles, Barth concedes, toward the end of his *Church Dogmatics*, that it is permissible for Christians to use what Barth refers to as a "supplementary, incidental and implicit apologetics."[56]

Balthasar: Aesthetic Apologetics

Hans Urs von Balthasar (1905–1988), who was influenced by Karl Barth,[57] developed an aesthetic apologetic because he believed that faith must be "felt" and "imagined."[58] Balthasar's apologetic centered on the scriptural construct of God's glory, understood as God's goodness, beauty, and truth.[59] Balthasar believed that the beauty of God's love was revealed most significantly in the self-emptying act of Christ's death on the cross and that the church, as the messenger of God's love, becomes a credible apologetic only insofar as its members base everything they do, say, and think on God's love.[60] Thus, the beauty of God's love revealed in the cross, presented and perceived in the life of the church, is the most effective apologetic.[61]

Newbigin: Christ and Culture

Lesslie Newbigin (1909–1998), a missionary, professor, and pastor, developed an apologetic approach for a twentieth-century, post-Christian, pluralistic society. Newbigin did not bend to the Western culture's rationality; rather, he asserted that apologetics cannot simply be based on rational arguments, because revelation is naturally unreasonable to a fallen person. In the development of his apologetic, Newbigin traveled back beyond Aquinas's proofs for the Christian faith, which were grounded in Aristotelian logic, to the earlier approach of Augustine, who asserted, "I believe in order to know." In his apologetic approach, Newbigin attempted to work out Augustine's maxim that one must begin with faith in order to reason rightly, aiming to build on the foundation of divine revelation rather than mere reason. Newbigin concluded that, at any rate, the cross—the

---

55. See Dulles, *History of Apologetics*, 365.

56. Quoted in Dulles, *History of Apologetics*, 307.

57. Balthasar wrote a book on Barth's theology titled *The Theology of Karl Barth*, which Barth regarded as the best summary of his work.

58. See Edgar and Oliphint, *Christian Apologetics Past and Present*, 2:492.

59. Anthony C. Thiselton, *The Thiselton Companion to Christian Theology* (Grand Rapids: Eerdmans, 2015), 116.

60. See Dulles, *A History of Apologetics*, 337.

61. See Thiselton, *Thiselton Companion to Christian Theology*, 110–11.

Son of God suffering and dying for sin he never committed—is not reasonable. And because no one can legitimately reason their way to the unreasonable, revelation and faith must precede true understanding.[62]

How does Newbigin's approach function practically? Newbigin himself did not articulate the mechanics, but Paul Weston suggests three interrelated perspectives, drawn from Newbigin's writings, that guide us in the application of his apologetic theory:

1. Preach the gospel as the culmination of the biblical story. The message of the incarnation, death, and resurrection of Jesus Christ is its own apologetic.
2. Demonstrate that Christianity is not unique in its acceptance of "faith commitments" that cannot be proven. Ultimately, every truth claim rests on tenets that must be accepted by faith.
3. Show that Christianity is more livable than other truth claims and proves itself as it is lived out. The trustworthiness of the gospel evidences itself through the course of faithful Christian living.[63]

CONCLUSION

There you have it—a brief history of apologetics. We are done. We have built the foundation of our apologetic house . . . almost. You probably noticed that we've made it to the end of the twentieth century, but we haven't covered how apologetics is done today. It may seem odd to end this chapter with Barth, Balthasar, and Newbigin—figures who died in the twentieth century—when several years have passed since then, and many other twentieth-century apologists are still very much alive, including William Lane Craig, Gary Habermas, John Frame, Alvin Plantinga, N. T. Wright, Timothy Keller, and many others. The reason we haven't mentioned these contemporary apologists and methods is that we have chosen to talk about them in a separate discussion. This will make more sense as we now transition together from building the foundation of our apologetic house to constructing its walls and exterior.

---

62. See Paul Weston, "Newbigin, Lesslie," in *New Dictionary of Christian Apologetics*, 485.
63. See Weston, "Newbigin, Lesslie," 485–86.

PART 2

THE THEOLOGICAL STRUCTURE FOR APOLOGETICS AT THE CROSS

CHAPTER FIVE

MAKING SENSE
OF THE METHODS

> If we are truly personal, as created by God, then each individual will differ from everyone else. Therefore each man must be dealt with as an individual, not as a case or statistic or machine . . . There is no set formula that meets everyone's needs, and if only applied as a mechanical formula, I doubt if it really meets anyone's need—short of an act of God's mercy.
>
> *Francis Schaeffer, "The Question of Apologetics,"*
> *in* The God Who Is There

DIFFERENT APPROACHES TO DRAWING APOLOGETIC MAPS

Imagine a friend asking you to draw her a map to your hometown so she can pay a visit. In the same way, we as Christians have opportunities to draw maps that lead people on a journey to our "hometown"—the Christian faith. Different apologetic approaches offer competing ways of drawing maps—different methods of what might be called "apologetic cartography." Consider this chapter as preparation for drawing these apologetic maps. The reason we've waited until now to dive into a discussion of contemporary apologetics is that we wanted to first lay a proper foundation, summarized as follows:

Chapters 1 and 2 demonstrate that Scripture does not outline any single, definitive apologetic method. Instead of offering some sort of systematized handbook for developing an apologetic method, the Bible makes many different kinds of apologetic appeals and persuades at various levels using contextualized arguments.

Chapters 3 and 4 reveal how the history of apologetics offers both positive and negative examples. Positively, the church has a rich history of developing biblical concepts to create different kinds of apologetic appeals appropriate for the needs of the day. Negatively, history warns us of the danger of allowing extrabiblical frameworks and a desire for relevancy to rule over Scripture.

Both the warnings of apologetic history and the diversity of apologetic appeals found in the Bible remind us, as we enter our discussion of methods, of the danger in allowing rigid, extrabiblical conceptual schemes to polarize us too sharply against competing camps. Yet despite this polarization, there is good reason to be optimistic. In recent years, more apologists have been charitably listening to alternative strategies, finding strengths in other approaches, and even acknowledging possible weaknesses in their own apologetic traditions.[1]

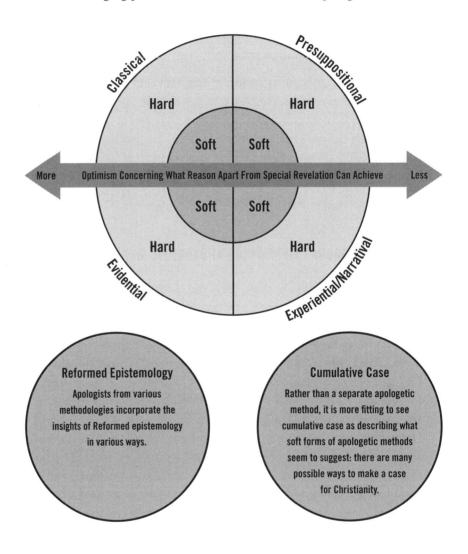

---

    1. David K. Clark points out how the various methods each have both valid points and blind spots that should be observed (*Dialogical Apologetics: A Person-Centered Approach to Christian Defense* [Grand Rapids: Baker, 1993], 103).

This chapter will summarize four apologetic approaches and discuss their potential strengths and weaknesses. As you look at the figure on the preceding page, which graphically represents the content of this chapter, keep in mind that the views of some apologists will not fit neatly in the center of one of the four major quadrants.[2] The reality is that apologists are often nuanced, putting them on slightly different places in the various quadrants. For example, some views may sit in one quadrant while gravitating toward another, and one may even lie on the line between two quadrants. The *soft* versions of each approach, which to some extent recognize the validity of other approaches, serve as a reminder that each approach is not necessarily sealed off from each other. The vertical axis divides the figure along a spectrum according to how optimistic each approach is toward the usefulness of reason apart from special revelation. The two circles below the four main quadrants—representing *Reformed epistemology* and the *cumulative case* approaches—signify schools of thought that have played valuable roles in methodological discussions. But for reasons we will discuss in sidebars later in this chapter, these two categories are distinct from the four approaches represented in the center of the graphic.

––––––––

The category of *evidence-based apologetics* encompasses both of the approaches represented on the left side of the graphic: classical and evidential apologetics. Due to their similarities, we will consider the two side by side.

CLASSICAL APOLOGETICS (OR THE TWO-STEP APPROACH)

Classical apologetics uses what is often referred to as a "two-step approach," which argues first for theism in general and then for Christianity as the most reasonable form of theism. The logic behind this approach is that a person must initially take the first step and accept the likelihood of a deity existing before they can accept that a specific God—the Christian God—exists. If a person has an assumed framework of naturalism and does not allow for the possibility of the supernatural, then they will often quickly dismiss core Christian claims. The first step (arguing for *a god*), therefore, makes room for the second step (arguing for *the Christian God*).

---

2. The apologetic taxonomy in this chapter, like other attempts to summarize apologetic camps, cannot be exhaustive. For examples of other ways to divide up the apologetic approaches, see Brian K. Morley, *Mapping Apologetics: Comparing Contemporary Approaches* (Downers Grove, IL: InterVarsity, 2015) and Steven B. Cowan, ed., *Five Views on Apologetics* (Grand Rapids: Zondervan, 2000).

Naturalism

In apologetic discussions, naturalism (or more specifically, ontological naturalism) normally refers to the view that everything develops from natural properties and causes.

Methodological naturalism is a framework for inquiry that does not claim that only the natural world exists, but nonetheless excludes the supernatural from consideration as unobservable and unprovable.

Compared to the approaches represented on the right side of the graphic, classical apologists tend to display a higher degree of confidence in what human reason can accomplish apart from special revelation. They assert that reason and evidence can be used to establish theism and the historical claims of Christianity. Unaided reason can demonstrate the high probability of realities such as God's existence, Jesus' crucifixion, and even Jesus' resurrection from the dead. However, most would still assert that special revelation is necessary for conversion.

Potential Strengths of Classical Apologetics

First, classical apologetics emphasizes the Bible's endorsement of using evidence and logic to persuade. Classical apologists do not shy away from the Bible's command that Christians be prepared to give reasons for the hope that they have, nor do they avoid the various instances in Scripture where logic and evidence are used to persuade.[3]

Second, classical apologetics has promoted the development of serious scientific, philosophical, and historical evidence for Christianity. In other words, classical apologists, rather than simply saying that Christians *can* use these types of arguments, emphatically assert that Christians *should* use and develop them. For this reason, classical apologetics has produced some of the most rigorous arguments for Christianity. Also, in the two-step approach they use to develop these arguments, classical apologists have rightly emphasized and shown the importance of integrating multiple disciplines in apologetics—specifically science, philosophy, and history.

Due to their similarities, we will wait to consider the potential weaknesses of classical apologetics together with the evidentialist approach below.

---

3. See, for example, Psalm 19:1; Luke 1:1–4; John 20:30–31; Acts 1:1–3; 26:26; Romans 1:19–20; 1 Corinthians 15:6.

EVIDENTIALIST APOLOGETICS (OR THE ONE-STEP APPROACH)

Evidentialism, also known as the "single-step approach," is similar to the classical approach in that it has a higher degree of confidence in human reason unaided by special revelation than the views on the left side of our graphic. However, unlike the classical apologist, the evidentialist does not believe that the first step in the two-step method—arguing for a general theism—is *necessary* in making a case for Christianity. Instead, evidentialists will start their apologetic by focusing on a historical case for either one of or a combination of the following: the general reliability of the Bible, the identity of Jesus, or the resurrection of Jesus. Evidentialists argue that this approach is simpler, in that it takes others straight to the central components of Christianity: the life of Jesus, the crucifixion, and the resurrection. In short, the evidentialist apologist believes that appeals to the traditional proofs for theism are unnecessary because historical evidence alone is strong enough to convince even those who deny theism.

Potential Strengths of Evidential Apologetics

First, evidential apologetics quickly takes others to the evidence for the historical elements of the gospel: Jesus, his death, and his resurrection. This fits well with the Bible's willingness to point to evidence and the way it emphasizes the centrality of the gospel (e.g., 1 Cor 15:1–8). As some evidentialists point out, the first step in the classical model can often lead to entanglement in long debates over complicated issues of science and philosophy, whereas the evidentialist model gets straight to the point: Jesus.

Second, evidential apologetics has promoted rigorous historical argumentation for Christianity. Christianity has a unique historic flavor to it. Unlike the gods of other religions, the Christian God did not just send a messenger to speak his revelation into human history; he himself entered into human history as the revelation! Thus, the heart of the Christian claim is, among other religions, uniquely historical. The best of evidential apologetics has stayed attuned to the latest historical scholarship and archaeology, not only to answer the questions of skeptics, but also to make a case for the historical reliability of the Bible and the life, death, and resurrection of Jesus.

Potential Weaknesses of Evidence-Based Approaches (Classical and Evidentialist Apologetics)

In pointing out the weaknesses of each apologetic tradition, we are not suggesting that everyone necessarily falls prey to these critiques—note the word *potential* in the heading above. There are, however, some concerns commonly expressed that appear to be a danger for at least some within each particular apologetic tradition. Usually such concerns are most applicable to those who have isolated themselves from the critiques and insights of other apologetic approaches. Each section in which we outline the most common critiques of a particular apologetic tradition will then be followed by exemplars who have offered softer versions of their tradition's apologetic approach, opening them up to the insights of other apologetic schools.

Keep in mind that in this particular section we will, because of their similarities, consider the potential weaknesses of classical and evidentialist apologetics together under the heading of *evidence-based approaches*.

The first danger of evidence-based approaches is that they can view humans as primarily thinking beings and singularly focus on persuasion that appeals cerebrally. This can happen either in the formal articulation of their methodology or, more likely, in its practical application. The danger is that evidence-based apologists may treat people like "cognitive machines, defined above all, by thought and rational operations"[4] and therefore see their job primarily as pouring the right information "into" non-Christians and getting the wrong information "out" so that they will assent to the propositions of Christianity. While most would not present this so crudely in theory, it is nevertheless a real danger in practice. Those within evidence-based traditions are vulnerable to falling into the trap of just "reasoning logically from the facts" without mastering the ability to appeal to people as believing and desiring beings. There are multiple and overlapping dimensions involved in human commitments. What we believe is determined not just by a process of logical reasoning we go through, but also by our feelings and desires.[5] People are far more than just a brain.

Moreover, the Christian faith is much more than just an acceptance of facts about God. The call of Christ is not to develop enough mental ability or academic rigor to figure out the pathway to truth. Rather, Christianity involves many different dimensions existing beyond a mere mental assent to facts, such as stepping out in faith, receiving grace, submitting to Jesus, accepting mystery, and partaking in the love of God.

However, we must not construct straw men. Many evidence-based apologists would agree with the statements the previous paragraph makes about Christianity. They would affirm that a mental assent to facts, while a necessary aspect of Christianity, does not encompass all that Christianity is. Still, because of their emphasis on reason, the danger remains that in practice, evidence-based

---

4. James K. A. Smith, *Desiring the Kingdom: Worship, Worldview, and Cultural Formation* (Grand Rapids: Baker, 2009), 42.

5. See Kelly James Clark, "A Reformed Epistemologist's Response," in *Five Views on Apologetics*, 85.

apologists may unintentionally make Christianity sound more like the answer to a math problem than a passionate call of a loving husband to his lost bride. The prudent apologist in both the classical and evidentialist traditions will be aware of these dangers and take into account a holistic view of human personhood and the Christian faith.

Second, evidence-based approaches can lack an appreciation for human situatedness. Sometimes evidence-based apologists will make it sound as if they are simply using common sense and reason recognized by all: "The truth is really obvious, so why can't everyone see it?" The problem is that with the advent of modern pluralism and the sociology of knowledge, it becomes clear there are plenty of very intelligent people who do not see the truth Christians do as "really obvious." In his important work on the development of doctrine, Alister McGrath makes this point when he writes that if apologetics is understood "as an attempt to justify the 'rationality' or 'reasonableness' of Christian beliefs *on the basis of the classic notion of universally valid patterns* of reason and thought," then the apologetic enterprise is in trouble.[6]

McGrath is not arguing for relativism, which can be dismissed as self-refuting. Nor is McGrath saying there are no points of contact between believers and those outside of the Christian community. There can be considerable "degrees of overlap" between competing frameworks of rationality. What McGrath *is* saying is that while we may be able to arrive at unquestionable, universal truths in fields such as basic logic and mathematics, nearly all the other frameworks of rationality we use to understand the world are shaped by our social and historical context.[7]

At play here is an important distinction between, on the one hand, what we might call *basic logic*—which in some sense is universal and is used, for example, in mathematics and entailed in the law of noncontradiction—and, on the other hand, the *larger frameworks of rationality and self-evident truths* held to by certain cultures and groups in history.[8] For instance, it seems self-evident to many Westerners that all humans are worthy of respect and dignity. Certainly, Christianity has taught this and has left its mark on Western culture to such an extent that it might seem like common sense. However, belief in the dignity and worth of all human beings is far from a universal norm embraced by all cultures in history.[9] Thus, as the Scottish philosopher Alasdair MacIntyre

---

6. Alister McGrath, *The Genesis of Doctrine: A Study in the Foundation of Doctrinal Criticism* (Cambridge, MA: Blackwell, 1990), 199, emphasis added.

7. See McGrath, *Genesis of Doctrine*, 199.

8. See McGrath, *Genesis of Doctrine*, 90; Charles Taylor, "Reason, Faith, and Meaning," in *Faith, Rationality, and the Passions*, ed. Sarah Coakley (Malden, MA: Wiley-Blackwell, 2012), 13–27.

9. See Nicholas Wolterstorff, *Justice: Rights and Wrongs* (Princeton, NJ: Princeton University Press,

has stressed, when we are speaking about these broader claims of justice or practical rationality—even those that are seemingly "obvious" to us—we must ask, "Whose justice and which rationality are we talking about?"[10] As Christians, we affirm there is a true rationality rooted in God and his gospel, but we should recognize that others assume different competing frameworks for rationality.

If you find yourself preferring the evidence-based apologetic approaches or are already working within classical or evidential apologetics, you ought to be aware of and avoid the "it's just obvious" mentality. For while your interpretation of the evidence may seem obvious to you, those who have not assumed a Christian framework—or at least a framework that has significant overlap to it—will often not see it as "common sense." The pluralism of the contemporary world, which includes a variety of assumed frameworks that weigh the significance of various types of evidence and reasoning differently, will frustrate those who are not willing to, along with making appeals based on evidence and logic, creatively challenge the larger interpretive frameworks that people have.[11]

Third, ultimately Scripture should assess what makes for a "good" argument. In determining the rules for a sound apologetic argument, some are pushing Scripture aside in favor of autonomous human reason. This critique pointedly asks, "Who determines what the ultimate standard is for what is true and false? How do we judge between competing systems of rationality? Can we line up more proofs and evidence to support our proofs and evidence?"

In addition to using reason, as evidence-based methods stress, _Christian_ apologists should acknowledge that God's Word has the final say in what makes for a "good" argument. This does not mean Christians have no connecting points

---

2008), 311–61; Charles Taylor, _Sources of Self: The Making of the Modern Identity_ (Cambridge, MA: Harvard University Press, 1989), 515–18. John Gray from a secular perspective argues that "cast-off Christian hopes" ground much of Western morality: "We inherit our belief—or pretence—that moral values take precedence over all other valuable things from a variety of sources, but chiefly from Christianity" (_Straw Dogs: Thoughts on Humans and Other Animals_ [London: Granta, 2002], 3, 88).

10. See Alasdair MacIntyre, _Whose Justice? Which Rationality?_ (Notre Dame, IN: University of Notre Dame Press, 1988), 399. MacIntyre is not denying there are some basic laws of logic (such as the law of noncontradiction) that are universal (see also McGrath, _Genesis of Doctrine_, 90). Lest they be misunderstood, neither MacIntyre nor McGrath are arguing for forms of fideism or blind faith against logic. For MacIntyre, the way forward is asking which truth claims within a particular tradition offer the most "explanatory power," as he points out in the last line in _Whose Justice? Which Rationality?_: "The rival claims to truth of contending traditions of enquiry depend for their vindication upon the adequacy and the explanatory power of the histories which the resources of each of those traditions in conflict enable their adherents to write" (403). See McGrath, _Mere Apologetics: How to Help Seekers and Skeptics Find Faith_ (Grand Rapids: Baker, 2012), for his view on how this should be developed in the field of apologetics. Also see Lesslie Newbigin's chapter titled "Reason, Revelation, and Experience," in _The Gospel in a Pluralist Society_ (Grand Rapids: Eerdmans, 1989), 52–65, and Alasdair MacIntyre, _After Virtue_, 3rd ed. (Notre Dame, IN: University of Notre Dame Press, 2007), xii–xiv.

11. For more on the inescapabilty of frameworks and their connection to the modern notion of identity, see Taylor, _Sources of the Self_, 19–21, 26–32, 105–7.

with the unbeliever or that the logic and morality of Scripture will *always* seem strange to outsiders. However, at times the Bible's logic and ethic will seem at odds with the world around us. For example, many would say that a perfect, sinless being suffering and dying on a cross is far from "good" or "rational." A divine being suffering as a human will seem foolish to many, and in fact, some critics, horrified, have remarked that this "sounds like divine child abuse." The apostle Paul reminds us that responses like this should not surprise us: "Christ crucified [is] a stumbling block to Jews and foolishness to Gentiles" (1 Cor 1:23). As Christians, we must be careful to allow God's Word to set the parameters for defining a "good" argument rather than allowing shifting cultural frameworks to decide (see 1 Cor 1:25).

Consider another example. An evidence-based apologist might appeal to the "current historical methods" as a supposed neutral arbiter of questions such as "Who was Jesus really?" and "Did Jesus really rise again?" However, such an apologist would be missing an important question: "What are these 'current historical methods' and who has defined them?" Historical methods can assume norms that work against the framework of Christianity. Furthermore, no method works independently of the persons applying it. That is why, for instance, twenty-first-century Western historians have produced such different portraits of Jesus.[12] Therefore, when referring to the "rules of history," it is important not to imply that either the current historical methodology or the historians themselves can operate as a neutral determiner of truth. Nor do historical events interpret themselves. Special revelation is needed to tell us what historical events ultimately mean.

However, we need to be balanced. Christian apologetics will at times rightly and productively employ what can be called "thin reasoning," playing by some of

---

12. The result of the various quests for the historical Jesus has not been a single historical Jesus, but instead a variety of competing portraits of the historical Jesus, which are too many to list here. Dale C. Allison Jr., who has made a career in writing extensively in the field of Jesus research, is an example of a growing trend among scholars to question historical Jesus research as it has traditionally been conducted. After noting some of the variety of the portraits of Jesus that are clearly "not complementary but contradictory," he points out that the quests have only achieved agreement on minimal and basic information about Jesus. He goes on to provide examples of how past scholarly opinions, which were at one time accepted basically as facts among critical scholars, are now out of favor and are viewed as misguided relics of the past. He then adds, "This is one reason why I am allergic to the phrase 'assured critical result'" (*The Historical Christ and the Theological Jesus* [Grand Rapids: Eerdmans, 2009], 10–11). For similar sentiments, see Scot McKnight, "The Jesus We'll Never Know," *Christianity Today* 54, no. 4 (April 2010): 26; Luke Timothy Johnson, *The Real Jesus: The Misguided Quest for the Historical Jesus and the Truth of the Traditional Gospels* (New York: Harper Collins, 1996). Jonathan T. Pennington also names Richard Bauckham, Markus Bockmuehl, Richard Hays, and Francis Watson as internationally respected scholars who "question historical Jesus studies as they have been practiced" (*Reading the Gospels Wisely: A Narrative and Theological Introduction* [Grand Rapids: Baker Academic, 2012], 93) Our point here is not that historical research is unimportant. Rather, the point is that scholars themselves ardently disagree on historical methodology, so appealing to this methodology uncritically as a kind of neutral arbitrator for determining the "facts" fails to do justice to the scholarly conversations that are actually occurring.

the rules of the current historical methodology. We should recognize with Jesus himself—who assumes that even those who are evil "know how to give good gifts" (Matt 7:11; Luke 11:13)—that knowing what is "good" is not an all-or-nothing affair. As we have said previously, one can appeal to human intuitions or a shared understanding of the "good" or "rational" without supplanting the Word of God as the final authority. The contextual nature of the Bible itself shows a willingness to accommodate an argument to its context. Nevertheless, it is important to understand that it is not as though the methodology of any discipline, including history, has dropped down from the sky in perfect form so that it can be appealed to uncritically as a neutral arbiter of truth. At times we should use "thick reasoning" and be willing to pull the rug out from underneath the very assumptions made by any given secular methodology.

Thin versus Thick Reasoning

Thin reasoning: persuading by operating within the assumed rationality and "common sense" assumptions of a given person or community.

Thick reasoning: persuading by pushing back against the broader framework of rationality and "common sense" assumptions of a given person or community.

Soft versus Hard Classical Apologetics

Some apologists, who we refer to as *hard* classical apologists, insist that a logical argument for theism *must* precede a historical argument for the reliability of the Bible or the resurrection. In their view, a non-Christian person will not even consider evidence for the supernatural events of Scripture unless they first adopt theism.

However, some well-known classical apologists, such as William Lane Craig, seem open to other approaches and could therefore be called *soft* classical apologists. Craig is well-known for using the kalam cosmological argument in support of God's existence and then proceeding by arguing that Jesus' bodily resurrection offers the best account of the historical evidence. In this way, Craig clearly fits into the standard classical model. However, he also emphasizes the need for various other types of arguments:

Of course, showing Christianity to be true will involve much more than the two arguments above: they are but two links in the coat of mail, and the positive case will need to be accompanied by a defensive case against objections. *The apologetic task, then, is perhaps best seen as a collective project taken on by the believing community.*[13]

An Excerpt from William Lane Craig as an Exemplar of Soft Classical Apologetics

"Now for those unfamiliar with the *kalam* cosmological argument, I'll provide a brief summary of it. The argument is a simple syllogism:

1. Everything that begins to exist has a cause.
2. The universe began to exist.
3. Therefore, the universe has a cause.

"The crucial second premise is supported by philosophical arguments against the infinitude of the past and by scientific evidence for the beginning of the universe. Having arrived at the conclusion, one may then do a conceptual analysis of what properties a cause of the universe must have. One is thereby brought to conclude that an uncaused, beginningless, changeless, timeless, spaceless, immaterial, enormously powerful, personal Creator of the universe exists."[14]

Craig also has expressed the merit of using historical evidence prior to moving on to the second step of the classical apologetics approach. For example, he writes, "I certainly agree that an argument from miracles can be part of a cumulative case for theism."[15] At another point, considering the evidence for the resurrection, Craig writes that the historian "may indeed rightly infer from the evidence that God has acted here in history."[16] So it seems that for Craig, the first step in the two-step classical argument is ideal, but it might not be absolutely necessary.[17]

Craig serves as an example of a leading apologist who prefers the two-step classical method, yet also shows openness by not strictly drawing a line between which types of arguments are allowed in each stage of the two-step approach.

---

13. William Lane Craig, "Classical Apologetics," in *Five Views on Apologetics*, ed. Steven B. Cowan (Grand Rapids: Zondervan, 2000), 53, emphasis added.

14. William Lane Craig "Objections So Bad I Couldn't Have Made Them Up (or, the World's 10 Worst Objections to the Kalam Cosmological Argument)," in *Come Let Us Reason: New Essays in Christian Apologetics*, ed. Paul Copan and William Lane Craig (Nashville: B&H, 2012), 53.

15. William Lane Craig, "A Classical Apologist's Response," in *Five Views on Apologetics*, 122.

16. William Lane Craig, *Assessing the New Testament Evidence for the Historicity of the Resurrection of Jesus* (Lewiston, NY: Mellen, 1989), 419.

17. This is what the evidentialist apologist Gary R. Habermas has argued, who writes that since Craig allows historical evidence as one of the indications for theism, "while the initial step [in the two-step approach] may be helpful, it is not mandatory" ("An Evidentialist's Response" in *Five Views on Apologetics*, 60).

Soft versus Hard Evidential Apologetics

In its ideal form, *hard* evidentialist apologetics would only need to include historical evidences for Jesus, the resurrection, and the Bible, and it would never appeal to philosophy or science to make a case for a theistic worldview in preparation for its historical case for Christianity. While there are some New Testament scholars who seem unconcerned with other types of arguments, the hard version of evidential apologetics is rarely adopted formally. Instead, most evidential apologists tend to be *soft* evidentialists, and only say that while the classical arguments for theism can be helpful, they are not *necessary*. In other words, most evidentialists believe that the historical arguments contain enough firepower to make the case for theism and Christianity without having to turn to the first step in classical apologetics. Gary Habermas explains, "Typical arguments for God's existence are frequently utilized [by evidentialists], but unlike classical apologists, not because they are necessary. Further, evidentialists often begin their discussions of evidence with these theistic arguments."[18] Thus, the soft form of evidentialism is not so much a "distinct apologetic methodology" that is never willing to use the classical two-step method as it is "a personally preferred style of argumentation."[19]

An Excerpt from Gary Habermas as an Exemplar of Soft Evidentialist Apologetics

"We have presented evidence for Jesus' resurrection, using a 'minimal facts' approach, which considers only those data that are so strongly attested historically that even the majority of nonbelieving scholars accept them as facts . . .

"Using our 'minimal facts' approach, we considered four facts that meet these stringent criteria and one additional fact that enjoys acceptance by an impressive majority of scholars, though not nearly every scholar. Let's look at what we now have. Shortly after Jesus' death [fact #1], his disciples believed that they saw him risen from the dead [fact #2]. They claimed that he had appeared to individuals among them, as well as to several groups. Two of those who once viewed Jesus as a false prophet later believed that he appeared to them risen: Paul, the church persecutor [fact #3]; and James, the skeptic and Jesus' brother [fact #4]. Both of them became Christians as a result. Therefore, not only do we have the testimony of friends; we have also heard from one enemy of Christianity and one skeptic. Finally, we have the empty tomb [fact #5].

"These facts point very strongly to Jesus' resurrection from the dead, which accounts for all five facts very nicely."[20]

---

18. Habermas, "An Evidentialist's Response," in *Five Views on Apologetics*, 60–61n.13.

19. These are Craig's words ("A Classical Apologist's Response," in *Five Views on Apologetics*, 122).

20. Gary R. Habermas and Michael R. Licona, *The Case for the Resurrection of Jesus* (Grand Rapids: Kregel, 2004), 75–76.

PRESUPPOSITIONAL APOLOGETICS

Found on the right side of this chapter's summarizing chart, presuppositionalists are less optimistic, if not altogether negative, about what reason apart from special revelation can achieve. Presuppositionalism, as its name suggests, asserts that reasoning does not take place in a vacuum; rather, a person's reasoning is colored by their presuppositions or assumptions—the lenses through which they see the world. There is no neutral realm where reason alone exists and operates; there is no perfectly objective vantage point from which a person can see and interpret the world without presuppositions. And because non-Christians deny the true God they know exists, they reason with unbelieving and sinful presuppositions.

Cornelius Van Til, the father of presuppositionalism, argued that we can know with certainty that the Christian God exists because we must presuppose him to be rational. Thus, for many presuppositionalists, probabilistic or "best explanation" arguments are off-limits because such arguments do not do justice to the power of the Christian case and would give unbelievers an excuse for their unbelief.

According to Van Til, apologists who appeal to human reason actually inflame human sinfulness. He argued that traditional apologetics reinforces human autonomy and makes unbelievers the judge of God, when instead, as presuppositionalists assert, unbelievers should submit to God as judge. The unbeliever's problem is not knowledge; it is submission.[21] This view accounts for why some of the most strident advocates of presuppositionalism refuse to use forms of the evidential or classical arguments for Christianity.

This raises an obvious question: *Should Christians just proclaim the gospel and forgo apologetics? What is an apologist to do?*

The presuppositionalist, taking seriously both the corruption of human reasoning and the inability of the unregenerate to comprehend spiritual realities, sets out to undermine the very framework of non-Christian thinking. The presuppositionalist asserts that the authority of the Bible should be the assumed starting point in apologetic discourse. As Van Til himself wrote, "The only 'proof' of the Christian position is that unless its truth is presupposed there is no possibility of 'proving' anything at all."[22] Thus, the goal of this apologetic approach is to undermine a non-Christian's worldview by demonstrating that without the Christian God, they cannot consistently claim meaning, truth,

---

21. See Morley, *Mapping Apologetics*, 72.
22. Cornelius Van Til, "My Credo," in *Jerusalem and Athens: Critical Discussions on the Philosophy and Apologetics of Cornelius Van Til*, ed. E. R. Geehan (Phillipsburg, NJ: P&R, 1971), 21.

or logic—and that to the extent that they *do* use such things, they are only "borrowing capital" from Christianity.

This method is referred to as the *transcendental argument*. By questioning an unbeliever's presuppositions and requiring them to justify their rationality, the apologist reduces their position to absurdity. Once the unbeliever realizes that their current worldview cannot provide sufficient justification, Christianity is then articulated as the only option that makes rational sense of the world.

Potential Strengths of Presuppositional Apologetics

Presuppositional apologetics helpfully emphasizes:

- the importance of Scripture
- that non-Christians assume presuppositions that negatively impact their reasoning ability
- that sin damages the whole person

Presuppositionalism offers an important reminder that the Word of God, rather than particular and local cultural frameworks of the day, should be the undergirding framework through which Christians view reality—charting a vision for what is good, rational, and meaningful. Scripture should be the "norming norm." Moreover, moral issues cannot be neatly separated from rational issues. Humans are not neutral agents out to discover God unimpeded; rather, they are sinful beings who are limited because they suppress the knowledge of God (Rom 1:18–32).

Potential Weaknesses of Presuppositional Approaches

First, most apologists do not find that the transcendental argument alone has the ability to demonstrate the truthfulness of Christianity. It seems too much to ask this argument to prove the existence of all the attributes of the Christian God. While Christianity provides a lens that makes sense of the world and our cognitive abilities, other worldviews are able to offer intelligible accounts, even though they explain less. Moreover, according to their own contrasting framework of rationality, many will find certain Christian doctrines themselves irrational (e.g., the full deity and full humanity of Christ existing as one person or the doctrine of the Trinity), so the claim that their non-Christian view is irrational could easily be turned back on the apologist. Thus, a variety of different kinds of arguments would be needed in support.

Second, presuppositionalists have lacked the ability to effectively transfer their methodology and arguments to a broad audience. Often their arguments have not been articulated in user-friendly ways, and they have lacked needed specifics.[23] It is one thing for philosophers to argue about how to ground rationality, but it is another thing when faced with a skeptic who is raising issues about the Bible's reliability, someone who is struggling to believe in Jesus' bodily resurrection, or a Muslim asserting the self-attesting nature of the Quran. This is why almost all biblical scholars and practitioners, no matter their apologetic tradition, end up using a variety of both positive and negative arguments.

The way some proponents articulate this apologetics system can make it sound like a narrow, circular argument. The presuppositionalist will rightly assert that in some sense all reasoning assumes an authority, whether it be the authority of a certain kind of rationality, a methodology that bases its standards on empiricism, or, in their case, Scripture itself. And yet if presuppositionalists do not modify their approach to commit to incorporating a variety of positive arguments for belief—as softer versions have done—it will continue to lack a broader appeal as a methodology.[24] And to their credit, some presuppositionalists themselves have admitted that a weakness in the presuppositional literature is that its authors have not paid sufficient attention to developing various types of specific arguments for Christianity.[25]

Soft versus Hard Presuppositional Apologetics

Hard presuppositionalists maintain that a transcendental argument should be rigidly distinguished from evidence-based arguments.[26] However, *soft* presuppositionalists, such as John Frame, argue that the transcendental argument, rather than simply being seen as one argument among many, should be seen as the *goal* of all apologetic arguments: "We should be concerned to show that God is the condition of all meaning, and our epistemology should be consistent with that conclusion." At the same time, Frame affirms that the transcendental argument is not a magic bullet, since its conclusion "cannot be reached in a single, simple syllogism." He concludes, therefore, that a transcendental argument "normally, perhaps always, requires many subarguments . . . some of [which] may be traditional theistic proofs or Christian evidences."[27]

---

23. John Frame admits this; see his *Apologetics: A Justification of Christian Belief* (Phillipsburg, NJ: P&R, 2015), xxxii–xxxiii.

24. While hardened forms of presuppositionalism claim an "absolute certain argument" for the biblical God, they lack the specifics of showing how this is done. For this critique, see John Frame, *Cornelius Van Til: An Analysis of His Thought* (Phillipsburg, NJ: P&R, 1998), 400.

25. John Frame writes, "As he [Habermas] points out, I too have acknowledged that weakness in the presuppositional literature . . . I am happy to recommend writings of Habermas, Craig, and others in these areas [for Christian evidences]" ("A Presuppositional Apologist's Closing Remarks," in *Five Views on Apologetics*, 358).

26. See Greg Bahnsen, *Van Til's Apologetic: Readings and Analysis* (Phillipsburg, NJ: P&R, 1998), 496–529.

27. Frame, "A Presuppositional Apologist's Closing Remarks," 360.

In contrast to proponents of hard versions of presuppositionalism, Frame does not expect "that all the elements of biblical theism are presupposed in intelligible communication."[28] Frame also denies that many core Christian doctrines can be demonstrated with just the transcendental argument alone.[29]

Furthermore, while affirming that Christianity is "absolutely compelling," soft versions of presuppositionalism allow that individual arguments can be helpful without being certain (i.e., probabilistic arguments) and that Scripture calls for evidence and arguments to be given in support of Christianity.[30] Thus, while Frame is clear that arguments should be part of a larger transcendental case where God is the very "presupposition of rational thinking," he argues that apologists can and should incorporate other types of arguments.[31]

While both hard and soft presuppositionalists emphasize that the believer should never advocate or accept "autonomous" thinking, they apply this emphasis differently. Hard presuppositionalists assert that only indirect arguments are acceptable (e.g., "without God you cannot have morality") because arguing directly (e.g., "there is morality, so there must be God") causes unbelievers to think they can know morality apart from God. Soft presuppositionalists like John Frame do not see much difference between direct and indirect arguments. While Frame sees promoting autonomous reasoning as a problem, he does not think that simply arguing in a more direct way necessarily means an apologist is doing so, for the apologist could well be correctly appealing to an unbeliever's repressed knowledge of God.

The result is that in this soft version of presuppositionalism, the presuppositional apologist is free to employ many, if not all, of the more traditional arguments of classical and evidentialist apologists.[32]

So, then, what distinguishes Frame's softer form of presuppositionalism from the other forms of apologetics? Frame acknowledges that on the surface there might not be much difference at all: "It may no longer be possible to distinguish presuppositional apologetics from traditional apologetics merely by externals—by the form of argument, the explicit claim of certainty or probability, etc. Perhaps presuppositionalism is more an attitude of the heart, a spiritual condition, than an easily describable, empirical phenomenon."[33]

The attitudes of our hearts clearly show how our allegiances affect the way we obtain knowledge, the degree of our commitment to present God as the sovereign

---

28. Frame, *Cornelius Van Til: An Analysis of His Thought*, 316.

29. See Frame, *Apologetics: A Justification of Christian Belief*, 56.

30. See Frame, *Apologetics: A Justification of Christian Belief*, 56.

31. Frame, "A Presuppositional Apologist's Closing Remarks," 357–58.

32. See John M. Frame, *Apologetics to the Glory of God: An Introduction* (Phillipsburg: P&R, 1994), 85.

33. Frame, *Apologetics to the Glory of God*, 87.

source of all meaning and rationality, and the belief that a non-Christian's thinking is impacted both by a sinful nature and a repressed knowledge of God.[34]

EXPERIENTIAL/NARRATIVAL APOLOGETICS

Similar to presuppositionalists, experiential/narratival (E/N) apologists stress that all evidence and reasoning depends on a person's particular framework, and they tend toward pessimism regarding human reason apart from special revelation.[35] But whereas presuppositionalists seek to undermine an unbeliever's rationality in order to show them that they must assume Christian propositions to be rational, E/N apologists interact with unbelievers by inviting them to participate in an experience and embrace a story that fits better with the actualities of life.[36]

Many E/N apologists tend to deemphasize the usefulness of the traditional proofs, and some even go so far as to question their propriety. E/N apologetics stresses that "proofs" for Christianity rest not in logical deductions or hard evidence, but in the lives of the community of faith and the power of the apostolic message. Traditional proofs for God are problematic because they can deny the essence of Christianity, which is a life and story to be lived out, not a series of propositional statements that can be proven.

E/N apologetics, while maintaining the importance of orthodox beliefs such as the incarnation, suffering, and resurrection of Christ, asserts that these truths come to us in story form and must be embraced and lived out in order to be truly understood. Human reason and logic can be helpful in understanding the proclamation of the gospel, but they do not ground the gospel.[37] As Myron Penner explains, "One of the serious problems for modern apologetics is that it treats Christianity as if it were an objective 'something' (e.g., a set of propositions or doctrines) that can be explained, proven, and cognitively mastered," when instead, "Christianity . . . is much more a *way* or an invitation to live (walk, grow) in the truth than it is a doctrine or set of beliefs (a position) whose truth we can grasp and cognitively master, as the modern apologetic paradigm seems to imply."[38]

At this point, you may be asking, "How does this practically play out in the apologetic task?" Christians are to "prove" the truth of Christianity not by offering people rational arguments but by ordering our lives around the gospel

---

34. See Frame, *Apologetics to the Glory of God*, 88.

35. See Myron Bradley Penner, *The End of Apologetics: Christian Witness in a Postmodern Context* (Grand Rapids: Baker, 2013), 53.

36. See Francis Spufford, *Unapologetic: Why, Despite Everything, Christianity Can Still Make Surprising Emotional Sense* (San Francisco: HarperOne, 2013), 67.

37. See Penner, *End of Apologetics*, 52, 132.

38. Penner, *End of Apologetics*, 66.

in ways that display the reality of Jesus. A faithful Christian life is the proof for the truth of the gospel because it "creates the conditions for the intelligibility of the truths of the Christian gospel by publically displaying . . . a way of being in which its claims make sense—a life that can only be made sense of in terms of those claims."[39]

This does not mean that offering reasons for belief in Christianity is off the table for the E/N apologist. However, their apologetic focuses primarily, and often exclusively, on internal, intuitive reasons. In other words, the gospel story is told, and the unbeliever is asked to try it on for size. Rather than offering proofs, the E/N apologist offers invitations for the unbeliever to see how Christianity harmonizes with their deepest human intuitions and life experiences.

Potential Strengths of Experiential/Narratival Apologetics

First, E/N apologetics rightly emphasizes the importance of human desire and imagination. The E/N approach warns against a dry rationalism, rightly recognizing that Scripture does much more than simply appeal to our brains. E/N apologists also point out that the vast majority of people in today's culture do not arrive at their deepest commitments through "proofs based on simple logic."[40]

Adhering to all or a combination of (1) an anthropology that emphasizes love as the primary human motivator, (2) their own observations about the current cultural moment, and (3) the example that Scripture sets, E/N apologists insist that story, images, and creativity are important elements in Christian persuasion. Through these insights, E/N apologetics makes a valuable contribution to apologetics.

Second, by stressing the importance of the corporate church as a living apologetic, E/N apologetics is recovering an ancient scriptural argument. As we have seen in previous chapters, one of the core arguments in the early church was that Christians lived and died better than anyone else. This type of argument finds a wealth of support in the pages of the New Testament.[41]

Third, E/N apologetics is concerned with understanding how living in different cultures shapes people's experiences in life. By understanding the framework of a particular culture, the E/N apologist can potentially be in a better position to explain the Christian faith and show how the gospel story both subverts and appeals to the deepest aspirations of that culture.

---

39. Penner, *End of Apologetics*, 128.

40. David Skeel, while being careful to point out that analytical arguments have their place, emphasizes this point. See *True Paradox: How Christianity Makes Sense of Our Complex World* (Downers Grove, IL: InterVarsity, 2014), 23.

41. Recall, for example, the opening explanation of 1 Peter 3:15 in the introduction.

Potential Weaknesses of Experiential/Narratival Apologetics

First, E/N apologetics can minimize propositional truths and cognitive appeals. Some apologists, perceiving what they see as overly rationalistic approaches dominating contemporary apologetics, perhaps swing the pendulum too far in the opposite direction. While humans are not merely thinking things, thinking is a part of their being. Similarly, while Christianity is not merely made up of propositional statements, propositional statements make up much of the Bible. As Christians, we must confess propositional statements—"Jesus is Lord" (Rom 10:9)—and call on others to do the same. In short, effective E/N apologists will be careful to avoid responding to an apparent reductionism with a reductionism of their own in the opposite direction.

Second, E/N apologetics can underutilize historical evidence and linear thinking. Historical evidence is not so conclusive that it can absolutely prove Christianity or coerce someone into acceptance. At the same time, part of Christianity's central message is the reality that God has acted in human history, entering into space and time in the person of Jesus of Nazareth. The New Testament itself clearly assumes that historical data is important.

It is one thing to prefer the E/N approach; it is another thing to completely avoid interacting with the historical and logical arguments for and against Christianity. Just as the effective evidence-based apologist will seek to understand the broader frameworks and cultures that form different backgrounds for reasoning and interpretation, so too will the effective E/N apologist acknowledge that competing frameworks can overlap and that historical and logical arguments can be offered—not to coerce anyone into faith, but to persuade them by supporting and confirming Christianity.

The works of the agnostic New Testament scholar Bart Ehrman illustrate the problem of ignoring the historical arguments for Christianity. Ehrman has written multiple bestsellers that have been absorbed by anxious Christians, former churchgoers, and hardened unbelievers. One of Ehrman's strengths is his ability to take readers on a tour of what he sees as all the Bible's problems while offering a story, a coming-of-age tale. Ehrman explains that he himself used to be a conservative evangelical Christian, but then he really started studying the Bible with an open mind, and he grew up. He admitted that the Bible was filled with errors and contradictions. It was a struggle, but he cast off the childish myths he had believed his whole life and faced up to the hard facts: The Bible doesn't really have the answers. Christianity isn't true.

Ehrman's appeal fits into what the E/N apologist's own narrative says about how persuasion works. In response, an E/N apologist might say, "See, a grand story is what is really appealing. We have to tell another story—a better story!"

and indeed, they would have a point. But Ehrman is not *just* telling a story. Ehrman's anti-Christian apologetic is persuasive because it also includes an examination of the biblical and historical evidence.

Effective apologists will not simply reply to someone who has absorbed Ehrman's argument with existential appeals and a proclamation of the gospel. Ehrman and his followers pose skeptical questions that require interaction with historical details:

- Doesn't the gospel of John's high view of Jesus' identity contradict the Synoptic Gospels' low view of Jesus' identity?
- Didn't Jesus' body just get left on the cross and eaten by animals?
- Wasn't the twenty-seven-book New Testament canon created because of a power play in the early church?
- Wasn't the New Testament forged?

Adequately answering questions such as these requires that an apologist be aware not just of the frameworks and existential appeals being used, but also of the evidence associated with these issues.[42]

Soft versus Hard Experiential/Narratival Apologetics

N. T. Wright's book *Simply Christian* serves as an example of what could be called *soft* experiential/narratival apologetics.[43] Four basic human experiences, namely, the quest for spirituality, a longing for justice, a hunger for relationships, and a delight in beauty (which Wright describes as the "echoes of a voice"), function as the threads that run through this apologetic.[44] Wright takes up each of these signposts, one at a time, connecting Christian belief with common human experience.

For instance, in reference to the echo of a longing for justice, Wright asserts that simply "being human and living in the world" means we have an intuitive

---

42. In responding to Bart Ehrman, my coauthors and I (Josh) sought to help readers see the problem with his narrative, offer a story that is more in line with reality, and interact with the historical evidence. See Andreas J. Köstenberger, Darrell L. Bock, and Josh D. Chatraw, *Truth in a Culture of Doubt: Engaging Skeptical Challenges to the Bible* (Nashville: B&H, 2014), and the more popular version, Andreas Köstenberger, Darrell Bock, and Josh Chatraw, *Truth Matters: Confident Faith in a Confusing World* (Nashville: B&H, 2014).

43. We are specifically using Wright's book *Simply Christian: Why Christianity Makes Sense* (San Francisco: HarperOne, 2006) as an example of an E/N apologetic approach rather than including Wright as a figure who necessarily represents this camp in all of his writings. Wright himself does not normally identify himself as an apologist, though he can easily be considered one of Christianity's leading apologists. However, unlike the other softer representatives in this chapter, he has not directly entered the apologetic methodology debate. In fact, the E/N approach is a general description for what we have observed a variety of different Christian authors doing, who have either not articulated their methodology in detail or, for various reasons, remain at the periphery of many of these methodological discussions.

44. Wright adds that these echoes "are among the things which the postmodern, post-Christian, and now increasingly postsecular world cannot escape as questions—strange signposts pointing beyond the landscape of our contemporary culture and out into the unknown" (*Simply Christian*, xi).

desire for justice.[45] Wright is leading his readers to ask the basic question, "Why do we have these feelings and desires?" As he moves along, he offers competing explanatory accounts. For example, justice could be just a childish dream. Some say the harsh reality is that we live in a world of naked power, and the only sin is to be caught grabbing what you can get. However, the Christian story offers a different explanation, suggesting that obtaining justice "remains one of the great human goals and dreams" because we have all "heard, deep within [our]selves, the echo of a voice which calls us to live like that." Moreover, the Christian story explains that the source of this voice, God himself, became human in the person of Jesus Christ and did what was necessary in order that justice could ultimately be done for all.[46]

In other words, Wright is saying something like, "Just about everyone has this sense that things are just not right with the world, that humans are at fault, and that we should do something about it. Now, what story best explains this intuition and provides the resources for us to respond appropriately? Which story about the world offers the most satisfying explanation?"

In addition to a longing for justice, Wright takes this same approach with the other three echoes—the quest for spirituality, hunger for relationships, and delight in beauty—commending the Christian story as the best account of the human experience.[47]

What you don't find in *Simply Christian* are the syllogisms or step-by-step arguments you encounter in traditional classical or evidential approaches.[48] Wright believes the world we live in is complex, made up of such realities as stories, rituals, beauty, work, and belief that intertwine to give life a rich texture. Because it is to this complex, richly textured world that Christianity speaks, becoming a believer in Christ and learning the deeper kind of truth—the source of what makes life mysterious and beautiful and profound—is more like getting to know a person and less like memorizing a series of propositions. The fundamental problem people have is not that they are "ignorant and need better information," but rather that they are "lost and need someone to come and find [them], stuck in the quicksand waiting to be rescued, dying and in need of a new life."[49] It is for this reason that Wright's apologetic approach in *Simply Christian* is not to introduce people to logical propositions, but rather to the Christian story and the person of Jesus. It is in Jesus and the story of redemption he made possible that people will be found, rescued, and given new life—that they will discover a "new world . . . a place of justice, spirituality, relationship, and beauty [which they] are not only to enjoy . . . as such

45. Wright, *Simply Christian*, 10.
46. Wright, *Simply Christian*, 15.
47. See Wright, *Simply Christian*, 55.
48. See Wright, *Simply Christian*, 48–50, 55, 57.
49. Wright, *Simply Christian*, 92.

but to work at bringing it to birth on earth as it is in heaven."[50] Expressed in this way—rather than as an acquisition of knowledge or a mental assent to a series of propositions—the Christian faith will resonate more deeply with unbelievers, because it will more clearly give a voice to the echoes they have been hearing their entire lives.

Simply Christian's softened approach is different from idealized versions, which could be called hard E/N apologetics, in that Wright sees the importance of making historical and evidentially based arguments. *Simply Christian* contains short sections offering arguments for both the reliability of New Testament gospel accounts and the historicity of Jesus' bodily resurrection, even asserting that "far and away the best explanation for why Christianity began after Jesus' violent death is that he really was bodily alive again three days later, in a transformed body."[51] But even here, Wright acknowledges that one can logically adopt other positions. He goes on to note the importance of how the assumptions that make up people's interpretive frameworks influence how they interpret evidence.[52]

Timothy Keller

An example of a book that fits near the line between the soft E/N and the soft presuppositional quadrants of the graphic is Tim Keller's *Making Sense of God: An Invitation to the Skeptical* (New York: Viking, 2016). While traces of the presuppositional tradition are discernable,[53] at the same time, much of *Making Sense of God* corresponds with what we have described as a soft E/N approach, namely, that Keller compares the explanatory power of Christianity to different forms of secularism, inviting skeptics to reconsider their assumptions about the world and see how Christianity actually makes better sense of their deepest aspirations. Still, Keller himself would also likely need to be placed close to the center of the graphic. For in the closing section of *Making Sense of God*, Keller—leaning into the work of evidence-based apologists—includes a quick survey of some of the positive evidences for the existence of God and the reality of Jesus' death and resurrection.

Making Sense of God is described as a prequel to Keller's first major apologetic book, *The Reason for God*, which deals more directly with various objections to Christianity ("defeaters") and spends more time explaining some of the traditional positive apologetic reasons for Christianity. Keller, with his willingness to contextualize and creatively retrieve various strands from different apologetic traditions, is a paragon of what we are describing as an apologist at the cross.

---

50. Wright, *Simply Christian*, 92.
51. Wright, *Simply Christian*, 113.
52. See Wright, *Simply Christian*, 114.
53. For more on the influence of the presuppositional tradition on Keller's approach, see Derek Rishmawy, "Mere Fidelity: Making Sense of God Interview with Tim Keller," Reformedish, December 13, 2016, https://derekzrishmawy.com/2016/12/13/mere-fidelity-making-sense-of-god-interview-with-tim-keller.

It is remarkable that when N. T. Wright, a world-renowned New Testament scholar, set out to write a book to, as he put it, "commend" the faith, he decided to make the reliability of the Bible and the historicity of the resurrection only minor points of his apologetic. *Simply Christian* serves as an example of soft E/N apologetics because it focuses—albeit not exclusively—on human experience and the explanatory power of the Christian story.

Reformed Epistemology

Some apologetic taxonomies include what has been called a Reformed epistemology approach to apologetics. While the Reformed epistemology approach is certainly an important voice that needs to be heard in apologetic methodology discussions, it does something different from what most people imagine when they think of "an approach to apologetics." This can be seen when Kelly James Clark, a representative of the Reformed epistemological approach, writes, "I do not have a well-worked-out strategy for defending Christian belief."[54]

The famous skeptic Bertrand Russell, in response to a question asking what he would say to God if he found out posthumously that he was wrong and God asked why he didn't believe, said he would simply reply, "Not enough evidence, God! Not enough evidence!" In a similar vein, some have argued that while they can't "prove" Christianity to be true or false (make a de facto argument), they can show that it is irrational to believe in Christianity (make a de jure argument). They argue that even if Christianity did happen to be true, it would not be rational to believe in it, because there is simply "not enough evidence" for Christianity. It is to this specific objection that Reformed epistemology responds.

Alvin Plantinga, the leading figure in the Reformed epistemology movement, has argued in response that the de jure and the de facto questions are linked. If Christianity is in fact not true, then belief in Christianity is irrational. However, if it is true, then it is entirely rational to believe Christianity, even if you don't have any conclusive arguments that everyone finds persuasive.

Plantinga claims that some beliefs are "properly basic." By properly basic, he means that even without any self-evident or incorrigible evidence, it is rational to accept some things as true. For example, I might make statements of fact or value that seem obvious, yet someone might argue against them. In response

---

54. Kelly James Clark, "Reformed Epistemology Apologetics," in *Five Views on Apologetics*, 278. Nicholas Wolterstorff, another one of the founding fathers of Reformed epistemology, uncovers misunderstandings of Reformed epistemology: "The project of Reformed epistemology is to answer the evidentialist critique of Chrsitianity. The project is not to say how religious beliefs are connected to each other. The project is not to say how religious beliefs are connected to experience. The project is not to say how religious beliefs are connected to life. The project is not to discuss how a religious way of life is taught. The project is not to explain what a religious way of life is. The project is not to offer a theory of the essence of religion. The project is not to consider what, if anything, can be said to an unbeliever to 'bring him around!' The project is not to discuss the role of argument in religion. The project is not to discuss the role of reason in religion—to offer a theory of rationality in religion. The project is not to develop a whole philosophy of religion of a certain stripe" ("What Reformed Epistemology Is Not," *Perspectives* 7, no. 9 [November 1992], 15).

to my saying, "I believe there is a tree outside my window," a skeptic might suggest that the tree is an illusion and I took the wrong medicine this morning or have been drinking too much. Or in response to my saying, "I believe it is wrong to lie about my colleagues to advance my career," they might respond that some worldviews actually assert that self-advancement should be prized over honesty.

Nevertheless, most people simply see a tree and believe it is actually there; most people "just know" that lying for self-advancement is wrong. They don't feel the need to form an argument for such beliefs—at least not initially. Even if someone disagrees with them about the tree's existence, they can't help but believe it's really there. Even if someone who denies the importance of truthfulness offers compelling reasoning and the person who believes that honesty should be prized over self-advancement has no incorrigible or self-evident reason to affirm their view, they still can't help but believe that lying is wrong.

Building on John Calvin and Thomas Aquinas, Plantinga argues that Christianity is properly basic in a way similar to the examples given above. God has made each person with a sense of the divine (Calvin refers to this as the "*sensus divinitatis*"). However, because of sin, humans suppress this sense of God. It is through the work of the Spirit that God restores this sense of the divine, enabling someone to believe in the gospel in a way that is properly basic. So while Reformed epistemology can still affirm that a variety of rational arguments can be valuable,[55] it correctly argues that a Christian does not need to "prove" Christianity (in the strong rational or empirical sense) for belief in Christianity to be considered rational.

A WAY FORWARD

Recall that at the beginning of this chapter, we asked you to imagine a friend inviting you to draw her a map to your hometown so she could visit. Of course, because you are delighted she wants to visit the town you love, you reply, "No problem!" and set out to sketch a map for her. As you do so, you can think of several different routes, but you are confident that you know which is the best way to get her there—after all, it's the way you've always traveled. You quickly get out a piece of paper and draw a detailed map of the roads, street names, and the points at which she should turn. Confident you've provided a map that will best get your friend to your hometown, you hand it to her.

---

55. See Plantinga's lecture notes titled "Appendix: Two Dozen (or so) Theistic Arguments," in *Alvin Plantinga*, ed. Deane-Peter Baker (Cambridge: Cambridge University Press, 2007), 210. Individuals from a variety of apologetic schools have embraced Reformed epistemology. For example, see C. Stephen Evans, *Why Christian Faith Still Makes Sense: A Response to Contemporary Challenges* (Grand Rapids: Baker Academic, 2015). For a proposal of how Plantinga's Reformed epistemology might be aided and advanced by the work of Charles Taylor, see Deane-Peter Baker, *Tayloring Reformed Epistemology: Charles Taylor, Alvin Plantinga, and the* de jure *Challenge to Christian Belief* (London: SCM, 2007). We are indebted to both Plantinga and Taylor for playing important roles in shaping our apologetic approach.

But as your friend peers down at the map, a strange look comes across her face. Shyly, she turns to you and says, "Sorry, but this doesn't really help me."

You are slightly frustrated, but you try to respond with patience. "I promise, this is the best route. I've been this way hundreds of times."

She senses you are trying to hide your frustration and doesn't want to come across as unappreciative, so she responds hesitantly, "Okay, well . . . thanks for taking the time to draw this map. Even though it isn't going to work for me, I'm glad it has helped you."

As she begins to walk away, you feel annoyed. *What does she mean by that?* you think to yourself. *What world is she living in? This is the best route to get home!* Exasperated, you catch up to her before she gets too far away and ask, "I swear this map shows the quickest way to get to my town, so for what possible reason could it not work for you?"

Letting her guard down, she replies, "You were so quick to want to draw me the *best* map that you never asked me any questions about my trip. I'm traveling from Richmond, not Washington D.C., where you had me starting from. And I'm actually traveling by bicycle, not by car, so I need to stay off the interstate. I also find my way much better with landmarks rather than road names."

This scenario depicts what often occurs in debates on apologetic method, when some apologists (who advocate the hard version of the apologetic method they adhere to) essentially say there is only *one* route—theirs—that really works when taking someone on the apologetic journey to Christianity.[56]

However, apologists who adhere to the soft versions of their respective apologetic method recognize there are other ways to draw the map. The interaction between advocates of the soft versions suggests that they still think their apologetic map offers the best explanation for Christianity, but they are (rightly!) open to other ways to get there. Their debates are not about whether other maps can be drawn, but rather about *which is the best map*. Finding the best map, however, is not contingent on copying some sort of eternal, universal apologetic map. No such map exists. What these discussions among the advocates of soft versions have not emphasized enough is that different types of apologetic maps not only *can* be drawn but *should* be drawn. The best apologetic map for any given situation depends on who will be using the map. An apologetic map can't be drawn before contextual information is gathered: Where is this person starting from? What are her past experiences with maps? How will she be traveling?

---

56. See David K. Clark, "Apologetics as Dialogue," in *Dialogical Apologetics: A Person-Centered Approach to Christian Defense* (Grand Rapids: Baker, 1993), 110.

A Cumulative Case Approach

A cumulative case approach offers a collection of arguments that interact and support each other, together making a more persuasive case than they would independently. In some ways, soft versions of apologetic methods can be described as cumulative case approaches because, while advocating for their particular form of argumentation, they recognize the merit of different links in the apologetic chain.

After hearing this, you may ask, "Is a cumulative case the approach this book suggests?" Offering a variety of different kinds of arguments for Christianity is certainly in line with the approach in this volume. And while the distinguishing features of a cross-centered apologetic will be explained further in chapters 6–9, one of the differences is the amount of focus given to the person we find ourselves in dialogue with. In other words, while there are times for offering numerous arguments that support and reinforce each other, apologetics at the cross stresses that different people find different arguments and collections of arguments more persuasive than others. In their personal encounters, New Testament exemplars such as Paul and Jesus do not simply add supporting argument upon supporting argument, but instead seem to pay particular attention to the person or audience they are in conversation with in order to offer a contextualized response. To use the analogy that has framed this chapter, we should not just throw a collection of maps at someone, but rather we should figure out what map(s) is best suited to them.

To put it more concretely, we might ask, "Am I drawing an apologetic map for a scientist who has a rigid methodology for determining truth? An academic philosopher from the West? A father whose son died of cancer at the age of seven? A devout Muslim who moved to America from the Middle East? A mother whose son came out of the closet? A Western businessman who has it all and adheres to a different vision of the good life than the one offered by Christianity? A first-generation Asian American who thinks about life in Eastern categories?"

As Edward Carnell wrote concerning apologetics more than a half a century ago, the *best* apologetic maps are person-specific:

> Philosophers err when they confine their attention to "universal man." There is only one real man: the suffering, fearing individual on the street; he who is here today and gone tomorrow; he whose heart is the scene of a relentless conflict between the self as it is and the self as it ought to be. Whenever a philosopher speaks of mankind in the abstract, rather than concrete individuals at home and in the market, he deceives both himself and all who have faith in his teaching.[57]

---

57. Edward J. Carnell, *Christian Commitment: An Apologetic* (Eugene, OR: Wipf & Stock, 1957), 2.

Thus, the best maps are not drawn for "mankind in the abstract" but for "concrete individuals." Nor are we drawing apologetic maps for ourselves. We are drawing maps for others, which means our apologetic should be others-centered.[58] It also means that while all of the maps should have the same final destination—the person and work of Jesus Christ—there are various types of maps that can and should be drawn.

WRAPPING IT UP

Throughout this book, our goal is to equip you to draw various types of maps and point you to resources that will enable you to fill in those maps with greater detail. It is important to note that if you already find yourself in a specific tradition we have surveyed, or you are gravitating toward one, *Apologetics at the Cross* can still be appropriated within the soft versions of that method.

Another goal of this book is to point you to the Word of God and the church, which are the means of grace that will enable you to become the type of apologetic cartographer suited for the task of drawing maps to the Christian faith. It is important that an apologist live as a faithful member of the body of Christ, the corporate apology for the gospel. The following four chapters will build on the foundation that has been laid, articulating a vision for apologetics centered on the gospel.

---

58. Of course, for Christians, everything we do, including apologetics, should first be God-centered.

CHAPTER SIX

TAKING PEOPLE TO THE CROSS THROUGH WORD AND DEED

> Christian witnesses are not only speakers but sufferers too . . . Christ's passion is a model for how we should stake truth claims today—as a suffering witness: "Christ is the truth [but] to *be* the truth is the only true explanation of what truth is." The witness to the truth is one whose life displays the rightness of the believing, and thus the rightness of the belief.[1]
>
> *Kevin J. Vanhoozer,* First Theology

TAKING PEOPLE TO THE CROSS THROUGH WORD

Jesus' life, death, and resurrection are the climactic events in salvation history. Following Paul's lead, we have seen that while the cross is not the only thing we should reflect on in apologetics, everything we reflect on should be viewed in light of the cross. In his seminal work on Christian ethics, Oliver O'Donovan makes a similar statement about ethics that can easily be applied to apologetics: "The foundations of Christian [apologetics] must be evangelical foundations; or to put it more simply, Christian [apologetics] must arise from the gospel of Jesus Christ. Otherwise it could not be *Christian* [apologetics]."[2] The centrality of the gospel to apologetics is the reason the approach in this book is called "apologetics at the cross," with the word *cross* serving as strategic shorthand for the entire gospel.[3]

---

1. Vanhoozer's quote in this epigraph is from Søren Kierkegaard, quoted in David J. Gouwens, *Kierkegaard as a Religious Thinker* (New York: Cambridge University Press, 1996), 218.

2. Oliver O'Donovan, *Resurrection and Moral Order: An Outline for Evangelical Ethics*, 2nd ed. (Grand Rapids: Eerdmans, 1994), 11. Where we bracketed *apologetics*, O'Donovan has the word *ethics*.

3. As mentioned previously, when we use *cross* as a shorthand for the gospel, we are not implying Jesus' life, resurrection, or ascension are less critical. Instead, following Paul in such passages as 1 Corinthians 1:16–27, Ephesians 2:16, and Philippians 3:18, we are capitalizing on the connotations of the symbol, while not narrowing the scope of Christ's saving actions.

Often the discussion between apologists concerning methodology has focused on issues that distinguish different approaches from each other. These debates are understandable and even necessary, but the amount of attention given to the differences has resulted in a tribalism that has perhaps diverted attention away from imagining how the gospel itself should provide the central emphases for apologetics. The remaining chapters in part 2 offer four gospel implications as unifying rallying points for apologetics. The centrality of the gospel to this approach raises a foundational question: *What is the gospel?*

Apologetics at the Cross

1. **Taking people to the cross through word and deed (ch. 6)**
2. Cruciform humility before God and others (ch. 7)
3. Appealing to the whole person for the sake of the gospel (ch. 8)
4. Contextualization through the lens of the cross (ch. 9)

WHAT IS THE GOSPEL?

In 1 Corinthians 15, Paul passes down one of the earliest creedal statements—likely from just a few years after Jesus' death—which summarizes the key themes of the gospel message seen throughout the New Testament: "For what I received I passed on to you as of first importance: that Christ died for our sins according to the Scriptures, that he was buried, that he was raised on the third day according to the Scriptures" (1 Cor 15:3–4).

The Gospel Announces Who Jesus Is

The gospel declares Jesus' identity. Notice that in 1 Corinthians 15:3, Paul refers to Jesus as "Christ"—a messianic title that means "anointed one" and refers to the hope of the Jews, expressed from the time of the Old Testament to the time of the gospels, that a king from the line of David would come and redeem the people of Israel and then bless the world through them. This hope sits well with the gospels' portrayal of Jesus as the messianic King. Throughout the New Testament, Jesus' kingship is attachd to his divine identity and his enthronement at the Father's side.

Jesus is the Christ, the Son of God.

The Gospel Announces What Jesus Did

The gospel describes Jesus' work. In 1 Corinthians 15:3–4, Paul stresses that the gospel he had received and passed on to the Corinthians—in one sense, an account of the work Jesus had done—was "of first importance." Paul also emphasizes that the events of the gospel all happened "according to the Scriptures," reminding his audience that the gospel is not a new story, but is in fact rooted in a story that began long ago. The grace that culminates in Jesus' ministry can be seen throughout the Old Testament—in God's promise that the woman's descendant will crush the head of the serpent (Gen 3:15), in his calling of Abraham and the promises made to him, in his deliverance of Israel from slavery in Egypt, and in the vision he gave to Isaiah (Isa 40–66), which prefigured the central role the atonement (Isa 52–53) would play in ushering in a new creation.

"Christ died for our sins." This declaration is representative of how Paul routinely connects language about death and dying with forgiveness. In the opening chapters of Scripture (Gen 3), because of man's disobedience, God issues the punishment of sin, separating humankind from himself. Harkening back to this event, Christ's death redeems humankind from the punishment of sin. Christ dies for the ungodly (Rom 5:6) to ransom us from our sins and enable us to be reunited with God (Gal 1:4; see Rom 5:8; Gal 2:20; 1 Tim 2:6).

"He was buried . . . he was raised on the third day." This part of the creed is not mindlessly tacked on at the end of the gospel events being recounted. In fact, without the resurrection, there would be no Christianity at all: "If Christ has not been raised, your faith is futile; you are still in your sins," and Christians "are of all people most to be pitied" (1 Cor 15:17, 19). The resurrection is at the heart of the Christian message, for it is only through the power of Christ's resurrection from the dead that death can be defeated and life can be renewed.

Jesus lived, died, and rose again. These historic events, which occur at the climax of the biblical narrative, are at the center of the message of good news.

The Gospel Promises What Jesus Secured

It is because of the gospel that all things will be renewed. After presenting the creedal statement outlined above, Paul continues by explaining what Christ's death and resurrection achieved: the ultimate defeat of death, the vindication of Christ himself, and the guarantee that in the future there will be a new creation. Because Jesus has secured victory over all evil powers and even death itself (1 Cor 15:24–26), everyone who is in Christ by faith will be made alive again (15:20–23). Through Jesus, God will make all the wrongs of the world right again and usher in a new creation.

Those who trust in Christ and turn from their sins will one day live with him in a new community and a new world.

In sum, the gospel (1) announces who Jesus is, (2) announces what Jesus did, and (3) promises what Jesus secured. Because there are many ways to describe sin, what God has done, and the hope to be found in Christ, these three gospel categories can be unpacked differently, depending on who you're talking to—and in fact, they *should* be. We shouldn't insist on a cookie-cutter approach to sharing the gospel. The New Testament authors certainly didn't; they felt free to hold up the gospel like a diamond, allowing its various facets to shine uniquely in different settings. Having a variety of categories at your disposal rather than simply adhering to a strict formulaic approach will allow you to tailor your presentation of the gospel message to your audience.[4]

THE GOSPEL

- Announces who Jesus is

- Announces what Jesus did

- Promises what Jesus secured

The Importance of Both Fidelity and Flexibility in Presenting the Gospel

Often when we attempt to engage non-Christians, we find that their objections to Christianity are based on misunderstandings of the gospel or other aspects of Christianity. Thus, one of the ways we can answer our contemporaries' objections to Christianity is simply by helping them understand what the gospel actually is and clarifying points of confusion. Unfortunately, an unbeliever's confusion is often exacerbated when a Christian either is *unfaithful* to the gospel message or is *inflexible* in the way they present the gospel.

When Jesus and the apostles proclaim the gospel throughout the New Testament, even though they consistently proclaim the essence of its message, they are flexible in which aspect of the message they bring to the forefront. Paul and Jesus both adjust their approach and emphasis, depending on the context. For this reason, they don't sound exactly alike—nor, for that matter, does Jesus or Paul in one context sound like Jesus or Paul in another. Examples of such contextualization abound in the New Testament: Jesus took a different approach with the Pharisees than he did with the social outcasts. His explanation to the rich young ruler of how to gain eternal life is quite different from his parable of the self-righteous Pharisee and the tax collector who went away justified before God. As for Paul, the way he engages the Thessalonian Jews at a synagogue with the gospel in Acts 17 is remarkably different from the way he approaches the Athenian philosophers of the Areopagus in the very same chapter.

---

4. For a survey of different gospel definitions, see Trevin Wax, "Gospel Definitions," Gospel Coalition, September 2012, https://blogs.thegospelcoalition.org/trevinwax/files/2009/09/Gospel-Definitions.pdf.

And the way he focuses on the law's relationship to the gospel when reminding the Galatians of what the gospel means is different from the way he focuses on the sin of idolatry when addressing those who don't accept the authority of the Hebrew Scriptures (Acts 14:15–17; 17:16–34). The biblical authors also use a myriad of different culturally bound metaphors when explaining the dimensions of the gospel.[5]

The point is that while the New Testament authors stress the importance of holding to the content of the one true, unchanging gospel (e.g., Gal 1:8–9; Jude 3), they do not adopt a strict formulaic approach to sharing the gospel that would exclude a consideration of the cultural context the gospel is being communicated in. Perhaps one of the strongest arguments for contextualization is that the gospel itself occurred and was recorded in a cultural context. It uses the languages and imagery of certain set of cultures. Thus, faithfully presenting the gospel means first understanding the message within the context of the Bible itself and its native culture and then applying the message in a way that those in your current context can understand.

The Relationship between Sharing the Gospel and Apologetics

It would be a grave mistake to think that apologetics is the same thing as the gospel. The Bible never makes statements like "*apologetics* is the power of God that brings salvation to everyone who believes." Nowhere in the Bible does Paul say, "God called you through our *apologetic*, that you might share in the glory of our Lord Jesus Christ," or does Jesus say, "By this they will know that you are my disciples, *if you have the right apologetic.*"

Instead, Paul in Romans 1:16 asserts that *the gospel* "is the power of God that brings salvation"; in 2 Thessalonians 2:14, he affirms that it is through *the gospel* that the people of Thessalonica were called to share in the glory of Jesus; and in John 13:35, Jesus teaches that the world will know his disciples by how they "love one another."

The absurd statements that result from substituting the word *apologetics* for the word *gospel* in such verses clearly demonstrate that they are not the same thing. However, while preaching the gospel and practicing apologetics may be different from each other, the Bible clearly emphasizes that both are important. This raises the question: What is the relationship between practicing apologetics and evangelism?

As stated previously, apologetics should be seen as a tool to clear the debris of doubt out of people's paths and propel them forward toward the gospel.

5. For an overview of some of these dimensions, see Brenda B. Colijn, *Images of Salvation in the New Testament* (Downers Grove, IL: InterVarsity, 2010).

Apologetics can both help non-Christians take the gospel seriously in the face of objections they may have (as Paul does in Acts 17) and also encourage Christians to *continue* taking the gospel seriously in the face of doubts they may be experiencing (which seems to be Paul's apologetic concern in 1 Cor 15).

Ravi Zacharias

In our contemporary setting, in many cases an unfortunate divide exists between apologists and evangelists, which would have been strange to both the New Testament authors and the early church. Among modern apologists, Ravi Zacharias (and his organization RZIM) has exemplified a way to reunite apologetics and evangelism.[6]

While a genuine saving knowledge of the true God is not available through reason and evidence alone, arguments can make individuals more open to an antinaturalist view of the world.[7] As philosopher Stephen Evans puts it, apologetic arguments do not "replace a full, special revelation of God (in particular, the Spirit working through the gospel)"; rather, they "[make] us open to the possibility of such revelation."[8]

Arguments and the Holy Spirit

As we've seen in chapters 1 and 2, the Bible is full of apologetic arguments. Yet the Bible also speaks of sin's effects on the human mind and heart, reminding us it is God who ultimately must enable someone to believe—for anyone to be saved, God's Spirit must work in them (e.g., John 3:5–6; 6:44; 1 Cor 2:14–16).

Unfortunately, there has been a popular misconception that apologists, by emphasizing the use of arguments, ignore the role of the Holy Spirit. This view, however, disregards what most apologists today are actually saying. While apologists from different theological traditions put the particulars together differently, nearly all of them agree that conversion is ultimately dependent on the work of the Holy Spirit. They simply see apologetics as a *means* through which the Spirit can accomplish his work.

For apologetics to successfully clear away intellectual, emotional, and

---

6. See Ravi Zacharias and Vince Vitale, *Jesus Among Secular Gods: The Countercultural Claims of Christ* (New York: FaithWords, 2017).

7. See C. Stephen Evans, *Why Christian Faith Makes Sense: A Response to Contemporary Challenges* (Grand Rapids: Baker, 2015).

8. Evans, *Why Christian Faith Makes Sense*, 27.

experiential debris in an unbeliever's path and lead them to the gospel and, ultimately, to a saving knowledge of God, the Spirit must work. This reality has two points of application for apologetics.

First, there is no need to pit apologetics against the work of the Holy Spirit. Always praying that the Lord will, through his Holy Spirit, make our persuasive efforts bear fruit, we should use a variety of appeals and evidences to make people more receptive to the gospel and invite them to believe in it.[9] Apologetics should not be seen as merely some secularized argument, as if we were arguing over data that people can simply "decide" on and then go on with life as usual. In our apologetic efforts, we are urging people to know the living, all-powerful, all-knowing God himself, and we are doing so in the midst of an ongoing cosmic battle. The demons stand against us, and we must pray for heavenly assistance; we must pray to God that his Spirit will go before us.

Second, both the fact that our arguments will often be rejected by the world and the fact that we are dependent on the work of the Holy Spirit for anyone to come to God will humble us. An apologist's chief weapon is not self-reliance, but rather *prayer*—persistent prayer to God for his Spirit to open the hearts of unbelievers and to sustain our own faith in the face of doubt. An apologist's job is not to create faith; it is simply to be faithful in prayer, in making a case for Christianity, and in more prayer.

TAKING PEOPLE TO THE CROSS THROUGH DEED

The debris blocking an unbeliever's path to the cross can be cleared by conversations; just as often, however, it is cleared by actions—specifically, the faithful lives of Christians corporately living out the gospel. Modern apologetics has often faltered in not stressing this point enough: Apologetics should never be severed from a strong doctrine of the church or careful reflection on the implications of the gospel. Christians should never set up word in opposition to deed. Our apologetic appeals are most faithful when they are embedded within a corporate witness marked by *long-suffering testimony*, *personal transformation*, and *holistic service*.

Long-Suffering Testimony

One of the ways the church has corporately cleared a path for gospel proclamation is seen in how it has responded and ministered to others in the face of trials and suffering. Consider what Paul said to the Philippians when they were facing hardships:

---

9. See C. Stephen Evans, "Evidentialist and Non-Evidentialist Accounts of Historical Religious Knowledge," *International Journal for the Philosophy of Religion* 35, no. 3 (January 1994): 174.

Whatever happens, conduct yourselves in a manner worthy of the gospel of Christ. Then, whether I come and see you or only hear about you in my absence, I will know that you stand firm in the one Spirit, striving together as one for the faith of the gospel without being frightened in any way by those who oppose you. This is a sign to them that they will be destroyed, but that you will be saved—and that by God. For it has been granted to you on behalf of Christ not only to believe in him, but also to suffer for him, since you are going through the same struggle you saw I had, and now hear that I still have.[10]

Paul instructs the church to corporately strive for the gospel, even as they suffer for Christ. The conduct, courage, and unity of the Philippian church in the midst of their God-ordained suffering would send a message to those who opposed the gospel: there is something powerful and supernatural that goes on in the lives of Christians. We've already seen in the introduction to this book that the apologetic proof-text 1 Peter 3:15 was written in the context of a letter addressed to a suffering community. Peter suggests that this community's joy and peace in the midst of trials will confound unbelievers, leading them to ask questions like "Why do these people have such hope?" and "How can they react to trials and suffering with such confidence and unity?"

This widespread confidence and compassion in the face of persecution and trials—first seen in Jesus and his disciples—were among the distinguishing marks of the church during the first three centuries of its existence when it experienced rapid growth. In his insightful study on the early church, the Oxford theologian Michael Green explains the strong impact the church made for a couple of centuries after its inception:

> The church had qualities unparalleled in the ancient world. Nowhere else would you find slaves and masters, Jews and Gentiles, rich and poor, engaging in table fellowship and showing a real love for one another. That love overflowed to outsiders, and in times of plague and disaster the Christians shone by means of their service to communities in which they lived.[11]

For example, in the third century during the terrible plagues that beset the Roman Empire, most people abandoned the sick and fled. Christians however, were known for refusing to leave their loved ones. They stayed in the face of

---

10. Philippians 1:27–30.
11. Michael Green, *Evangelism in the Early Church*, rev. ed. (1970; repr., Grand Rapids: Eerdmans, 2004), 19.

likely death and even cared for pagans whose families had abandoned them.[12]

One of the reasons Christianity grew is that Christian men and women knew how to suffer and die well. Instead of hating their executioners, the early Christians forgave them. Their faith in the midst of persecution was so strong that they even sang hymns as they were being tortured. The earliest Christians understood something we too often forget: Christ's glory in his resurrection was first achieved through his suffering on the cross.

The concepts on which apologetics at the cross are built appear not only to have begun with Jesus' teachings, but also to stretch into the corporate witness of the early church. As theologian Peter Leithart remarks, "The first and chief defense of the gospel, the first 'letter of commendation' not only for Paul but for Jesus, is not an argument but the life of the Church conformed to Christ by the Spirit in service and suffering."[13] Christians do not, however, develop into long-suffering witnesses by way of brute force or their own willpower. As we live in the body of Christ and worship God under the guidance of his Word, it is the Spirit of God who transforms us into apologists able to persevere in the face of difficulties.

On Truth and Suffering

This, in short, is the difference between us and the others who know not God, that in misfortune they complain and murmur, while adversity does not call us away from the truth of virtue and faith, but strengthens us by its suffering.

Cyprian, De mortalitate (Mortality)

Personal Transformation

After instructing his audience to "always be prepared to give an answer to everyone who asks you to give the reason for the hope that you have," Peter adds, "But do this with gentleness and respect, keeping a clear conscience" (1 Pet 3:15–16a). Those who have been transformed by the Spirit of God are to display "gentleness" and "respect" in response to skeptical critics.

In this way, Peter not only calls us to be prepared to defend the faith, but also gives instructions for the *manner* in which we are to defend it. The tone and conscience of an apologist matter to God, but they also matter to the unbeliever. Peter states that the reason we ought to speak with a gentleness and respect is "so that those who speak maliciously against your good behavior in Christ may be ashamed of their slander" (1 Pet 3:16b). In other words, an apologist must speak from a cruciform life.

Even more than a gentle, respectful tone, personal transformation gives credibility to our words. The virtues of a faithful Christian—such as love, hope, faith, charity, justice, and courage—will often serve as a catalyst for apologetic conversations and even be a kind of apologetic in and of themselves.

---

12. See Rodney Stark, *The Rise of Christianity: How the Obscure, Marginal Jesus Movement Became the Dominant Religious Force in the Western World in a Few Centuries* (San Francisco: HarperSanFrancisco, 1997).

13. Peter J. Leithart, *Against Christianity* (Moscow, ID: Canon, 2003), 99.

Theologian Kevin Vanhoozer stresses that "good apologetics is less a matter of having mastered certain intellectual procedures than it is of character formation, of having become the right sort of person, a person of apologetic virtue."[14] Vanhoozer's aim is to recast a vision for cross-centered apologetics that emphasizes the importance of virtues—in particular, Christian wisdom—playing a central role. "Christian wisdom" refers to *the knowledge that embodies the wisdom of the cross and is lived out and cultivated through discipleship within the body of Christ.* Vanhoozer's thesis is that "the truth apologists defend is not simply the existence of God but, in particular, the *wisdom* of God, especially as this comes to historical expression in the cross of Jesus Christ. More generally, we are to defend the wisdom, truth, and power that is in Christ. Jesus, his person and work, is God's primary truth claim."

The problem with contemporary universities and many apologetic training programs is that while they certainly equip students with knowledge, they don't equip them with the kind of true, godly wisdom Vanhoozer is calling for. Knowledge often only amounts to the brute memorization of facts and can easily be obtained by looking in dictionaries or how-to books or by using internet search engines. In contrast, true wisdom is only gained as we plant our lives within the community of faith, following exemplars; living the day-in, day-out struggle of the cruciform life; feasting on God's Word; and breaking bread as the body of Christ.

Living out this godly wisdom equips the apologist to defend three central elements of the gospel: goodness, beauty, and truth. First, the wisdom of God teaches us how to live the good life so that we can persuade in both theory and practice. Second, godly wisdom expands our imagination, enabling us to see how the individual pieces of our lives fit into the grand redemptive narrative presented in the Bible. The idea that our story is a part of a greater story appeals to the deep human desire for harmony and the joy which is found in discovering ultimate meaning and purpose. Third, wisdom enables us to live out the truth we defend. Vanhoozer sums up the value of an apologist who doesn't just speak the truth but also *lives it out*: "In our age of irony and cynicism, market-savvy millennials are not buying 'they lived happily ever after.' It is not that they are rejecting our arguments. Rather, they do not perceive our claims as being authentic. Ideas (and theoretical arguments) are cheap. Show me a changed life."[15]

Lives of virtue and wisdom will make Christians stand out from everyone

---

14. The quotes attributed to Kevin Vanhoozer in this section come from a prepublished paper, a version of which later appeared in his *Pictures at a Theological Exhibition: Scenes of the Church's Worship, Witness and Wisdom* (Downers Grove, IL: InterVarsity, 2016).

15. Vanhoozer, *Pictures at a Theological Exhibition*, 232–33.

else in the culture, and that is how it should be. However, there is another sense in which the life of a Christian should *not* stand out. This paradox may seem confusing at first, but it is important that we grasp its meaning. Consider the following two passages.

On the one hand, Paul insists in 1 Thessalonians 4:11–12 that Christians "make it your ambition to lead a quiet life: You should mind your own business and work with your hands . . . so that your daily life may win the respect of outsiders." On the other hand, Paul says in Ephesians 4:17, 19 that Christians "must no longer live as the Gentiles do, in the futility of their thinking . . . Having lost all sensitivity, they have given themselves over to sensuality so as to indulge in every kind of impurity, and they are full of greed." Paul advises believers in 1 Thessalonians 4 to live "quiet" lives that earn the respect of outsiders, and yet he turns around in Ephesians 4 and says that Christians shouldn't be like everyone else (i.e., unbelievers). What are we to do with this Pauline paradox?

The context that surrounds these two passages explains how we are to be both similar and dissimilar to the culture around us. We should look similar to those around us in the way we work, play, and interact. Like anyone else, for much of our daily and weekly routines, we are caught up in the mundane: going to the grocery store, sitting in bumper-to-bumper traffic, doing paperwork, studying, paying bills, and so on. Christians, just like anyone else, must tend to the "normal" stuff of life. In fact, it is actually unnecessary and unwise apologetically for Christians to live lives that repudiate nonsinful norms of the surrounding culture. When we engage in normal activities with a "quiet" excellence, "as working for the Lord" (Col 3:23), our apologetic and our message is more likely to be taken seriously. In this sense, most Christian lives will look rather *ordinary*.[16]

Much of faithful Christian discipleship depends on a Christian's understanding of day-to-day obedience and the practices that direct our affections to the kingdom of Christ. And this, of course, is how we as Christians are to look different from the culture around us. As Paul tells us, we "no longer live as the Gentiles do." Though sin remains, we no longer have hardened hearts and darkened minds. We are no longer enslaved by money, sex, or any other worldly idol. Instead, we fight counterculturally to live holy lives; we sacrificially give of ourselves for others. As Paul goes on to say in Ephesians 4:22b, 24, "Put off your old self, which is being corrupted by its deceitful desires . . . and . . . put on the new self, created to be like God in true righteousness and holiness." In this sense, our lives should look *radical*.

---

16. See Michael Horton, *Ordinary: Sustainable Faith in a Radical, Restless World* (Grand Rapids: Zondervan, 2014).

A countercultural ethic combined with a quiet excellence is honoring to God and will often leave a powerful impression on those we are seeking to engage.

Holistic Service

Apologists can run the risk of failing to see the individual they are speaking to as having both cognitive and physical needs. Humans are whole beings, and a person's brain cannot be neatly separated from their body. Thus, the way an apologist's nonbelieving friends will respond to their case for Christianity will be strongly affected by how that apologist cares for them both emotionally and physically.

Although we must be careful when using Jesus as a model for apologetics—after all, the gospels were not written primarily to give us a guide to apologetics—it would be wrong not to look to Jesus for guidance. While acknowledging that we aren't the second person in the Trinity and that the first-century context Jesus lived in is not the same as our own, we should always ask, "How do Jesus' actions and words apply to our situation?" Jesus' ministry certainly has something to teach us about how we should engage the people around us.

Jesus didn't ever show up on the scene and simply say, "Okay, since I'm the smartest guy in the world [though he surely was!], I'm going to fill your head with reasons so convincing that you will be *forced* to believe in the gospel!" Yes, Jesus spoke with authority and was a master teacher. He could go toe-to-toe with the highly trained religious establishment, and the gospels make it quite clear that people were impressed with and even jealous of his ability.

However, Jesus' teaching ministry was marked by a genuine concern for the whole person. In the Bible, it is clear that Jesus' teaching ministry cannot be separated from the care he shows to those he speaks to. Jesus not only forgives people's sins, but he also heals their bodies.[17] He makes the sick well, mobilizes the paralyzed, frees the demon-possessed, and raises the dead to life. He gives sight to the blind, hearing to the deaf, speech to the mute, and food to the hungry.[18] In Matthew 8:16–17, the Evangelist makes a statement summarizing Jesus' healing ministry and then grounds his beliefs about Jesus' care of the whole person in Isaiah 53:4: "This was to fulfill what was spoken through the prophet Isaiah: 'He took up our infirmities and bore our diseases'" (Matt 8:17).

Isaiah 53 is a prophecy about how Jesus' death on the cross would atone for humankind's sin, but Matthew makes it clear that it also points to how Jesus' death would heal the whole human person, both soul and body. Jesus' healing ministry points to the cross, which will ultimately do away with all sickness; and

---

17. Psalm 103:3; Matthew 9:1–7; Mark 2:1–12.
18. Matthew 4:23–25; 8:28–34; Mark 5:21–43; 7:31–37; Luke 9:10–17; John 9:1–12.

in this way, when Jesus heals a person, the future breaks into the present.[19] As the New Testament scholar Leon Morris writes, "The final answer to sickness is in the cross."[20] Bodily resurrection is promised to all those who trust in Jesus as a part of his ministry to their whole person, and Christians will experience it most completely at Jesus' second coming, when both their body and soul will be entirely healed and perfected.

Salvation touches the entirety of our lives. This is made especially clear in Luke's decision to use the word *save* frequently to describe Jesus' healing ministry.[21] The first-century reader of the Greek text would not have missed the clear implication of Luke's word choice: the salvation offered by Jesus Christ includes the ultimate well-being of our bodies—our entire persons. Salvation is more than just getting your sins forgiven or your soul saved; it involves being made whole in soul *and* body. The healings or "salvations" Luke describes should encourage us that Jesus cares for the whole person and that such a salvation will one day come to all who believe in Jesus.

Jesus, not us, is the one who heals people, but in our apologetic approach, we must care about the whole person, just as Jesus did. Caring for the hurts, pain, and hunger that people experience is a vital part of defending the faith. Doing so brings into the present the reality of the final healing that will occur in the future. It not only makes an apologetic appeal to the whole person, but also gives hope for the present and the future, which stands in stark contrast to the bleak naturalistic explanations of the world that so many people have today.

This care for the whole person should also extend to societies, communities, and institutions. Seeking peace and the good of our communities and the world is a worthy pursuit that is mandated by God.[22] So while the pursuit of *peace* (*shalom*), in offering a foretaste of the coming kingdom, is certainly much more than an instrument that provides a platform for the corporate apologetic witness of the church, it nonetheless does function as an important aspect of our apologetic.[23]

In the past, it has often been Christians' care for the whole person and aspects

---

19. See Craig Blomberg, *Matthew*, New American Commentary (Nashville: Broadman & Holman, 1992), 22:145.

20. Leon Morris, *The Gospel according to Matthew*, Pillar New Testament Commentary (Grand Rapids: Eerdmans, 1992), 198.

21. See Darrell Bock, *A Theology of Luke and Acts: Biblical Theology of the New Testament* (Grand Rapids: Zondervan, 2012), 230.

22. See, for example, Genesis 1:26–28; Psalm 85; Isaiah 2:2–3; 11:1–2, 6–8; 25:6; 58:6; John 14:10–12; Acts 10:36; Ephesians 2:17.

23. See Nicholas Wolterstorff, *Until Justice and Peace Embrace: The Kuyper Lectures of 1981 Delivered at the Free University of Amsterdam* (Grand Rapids: Eerdmans, 1983), 69–72; Lesslie Newbigin, *The Gospel in a Pluralist Society* (Grand Rapids: Eerdmans, 1989), 232–33.

of their vision for *shalom* in the midst of a fallen world that has had such a powerful effect on unbelievers. To note just one example, Peter Brown has demonstrated how in the early centuries of the church, it was because Christian leaders showed this kind of concern for the needs of the poor that they had authority and influence in the broader community.[24] In the middle of the fourth century, the influence of Christians even led Julian the Apostate, the last pagan emperor of the Roman Empire and a critic of Christianity, to write these words:

> These impious Galileans not only feed their own poor, but ours also; welcoming them into their *agape*, they attract them, as children are attracted, with cakes . . . Whilst the pagan priests neglect the poor, the hated Galileans devote themselves to works of charity, and by a display of false compassion have established and given effect to their pernicious errors. See their love-feasts, and their tables spread for the indigent. Such practice is common among them, and causes a contempt for our gods.[25]

In our context, in which modern "gods" and worldviews compete with Christianity, the modern church and her apologists have much to learn from the commitments of the early church. Even this early critic of the Christianity recognized that an ethic driven by the principles of the cross makes for a powerful apologetic appeal.

CONCLUSION

The gospel is "of first importance" (1 Cor 15:1–3) and should therefore ground and form our apologetic. Apologetics is not the same thing as the gospel, nor does it hold the same status; rather, apologetics should function as the gospel's servant. Apologetics' purpose is to, by the grace of God, clear the faith-obstructing debris out of people's paths and move them toward considering the gospel. Additionally, apologetics can encourage Christians to continue taking the gospel seriously in the face of doubts. We've seen that while the Spirit can work through *our words* we use in our apologetic, he ultimately works to bring salvation and maintain faith through the gospel—*God's Word*. Furthermore, the Spirit not only uses our words; he also uses *our deeds*; the corporate actions of the church, as it is transformed through the Spirit, serve as an apologetic for the gospel.

---

24. See Peter Brown, *Power and Persuasion in Late Antiquity: Towards a Christian Empire* (Madison: University of Wisconsin Press, 1992).

25. Emperor Julian, *Epistle to Pagan High Priests*, quoted in Kelly M. Kapic, *God So Loved, He Gave: Entering the Movement of Divine Generosity* (Grand Rapids: Zondervan, 2010), 204.

CHAPTER SEVEN

CRUCIFORM HUMILITY BEFORE GOD AND OTHERS

> Apologetics is not, primarily, about me . . . I ought to be commending the faith to my neighbor primarily for her benefit, to the glory of God. I ought *not* to be engaging in apologetic conversation out of some need of my own, whether a need to save face, or show up an enemy, or congratulate myself on my fervor. Apologetics, again, is a form of Christian speech, and as such it is always and only to offer a gift to the recipient—not aggrandize the speaker.
>
> *John G. Stackhouse Jr.,* Humble Apologetics

APOLOGETICS AT THE CROSS VERSUS AN APOLOGETIC OF GLORY

This book's introduction and opening chapter examined how two key biblical texts, 1 Peter 3:15 and 1 Corinthians 2:1–5, lay the foundation for an apologetic built around the cross. As we saw in chapter 6, the cross is central not only to biblical theology but also to the way we do apologetics—to the way we interact with the world in what we say and do. In this chapter, we will see how the cross also paradoxically serves as a symbol of both strength and humility. Drawing on the work of Martin Luther (who contrasted theologians of the cross with theologians of glory), we will contrast an *apologetic at the cross* with an *apologetic of glory* to emphasize the importance of humility to apologetics.[1]

When apologists of glory engage others in apologetic encounters, they are seeking honor, power, and personal satisfaction. They feel a surge of pride when they confidently rattle off all the answers to any questions thrown at them and get a thrill out of intellectually checkmating their "opponents." Moreover, they can be tempted to reduce Christianity to something more palatable for the sake of their own success.

---

1. Martin Luther's classic statement on the theology of the cross versus the theology of glory is found in the Heidelberg Disputation of 1518. We do not follow Luther in all of his polemic against philosophy. Rather, we recognize that philosophy is a vital discipline that should operate within a theology of the cross.

Apologetics at the Cross

1. Taking people to the cross through word and deed (ch. 6)
2. **Cruciform humility before God and others (ch. 7)**
3. Appealing to the whole person for the sake of the gospel (ch. 8)
4. Contextualization through the lens of the cross (ch. 9)

In contrast, apologists at the cross will engage others with humility, honesty, and a bold confidence in the apparent foolishness of the cross. The cross calls us to sacrifice our own personal triumphalism. Of course, Christ has triumphed, and the day will come when every knee will bow to him and we will be vindicated. But that day has not yet come, and we are not above our Master. On his road to glory, Christ traveled through the cross, and so must we. Awaiting the future glory we will have in Christ, we must carry our cross with bold humility as we live in and engage the world.

Another aspect of Martin Luther's work relevant to apologetics today was his fear that some would compromise the message of Christianity for the sake of the fashionable intellectual trends, or "wisdom," of his day.[2] An apologetic at the cross is aware of this danger, and thus, while it recognizes the importance of making arguments that appeal to the thought and forms of reasoning of a particular culture, it resists the temptation to bypass whatever the particular historical context views as the "foolishness of the cross."

Apologists at the Cross	Apologists of Glory
✝	♔
• Engage others with humility, honesty, and confidence in the apparent foolishness of the cross	• Seek honor, power, and personal satisfaction from an apologetic encounter
• Sacrifice personal triumph	• Exhibit pride and triumphalism
• Submit to God and his word	• Diminish the scandal of the cross to make it more palatable to the current culture

Therefore, while humbly engaging others, the apologist at the cross also boldly submits to Christian revelation. In what may seem to the world like a strange combination, the Spirit working through the Word produces in a believer both *humility before God* and *humility before others*. This chapter will explore these two tiers of humility, starting with the upper level: humility before God.

---

2. See Martin Luther, *Martin Luther's Basic Theological Writings*, ed. Timothy F. Lull and William R. Russell (Minneapolis: Fortress, 2012), 32.

HUMILITY BEFORE GOD: Submitting to God's Transcendence

God and his Word can often make us uncomfortable. C. S. Lewis once quipped, "I didn't go to religion to make me happy. I always knew a bottle of Port would do that. If you want a religion to make you feel really comfortable, I certainly don't recommend Christianity."[3]

The apostle Paul certainly knew nothing of a comfortable Christianity. Yet neither the trials he experienced nor what humans thought about him was of primary importance to Paul, because he viewed his ministry in light of a future day when he would stand before Christ. In 2 Corinthians 5, after Paul tells the Corinthians that his foremost purpose in life is to please Jesus, he goes on to add, "For we must all appear before the judgment seat of Christ, so that each of us may receive what is due us for the things done while in the body, whether good or bad" (v. 10). Paul then shows how his Christ-centered perspective drives the way he interacts with people: "Since, then, we know what it is to fear the Lord, we try to persuade others" (v. 11). It is this fear of (or we might say reverence or humility before) the Lord (cf. Prov 22:4) that is the catalyst for Paul's primary concern with what humans think about Christ.

Thus, the reason we seek to persuade others to change their views is that we fear God. We cannot afford to get this backward: we must seek to change others because we fear God, not seek to change God because we fear others.

As we've seen in chapters 3 and 4, a trap we can fall into as apologists is that in trying to persuade we end up trimming Christianity down to make it more palatable to the context we find ourselves in. In the Western world specifically, the temptation tends to be to present a God who is only loving instead of a God who is loving but is also holy and just. It is far easier to present a tepid, vaguely benevolent God who is trying his best rather than an all-powerful, holy God. Another temptation for apologists is, instead of humbly acknowledging certain mysteries and limits in our knowledge, to construct a facade of glib answers and dogmatic replies. People may like things to be cut and dried, but many important questions aren't; they're difficult and call for nuanced replies given in a spirit of humility.

The Idol of Cultural Acceptance: Ethics

The apologist at the cross humbly submits to God and his Word. This will at times look foolish to the world. It certainly did to people living in the first century. The word *cross* itself was impolite to speak of in well-mannered

---

3. C. S. Lewis, *God in the Dock: Essays on Theology and Ethics* (1970; repr., Grand Rapids: Eerdmans, 2014), 48.

society, and in response to a Christian's faith most would have scoffed, "World changers don't die on crosses. A great king, dying on a cross—what a ludicrous idea!" In this way, just as Paul wrote, the symbol at the heart of the Christian proclamation was "foolishness" to the world.

Currently in Western cultures, one of the greatest temptations is for Christians to modify the Bible's ethics in favor of one that is more acceptable, to an ethics based on self-gratification or personal freedom as the highest good. If, however, an apologist allows a particular culture's sensibilities to hollow out the ethics of the Bible in this way, then a fundamental call of Christianity will be hollowed out as well: "Whoever wants to be my disciple must deny themselves and take up their cross and follow me. For whoever wants to save their life will lose it, but whoever loses their life for me and for the gospel will save it. What good is it for someone to gain the whole world, yet forfeit their soul?" (Mark 8:34–36).

At the same time, it is important to note that the fault does not always lie with the culture. When trying to relate the Bible's morality to the culture around them, apologists must first be willing to humbly go back and examine the Bible to make sure they are not just defending the view or interpretation of their particular tradition, because it could be their tradition that missed the mark.

As Christians, we know that since God transcends culture, our faith will at different points offend the sensibilities of every culture. If the shifting winds of culture are what ultimately steer an apologist, then the standards of Christianity will always be changing, from year to year and culture to culture. For example, traditional societies in the Middle East have very different ethics regarding sexuality and gender than Western cultures. Should Christian ethics change between these two cultures, conforming to each in turn? In the name of relevancy, should the biblical standard change from one culture to another, or even within one culture as it changes over time? This does not sound like "the faith that was *once for all* entrusted to God's holy people" (Jude 3, emphasis added).

The job of the apologist is not to alter God to fit culture's changing conception of what is "good," but rather to help those in the culture understand and see that God is the one unchanging ultimate Good. Making this sort of appeal takes hard work. It's much easier to simply change biblical ethics to fit the ethics of a particular culture. Helping others see the goodness of God and his ways requires that you put yourself in their shoes and understand where they are coming from so that you can then figure out how to best relate to them. In later chapters, we will explore how to do this, but first things first: a believer cannot seek to be culturally relevant unless he or she first humbly submits to God over and against the idol of cultural acceptance.

Knowledge

It is not just the morality of God that people can find off-putting. Humans not only lust for moral independence, but also for autonomous, exhaustive knowledge. The temptation in the garden, after all, was that humans would seek to be like God and know as he knows (Gen 3:5). Because we are prone to rail against our creatureliness and the limits that come with it, it is important to acknowledge that there are certain mysteries in the world that God has not filled us in on, and that we will never have the independent, all-encompassing view on reality that God does. As creatures, we are contingent beings.

It's easy to see why apologists would feel uncomfortable with this point. You might have even picked up this book because you wanted to be able to give unbelievers definite, satisfying, and exhaustive answers to all their questions. After all, isn't that the whole point of apologetics?

No. We are called to give an answer for our Christian hope, and God has graciously revealed himself to us in the Scriptures. Yet the Bible does not answer every question an unbeliever might ask of us. Also, while Scripture is infallible, our interpretation of it is not.

Nor is accepting our finitude and the inexhaustible depths of God an excuse for refusing to think deeply. As the celebrated British pastor John Stott once said, "Christ calls human beings to humble, but not to stifle, their intellect."[4] We should think deeply about the various questions unbelievers have and how we might answer them, depending on the context. Being able to give reasons for Christianity does *not* mean, however, that we will be able to answer every question with certainty and in a way that will satisfy everyone.

A humble acceptance of both our dependence on God and our inability to know truth exhaustively is important to honoring the Lord as we do apologetics. A Christian, while operating within the larger framework of a Christian worldview, should recognize that although it offers a coherent, beautiful, multilayered, and true view of reality, our knowledge is not exhaustive. Unfortunately, this has not always been appropriately emphasized in apologetics. To understand why apologetics has often failed on this point, we must consider an important development that occurred in the West, which has strongly affected the expectations we have concerning how much we can and should know.

The term *modernism* refers to a period of thought that began in the early seventeenth century with René Descartes and is commonly associated with his dictum "I think, therefore I am." As this familiar quote implies, a key feature of modernism is that it sought to cast aside past authorities—such as the church,

---

4. John Stott, *The Message of Acts: The Spirit, The Church and the World* (Downers Grove, IL: InterVarsity, 1990), 281.

Scriptures, and tradition—in favor of individual logic and empirical observation. Humankind, the modern would assert, had come of age and no longer needed such authority figures to guide them to truth. Absolute certainty was not only to be pursued through reason alone, but this certainty was believed by some to be an attainable goal. Like a machine processing raw data, if an individual followed the proper methods and freed themselves from bias, then the results they came up with would be unquestionable, absolute truth.

The modern period championed approaches to discovering truth—most notably, the scientific method—which led to amazing, unprecedented results in a wide array of disciplines. However, when people began to universalize these approaches and apply them to all disciplines, many came to question some of the basic axioms of modernism, leading to what most today call postmodernism (though, as we will see in chapter 10, a more helpful label might be late modernism). Two "leftovers" of modernism are still being served today, especially in popular contexts: *strong empiricism* and *unrealistic expectations* of what humans can know.

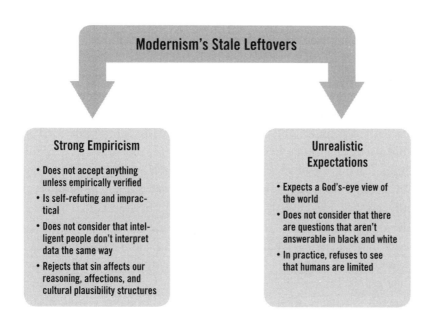

Modernism's Stale Leftovers

Strong Empiricism

- Does not accept anything unless empirically verified
- Is self-refuting and impractical
- Does not consider that intelligent people don't interpret data the same way
- Rejects that sin affects our reasoning, affections, and cultural plausibility structures

Unrealistic Expectations

- Expects a God's-eye view of the world
- Does not consider that there are questions that aren't answerable in black and white
- In practice, refuses to see that humans are limited

Strong Empiricism

"If you can just prove the existence of God, then I'll believe." We've heard this sort of comment many times, from both skeptics challenging Christianity and church members desperate to pull themselves together in the face of their own doubts. Oftentimes, people expressing this sentiment have no idea they are actually operating from a framework of *strong empiricism*.[5]

Strong empiricism stipulates that we should not accept anything as true unless it is empirically verified or demonstrated logically. This limits proofs to statements such as "five plus five equals ten" or step-by-step syllogisms like "James is a boy in this class; all the boys in the class are teens; therefore, James is a teen." Many nonbelievers reject Christianity (and for that matter, any religion) because it cannot be "proven" with this type of reasoning. We've also watched many Christians go through a crisis of faith seeking this kind of universal proof based on evidence that every seemingly rational person will agree on.

The impulse of some Christians is to accept without hesitation the challenge thrown down by skeptics who adhere to a strong empiricism: "Okay, if you want proof, I'll give you proof!" Yet we need not allow a strong empiricist to set the terms like this. Far too often, novice apologists (and perhaps a few more experienced apologists who should know better) eagerly set out to respond to demands for "proof," confident that they will be able to "prove" Christianity by compiling a list of evidence.

The problem is that not everyone finds these lists of evidence convincing. In what sense can we say we have *proven* Christianity if our "proofs" are not universally accepted by all who examine them? And will anyone ever really be able say they have *proven* Christianity once and for all? Intelligent people often disagree on important issues. Some may find a certain set of evidence thoroughly convincing, while other equally intelligent people find that very same evidence significantly less convincing. This not only suggests that it's not our IQ level that ultimately determines how we process evidence, but also that we should be careful not to put too much stock in what reason *alone* can achieve.

In his important work *Knowledge and Christian Belief*, philosopher Alvin Plantinga writes that while there are many strong arguments that can be made for the truth of Christianity, there is no argument that will fully persuade everyone or absolutely prove Christianity.[6] In this way, Christian philosophers are increasingly rejecting an adherence to strong empiricism and the demand for absolute proof.[7] Yet strong empiricism is still what many people, whether they are skeptics seeking to disapprove Christianity or believers trying to prove it,

---

5. A classic expression of this approach to knowledge is William Kingdon Clifford, "The Ethics of Belief," *Contemporary Review* 29 (December 1876–May 1877): 289. We are using the term *strong empiricism* to include *strong rationalism*, which highlights the logic necessary for belief. For the sake of simplicity, we are using *strong empiricism* to capture the sense of both terms.

6. Alvin Plantinga, *Knowledge and Christian Belief* (Grand Rapids: Eerdmans, 2015), x.

7. See Lesslie Newbigin, *Proper Confidence: Faith, Doubt, and Certainty in Christian Discipleship* (Grand Rapids: Eerdmans, 1995), 94–96.

base their belief or disbelief on—even if they are not aware of their perspective's intellectual roots.

There are several reasons strong empiricism is problematic.

First, it is self-refuting. Strong empiricism works on the premise that we should only accept something as true if it can be proven by observation or logic, yet that premise itself cannot be proven by observation or logic. Thus, according to strong empiricism's own logic, there is no reason to accept it as true.

Second, it is impractical. Many things that are obviously true cannot be "proven" in a rationalistic way. For example, you can't prove empirically or logically that the people around you have minds—it's simply the way it seems to be. Likewise, I might wonder, *Can I prove that I existed ten minutes ago? I remember that I ate a snack, but why should I trust my memory?* Memories sometimes fail us. Even though I cannot prove I ate a snack in my office ten minutes ago, is it irrational to believe it happened?

Certain ethical norms fall into this category as well. One cannot "prove" that rape is wrong—at least, not with empirical research or logic alone. Most people have a deep sense that it is wrong. Though they would admit they haven't formulated a foolproof logical or empirical argument for it being wrong, they still believe it to be so and live their lives accordingly.

Beliefs like these—that other minds exist or that rape is wrong—cannot be strictly proven in strong rationalistic terms, and most people don't even attempt to do so. Yet to people who hold these beliefs, they are obviously, undeniably true. Most of our day-to-day decisions are made like this. We can't "prove" the assumptions we base our decisions on, and we normally don't even feel the need to try.

Similarly, Michael Polanyi advanced the thesis that even scientific knowledge is not simply proven by a mechanical process, but rather must take place in a fiduciary (faith-like) framework that involves personal trust and assent to a larger tradition.[8] All people, both religious and irreligious, live on the basis of both faith and reason.

Third, not all intelligent people reason and interpret data in the same way. It is not as though the only requirement for someone accepting the best arguments for Christianity is a willingness to examine the evidence. Belief in Jesus can't simply be boiled down to a cognitive decision made as people consider evidence for and against Christianity from a perfectly neutral position. We are not blank slates, and we do not reach decisions simply by logically processing data. Humans

---

8. See Michael Polanyi, *Personal Knowledge: Towards a Post-Critical Philosophy* (Chicago: University of Chicago Press, 1962); see also Esther Meeks, *Loving to Know: Covenant Epistemology* (Eugene, OR: Cascade, 2011), who builds on Polanyi's work, emphasizing the "personal" aspect of knowing.

are multifaceted beings, and we approach data from our own unique set of cultural perspectives, traditions, and basic assumptions (see ch. 8). Thus, not everyone is going to look at the evidence in the same way. We each have our own perspectives and interpretations. Not every perspective, however, is ultimately correct—which leads to the fourth factor.

Fourth, all individuals are born with a fallen human nature. This is a significant theological point consistently raised throughout the Bible, and since it is crucial for apologetics in general, we will need to linger on it longer than we did on the previous three points. Using Romans 1:18–32 as our guide, we can observe three ways a recognition of humankind's sinful nature should chasten any overly rationalistic reflexes we may have.

1. Sin affects our reasoning structures (e.g., the way we think and reason). Paul makes clear in Romans 1:18–32 that humankind, despite its fallen nature, has a knowledge of God and is therefore without excuse. He insists that even unbelievers have a true knowledge—though not a saving knowledge—of God: "what may be known about God is plain to them, because God has made it plain to them"; thus when they sin, it is in spite of the fact that "they [know] God" (1:19, 21). This knowledge is what theologians have referred to as the "sense of God," which God has implanted in every person he has created. This knowledge of God is not simply a vague, abstract sense of a general deity. For, as Paul describes, we are creatures living in God's creation, and thus by looking at ourselves and the creation around us, we obtain specific knowledge of the one true God.

Anyone can see God's eternal power and divine nature through creation. Accordingly, Paul appeals to creation as part of his apologetic strategy toward the Gentiles (Acts 14:15–18; 17:24–29). In appealing to the knowledge all people can obtain from creation, Paul is appealing to what is called *native rationality*, the universally shared internal mechanisms that work to produce the sort of basic beliefs people hold that we mentioned above. Although people debate the exact number and character of these basic beliefs, all humans have them in one form or another. These beliefs seem to derive instinctively or spontaneously, such as the idea that other people and the external world we perceive are real rather than an illusion and the conviction that certain things are right or wrong.[9] The reason humans have this native rationality is that they were created by God. As theologian Richard Lints observes, it makes sense "to suppose that if God creates us, then he creates us to interact intellectually with the rest of the created order in certain prescribed fashions."[10]

---

9. See Richard Lints, *The Fabric of Theology: A Prolegomenon to Evangelical Theology* (Grand Rapids: Eerdmans 1993), 118.

10. Lints, *Fabric of Theology*, 120.

Lints goes on to argue that if it were not for the effect of sin, everyone would have the exact same number and character of basic beliefs, and everyone would believe in God. In other words, if it weren't for sin suppressing the truth, then everyone would affirm a belief in God in a similar spontaneous, instinctive fashion to the way they affirm that other minds exist and that the external world is real. The problem is, however, that humans *do* suppress this knowledge of God—often to such an extent that they (unnaturally) do not recognize, let alone accept, that they have it.

Paul asserts that the fall has affected our cognitive functions. Wickedness suppresses the truth. All humans know God, but their thinking is futile. They might think they are wise, but they are actually fools. Instead of embracing the truth about their Creator, people unnaturally embrace lies. Alvin Plantinga writes that sin brings with it "a cognitive limitation" that hampers people both in the accuracy and extent of what they know—in particular, their "knowledge of God and his beauty, glory, and love"—and in their ability to make right value judgments—to discern "what is worth loving and what worth hating, what should be sought and what rejected."[11] This alone sounds bleak enough, but in the opening chapter of his letter to the Romans, Paul goes even further in showing the pervasiveness of sin.

2. Sin affects our affections; it misdirects our desires and loves. We must first note that emotive structures cannot be neatly separated from reasoning structures. Paul weaves the two together; we only separate them here for the sake of clarity. Paul links "[exchanging] the truth about God for a lie" with worshiping and serving the created instead of the Creator (Rom 1:25). When people sin, they are given over to a depraved mind, leading them into further immorality (vv. 28–32).

Thus, in addition to our reason being distorted due to the fall, our desires are distorted as well. We love what we should not and fail to love what we should. We love God's creation and fail to love God himself. It is easy to see these distorted desires in ourselves today. A strong example is the way we often consciously or unconsciously view God as a threat. We make the giver of every good gift and the sustainer of all into a competitor who restricts our independence and freedom. We think to ourselves, *Why does he get to do whatever he wants and to make all the rules? That's what I want to do.*[12] Instead of loving God as the provider and the person in whom ultimate joy is found, we resent him because he threatens our access to what we really want: happiness on our own autonomous

---

11. Plantinga, *Knowledge and Christian Belief*, 49.

12. See Ron Highfield, *God, Freedom, and Human Dignity: Embracing a God-Centered Identity in a Me-Centered Culture* (Downers Grove, IL: InterVarsity, 2013).

terms—terms in which we worship his gifts as our gods. In this way, when it comes to belief in God, "the crucial issues are never narrowly epistemological: they are profoundly moral."[13]

3. Sin affects cultural plausibility structures. Part of what shapes the way people interpret evidence is what sociologist Peter Berger calls "plausibility structures,"[14] a term referring to how we are much more inclined to believe something if the people around us believe it too.[15] The sins described in Romans 1:18–32 are social sins that affect not just individuals, but the culture that surrounds them: "they not only continue to do these very things but also approve of those who practice them" (1:32). Because we humans are relational beings, we acquire beliefs, ideas, attitudes, and affections—both loves and hates—from those around us. These *cultural plausibility structures* determine both the sort of things we would even consider believing and the beliefs that many in any given culture or subculture take for granted. (Note that Richard Lints refers to these plausibility structures as *cultural rationality*, which contrasts with the *native rationality* mentioned above.)[16]

For example, in some cultures, many would deny the existence of the supernatural. In other contexts, people may see the belief that there are many paths to God as a universal axiom. Or in yet another context, the pursuit of sexual freedom may be taken for granted. Often for belief in the true God to become plausible to someone, an apologist must not only overcome sin's effect on their reasoning and on what they desire, but also the effect of the cultural plausibility structures they operate within.

Summarizing the problems with strong empiricism. In summary, strong empiricism fails because it is self-refuting, impractical, neglects our situatedness (that we assume the basic frameworks our culture and traditions assume), and cannot be reconciled with the pervasive effects of sin. Therefore, instead of adhering to strong empiricism, we ought to affirm that some beliefs are more coherent and reasonable than others, but that arguments can be avoided.[17] Accordingly, we can evaluate beliefs. Because we were created by God with native rationality, the intuition we have that we ought to use our cognitive abilities to figure out what makes the most sense is correct, yet we should not expect to have rationally

---

13. D. A. Carson, *The Gagging of God: Christianity Confronts Pluralism* (Grand Rapids: Zondervan, 1996), 184.

14. Peter L. Berger, *The Sacred Canopy: Elements of a Sociological Theory of Religion* (1967; repr., New York: Anchor, 1990), 45.

15. See "Rethinking Secularization: A Conversation with Peter Berger," AlbertMohler.com, October 11, 2010, www.albertmohler.com/2010/10/11/rethinking-secularization-a-conversation-with-peter-berger.

16. Lints, *Fabric of Theology*, 118–19.

17. Timothy Keller makes a similar point in *The Reason for God: Belief in an Age of Skepticism* (New York: Penguin, 2008), 120.

coercive proof for God. Even those in the hard sciences, which have proliferated since the Enlightenment, do not demand conclusive "proof" in order to reach all their conclusions. Instead, scientists accept whatever theory they feel has the best explanatory power, and, of course, they sometimes disagree.[18]

In sum, the apologist at the cross recognizes that absolute or coercive proof for Christianity is not available. And while we as Christians find various arguments for Christianity to be persuasive, for someone who has assumed a non-Christian framework and has not been transformed by the Holy Spirit, those arguments are avoidable. Our apologetic is ultimately not dependent on ourselves but on the Holy Spirit. This should both humble us and give us great confidence before God as we seek to convince others and work through our own doubts. God himself is the apologist par excellence.

A strong case—in fact, *various* strong cases—can be made for Christianity. This does not mean, however, that others will never find any of the strands of our apologetic cord to be wanting. Being humble means being open to learning from others—even our harshest critics. We must also keep in mind that, as we will discuss in the next section, not every question can be answered with absolute certainty. Yet even though arguments aren't so strong as to be coercive, they are still worth making, because the Spirit can use them to "bolster," "confirm," and even "convince."[19]

Unrealistic Expectations

The modernistic expectation that humans can attain a "God's-eye" view of the world is problematic, because there are questions surrounding any worldview—not just Christianity—that aren't answerable in black-and-white terms. Oftentimes, Christians and non-Christians alike will expect or even demand as a qualification for belief that the Bible answer all their questions. This is curious, because from a Christian perspective, we are obliged to admit we aren't in a position to see all and know all.

In Deuteronomy 29:29, the Lord reminds us that while he has revealed truth to us—"the things revealed belong to us and to our children forever, that we may follow all the words of this law"—he has not revealed all things to us: "The secret things belong to the Lord our God." The Bible presents God as a figure who is beyond us. His ways are not our ways.

The book of Job teaches how important it is that we humbly submit to God

---

18. See Alister McGrath, "The Natural Sciences and Apologetics," in *Imaginative Apologetics: Theology, Philosophy, and the Catholic Tradition*, ed. Andrew Davison (Grand Rapids: Baker Academic, 2012).

19. Alvin Plantinga, "Appendix: Two Dozen (or so) Theistic Arguments," in *Alvin Plantinga*, ed. Deane-Peter Baker (Cambridge: Cambridge University Press, 2007), 210.

in the face of the mystery of suffering. Job, in view of all the evils that fall on him, calls on God to hear his case, knowing that he is (compared to others, at least) a righteous man. At times, Job's call for justice seems to border on irreverence. Remarkably, at the end of the book, God does come down and speak to Job, though it does not go quite the way Job expected. In essence, God asks Job a series of pointed rhetorical questions: "Where were you when I was forming the universe? What knowledge do you have of the things of God?" (see Job 38:1–7). God goes on poetically asking questions for four chapters. Of course, the answer Job would have to give to these questions is that he was not around when God made the world and that he does not have the mind of God.

Notice that what God *doesn't* do here is explain to Job in great detail all the answers to his questions. After God has revealed himself to him, Job, far from asking more questions, musters a very different type of response: "Surely I spoke of things I did not understand, things too wonderful for me to know . . . My ears had heard of you, but now my eyes have seen you. Therefore I despise myself and repent in dust and ashes" (Job 42:3b, 5–6).

According to the book of Job, believing in God means *trusting in a personal being who is infinitely wiser and whose ways are beyond our full understanding.* If a person rejects God because they can't understand what he is doing, they are not really rejecting the God presented in the Bible. The God of the Bible promises us that, while he has reasons for all he does, we often will not understand them. Job offers the proper response to a God who is infinitely beyond him: he worships.

The apostle Paul echoes this sentiment in his doxology in Romans:

> Oh, the depth of the riches of the wisdom and knowledge of God!
>> How unsearchable his judgments,
>> and his paths beyond tracing out!
> "Who has known the mind of the Lord?
>> Or who has been his counselor?"
> "Who has ever given to God,
>> that God should repay them?"
> For from him and through him and for him are all things.
>> To him be the glory forever! Amen.[20]

The inexhaustible mysteries of God lead Paul, just as they do Job, to worship. However, because of the expectations modernism has created, mysteries that once led people to worship God now can lead them to doubt instead.

---

20. Romans 11:33–36.

The Bible clearly speaks to the fact that, as human beings, we are limited by our finitude and sinfulness. Yet many—especially nonbelievers, but also some confessing believers—succumb to "the lust of the mind."[21] They start poking around at a Christian worldview, thinking, *It had better answer all my questions, or else.* In response to critics like these who demand answers to all their questions, it can be tempting to trim Christianity down to argue for a more generic deity.

We will argue as this book moves forward that Christianity provides a worldview that has more explanatory power than any other worldview and that we find a variety of arguments for it compelling. But some may wonder, *What should I do if an unbeliever expects me to answer all their questions on their own terms, demanding that I provide them with a "God's-eye view"?* When questions arise that seem to be beyond the scope of what has been revealed or what we can fully understand—questions on such topics as the Trinity, a God who is both transcendent and personal, or a God who became a baby—how are we to reply?

What Do We Do with the Gaps in the Puzzle?

As we've seen, the Bible includes certain tensions or mysteries we are called to accept rather than resolve artificially by trimming God's Word down into something more palatable to either ourselves or our cultural context.

The data the Bible gives us is analogous to all the separate pieces we have when we open a puzzle box. The pieces (the biblical information) can be arranged in various ways, yet it is clear there is only one way for them to fit together to form an image that makes sense. When we arrive at the end of putting all the pieces together, however, we find there are gaps in our puzzle. It is not that the entire puzzle is illogical or that we can't basically see the picture—we simply don't have all the pieces. In other words, God has revealed himself sufficiently, just not exhaustively.

Consider these Christian mysteries: God is sovereign, and humans are responsible for their actions. God has eternally existed as three Persons, but has always remained one God. Jesus is both fully God and fully man. These biblical tensions are at the very heart of Christianity.

What do we do when there are gaps in our theological puzzle? The temptation can be to rearrange the puzzle in a way that changes the image. Or we may try to make our own pieces and force them into the holes, pretending they were a part of the original puzzle (as if no one could tell).

---

21. Kevin Vanhoozer, "From Canon to Concept: 'Same' and 'Other' in the Relation Between Biblical and Systematic Theology," *Scottish Bulletin of Evangelical Theology* 12, no. 2 (1994): 119, https://biblicalstudies .org.uk/pdf/sbet/12-2_096.pdf.

G. K. Chesterton on the Importance of Mystery

"Mysticism keeps men sane. As long as you have mystery you have health; when you destroy mystery you create morbidity. The ordinary man has always been sane because the ordinary man has always been a mystic. He has permitted the twilight. He has always had one foot in earth and the other in fairyland. He has always left himself free to doubt his gods; but (unlike the agnostic of to-day) free also to believe in them. He has always cared more for truth than for consistency. If he saw two truths that seemed to contradict each other, he would take the two truths and the contradiction along with them. His spiritual sight is stereoscopic, like his physical sight: he sees two different pictures at once and yet sees all the better for that. Thus he has always believed that there was such a thing as fate, but such a thing as free will also. Thus he believed that children were indeed the kingdom of heaven, but nevertheless ought to be obedient to the kingdom of earth. He admired youth because it was young and age because it was not. It is exactly this balance of apparent contradictions that has been the whole buoyancy of the healthy man."[22]

The limits placed on us by our finitude and sinful nature do not mean we cannot suggest ways to fill in the gaps and explain these mysteries. It is important, however, that when we make such suggestions, we do so with a large dose of humility and caution. If we don't—if we try to fill the gap by forcing a piece into it—we will only leave a larger gap somewhere else and distort the picture the puzzle is supposed to present.

If we acknowledge that the Bible does not explicitly solve a certain tension, then we can legitimately suggest how things *might* fit together. By offering these suggestions as possibilities rather than dogmatic assertions, we display an appropriate amount of humility. And by offering suggestions rather than nothing at all, we can show that even with our limited knowledge, it is possible to think of plausible reasons for the way things are, which can often help people when they are distressed about a particular theological problem.

A salient example of how the modern shift to expecting exhaustive answers has affected our thinking is in the way we wrestle with the problem of evil and suffering. Modern Westerners are often dissatisfied with Christianity and may even completely dismiss it because they have both seen suffering and experienced it firsthand. Yet as Oxford professor Alister McGrath observes, it is not only Christianity that cannot completely explain the problem of evil; no worldview can. The real question, then, is which worldview offers the *most satisfying* explanation of the problem of evil, which is both livable and intellectually

---

22. G. K. Chesterton, *Orthodoxy* (1908: repr., New York: Image, 2001), 23.

defensible, even though that explanation will inevitably leave important questions unanswered. Speaking to this point, McGrath concludes, "A willingness to live with unresolvable questions is a mark of intellectual maturity, not a matter of logical nonsense as some unwisely regard it."[23]

Later we will explore more about how to respond to the problem of evil, along this trajectory of thought (see ch. 12). For now, we may review the major point of this section. If apologists, in attempting to meet the modernistic expectation that every question be answered and a complete panoramic view of truth be produced, "solves" the problem by discarding pieces of the biblical data to make the pieces fit better (at least according to their own structures of thought), then they are ironically destroying the very picture they are trying to complete. In other words, when apologists minimize or ignore certain biblical teachings in order to resolve mysteries, then they are jeopardizing the Christian faith itself. For this reason, we must avoid playing into the hands of a modernistic pride that expects humans to be able to attain a "God's-eye view" on reality and demands that we prove Christianity in a way that will satisfy strong empiricism.

HUMILITY BEFORE OTHERS: Loving Your Neighbor

In his 1993 book on apologetics, David K. Clark, a vice president and dean at Bethel Seminary, writes, "Sometimes a person who speaks to an apologist feels like an object—like yet another notch on the handle of a gunslinger's six-shooter. An apologist's dialogue partners do not always sense genuine concern for them. This negative feeling can build tremendous resistance. People pull hardest when they are pushed hardest."[24]

As Clark points out, a "gunslinger" approach is rarely effective in persuading the unconvinced. It is not often that you will talk to someone who became a Christian because they were backed into an intellectual corner by an apologist and forced to concede defeat. Most apologists, at least in *theory*, recognize this; nevertheless, too often in *practice*, apologetics can eerily resemble an old western. Gunslinger apologists may have the best of intentions, but their approach to defending their town results in bullets being fired all over the place. They may successfully defend the town, but not because anyone on the other side has decided to lay down their gun and put on a white hat.

It's not simply that this "gunslinger" approach normally proves ineffective

---

23. Alister E. McGrath, *Mere Apologetics: How to Help Seekers and Skeptics Find Faith* (Grand Rapids: Baker, 2012), 166–67.

24. David K. Clark, *Dialogical Apologetics: A Person-Centered Approach to Christian Defense* (Grand Rapids: Baker, 1993), 124; see Os Guinness, *Fool's Talk: Recovering the Art of Christian Persuasion* (Downers Grove, IL: InterVarsity, 2015), 172.

in winning others over; it also denies the humility and love that ought to characterize people of the cross. In other words, an apologetic of glory is not only impractical for winning others over, but it also doesn't fit well with New Testament theology.

The New Testament Pattern for Tone

As we'll see in chapter 9, the apostle Paul took a very different tone when he was addressing the Christian community about idols in Romans 1 than when he sought to persuade the Athenian philosophers in Acts 17.

For example, when Paul addresses the Corinthians about how the church should handle moral issues, he makes a distinction between insiders and outsiders: "What business is it of mine to judge those outside the church? Are you not to judge those inside? God will judge those outside. 'Expel the wicked person from among you'" (1 Cor 5:12–13). At times, Paul speaks very bluntly to those inside the church—especially toward false teachers and teachings that have made their way into the church—yet at other times, he is remarkably gentle and advises the church to be gentle as well.

Of course, the classic example of a dramatic change in tone is how Jesus' language to the religious Jewish insiders of the day—"Woe to you . . . You brood of vipers!" (Matt 23:29, 33)—contrasts with his words to social outcasts and children. Just like Paul, Jesus has quite a range of tone.

These passages, among others, suggest that while no rigid system exists in the New Testament, there seems to be a pattern that, with godly wisdom, can be applied to our context today.

In the New Testament, we have *insiders*—people who were at least claiming to be a part of God's people. For example, this included many of the religious leaders of Jesus' day, those who entered the community claiming to be a teacher from God, the disciples, and those who had been baptized into the church. Like the tone of parents correcting their children, Jesus' and Paul's tone with insiders could be gentle at times and sharp at other times, either when Jesus and Paul were disciplining their children in the faith or protecting them from the "child abuse" of false teachers.

And we also have *outsiders*—people not claiming to be in the know or those seen as on the outside of God's people. This included, among others, social outcasts and the Athenian and pagan philosophers. With outsiders, Paul and Jesus seem to regularly demonstrate a tone of gentleness and patience.

Of course, we can think of some puzzling examples that resist an attempt to turn this general pattern into a rigid system. For example, in Mark 7:27, Jesus addresses harshly a Syrophoenician woman, an outsider: "First let the children eat all they want . . . for it is not right to take the children's bread and toss it to the dogs." Commentators have various theories for why Jesus responds like this, but most do not deny the bluntness of Jesus' tone. Referring to someone as a "dog" is hardly a term of endearment today, and it certainly wasn't in first-century Palestine either. We would assert, however, that exceptions such as this prove the general rule. In summary, it's important for apologists to be aware of the New Testament pattern outlined above—coupled with Spirit-endowed wisdom—as they seek to respond in a given context with the proper tone.

Recall that 1 Peter 3:15 emphasizes that our defense should be given with "gentleness and respect." It is no wonder that Peter would stress this, for Jesus himself taught Peter that he "did not come to be served, but to serve, and to give his life as a ransom for many" (Mark 10:45). Peter's and Jesus' words also sit well with Paul's instructions in Colossians 4:5–6: "Be wise in the way you act toward outsiders; make the most of every opportunity. Let your conversation be always full of grace, seasoned with salt, so that you may know how to answer everyone."

Humility and Wisdom: Practical Apologetic Lessons from Proverbs

The proverbs in Scripture connect wisdom with humility: "When pride comes, then comes disgrace, but with humility comes wisdom" (Prov 11:2). Wisdom does not necessarily entail a vast accumulation of facts or an above-average IQ; rather, wisdom is a practical knowledge of living rooted in the fear of God. Thus, using wisdom in apologetics does not mean following seven-step plans or plugging facts into an equation in order to produce effective persuasion. The Bible demonstrates that using wisdom, rather than pointing us to simply use a mathematical formula for engagement, requires that we assess our context and respond appropriately. Notice, for example, how Proverbs 26:4–5 instructs us *not* to "answer a fool according to his folly" because "you yourself will be just like him," and then turns around in the very next verse and tells us that we *should* "answer a fool according to his folly" because otherwise "he will be wise in his own eyes." Rather than being a contradiction, these two verses serve to remind us that different situations call for different types of responses. Jesus himself, the embodiment of wisdom, taught us, "Be as shrewd as snakes and as innocent as doves" (Matt 10:16).

First, listen and take others seriously. "To answer before listening—that is folly and shame" (Prov 18:13). We shouldn't expect others to take us seriously if we're not willing to take them seriously. It is important to understand what someone else is saying, not only because it enables us to answer what they are actually asking, but also because being quick to listen and demonstrating a commitment to look at things from an opposing perspective is one of the most disarming things we can do. Being able to communicate that we understand, and thus have actually been listening, puts us in a better position to empathize with and respond redemptively to the unbeliever.

Second, avoid falsely representing the other side. When someone's argument describes the opposing position in a way that misrepresents it or is simply inaccurate, it is called a "straw man" argument. People build straw men because they are far easier to tear down than the real position and thus make it easier to paint another's view as unreasonable.

The Golden Rule, however, demands that we tear down any straw men we have created—or better yet, that we never build any straw men to begin with.

Building straw men can create fervor and perhaps a false confidence among those who already agree with us, but normally it only engenders distrust and animosity in those we are trying to reach. Here again, the proverbs guide us in our engagement: "A false witness will perish, but a careful listener will testify successfully" (Prov 21:28).

Third, resist assuming motives. The problem with assuming the motives of those who oppose us is that we are not normally in the position to know them, so we can only speculate. Speculating that the other person has negative motives may certainly have the effect of demonizing their position in the eyes of others listening, but just consider how you would feel if someone led off a discussion by explaining to you that you believe what you believe because "you can't handle the truth!" That sort of comment may make for a dramatic movie scene, but it rarely opens the door for gospel conversations. Humans are incredibly complex and normally have multiple motives for their decisions. As Proverbs 16:2 reminds us, people's "motives are weighed by the LORD." Yet Proverbs 20:5 teaches, "The purposes of a person's heart are deep waters, but one who has insight draws them out." So rather than being overly quick to judge the motives of others, it is best to always be seeking to discern the deeper issues, while avoiding jumping to conclusions and serving as the ultimate judge of motives.

Fourth, when you can, find points of agreement to affirm. If the goal of apologetics were simply to win over an audience in a debate, this point might not matter. After all, one might think, *Who cares what we agree on; we are here to wrestle over what we disagree on. Let the best arguments win!* Yet because the goal of apologetics is not simply to demonstrate that the other person is wrong, but rather to win the other person over for the sake of the gospel, it is important that, when we can, we find connecting points.

When we talk about "finding common ground" in this way, we're not referring to some kind of neutral, unbiased space that both believers and unbelievers can inhabit together. No such "neutral space" exists. However, as we've seen in this chapter, the Bible teaches that although humans suppress the truth, they still have certain intuitions about life, God, and meaning that are deeply implanted within them. One example is the way that, because of God's grace on humans, all people worship—that is, seek to find meaning and identity in—something and have an intuition (even if they deny it!) that there is a right way to live that should be followed and a wrong way to live that should be avoided. Points such as these often serve as common ground that we can start with. Beginning with points we agree on allows us to have a footing to challenge points we disagree on, while at the same time living out the wisdom of the proverb: "A gentle answer turns away wrath, but a harsh word stirs up anger" (Prov 15:1).

Fifth, resist focusing on the periphery. It is important to stay focused. At times, the people we are speaking to will bring up something we think is silly, irrelevant, or just plain wrong. The tendency can be to respond to every single point we don't agree with. Yet if we don't pick and choose what we will address, our conversations can easily become fifteen-round sparring matches. Usually it is pride that fosters in us the need to hoist our every opinion over the person we are speaking with every time they say something—even something relatively minor—we disagree with. As Proverbs 13:10 warns us, "Where there is strife, there is pride."

Paul calls the gospel "the power of God that brings salvation" and that which is of "first importance" (Rom 1:16; 1 Cor 15:3). A helpful image is "apologetic triages," similar to what medical professionals refer to as "medical triages." I (Josh) recently took my daughter to the ER after she sustained a head injury that caused her to black out for a few seconds. Upon our arrival at the ER, the hospital staff quickly began to ask my daughter questions like, "From 1 to 10, tell us how much it hurts." They were trying to figure out how critical her injury was compared to those of other patients. A head injury in a child can be very serious, so she was probably put before any patient who came in that night with, say, a sprained ankle. Someone who was having a heart attack, however, would probably have been treated before my daughter. Medical triaging determines which patient's injury is most critical and needs to be given priority.

Similarly, an apologetic triage recognizes that not every objection to what we think of as "correct doctrine" should be treated with the same priority. In other words, we must decide what is most critical to the gospel.[25] Many times, believers and skeptics alike who are experiencing deep doubts have not learned to triage their questions in order to distinguish the essentials of Christianity from the periphery. When someone is considering a belief in Christianity, they ought to begin with some basic questions: What do you believe about Jesus and the gospel? Can you trust Jesus and the gospel accounts? Did Jesus rise from the grave? Is he Lord?

Sometimes the challenging questions believers face aren't about an essential doctrine but a doctrine inherited from their theological tradition. Because these believers have been taught that such doctrines "are just the way it is," their house of faith begins to crumble when they encounter skeptics who challenge one of these doctrines. Part of the problem is they were never taught the difference between core Christian beliefs and beliefs that are important yet nonessential for conversion or orthodox theology.

---

25. For more on how one goes about understanding the difference between indisputable and disputable matters for believers, see D. A. Carson, "On Disputable Matters," *Themelios* 40, no. 3 (December 2015): 283–88.

This lack of nuancing can affect an apologist's dialogue with the person they're attempting to minister to. If every doctrine is triaged at the "critically important" level, then the result will be dialogues with nonbelievers—who obviously see the world very differently—that will inevitably devolve into arguments that never build a bridge to the gospel.

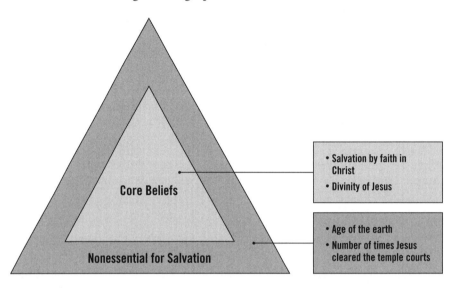

Questions about Genesis 1 and 2

We are suggesting an approach similar to what Francis Schaeffer modeled some time ago in his work *Genesis in Space and Time*.[26] As D. A. Carson points out, Schaeffer, rather than getting caught up in the various Christian debates, asks the question: "What is the least that Genesis 1 and the following chapters must be saying for the rest of the Bible to make any sense?"[27] It seems that Christians can and should be willing to say more than this in certain contexts, but if this subject is brought up in apologetic conversations, we suggest that in most cases the wisest course will be to (1) explain the essential elements of what Genesis 1 and 2 are saying and then (2) explain some of the interpretive options that exist within the Christian tradition. This approach gives the person you are speaking to the opportunity to consider the gospel without feeling as if they have to agree with you or immediately make up their mind on certain specifics in Genesis 1 and 2.

26. Francis A. Schaeffer *Genesis in Space and Time: The Flow of Biblical History* (Downers Grove, IL: InterVarsity, 1972).

27. Quoted in D. A. Carson, *The God Who Is There: Finding Your Place in God's Story* (Grand Rapids: Baker, 2010), 17.

When an apologist acknowledges to the skeptic that there is a legitimate and extensive history of diversity among Christians on certain non-gospel related issues, it helps keep the discussion open and avoids creating unnecessary boundaries between the skeptic and the gospel.[28]

Sixth, avoid being unnecessarily antagonistic. Avoid unnecessary pejorative language. Describing another person's position in a way that mocks them and makes their position seem silly may win points with others listening who are already on your side, but it will only alienate the person you are trying to reach. As Proverbs 20:3 observes, "It is to one's honor to avoid strife, but every fool is quick to quarrel."

New York Times columnist David Brooks sums up well the danger of using unnecessary antagonism: "If one person in a conversation takes the rhetorical level up to 10 every time, the other person has to rebut at Level 10 and turn monstrous, or retreat into resentful silence. Rhetorical passion, which feels so good, can destroy conversation and mar truth and reconciliation."[29]

There is, of course, a time to speak bluntly and with tough language. To do so requires godly wisdom and sensitivity to the context. And yet the gospel reminds us that we are to love and pray for our enemies—even those who are publically antagonistic toward Christianity. Most of us will not engage high-profile atheistic and agnostic critics in public debate and writing. Instead, we will find ourselves in dialogue in real-life relationships. Careless words may not break an unbeliever's bones, but careless words will often hurt them emotionally, detract from our ability to be heard, and neglect to win them over.

CONCLUSION

The last point brings us full circle to the beginning of this chapter. Love and humility must not be confused with compromise. Just like Jesus, who modeled both grace and truth in his life and teaching (John 1:14), we must be willing to engage one another with humility and love, and also to proclaim truth boldly. At the points in which the truth of the gospel collides with the sensibilities of our culture, we must have the humility before God to stand under his Word.

As we make our case, we must humbly submit to what God's Word tells us: that our apologetics, our evangelism, and our saving knowledge of God are

---

28. Of course, what is to be included as "essential" is itself debated. Here we are not attempting to resolve such debates, but rather to give you a paradigm to begin sorting through what doctrines are essential to the gospel.

29. David Brooks, "The Year of Unearthed Memories," *New York Times*, December 15, 2015, www .nytimes.com/2015/12/15/opinion/the-year-of-unearthed-memories.html.

ultimately dependent on the redeeming work of the Holy Spirit. We must not only humble ourselves to our limitations; we must also instill a recognition of humanity's limitations into others, because no one comes from a neutral perspective, and no one has a full "God's-eye view." We now turn to explore why people end up making the commitments they make and how this should shape our case for Christianity.

CHAPTER EIGHT

APPEALING TO THE WHOLE PERSON FOR THE SAKE OF THE GOSPEL

> The reality is that every person embraces his or her worldview for a variety of rational, emotional, cultural, and social factors.
>
> *Timothy Keller,* Making Sense of God

A HOLISTIC APOLOGETIC

We have already seen in chapter 6 how Jesus ministered to people not only spiritually but also physically—in other words, to their whole person, foreshadowing a future, embodied salvation. In line with this holistic understanding of salvation, Scripture often uses the word *heart* to describe the center of a person's entire being. In contemporary usage, *heart* is often used to refer to how we intuitively feel or desire, in contrast to the *head*, which is used to refer to how we rationalize. Thus, normally when someone says something like, "My head told me one thing, but my heart told me another," they mean that logically they knew they should do one thing, but that they desired to do something else.

Apologetics at the Cross

1. Taking people to the cross through word and deed (ch. 6)
2. Cruciform humility before God and others (ch. 7)
3. **Appealing to the whole person for the sake of the gospel (ch. 8)**
4. Contextualization through the lens of the cross (ch. 9)

The biblical usage of the words *heart* and *mind*, however, is quite different. It reminds us that we are not compartmentalized beings. In biblical usage, the word *heart* usually refers to *all* aspects of the human psyche.[1] And in Matthew 22:37, when Jesus, referencing the Old Testament, commands, "Love the Lord your God with all your heart and with all your soul and with all your mind," it seems that the meaning of these terms—*heart*, *soul*, and *mind*—overlaps in such a way that they cannot be completely separated. Thus, Scripture calls for a holistic understanding of human beings; it does not allow us to separate desire, will, and intellect from each other.

WHAT DOES THIS HAVE TO DO WITH APOLOGETICS?

As far as apologetics is concerned, Scripture, by informing us that humans are holistic beings, reminds us that in our persuasive efforts we cannot force someone to convert simply by using logic to back them into a corner. In the previous section, we already discussed the importance of a *holistic* view of human beings in contrast to a view of humans as one-dimensional or purely logical, and we will come back to reflect on that concept more. First, however, we need to direct our attention to three specific aspects of a theological anthropology, namely, that humans are (1) *intellectually reflective* and (2) *moral* beings who (3) *worship*.

Intellectually Reflective Beings

We spent chapter 5 learning from the methods of contemporary apologetic models, and in chapters 12 and 13, we will incorporate insights from evidence-based methods as we deal with objections to the faith ("defeaters") and build a case for Christianity. These approaches have much to offer, particularly in the strength of their defense of the rational and historical cogency of Christian faith. But as we saw in chapter 5, these evidence-based appeals should not be separated from appeals to tradition, desire, and imagination. Focusing primarily on more analytical and empirical apologetic methods can leave the false impression that apologetics is exclusively an intellectual activity in which people make a decision for or against Christianity just by sorting out all the facts.[2] And while persuasion is certainly a cognitive activity, it is also a personal and existential

---

1. The Greek word *kardia* is often used in the New Testament as the "center and source of the whole inner life, with its thinking, feeling, and volition" (Frederick William Danker, ed., *A Greek-English Lexicon of the New Testament and Other Early Christian Literature*, 3rd. ed. [Chicago: University of Chicago Press, 2000], 508).

2. For more on this, see David K. Clark, *Dialogical Apologetics: A Person-Centered Approach to Christian Defense* (Grand Rapids: Baker, 1993), 112–14.

activity. Apologetics is not done in some abstract theoretical realm; it is done in the real world, with real people who have unique perspectives and outlooks and are driven to their deepest commitments for a complexity of reasons. Considered alongside our discussion of contemporary apologetic theories in chapter 5, our focus on the whole person reminds us that while we do use our intellect when we make commitments and decisions, we never make them on a purely intellectual basis.

Moral Beings

God created humans as moral beings who are responsible for the decisions they make. Because God made us this way, we cannot help but make decisions based on what we sense is "right" and "good."[3] As humans we not only have desires, but also, unlike animals, we reflect on these desires and evaluate them, making moral judgments. A lion does not ponder the morality of his selfish desire to keep all to himself the zebra he just mauled and not share it with his fellow lions. Humans, on the other hand, have the capacity to evaluate their own desires. For example, I (Josh) once had a student confess to me, "I really hate him, but I know it's not right." Even the fact that we almost always attempt to rationalize our decisions to follow our impulses (the student who spoke to me may well have thought something like, *I have every right to hate him, because he stole my girlfriend*) is a sign we were created as moral beings. Only humans are capable of losing their temper and then, after reflecting on the situation and realizing their anger was illegitimate, feeling bad about it. Our propensity as human beings to evaluate the desires and motives of ourselves and others—to make moral judgments—is both unique to us and universal among us.

The point is not that all humans and, by extension, cultures, *agree on* a particular moral standard, but that all humans and cultures *have* a moral standard and make moral judgments about what is good, bad, appropriate, inappropriate, meaningful, and inconsequential.[4]

Worshiping Beings

Humans are worshiping beings. All people worship something, no matter how irreligious they may appear to be. Jesus himself taught that each of us inevitably serves a master—whether it be God or money—and that we will ultimately be devoted to one master alone: "No one can serve two masters. Either you will hate the one and love the other, or you will be devoted to the one and

---

3. See Christian Smith, *Moral, Believing Animals: Human Personhood and Culture* (Oxford: Oxford University Press, 2003).

4. See Smith, *Moral, Believing Animals*, 7–13, 28–29, 148.

despise the other" (Matt 6:24). The thing we love most is what we will serve, and what we serve is what we will love most.

Modern gods—the most prevalent being sex, money, and power—appeal to the deepest desires of the human heart and find their way into the very recesses of our inner being. We cling to these gods with a deep devotion, hoping to find in them meaning, healing, significance, physical comfort, and identity. They should not be taken lightly, for they can seductively determine the very course of our lives and are very difficult to cast aside. An apologetic that is one-dimensional and fails to appeal to the whole person is no match for modern gods that appeal to our most deeply rooted desires.

WHAT'S LOVE GOT TO DO WITH IT?

One danger in apologetics is that, in seeking to clear people's pathway to the gospel, we appeal solely to their intellect. When we do so, we are mistakenly assuming that humans are primarily thinking beings rather than holistic, embodied beings who, yes, think, but who also believe, desire, and imagine.

We have already noted how in the New Testament the word *heart* is usually used to refer to the center of a person's whole being—a combination of what we would now in contemporary usage separate into two words: *head* (how we think) and *heart* (what we feel). When Jesus explains, "Where your treasure is, there your *heart* will be also" (Matt 6:21, emphasis added), he is implying that what we treasure most will ultimately control not merely our feelings, but our entire direction and purpose in life.[5]

This point has been emphasized across a long history of Christian thought. For instance, after pointing out that the distinguishing mark between believers and demons is not a knowledge of God, but rather an affection for him, philosopher Alvin Plantinga, building on Martin Luther and John Calvin, writes, "There is an intimate relation between revealing and sealing, knowledge and affection, intellect and will; they cooperate in a deep and complex and intimate way in the person of faith."[6] This is in line with Jonathan Edwards, who famously argued that the affections are primary in true religion. For Edwards, the term *affections* includes emotions, but more broadly refers to our whole sense of beauty and the good and is far more enduring than the fleeting feelings we experience from moment to moment.[7]

---

5. See D. A. Carson, "Matthew," in *Expositors Bible Commentary: Matthew-Mark*, rev. ed. (Grand Rapids: Zondervan, 2010), 212.

6. Alvin Plantinga, *Knowledge and Christian Belief* (Grand Rapids: Eerdmans, 2015), 79.

7. See Jonathan Edwards, *Religious Affections: In Three Parts* (Philadelphia: Chrissy, 1821).

C. S. Lewis

There are exceptional examples of apologetics that have appealed to more than just the head, and perhaps the most well-known is the apologetic approach of C. S. Lewis. As Alister McGrath explains, Lewis's works appeal not only to reason (as in *Mere Christianity*, which builds a logical case for Christianity), but also to human longing and the imagination. For example, Lewis uses allegory in *The Pilgrim's Regress* and his own life experience in *Surprised by Joy* to vividly illustrate how Christianity fulfills humanity's deepest innate longings. And in his *Chronicles of Narnia* series, Lewis creates a world that so enthralls the reader's imagination that it opens up their very soul to the beauty and truth—the deeper magic—of the Christian story.[8]

Theologian and philosopher James K. A. Smith has sought to recover this emphasis on desires. His specific focus is in the areas of education and worldview, but because his project has important implications for apologetics as well, we can apply his work to apologetics.

When frameworks for Christian apologetics overemphasize the role of the mind, they "[reduce] Christian faith primarily to a set of ideas, principles, claims, and propositions that are known and believed," all with the goal of "'correct' thinking." The problem with this approach is that it makes humans out to be merely "thinking things that are containers for ideas."[9]

Smith describes three anthropological models, the first of which is the model just described, which views the person as fundamentally a thinking being: our mind is who we are; our body is merely incidental.[10] As thinking beings, we process information and decide how we will live with primarily our cognitive faculties. Thus, according to this model, practicing apologetics mainly consists of disseminating ideas and information to others.

The second model views people primarily as believers and thus describes people in terms of what they *believe* instead of what they *know*. In Smith's own words, this model views humans as "believing animals, or essentially

3 Anthropological Models

Humans as primarily "thinking" beings
Humans as primarily "believing" beings
Humans as primarily "desiring" beings

---

8. See Alister E. McGrath, *Mere Apologetics: How to Help Seekers and Skeptics Find Faith* (Grand Rapids: Baker, 2012), 69.

9. James K. A. Smith, *Desiring the Kingdom: Worship, Worldview, and Cultural Formation* (Grand Rapids: Baker Academic, 2009), 32; for a more popular version, see his *You Are What You Love: The Spiritual Power of Habit* (Grand Rapids: Brazos, 2016).

10. See Smith, *Desiring the Kingdom*, 41–43.

religious creatures, defined by a worldview that is pre-rational or supra-rational."[11] Smith asserts that while this model is stronger than the first, it just replaces a "clash of ideas" with "a clash of beliefs" and "still tends to operate with a very disembodied, individualistic picture of the human person."[12]

Consequently, Smith suggests a third model: a human being as primarily a lover, as "embodied agents of desire or love." Smith, channeling Augustine, argues that "we inhabit the world . . . not primarily as thinkers, or even believers, but as more affective, embodied creatures who make our way in the world more by feeling our way around it."[13]

Augustine believed that sin is rooted in disordered love. Our problem is not that we love the things of the world; after all, God has designed us to love.[14] The problem is that we love things in the wrong order—with the wrong priority: We love created things more than the Creator, and our own kingdoms rather than God's kingdom.

It is these loves, disordered as they often are, that drive us to live our lives the way we do. What we love or desire "pushes (or pulls) us to act in certain ways, develop certain relationships, pursue certain goods, make certain sacrifices, enjoy certain things."[15] If someone were to press us, asking us to explain why we live life the way we do, we would likely have trouble articulating logical reasons or even beliefs that entirely (or accurately) explained our behavior. If we are honest and self-reflective enough, however, we will respond that we act the way we do, not because of what we logically assent to or even say that we believe, but because of what we desire most in life.

The thinking and believing aspects of humanity are important, but as James K. A. Smith has pointed out, they do not tell the whole story: humans are also desiring beings. On the other hand, there is the danger of treating thinking, believing, and desiring as though they are independent from each other.

Marriage serves as a fruitful analogy that demonstrates the interplay between thinking, believing, and desiring, and in doing so, it offers a balanced and holistic approach. In my own marriage, for example, the more I (Josh) have *known* my

---

11. Smith, *Desiring the Kingdom*, 43.

12. Smith, *Desiring the Kingdom*, 44. Considering the significance of faith in the New Testament, we suggest that close attention to "correct belief" is warranted. But to Smith's point, there does seem to be a disproportional amount of attention to reason and faith over desire in worldview and spiritual formation—and, we would add, in the area of apologetics as well.

13. Smith, *Desiring the Kingdom*, 47.

14. See Augustine, *On Christian Doctrine* 1.26.27–27.28, www.newadvent.org/fathers/12021.htm.

15. Smith, *Desiring the Kingdom*, 52. Smith himself acknowledges, "This isn't to say that the cognitive or propositional is a completely foreign register for us . . . however, it doesn't get into our (noncognitive) bones in the same way or with the same effect" (p. 53). In his second volume of this series, *Imagining the Kingdom: How Worship Works* (Grand Rapids: Baker Academic, 2013), he further clarifies: "My criticism here is not that worldview is wrong, but only that it is inadequate" (p. 8).

wife, the more I have *believed* in her high character and grown more deeply in *love* with her, which have both increased my *desire* to serve her. Love, knowledge, and belief all work together in a healthy relationship.

Even in marriage, though, when we use the word *knowledge*, we're implying something much more than an intellectual awareness of facts. A mere description of facts about my wife (she has brown hair, likes the beach, and enjoys romantic comedies) could hardly do justice to the "knowledge" I have of her. Clearly, there is at a deeper level an aesthetic knowledge of my wife's beauty—the way she laughs, the way she tells a story to our kids, her smile, and other things about her that I can't find the words to articulate—that has captured me.[16]

Like any analogy, this one will fail if you push it too far, but our point is that we were not primarily driven to marry our spouses by the facts we knew about them (as interesting as they are!) or by our belief or trust in them (though we deeply trust them!). We were driven to marry them and make a lifelong commitment to them, through all the ups and downs, because of a deep affection we have for them that is far more than just a feeling.

Believing truth is essential. Yet a list of facts alone is not what fuels a healthy marriage, nor, for that matter, what most would consider a proper motivation to marry someone in the first place. Likewise, a list of evidences alone does not fuel a healthy apologetic. However, evidences are still relevant.

Placing trust in the personal God of the Bible and having knowledge of his truth are essential to Christianity. This means that part of the role of apologetics is to explain why someone should take truths about God seriously, to provide reasons for faith, and to answer why this covenantal God should be trusted. But as in a commitment to a spouse, it is not simply a list of facts and evidences that drives people to turn from their current way of living and commit to follow Christ. Timothy Keller writes, "People . . . change not by merely changing their thinking but by changing what they love most. Such a shift requires nothing *less* than changing your thinking, but it entails much more."[17] Thus, a healthy apologetic makes truth claims and provides evidences, but it also offers much more.

The circular diagram pictured above reminds us that the three anthropological models (humans as thinking, believing, and

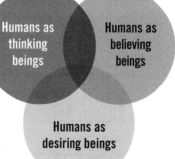

A Healthy Apologetic

Humans as thinking beings

Humans as believing beings

Humans as desiring beings

---

16. See Smith, *Imagining the Kingdom*, 126.
17. Timothy Keller, *Preaching: Communicating Faith in an Age of Skepticism* (New York: Viking, 2015), 159.

desiring beings) overlap to form the core of the human volition.[18] We are holistic beings who think, believe, *and* desire. The Bible, recognizing the complexity of human beings, appeals to us in different ways, and an apologetic at the cross will do the same. An apologist should have a tool belt full of different apologetic appeals, some aimed more at the head and others more at the heart, which ideally can be woven together to create a holistic apologetic.

IDENTITY AND PURPOSE: Lessons from Nike and Augustine

James K. A. Smith and others have pointed to the marketing industry to illustrate the importance of human desires. Marketers make their living by persuading, and therefore they've made it their business to understand what most strongly drives human decisions. With this in mind, it is interesting to note how rare it is that we see marketing campaigns targeting the intellect. Notice how you never hear commercials provide, for example, five reasons to buy a certain type of shampoo or a logical progression of statements that lead to the conclusion that you should buy a particular kind of automobile. Instead, marketers sell an *image* of who they think you would want to be, an *identity* that would seemingly provide fulfillment, or a *vision* of what life could be like . . . if you purchase their product.[19]

Consider, for example, how successful Nike has been in persuading people to buy their shoes. Nike advertisements don't give "just the facts," and they aren't simply selling a shoe. Instead, Nike, with its long line of famous athletes and famous slogan—"Just Do It"—is selling an identity, a life full of meaning and purpose. Nike has been successful because they know how to capture the imagination of their clients.

Modern marketing agencies have learned from practice what theologians such as Augustine and John Calvin have said for centuries: the human heart is restless, and it is a "factory of idols." While there are many ways in which we should avoid mimicking marketing agencies, the importance of appealing to humans as worshipers—and thus to such issues as identity and purpose—should not be lost in apologetics.

WHEN "REASONS" AREN'T ENOUGH

It often seems that someone has to *want* to believe before they will seriously listen to reasons why they should believe. This is because, as one recent author observed,

---

18. For a philosophical reflection on the "close relation between reason, faith and feeling," see Charles Taylor, "Reason, Faith, and Meaning," in *Faith, Rationality, and the Passions*, ed. Sarah Coakley (Malden, MA: Wiley-Blackwell, 2012), 26.

19. See Smith, *Imagining the Kingdom*, 76. To make this point in class, I (Josh) often use excerpts from a fascinating series produced by PBS titled *The Persuaders*.

it is human nature to "change our beliefs to fit our loves," and to be "less ready to change our loves to fit our beliefs."[20] We recently spoke with a student who had approached a skeptical friend from his hometown armed with a step-by-step argument for Christianity written by one of Christianity's foremost apologists. He was very excited to guide his friend through the impenetrable argument he had found, but he returned to school disappointed. His friend wasn't convinced at all.

The student's problem wasn't so much that he didn't prepare a thoughtful enough presentation; it was more that his expectations for what the logical argument he had found would achieve. The student wasn't wrong in thinking that presenting evidence is an important aspect of apologetics, but, as he discovered, when it came down to it, what made or broke his argument was the fact that his friend just didn't *want* to believe.

What makes someone *want* to believe? How do we, to refer back to Augustine, appeal to someone who has disordered desires—disordered loves? If apologetics has too often overemphasized the head and neglected the heart (to use the popular modern distinction), what might a holistic apologetic that appeals to people as thinkers, believers, and, ultimately, worshipers look like?

Oxford professor of science and religion Alister McGrath offers a balanced, holistic approach to apologetics, explaining that although rational argumentation will always be an essential part of apologetics and was especially important during the modern era, in our late modern context "other aspects of the Christian faith need to be recognized—above all, its powerful imaginative, moral, and aesthetic appeal." McGrath points out that emphasizing such aspects of Christianity is certainly not an innovation to be eyed with suspicion, for "older Christian writers, particularly those who lived during the Middle Ages and Renaissance, placed a high value on biblical stories and images in teaching the faithful." And although "the rise of modernity caused these both to be devalued . . . the later rise of postmodernity has led to a rediscovery of their power."[21]

As McGrath is careful to explain, we are not suggesting that an apologetic approach should exclude any rational argumentation and focus merely on telling stories and sharing personal experiences. Far from it. Yet in view of the tendency of many modern forms of apologetics to confuse the ability to make an argument with the ability to persuade, it is necessary to highlight other forms of persuasion, for the art of persuasion can't be boiled down to simple logic or a list of the evidences. The complexity and diversity of the world we live in calls for the Christian to think deeply about how to engage the world from a diversity of angles.

---

20. Gregory E. Ganssle, *Our Deepest Desires: How the Christian Story Fulfills Human Aspirations* (Downers Grove, IL: InterVarsity, 2017), 6.

21. McGrath, *Mere Apologetics*, 128.

Story and Imagination

Scripture is full of encounters in which one person appeals to others' imaginations in order to make a point in a way that will capture their hearts. For instance, after David sinned with Bathsheba, the prophet Nathan could have simply confronted him with a list of his sins and their logical consequences: "You, king, are a liar, an adulterer, and a murderer, and you will reap what you have sown!" In doing so, Nathan would have been speaking truthfully. Yet he took a different route: he made an appeal to David's heart by telling him a story (2 Sam 12:1–13).

Likewise when Jesus, during his earthly ministry, spoke of the Father's love and commanded his disciples to love their enemies, he could have simply stated those concepts as propositions. Instead, however, he illustrated them by telling the parables of the good Samaritan and the prodigal son (Luke 10:25–37; 15:11–32).

Most remarkably of all, the entire Bible itself does far more than present propositional statements and rules. God not only inspired his Word to include propositional truths, appealing to us with arguments and evidences; he also inspired his Word to include appeals made with poetry, songs, wisdom, and stories. Among these appeals, the narrative form of the Bible particularly stands out.[22] Much of Scripture is made up of different kinds of stories, and in fact, the entirety of Scripture itself tells one grand story of redemption. This in no way puts propositions in a backseat. As Kevin Vanhoozer writes, "The truth of God's word is not merely but *richly* propositional. Scripture summons the intellect to accept its propositions, but it also summons the imagination to *see*, *feel*, and *taste* them as well."[23] The diversity of approaches presented in the Bible reminds us of one of the themes you'll find throughout this book—that you should be equipped with a diversity of apologetic tools that appeal not only to different kinds of people but to different facets of the same person.

Stories are not simply something for children or less intellectual types of people. Nor do stories just function as an illustration or metaphor for the "real thing." Biblical scholar N. T. Wright has explained that stories are important because, by affecting how we see and relate to the world around us, they ultimately have a strong effect on how we live our lives. Stories are "a basic constituent of human life; they are, in fact, one key element within the total construction of a worldview."[24] Foundational to our worldview—the way we see and interpret the

---

22. Scholars have pointed out that even in the epistles, there is often a narratival substructure. This is especially true in many of Paul's letters. See Richard Hays, *The Faith of Jesus Christ: The Narrative Substructure of Galatians of 3:1–4:11* (Grand Rapids: Eerdmans, 2002).

23. Kevin J. Vanhoozer, *The Drama of Doctrine: A Canonical-Linguistic Approach to Christian Theology* (Louisville: Westminster John Knox, 2005), 291.

24. N. T. Wright, *The New Testament and the People of God: Christian Origins and the Question of God* (Minneapolis: Fortress, 1992), 38.

world—are the stories we believe we are in. Ask someone a universal question like, "Why are we here?" or "What should we be doing?" and if you listen closely, you'll hear them tell a story.[25] Listen to a scientist explain a theory, and you'll hear him tell a story that pieces all the information together. Listen to a song, look at a piece of art, or try to understand the actions of a friend, and you'll find yourself thinking in terms of a story. Thus, Wright, far from presenting an idiosyncratic view, makes his point based on a universal aspect of human nature: we all tell stories because they are foundational for how we perceive and relate to the world.[26] Alasdair MacIntyre makes a similar point in his seminal book *After Virtue*: "Man is in his actions and practice, as well as in his fictions, essentially a story-telling animal . . . [We] can only answer the question, 'What am I to do' if [we] can answer the prior question 'Of what story or stories do I find myself a part?'"[27]

Charles Taylor on Narrative

Canadian philosopher Charles Taylor also stresses the importance of story, explaining that everyone believes a story about their life and about history itself: "We can't avoid . . . [master] narratives. The attempt to escape them only means that we operate by an unacknowledged, hence unexamined and uncriticized, narrative. That's because we (modern Westerners) can't help understanding ourselves in these terms . . . Our narratives deal with how we have become what we are; how we have put aside and moved away from earlier ways of being."

Taylor explains that when people say things like "that approach is medieval" or "that's a progressive thought" or "she is ahead of her time," and so on, they are speaking from a narrative—a coming-of-age story about humankind developing from a corrupt and barbaric way of life into one that is sophisticated and enlightened. Likewise, when people bemoan that things aren't like they used to be in the good old days and that people no longer have the moral fiber or a clear sense of meaning they used to, they are speaking from a "reactionary" narrative.

How does one counter master narratives such as these? Taylor explains that because "various tellings of the story of how we have become carry this sense of secularity as an inevitable consequence," we must challenge these narratives with "another story."[28]

---

25. See Alasdair MacIntyre, *After Virtue: A Study in Moral Theory*, 3rd ed. (Notre Dame: University of Notre Dame Press, 2008), 204–18.

26. Wright, *New Testament and the People of God*, 40; see McGrath, *Mere Apologetics*, 138–48.

27. MacIntyre, *After Virtue*, 216; also 212–13. See Charles Taylor, *Sources of the Self: The Making of the Modern Identity* (Cambridge, MA: Harvard University Press, 1989), 47–52.

28. Charles Taylor, "Afterword: *Apologia pro Libro suo*," in *Varieties of Secularism in a Secular Age*, ed. Michael Warner, Jonathan VanAntwerpen, and Craig Calhoun (Cambridge, MA: Harvard University Press, 2010), 300 301.

For this reason, stories are a particularly important avenue for Christians to challenge how unbelievers view the world.[29] By telling an effective story, a Christian can invite an unbeliever to drop their weapons, come in, and listen with an open mind and heart. In this way, stories grant an unparalleled opportunity to challenge an unbelievers' basic assumptions about life.[30] An excellent example of this is the way C. S. Lewis, in his series *The Chronicles of Narnia*, portrays Christ in the character Aslan, capturing the reader's imagination while their defenses are down. Part of the reason Aslan the lion is such a powerful character is that people don't see him coming.

In apologetics, stories are not only effective for subverting other false stories, but perhaps even more significantly for striking at people's hearts and casting a vision of the good life that appeals to the end for which we were created. Here again James K. A. Smith is helpful:

> A vision of the good life captures our hearts and imaginations not by providing a set of rules or ideas, but by painting a picture of what it looks like for us to flourish and live well. This is why such pictures are communicated most powerfully in stories, legends, myths, plays, novels, and films rather than dissertations, messages, and monographs . . . This isn't to say that the cognitive or propositional is a completely foreign register for us . . . [However, it] is easily reduced and marginalized as just more 'blah-blah-blah' when our hearts and imaginations are captured by a more compelling *picture* of the good life—the way it's hard to listen to someone talking when the television is on, with its blinking images functioning as magnets for our attention.[31]

Have you ever been talking to someone about Christian evidences and felt like all they hear you saying is "blah-blah-blah"? It has happened to us on numerous occasions. You may think the answer is to dump more evidence on them, but we remind you of the story we told above about the student who was disappointed because his friend didn't find his evidence convincing. If someone is blowing off the evidence you are presenting or is lethargic about your argument, simply rattling off more evidence or logical syllogisms will often only make the "blah-blah-blah" sound louder (and probably just more annoying!). We often

---

29. For a more detailed argument for how narrative is central to all of life and cannot be simply translated into other forms without losing something, see Charles Taylor, "How Narrative Makes Meaning," in *The Language Animal: The Full Shape of the Human Linguistic Capacity* (Cambridge, MA: Harvard University Press, 2016), 291–319.

30. See Wright, *New Testament and the People of God*, 40; Smith, *Imagining the Kingdom*, 58.

31. Smith, *Desiring the Kingdom*, 53–54.

have to give people reasons to want to believe before we can give them reasons for why they can believe.

Apologetics in Corporate Faithfulness and Communion

In chapter 6, we saw how the corporate faithfulness of the church serves as its own apologetic. The church doing life together—a visual and experiential apologetic for the gospel—is especially powerful because, as Kevin Vanhoozer observes, "It is easier to dismiss abstract theological concepts or argue against what appear to be outmoded doctrines; it is something else altogether to ignore real-life scenes that enact the truth of the gospel through racial reconciliation, familial forgiveness, social justice, and sacrificial love. It is difficult to contradict the ministry of reconciliation."[32] As holistic beings, humans are not simply, or even most fundamentally, looking for answers to their lists of questions; they are looking to love and be loved. This is why it is integral that individual Christians be planted within the church, for it is only in the church that the individual Christian, by communing together with other Christians in love and "proving" the wisdom of Christ by practical corporate demonstrations, can offer an apologetic that demonstrates the love of Christ in a way that no other apologetic can.[33]

Furthermore, the apologist should see the corporate practices of the church, including worship, baptism, and the celebration of the Lord's Supper, as visual apologetics for the gospel. As mentioned above, all humans worship and desire something ultimate, and oftentimes that object is the wrong thing. A well-led service reorients our desires, turning us from false idols and aiming us beyond this world to the God we were created for. Baptism, as a part of worship, is a visual display of Christ washing away our sins and guilt so that we can live transformed lives in deep community with other believers. We should also not forget the picture Jesus has commanded us to reenact in order that we might remember him and proclaim his return:

> The Lord Jesus, on the night he was betrayed, took bread, and when he had given thanks, he broke it and said, "This is my body, which is for you; do this in remembrance of me." In the same way, after supper he took the cup, saying, "This cup is the new covenant in my blood; do this, whenever you drink it, in remembrance of me." For whenever you eat this bread and drink this cup, you proclaim the Lord's death until he comes.[34]

---

32. Kevin Vanhoozer and Owen Strachan, *The Pastor as Public Theologian: Reclaiming a Lost Vision* (Grand Rapids: Baker, 2015), 175.

33. See Vanhoozer and Strachan, *Pastor as Public Theologian*, 174.

34. 1 Corinthians 11:23–26.

By celebrating the Lord's Supper, the church points to and enacts for the world our unity in Christ, the sweetness of fellowship with him, and the life-giving hope of the gospel and the Lord's promises.

The visible appeals the church makes as a body—worship, baptism, and Communion—are actually more traditional than what have sometimes been called the "traditional proofs." Not all will find the corporate gathering and practices of the church convincing, but as we've already seen, no proof of any kind is convincing to everyone. For many people, the communal practices of the church can serve as a powerful visual appeal to humans as worshiping beings.

APOLOGETICS, REASON, AND EVIDENCE

What we are offering in this book is not a narrowing of apologetics, but rather a wider, holistic apologetic vision in which the people of God demonstrate the truth of the gospel by living out the implications of the cross in word and deed, presenting rigorous arguments, continuing in our faithful practices, showing compassion for others, and persevering in the truth.[35]

Unfortunately, some who resonate with an apologetic that emphasizes that people are more than just brains have swung the pendulum too far in the other direction, rejecting the use of evidence-based appeals altogether. Some have claimed that we simply need to tell the gospel story and allow God to change hearts. Others, sounding the siren of a postmodern age, have declared that in this new era, logic or evidence given in defense of the truth of the gospel will no longer be effective, and so we should limit ourselves to telling Christian truth in story form. There is substance to some of these objections and much truth to be taken from them, but, as already stressed, entirely dismissing evidence-based appeals is not wise.

Native Rationality versus Cultural Rationality

In chapter 7, we introduced the distinction between *native rationality* and *cultural rationality*. Native rationality describes the universally shared internal mechanisms that work to produce basic beliefs such as "the reality of the external world, the existence of other human beings, and perhaps . . . a basic distinction between right and wrong as well."[36] People seem to develop these beliefs instinctively or spontaneously rather than through logical deduction. The reason humans have this native rationality is that they are created by God and

---

35. See Kevin Vanhoozer, "Theology and Apologetics," in *New Dictionary of Christian Apologetics*, ed. W. C. Campbell-Jack and Gavin McGrath (Downers Grove, IL: InterVarsity, 2006), 42.

36. Richard Lints, *The Fabric of Theology: A Prolegomenon to Evangelical Theology* (Grand Rapids: Eerdmans 1993), 118.

live in the world he created. If it were not for the corruption of sin, we would not suppress our knowledge of God (Rom 1:18–32) and all would believe in God in the same spontaneous way. As you may recall, cultural rationality refers to the frameworks assumed by a culture that "further define the sorts of things" those in that culture "consider it plausible to believe."[37]

Basic Logic versus Frameworks of Rationality

Similar to the difference between native rationality and cultural rationality is the difference noted in chapter 5 between *basic logic* and *frameworks of rationality*. Basic logic is what is used in elementary mathematics and in certain assumed rules for communicating and thinking that seem to be universal. Frameworks of rationality (or patterns of rationality) are broader assumed systems of thought linked to specific historical and social locations that people (consciously or unconsciously) operate under, influencing how they make and receive arguments.

Here's an example of what we're talking about. All humans, because they are created by God and live in his creation, have certain things in common. Imagine traveling to a premodern tribe untouched by the modern world. There will be a cultural distance that will make communication and persuasion difficult, but not impossible. If you try to communicate certain ethical values or beliefs, it will likely require long discussions in which you learn the foreign premodern framework, thus enabling you to make contextualized appeals.

However, if you try to communicate with more basic types of logic, then it will be far easier. For example, if you give tribespeople two pieces of food and then two more pieces of food, the result will be the same cross-culturally: they will have four pieces of food. Likewise, if you establish that a spear is longer than a knife, everyone will rightly assume that the spear cannot at the same time be shorter than the knife.

As demonstrated in the examples above, when we attempt to discover and articulate some basics of logic that exist across cultures, we are in some sense asking the questions, "Across the experience of those in all cultures, what functions as native rationality? Where do different cultural frameworks all tend to overlap?" These questions take us to three basics of logic.

1. **Law of identity**—"A is A" (or "whatever is A is A"). What is this getting at? The law means that all things have certain qualities that can be described—qualities that set them apart from everything else. Without such qualities, we could not identify something in the first place.

---

37. Lints, *Fabric of Theology*, 118.

2. **Law of noncontradiction**—"A is not non-A." A baseball bat cannot be at the same time taller than a yardstick and shorter than a ruler. In other words, "If A is true, then A is not false." Note: This does not mean that paradoxes, which initially appear to be contradictory yet ultimately express something that is true, ought to be rejected. We find many truths expressed in the form of paradox in Scripture.[38]

3. **Law of the excluded middle**—"Either A or non-A" (or "something must be either A or it is not A"). Something is either true or it is false.

To deny these basics of logic is to preclude basic communication and persuasion. In chapter 5, we discussed the need to use different apologetic maps to lead people to the gospel. Denying basic logic would be like denying the basics needed to read any type of map. If you deny that there is any such thing as "right" and "left" or "north" and "south," it doesn't matter what type of map you draw—it won't help. Maps can and should be drawn differently, depending on the circumstances, yet all maps require that some baseline universal assumptions be made.

To use a different analogy, someone might, swerving into the opposite lane of traffic, say, "I choose not to believe the car that I appear to be heading toward is really there." Regardless of what that person believes, the basic reality is that they are going to run into another car and either die or be seriously wounded. Reality does not bend for sincere but wrongheaded beliefs. Some basic logic is generally assumed cross-culturally.

A person can be intelligible within a variety of frameworks of rationality, but only if they accept the basics of logic outlined in the previous section. As Alasdair MacIntyre explains, basic laws of logic are a *necessary* condition for rationality. At the same time, however, they are not a *sufficient* condition for rationality. Whenever someone attempts to justify any action, philosophy of life, or religious belief as "rational," they must appeal to something more than just the basic laws of logic. Disagreement about what is or is not "rational" or even how a "rational discussion" should proceed in such matters centers not on the basic laws of logic but on this "something more" that must be appealed to over and above those laws.[39] This is one of the reasons, as we will see in the forthcoming chapters (especially in ch. 10), that what we will call an "inside out" approach is important.

---

38. For a noteworthy work on paradox, see Richard P. Hansen, *Paradox Lost: Rediscovering the Mystery of God* (Grand Rapids: Zondervan, 2016).

39. See Alasdair MacIntyre, *Whose Justice? Which Rationality?* (Notre Dame, IN: University of Notre Dame Press, 1988), 4. For a similar point in regard to morality and laws, see Michael J. Sandel, *Justice: What's the Right Thing to Do?* (New York: Farrar, Straus and Giroux, 2009); Steven D. Smith, *The Disenchantment of Secular Discourse* (Cambridge, MA: Harvard University Press, 2010).

If someone denies the basics of logic outlined above, which some have attempted to do, it can be helpful to attempt to explain the self-refuting nature of their claim by asserting that in the course of the conversation they have to assume basic logic in order to argue against it. Reality pushes against their claim.

As we've seen so far, in apologetics the question "why" is very important, because there are a wide variety of factors that lead people to believe what they do. In this particular case, we must explore why someone would deny basics of logic while also assuming them. Intellectual questions can often mask the emotional and experiential struggles that people face, and the wise will seek to get to the heart of the issue. At the same time, however, ignoring a person's intellectual questions will often only build a thicker wall between you and them and actually inhibit conversations about internal struggles they may be experiencing. We are much more than simply thinking beings, but we surely are not less; even though we don't *simply* think our way through life, we do *think*. Regardless of what might be driving someone internally, at times we must first help them work through their intellectual issues and show them the internal contradictions in their logic or worldview in order to give us opportunities to draw out the deeper issues plaguing them and causing their unbelief.

CONCLUSION

An important part of apologetics is to listen and learn about the person or people to whom you are speaking. This chapter has emphasized the need to recognize each person we talk to as a *holistic* being. We've seen that reasons and evidences are important to making a case for Christianity, but that at times apologetics has, in emphasizing the use of reason and logic to persuade, neglected the reality that humans are worshiping and desiring beings. Thus, we have emphasized the importance of combining appeals based on logic and evidence with the appeals of story, imagination, and identity. Because we minister to multidimensional people, we should adopt a multidimensional apologetic approach.

CHAPTER NINE

CONTEXTUALIZATION THROUGH THE LENS OF THE CROSS

> The gospel provides the stance from which all culture is to be evaluated;
> but the gospel . . . is always embodied in some cultural form.
>
> *Lesslie Newbigin,* Foolishness to the Greeks

UNIVERSAL TRUTH AND CONTEXTUALIZATION

The gospel message is true for all people and is the standard by which all cultures should be assessed. But the gospel message was revealed in a particular culture, and whenever it is shared, it is translated into the language and thought forms of the culture it is being shared in.

Apologetics at the Cross

1. Taking people to the cross through word and deed (ch. 6)
2. Cruciform humility before God and others (ch. 7)
3. Appealing to the whole person for the sake of the gospel (ch. 8)
4. **Contextualization through the lens of the cross (ch. 9)**

One of the threads that has run throughout this entire book is that while there is universal truth—manifest in the triune God and his revelation of himself—God has revealed himself in space-time history, that is, within human culture. For this reason, the Bible itself is full of examples of contextualization.

PAUL'S PHILOSOPHY OF MINISTRY

In the Bible, the apostle Paul's ministry offers some of the most immediate examples of contextualization. No single passage can comprehensively describe how Paul approached his ministry to unbelievers. However, for our particular purposes, 1 Corinthians 9:19–23 serves not only as a key text in understanding Paul's ministry but also as an important capstone to the previous eight chapters in our study of apologetics and a bridge to a survey of some of the major speeches given in the book of Acts:

> Though I am free and belong to no one, I have made myself a slave to everyone, to win as many as possible. To the Jews I became like a Jew, to win the Jews. To those under the law I became like one under the law (though I myself am not under the law), so as to win those under the law. To those not having the law I became like one not having the law (though I am not free from God's law but am under Christ's law), so as to win those not having the law. To the weak I became weak, to win the weak. I have become all things to all people so that by all possible means I might save some. I do all this for the sake of the gospel, that I may share in its blessings.

Paul wrote this to the Corinthian church as part of an explanation concerning how they should handle the question of eating meat sacrificed to idols and participating in banquets held in pagan temples. At first glance, a discussion about pagan sacrifices and banquets may seem to be irrelevant to apologetics, yet because Paul in this passage is giving certain guidelines for how he approaches ministry (for Paul, *ministry* meant a synthesis of missions, evangelism, apologetics, and theology applied to real-life situations), it provides principles that can be applied in support of cross-centered contextualization. In fact, New Testament scholar Eckhard Schnabel has derived from this passage two important principles that can be applied to apologetics.[1]

Apologists are "to take [their] listener seriously in a fully consistent manner" (see 1 Cor 9:19).[2] Though we are free to persuade in a wide variety of ways, we are to give up our rights and become "all things to all people" for the sake of winning others to Christ. As Georg Eichholz observes, Paul's determination to become all things to all people is not simply "tactical behavior," but rather "a consequence of the gospel" itself.[3]

---

1. See Eckhard J. Schnabel, *Early Christian Mission: Paul and the Early Church* (Downers Grove, IL: InterVarsity, 2004), 953–60.

2. Schnabel, *Early Christian Mission*, 953.

3. Georg Eichholz, *Die Theologie des Paulus im Umriss* (Neukirchen-Vluyn: Neukirchener Verlag, 1972), 49.

Schnabel elaborates on this point, explaining that when Paul uses the phrase "all things to all people," he means he will "[go] to people wherever they are at 'home' in terms of space, language or history."[4] Schnabel notes that because Paul seeks to identify with his listeners, he decides on the language he uses based on his audience's situation. Paul's goal is to take everyone to the gospel message, but he recognizes the need to distinguish between different groups of people, because people aren't inanimate objects we speak the gospel at; they are unique individuals who have, for example, different life experiences and need to be spoken to differently.[5]

Furthermore, the gospel rather than pragmatics sets the limits of and propels contextualization.[6] Paul is clear that to contextualize is not to abandon the gospel, since the very reason the Christian contextualizes is "for the sake of the gospel" (1 Cor 9:23). Throughout Paul's ministry, the gospel is central to his theology, witness, and persuasive efforts (Rom 15:6; 2 Cor 2:12; Gal 2:7; Phil 1:5; Col 1:23; 1 Thess 2:4). Paul's mode of operation is to adjust his style of living—without violating his theological or moral beliefs—in order to win over all different types of people.[7]

Thus, it should come as no surprise when we see Paul and the other apostles display the principles from 1 Corinthians 9 and take different approaches when addressing different audiences. This accommodation is especially apparent in the major speeches that Peter and Paul delivered to non-Christian audiences in the book of Acts.

A SURVEY OF THE MAJOR SPEECHES IN ACTS

Peter's Apologetic to the Jews[8]

In Acts 2:14–36, because Peter is addressing a diverse Jewish audience on the day of Pentecost, he builds his entire speech to be persuasive and understandable to the Jews in particular. Alister McGrath outlines three specific ways in which Peter reaches out to his Jewish listeners:

---

4. Schnabel, *Early Christian Mission*, 954.

5. See Schnabel, *Early Christian Mission*, 955.

6. Schnabel, *Early Christian Mission*, 959.

7. See Ben Witherington III, *Conflict and Community in Corinth: A Socio-Rhetorical Commentary on 1 and 2 Corinthians* (Grand Rapids: Eerdmans, 1995), 211.

8. For this and the following two sections, we owe a debt of gratitude for the four-part series of journal articles written by Alister McGrath: "Evangelical Apologetics," *Bibliotheca Sacra* 155, no. 617 (January 1998): 3–10; "Apologetics to the Jews," *Bibliotheca Sacra* 155, no. 618 (April 1998): 131–38; "Apologetics to the Greeks," *Bibliotheca Sacra* 155, no. 619 (July 1998): 259–65; "Apologetics to the Romans," *Bibliotheca Sacra* 155, no. 620 (August 1998): 387–98.

1. Peter establishes that Jesus has ushered in specific scriptural expectations of the Jewish people for events that would occur at the restoration of the kingdom.
   - The Spirit has been poured out.
   - Wonders and signs have occurred.
   - Jesus fits the criteria expected of "the king greater than David" (i.e., the Messiah).
2. Peter appeals to an authority relevant to the Jews: the prophetic passages of the Old Testament. Specifically, Peter refers to Joel 2:28–32; Psalm 16:8–11; and Psalm 110:1.
3. Peter uses language that would have been accepted and understood by his audience. In view of his Jewish audience, Peter uses certain loaded theological words—such as "Lord," "Christ," and "Holy Spirit"—without explaining them because he knows his audience will understand.

Peter, while keeping Jesus' life, death, and resurrection as the essential climax of his proclamation, speaks to his Jewish audience in ways they can understand. In this way, his persuasion is others-centered.

Paul's Apologetic to the Greeks

At the beginning of Acts 17 (vv. 2–3), we see Paul, in a similar fashion to Peter in Acts 2, using the Hebrew Scriptures in dialogue with Jews in order to support his proclamation of Jesus' death and resurrection. Later in Acts 17 (vv. 16–34), as Paul moves from the Jewish synagogue to the Greek Areopagus, he maintains his emphasis on Christ while changing his approach. First, as a starting point, he finds common ground with the Greeks. Then, after finding things he can affirm, he transitions to a proclamation of the gospel by subverting the assumptions they hold about the divine.[9]

The story begins in verse 16, when Paul, as he waits for Timothy and Silas, decides to walk around the renowned city of Athens. Paul finds himself provoked by the rampant idolatry of the city, so he soon makes his way to the marketplace and continues to visit there daily to dialogue with the people of Athens—in particular, the intellectuals of the day (v. 18). These intellectuals don't understand what Paul is talking about, so they do what many people do when they don't understand someone else's view: they make fun of him, and some even call him a "babbler." Yet because they are intrigued by the strange

---

9. Thanks to Darrell Bock, whose lectures and personal conversations about this passage have informed and spurred reflection that resulted in this section on Acts 17.

things Paul has to say, they decide to take Paul before the prestigious council called the Areopagus so that he can explain his teaching further.[10]

In the second half of verse 22, as Paul stands before the Areopagus, he begins his speech: "People of Athens! I see that in every way you are very religious." The Greek word translated in the NIV as "very religious" is actually a bit ambiguous, because it has a range of possible meanings. In some contexts, it can be used positively and mean something like "religious" or "devout," while in other contexts, it can mean something akin to "superstitious." Paul might have even chosen the word because of its flexibility—such a choice would certainly align with the way Paul seems to be doing what he can in order to connect to his audience, and yet at the same time not give them a wholesale endorsement either.

Despite being provoked and mocked, Paul doesn't simply dismiss the Athenian culture; instead, he builds a bridge to it, even quoting the Athenians' own pagan philosophers and poets. As Paul delivers his speech, he uses three major strategies:

First, Paul relates to the culture. Paul has walked around Athens and studied the Athenian culture, so he knows how to build a bridge to relate to his audience.

- He relates to their *belief in supernatural beings.* The widespread presence of idols and temples in Athens testifies to a belief in a higher world. Paul can affirm this belief, for he knows from Scripture and experience that there is a supernatural world (Acts 17:22).
- He relates to their *desire to worship.* The Athenians both worship and see themselves as worshipers, which is a right desire, though Paul knows their worship is directed to the wrong object (Acts 17:23, 29).
- He relates to their *sense that they might be missing something.* In Acts 17:23, Paul points to their altar "TO AN UNKNOWN GOD," which they made because they recognized they might have been missing a god. Paul picks up on this and essentially says, "You're exactly right—you are missing a God! Let me tell you about him."
- He relates to their *belief in a god who is the source of all life.* In Acts 17:28, Paul quotes one of their philosophers and then one of their poets in reference to Zeus: "For in him we live and move and have our being," and "We are his offspring." Even though both statements were written in reference to Zeus, Paul sees that there is truth in them only if they are applied to the true God, who is the creator and sustainer of all humankind.

---

10. See F. F. Bruce, "Areopagus," in *New Bible Dictionary*, 3rd ed., ed. I. H. Marshall et al. (Downers Grove, IL: InterVarsity, 1996), 79.

Second, Paul challenges the culture. Paul subverts aspects of the Athenian culture's central beliefs: he first affirms that they have some things right, but then he demonstrates that other behaviors and beliefs they hold contradict those correct beliefs.

For example, drawing on the opening chapters of Genesis, Paul challenges the Athenian culture by using one of their own beliefs to demonstrate that God must, despite their attempt to suggest otherwise, be independent from his creation. In so many words, Paul reasons as follows: "Since you affirm that there is a God who made us and is therefore greater than us, then how can any of you build a temple that would house him or serve him, as if he needed anything?" (see Acts 17:24–25). Paul is not saying that God can't reveal himself in a particular place, like a temple or tabernacle. Instead, Paul's critique is aimed at a quid pro quo type of religion, which, by suggesting that humans can solicit favor from God by creating temples for him and offering sacrifices to him, puts God in humans' debt and allows them to limit and control him. Yet if God made this world and the creatures in it, surely he wouldn't need his creatures to take care of him (rather, he would need to care for his creatures!). Paul makes a similar point in verse 29, where after quoting the Greeks' own poet, who says that all people are children of God, Paul reasons that if that's the case—if humans are made by God and are therefore created beings—then it doesn't make any sense for them to try to make their own gods.

Paul also challenges the Athenians' ability to see the divine clearly. He points out that their claim to intellectual superiority is inconsistent with the uncertainty about the divine that led them to build an altar to an unknown god. He asserts that they are right to sense an unknown God because they do not yet know the true God. In verses 26 and 27 in particular, Paul emphasizes the uncertainty of the citizens of Athens (as reflected by the NASB's translation of verse 27: "if perhaps they might grope for Him"). The overall picture in verse 27 is not positive, especially where Paul speaks of humankind groping, as if in the dark, after God. Yet Paul knows what the Athenians do not yet know: God is near. He has not left humankind groping in the dark, but has revealed himself to humankind in the person of his Son. This leads us to Paul's third strategy.

Third, Paul connects his audience to Jesus. Paul concludes by calling the Athenians to repent and turn from their idolatry (Acts 17:30). Notice how in contexts where his audience accepted the authority of the Hebrew Scriptures, Paul speaks about the law (e.g., in Romans and Galatians) and reasons directly from the Scriptures (Acts 17:1–15), but here, Paul focuses on idolatry.

Even though Paul has been careful to study the Athenians and speak in a way that is relevant to them, relevance is not his primary concern—nor is acceptance.

Speaking before the Areopagus is no mere intellectual exercise for Paul. He is not fulfilling a lifelong dream of getting a seat at the academic table, nor is his ambition to be esteemed by the cultural elites. Because relevance and acceptance are not his primary concerns, Paul isn't afraid to confront the Athenians with a strong warning: a day is coming when Jesus, who rose from the dead, will return, and when he does, he will "judge the world" (Acts 17:31).

Relevance should not be an end to itself. Not only is making relevance one's ultimate goal one of the quickest ways to become irrelevant, but it also debases contextualization, transforming it into a sinful attempt to be accepted by the world.

Paul's Apologetic to the Romans

Another example of the way Paul contextualizes the gospel message can be seen in his defense of Christianity before Roman authorities. The Romans viewed early Christians as immoral and seditious, partly because they misunderstood Christian worship and practices and partly because the Christians refused to participate in their "imperial cult." The Romans' negative view of Christians meant that as Paul defended Christianity before them, he would need to address certain pragmatic concerns—specifically, he would need to make it clear that Christianity was not dangerous to the empire and that logic demanded that Christians be granted similar allowances for worship as the Jews.

Studies have demonstrated how Paul's speeches to Roman officials in Acts 24–26 conform to patterns that were common in Roman legal proceedings.[11] Paul, himself a Roman citizen, understood the Roman authorities' domain of discourse and what form of argumentation they would respond to.

Paul before Felix—Acts 24:1–26. Brought before the Roman governor Felix by a lawyer named Tertullus for allegedly stirring up trouble and participating in a "sect," Paul responds to each accusation by engaging within the rules of the Roman legal context he found himself in. Paul first explains that it can be easily verified that he was not stirring up trouble, and then he asserts that in the eyes of the Roman law, his religious practices are no different from those of the Jews bringing charges against him: he too worships the God of the Old Testament Scriptures and believes in a future resurrection. Significantly, in his defense Paul appeals to Roman "rules of evidence" when he states that, as Alister McGrath writes, "his accusers (some Asian Jews) were not present to witness against him."[12]

---

11. See, for example, Bruce W. Winter, "Official Proceedings and the Forensic Speeches in Acts 24–26," in *The Book of Acts in Its Ancient Literary Setting*, ed. Bruce W. Winter and Andrew D. Clarke (Grand Rapids: Eerdmans, 1993), 305–26; cf. McGrath, "Apologetics to the Romans," 387–98.

12. McGrath, "Apologetics to the Romans," 391.

Paul before Festus—Acts 25:1–12. A few years later, Felix is succeeded by Festus, and Paul must again defend both himself and the gospel itself against misrepresentation. Paul makes his defense by repeating familiar elements of the appeal he had made to Felix. He says he has done "nothing wrong against the Jewish law or against the temple or against Caesar" (Acts 25:8). Again, in making an appeal to Caesar, Paul is operating within the "rules" of his context.

Paul before Agrippa—Acts 25:23–26:32. Festus seeks the advice of the Jewish political leader Agrippa, who is interested in hearing Paul, so Paul is brought before Agrippa in a judicial hearing. In order to offer a persuasive apologetic, Paul carefully constructs it based on the "judicial rhetoric" his audience would be familiar with.[13] Beyond the judicial form of his argument, Paul also appeals to Moses and the prophets, since he knows Agrippa, himself a Jew, believes in them. As New Testament scholar Ben Witherington notes, "The form of [Paul's] speech is determined by the social context, but the content is largely determined by the primary audience and what the orator Paul wants to accomplish by his testimony."[14] Paul's aim is not simply to defend himself and the Christian faith, but also to lead his audience to the gospel so that they might repent and believe.

Like most Christians today, you probably won't find yourself being brought before government authorities in hearings or trials any time soon. However, many people you encounter, like the Roman authorities of Paul's day, will have rejected Christianity based on misunderstandings and false portrayals of the faith, and it will be important for you to be able to clear up those misunderstandings, just as Paul did. Also, just like the "rules of engagement" in the Roman Empire, there are rules of engagement in every contemporary context that apologists must pay careful attention to if they want to successfully convey the gospel message to the audience.

The book of Acts displays the principles of 1 Corinthians 9 in action. When sharing the gospel, the early church faithfully drew different apologetic maps for different apologetic audiences. As Alister McGrath asserts, it is crucial for us in the pluralistic age we live in to recognize that "we cannot simply treat all those who dislike or reject Christianity as being one homogeneous group."[15] No two people have the exact same reasons for rejecting Christianity, and as a result, no two people will find the same arguments for accepting Christianity equally persuasive. The very same argument one person finds extremely compelling,

---

13. See W. R. Long, "The Trial of Paul in the Book of Acts: Historical, Literary, and Theological Considerations" (PhD diss., Brown University Press, 1982), 237–39; Ben Witherington III, *The Acts of the Apostles: A Socio-Rhetorical Commentary* (Grand Rapids: Eerdmans, 1998), 736–38.

14. Witherington, *Acts of the Apostles*, 736.

15. Alister McGrath, *Mere Apologetics: How to Help Seekers and Skeptics Find Faith* (Grand Rapids: Baker, 2012), 67.

another person will find utterly unconvincing, which is why understanding your audience—whether it's a group or an individual—is so important.

In their speeches, the apostles, while embracing universal truth—namely, the gospel of Jesus Christ—did not use a universal apologetic. The apostles did not appeal to a one-size-fits-all apologetic that could be applied to whomever and whatever situation they found themselves in. Rather, they tailored their presentation of the *universal* truth of the gospel to a *particular* audience.

The more we've interacted with people through the years, the more we've come to appreciate the diversity of opinions concerning what constitutes a persuasive case. Different people simply find different things convincing. An apologist with a "me-centered" approach to apologetics says, "I find this argument the most persuasive to me personally, so I am going to use it," but an apologist with an "others-centered" approach will be willing to adjust depending on the person or the context that he is speaking into.

We'll return to the topic of contextualization and culture in the next chapter. However, the idea that your apologetic approach should differ depending on the culture is likely new to many of you, and therefore requires that we first address two important questions: (1) What do we mean by the term *culture*? and (2) How significant are cultural assumptions to apologetics?

CAN'T YOU SMELL THAT? UNDERSTANDING CULTURE

The assumptions and attitudes of the culture we live in orient and shape us so deeply that we usually don't give much thought to them. Without us normally being aware of it, our culture provides a grid by which we live and interact with the world around us. While the term *belief* is a convenient way to describe these basic commitments we hold, using this term may be misleading. When someone says "I believe such-and-such," they are normally referring to a proposition they have thought about (at least to some extent) and can articulate. However, what we are referring to is a little different. It's more under the radar. We are referring to not simply a set of beliefs, but our sense of things, a world we inhabit, the interpretive frameworks we simply take for granted. As philosopher Charles Taylor puts it, these "taken for granted" frameworks are "not usually, or even mainly a set of *beliefs* which we entertain" but rather "the sensed context in which we develop our beliefs." In other words, these assumptions have "usually sunk to the level of such an unchallenged framework, something we have trouble often thinking ourselves outside of, even as an imaginative exercise."[16]

---

16. Charles Taylor, *A Secular Age* (Cambridge, MA: Harvard University Press, 2007), 549.

Let's start small to try to get a better handle on this concept. Growing up, I (Josh) never really gave much thought to eating with a fork and knife. I just assumed it was how everyone ate—that is, until my parents took me to a Chinese restaurant. Chopsticks forced me to rethink the assumptions I held about what constituted proper eating utensils. Later in life, a trip to Zambia similarly opened up another framework for proper dinner manners: no utensils were even necessary.

Alternatively, cultural frameworks can be compared to the fragrance within someone's own home. People rarely notice the smell of their house because they are used to smelling it; they grow accustomed to it. I can remember when I pastored a church in a rural area and visited some members who lived right beside cows grazing in a field. I asked them, "How can you stand the smell?" (I know, looking back on it, it probably wasn't the most sensitive thing to ask.) They replied, "What smell? Oh"—it took them a second to figure out what I was talking about—"the cows. We don't notice it anymore, unless we go on a trip for an extended time and then return home." *What smell?* I thought. *How can they possibly not smell it?*

In the same way that we don't notice familiar odors until someone says something about them, we usually don't notice many of the assumptions, attitudes, and beliefs we hold that have been formed by the culture we live in. Our culture is, in a sense, the very air we breathe. It gives us a framework for thinking, believing, and desiring that is so natural that we simply take it for granted. As apologists, it is important that we understand how people's assumptions and beliefs are often *historically* and *culturally* conditioned. As we mentioned earlier, the term *cultural plausibility structures* refers to the beliefs we deem plausible because the people around us support them. Consider the following illustration from Timothy Keller:

> Imagine an Anglo-Saxon warrior in Britain in AD 800. He has two very strong inner impulses and feelings. One is aggression. He loves to smash and kill people when they show him disrespect. Living in a shame-and-honor culture with its warrior ethic, he will identify with that feeling. He will say to himself, *That's me! That's who I am! I will express that.* The other feeling he senses is same-sex attraction. To that he will say, *That's not me. I will control and suppress that impulse.* Now imagine a young man walking around Manhattan today. He has the same two inward impulses, both equally strong, both difficult to control. What will he say? He will look at the aggression and think, *This is not who I want to be*, and will seek deliverance in therapy and anger-management programs. He will look at his sexual desire, however, and conclude, *That is who I am.*[17]

---

17. Timothy Keller, *Preaching: Communicating Faith in an Age of Skepticism* (New York: Viking, 2015), 135, emphasis in original.

Where does each man in this illustration get the external grid he uses to sort through the impulses he experiences? The answer is that neither of these two men are rejecting or accepting their impulses based on their "true selves," or are just doing what pleases them, irrespective of external influences. Both are choosing to express or suppress certain feelings and desires based on what their cultures and the people around them praise or censure: "They are choosing to be the selves their cultures tell them they may be."[18] This concept applies not only to the way people respond to competing internal desires, but also to how they determine what they consider a "good" or "persuasive" case for Christianity. Thus, the persuasive power of a Christian's apologetic approach depends on the assumed cultural grid of the individual they are speaking to.

For this reason, understanding cultural plausibility structures is vital for apologetics. When we interact with others, we are not engaging blank slates. We are talking to people who have adopted certain assumptions about the world—assumptions about how we should understand it and live in it. A person's cultural framework shapes their view on any given issue, the way they interpret evidence, and the way they receive an explanation. Thus, settling a disagreement is often not simply a matter of providing enough evidence to support some historical claim or proposition about reality. The person you're speaking with may not see your evidence as important or interpret it in the same way as you, because they have a different cultural lens that has caused them to see the world a certain way.

The challenging aspect of this is that these webs of beliefs are largely prereflective; in other words, they are unconsciously taken for granted as axiomatic truth: "Of course we use a fork and knife to eat. What else would we do?" Or to offer examples relevant to apologetics, "Of course my sexual impulses are trustworthy. Of course there are multiple ways to God. Of course a loving God would not condemn. Of course miracles can't happen. Of course science has disproved religion!" A list of these cultural "of course" statements could go on ad infinitum. To those who hold them, they seem obvious. Yet if one were to visit another culture or time, these "of course" statements (and the plausibility structures they are based on) would be different and, in fact, sometimes exactly the opposite of their modern Western counterparts: "Of course we use our hands to eat our food. Of course I can't always trust my sexual impulses. Of course there is only one way to God. Of course God will condemn the guilty. Of course miracles are real. Of course science has its limits in what it can teach us."

---

18. Keller, *Preaching*, 136. What we are getting at in this section is similar to what Charles Taylor refers to as our *social imaginary*. It is "our *sense* of things" and not simply what we believe, but rather "the way the universe is spontaneously imagined, and therefore experienced" (Taylor, *A Secular Age*, 325); see also Charles Taylor, "Afterword: *Apologia pro Libro suo*," in *Varieties of Secularism in a Secular Age*, ed. Michael Warner, Jonathan VanAntwerpen, and Craig Calhoun (Cambridge, MA: Harvard University Press, 2010), 308.

It is vital to learn how to point out the way these prereflective statements are different from culture to culture. In the West, when so many want to avoid ethnocentrism, helping unbelievers see that their baseline assumptions are not universal is an effective way to create some space for a deeper conversation about their beliefs.

WHAT'S NEXT?

Building on the work of Charles Taylor, Tim Keller points out that Christians too often do not recognize the existence of cultural frameworks through which even secular people filter evidences and proofs: "Secularity is not simply an absence of belief. Christians often accept this claim and respond by getting out their proofs and other rational bona fides. Not so fast . . . Secularism is its own web of beliefs that should be open to examination."[19] Once you've recognized that all people have frameworks, the question then becomes, "How do I get someone to open up and examine their own web of beliefs and assumptions?" The answer, which we will explain in great detail in the next chapter, is that you need to learn to step inside an unbeliever's cultural framework and work from the *inside out*.

---

19. Keller, *Preaching*, 126.

PART 3

THE PRACTICE OF APOLOGETICS AT THE CROSS

CHAPTER TEN

PREPARING TO ENGAGE (NOT SPIN) IN LATE MODERNISM FROM THE *INSIDE OUT*

Christianity does not set faith against thinking. It sets faith against assuming.

Timothy Keller, Twitter, August 28, 2014

LOOKING BACK AND PICKING UP WHERE WE LEFT OFF

To return to the house metaphor from the introduction, we are now approaching the final stage of our building project. In chapters 1–2, we built the biblical foundation of our apologetic house, and in chapters 3–4, we finished the base with a brief sketch of the history of apologetics. In chapters 5–9, we erected the walls and exterior of our house: chapter 5 discussed the various contemporary apologetics maps, and chapters 6–9 outlined a theological vision for apologetics assembled around the gospel itself.

We enter now the final section of the book, in which we will construct the most visible aspect of apologetics at the cross: the practical outworking and application of all we have discussed thus far. Returning to our home metaphor, it is time to install the most visible aspects of the building project: the paint, the flooring, and the furnishings—the features that everyone sees.

At the end of the last chapter, we discussed how culture subtly shapes us and provides us with an assumed framework through which we interpret life. In this and the subsequent chapter, we'll explore some significant cultural trends within late modernism and offer an approach for engaging with those trends.

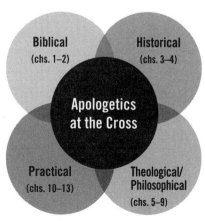

Biblical (chs. 1–2)

Historical (chs. 3–4)

Apologetics at the Cross

Practical (chs. 10–13)

Theological/ Philosophical (chs. 5–9)

Yet before providing some specific strategies for responding to the cultural trends of late modernism and the plausibility structures those trends have created, we need first to examine three general historical shifts—premodernism, modernism, and late modernism—and then discuss two salient aspects of late modernism: the *immanent frame* and what we've termed "the age of the spinmeister." At first it may seem that in exploring these three historical shifts and two aspects of late modern culture, we are taking an unnecessarily circuitous route to our destination, but stay with us: this is a strategic trip that will serve as an important backdrop for our discussion of how Christians can better engage unbelievers in this late modern era.

Once the backdrop has been set and you've learned how to engage others using what we have termed "inside out," the next chapter will survey some significant features of the current cultural situation in the West and apply what we have learned in this chapter in response to those cultural trends.

THREE GENERAL HISTORICAL SHIFTS: The Road to Late Modernism

Before we outline three basic periods in the history of Western culture, we must note that their boundaries are not etched in stone. Historical movements are never so neat that they can be encapsulated within a simple set of characteristics—nor, for that matter, are the people who live during those periods. The people who identify with these periods are diverse and do not agree with or exhibit every assumption of the period they live in. These admittedly simplified divisions are intended to help you get your feet on the ground as you embark on a deeper study of history and culture.

Premodernism

In the first period, the premodern era, people believed in the supernatural. People assumed that God or the gods had created the world and that there was a spiritual realm beyond nature; in fact, they saw nature as pointing beyond itself to a transcendent reality. Society took for granted that there was a purpose in the universe. Traditional and religious institutions were viewed as authorities that should be revered; they provided the ultimate frameworks through which people lived their lives.

These institutions were also central in forming closely knit communities. People did not see themselves simply as individuals, but rather as members of a corporate whole; the faith and obedience of individuals were viewed in light of how they impacted the community.

Many of these assumptions of the premodern era align well with Christianity—

particularly the belief in the supernatural, the emphasis on community, and the appreciation for tradition and religious institutions. However, during the premodern period, a more critical posture toward certain claims would have at times been advantageous. When fanciful myths went unchecked and traditional institutions slipped into a corrupt authoritarianism and oppression, some questioning was in order. But what emerged went far beyond simple reform; an intellectual revolution ensued.

Modernism

In the middle of the second millennium, significant thinkers began to question whether traditional authorities—the church, tradition, Scripture, and even community—could be trusted. Rejecting the truth propagated by these traditional authorities, individuals attempted to discover truth by laying aside all presuppositions and only believing what was self-evident. But naturally, the questions became, "What is self-evident? How can anyone know that what they see is reality? How does one know there is a God? How does anyone know anything?"

René Descartes, a defining figure of modernism, came to the conclusion that to know anything for certain, he would need to reject everything he thought he knew and start from the ground up. Ultimately, he determined that the basis for building knowledge needed to be the self. After all, Descartes reasoned, he could doubt everything he thought he believed to be true and even everything he perceived with his senses, but the one thing he could not doubt—the one thing he could be sure of—was that he was thinking, which meant that at the very least, he could be sure he existed. It was this line of reasoning that concluded in the familiar phrase, "I think, therefore I am." Modernism's turn from traditional, external institutions to the individual's own reasoning as the ultimate authority—widely referred to as "the turn to the subject"—was the spirit undergirding the Enlightenment's search for certainty.

Recall Immanuel Kant from chapter 4, another key figure of this period who represents the intellectual ethos of the Enlightenment. Kant declared his current age to have marked "man's emergence from his self-imposed immaturity," and he enjoined humankind: "Have the courage to use your own understanding!"[1] The ancient sources of wisdom were dethroned and in their place was crowned a new source of ultimate authority: individual reason. Humankind, the modern asserted, had come of age, and such authority figures as the church, tradition, and the Scriptures were no longer needed to guide them. People were now obligated to substantiate the beliefs they held by using reason alone.

---

1. Immanuel Kant, *An Answer to the Question: "What Is Enlightenment?"* (London: Penguin, 2013), 1.

A Cultural Shift and Apologetics

Alister McGrath explains how a major cultural shift in the West has rendered what used to be an effective approach to apologetics ineffective. During the modern era, which extended into the mid-1900s, apologists appealed primarily to reason, because reasoned arguments were considered most persuasive in their cultural context. Now, however, reason is no longer seen as supreme, and Christianity "faces a cultural context more complex and varied than that known by apologists in the middle of the twentieth century."[2] In such a context, McGrath asserts, it is "neither right nor possible" to share the gospel effectively with postmoderns by first getting them to see the world from a modern framework.[3]

In line with the approach we present in this book, McGrath proposes that instead of seeking a return to modernity as if it were a superior framework for viewing the world, Christians simply view modernity and postmodernity as two different cultural perspectives, both with strengths and weaknesses they will need to navigate.

Scientific methods were developed in the modern era and became a defining means of obtaining truth. One could discover all truth by following certain steps: ask a question you want the answer to, state a hypothesis, and plan a method to test your hypothesis with logic or empirical observation. Based on the data you obtain, your hypothesis will have either been proven or disproven, meaning you will need to form another hypothesis and repeat the process. In other words, after an individual carefully analyzed and tested the raw data with this carefully crafted system, the result they obtained would be unquestionable, absolute truth.

This method produced unprecedented results, as evidenced by the myriad of new scientific discoveries and technological advancements that followed its development. These breakthroughs engendered a confidence in this new enlightened rationality that spread to other areas, such as politics and ethics. For instance, some began to think that violent wars—often fought for perceived religions reasons—could be largely avoided. While wars based on religion formerly had no universal tool that could be used to seek resolution, now the apparently neutral ground of universal reason could be used to mitigate the bloodshed.

However, a problem arose when people began to universalize these scientific principles and expect the operation of the scientific method to produce truth in all areas of life. When this happened, many began to grow skeptical of modernism and started questioning some of its basic axioms. Most notably, adherents of

---

2. *Alister McGrath, Mere Apologetics: How to Help Seekers and Skeptics Find Faith* (Grand Rapids: Baker, 2012), 29.

3. McGrath, *Mere Apologetics*, 31.

Romanticism responded by critiquing the Enlightenment's mechanistic flattening out of life, choosing instead to emphasize emotion, nature, and aesthetics alongside the individual's primacy.

Another shortcoming of modernism also became apparent: In the wide scope of human experience and knowledge, there is very little that can be considered "raw facts"—basic math is perhaps the closest we can come. Furthermore, humans are not simply computer processors, and the most important questions in life cannot be solved by running them through an algorithm. As we emphasized in chapter 8, humans aren't just brains; they are complicated, holistic beings each with their own unique personalities, biases, traditions, and cultural perspectives on the world.

One of the hopes of the Enlightenment—that this new kind of knowledge rooted in universal reason and observation would lead to an orderly and peaceful society—was dashed when it eventually became apparent that human reason alone was unable to curb violence or provide a universal system of morality. Eventually, even beyond being disappointed in what Enlightenment rationality could achieve, people began to fear that the totalizing claims of the Enlightenment had actually become tools for oppression.

Late Modernism

The most widely used term for the period of time extending from the middle of the twentieth century to the present, *postmodernism*, tends to give the impression that the period we are now living in is the very opposite of modernism.[4] However, this is not the case, for while aspects of modernism have been called into question, key principles of the Enlightenment are still at work and, in fact, have only intensified. It is for this reason we think it best to refer to this period as *late modernism* rather than *postmodernism*.[5]

While history and culture are complex and resist singular explanations, it is safe to say that the present late modern culture has been profoundly shaped by the modern turn to the self. Like moderns, late moderns still set the autonomy of the individual and personal freedom over against the claims of tradition, religion, family, and community. The "self" still rules, but the shift to late modernism began to expose the alleged "neutrality" of early modernism as a myth and the notion that humans could control nature through precise reasoning and science as an illusion.

---

4. The terms *postmodernism* and *postmodernity* can at times be distinguished by writers, with postmodernism referring to developments in theory and culture and postmodernity to actual conditions in the culture. Yet it is our opinion that these two cannot be neatly separated.

5. See Charles Taylor, *A Secular Age* (Cambridge, MA: Harvard University Press, 2007), 716–17.

Some late moderns followed this critique of Enlightenment principles all the way to its extreme. They reasoned that since everyone approaches the external world with a preconceived framework for understanding it (created by everything from their own genes to the biases of their cultural environment), all that exists are individual perspectives. There is no universal *Truth* (with a capital "T") that we can know; we can only know what the *truth* (little "t") is for ourselves. At worst, this view leads to either arbitrary relativism (truth is totally dependent on the individual person) or hopeless skepticism (truth cannot be found). Thus, ironically, as James Hunter puts it, "The Enlightenment's own quest for certainty resulted not in the discovery of new certainties but rather in a pervasive astringent skepticism that questions all, suspects all, distrusts and disbelieves all."[6]

Taken to an extreme, radical skepticism leads to radical nihilism, the belief that there is no meaning. Though it may be the logical outworking of radical skepticism, radical nihilism is a difficult pill for most to swallow. It is impractical. While some accept radical nihilism in theory, the way they live their lives—as if they had purpose—is inconsistent with what they claim to believe. Notwithstanding the inconsistency issue, most people who adhere to relativism do so by degrees and do not completely deny all meaning or morality.

The portrait of a "liberal ironist" offered by philosopher Richard Rorty is an incisive picture of a paradox of our current age. In this term, the word *liberal* refers to the firm conviction of the late modern that violence against other people is morally repugnant, while the word *ironist* refers to the irony of them also asserting that no belief or desire can be held as decisively true.[7] Though the late modern concedes that people can adhere to a creed, they say it must be held loosely. To assert that you have personal access to *Truth* (with a capital "T") is not only intellectually suspect; it is morally wrong, because it will eventually lead to cruelty toward those who hold different beliefs. This is a portrait of the prototypical late modern: someone who has deep convictions about universal benevolence toward others yet is also averse to claiming they have access to Truth in any definitive sense.[8]

---

6. James Davison Hunter, *To Change the World: The Irony, Tragedy, and Possibility of Christianity in the Late Modern World* (New York: Oxford University Press, 2010), 206–7.

7. Richard Rorty, *Contingency, Irony, and Solidarity* (Cambridge: Cambridge University Press, 1989), xv. Thanks to Todd Wilson for directing us to Rorty's "liberal ironist."

8. The point being made by describing the liberal ironist is similar to what Charles Taylor refers to as the modern theorists' "strange pragmatic contradiction": "It seems that they are motivated by the strongest moral ideals, such as freedom, altruism, and universalism. These are among the central moral aspirations of modern culture, the hypergoods which are distinctive to it. And yet what these ideals drive the theorists towards is a denial of all such good. They are caught in a strange pragmatic contradiction, whereby the very goods which move them push them to deny or denature all such goods" (*Sources of Self: The Making of the Modern Identity* [Cambridge, MA: Harvard University Press, 1989], 88).

The late modern response to the hubris of modernity's quest to obtain certainty through human reason can certainly be viewed as a relief to Christians. Scripture is clear that humans are finite and sinful, and as a result, their perspectives are limited. Christians can also affirm the universal benevolence promoted in late modernism (which is itself actually an outgrowth of Christianity). And yet, even though Christians can draw on some important lessons and affirm aspects of late modernism, we must remember that most late moderns did not derive their rejection of modernism from Scripture and that, as we have seen, some have taken their critique of modernism too far. Ultimately, the gospel must supersede the prevailing assumptions of any period. With this in mind, the following chapter will survey how Christians ought to interact with salient features of late modernism.

Why It Matters

It would be a mistake to think all this talk of culture, traditions, and truth is something that only plagues graduate-level philosophy students or academics in tall ivory towers. The existing social structures and frameworks of belief that accompany late modernism have led to a far-reaching distrust of traditional authorities and a disdain for anything that seems to suppress personal desires.

Several years ago during my (Josh's) pastorate, a small group leader came to me and told me about a conversation she had with a high school student after a group meeting. She had confronted the girl about the guys she had been, to use the girl's phrase, "hooking up with." She had asked the student, "Why do you even go out with those sort of guys? They're clearly no good." The girl snapped back, "Who are you to tell me what the Bible says? Doesn't the Bible teach us not to judge others? And after all, who can really say that they're good or bad? I'm doing what I feel is right."

That response would sound strange to premodern or modern ears, yet today it is normal. We all know stories like that because they happen all the time—and not just in the secular corners of the country. That young woman grew up, not in a large city, in, say, the northeast, but rather in a small town in the Bible Belt. It's safe to say she had never read an academic treatise on post or late modernism, nor did she respond in the way she did because she was led to that perspective by deep reflection. She had not thought her way to her point of view; she had been led to it by cultural influences and social structures. It was just the air she breathed.

TWO INFLUENTIAL ASPECTS: Immanent Frame and the Age of the Spinmeister

Immanent Frame

Charles Taylor uses the term *immanent frame* to refer to how in the current cultural context people view everything in terms of a natural rather than a supernatural order. The modern social imagination, which is deeply imbedded in much of our culture, works from the assumption that while people can find significance or meaning in life (immanence), there is no higher, divinely given purpose that has been assigned to them (transcendence).[9]

A helpful way of understanding the immanent frame is to picture a two-story building. Our premodern ancestors lived in a two-story world. Humans lived on the first level but believed in the existence of a second floor—a higher realm. Theirs was an enchanted world where higher beings were assumed to be active and relevant to the affairs of everyday life. There was something greater beyond this life, a higher realm of existence that gave meaning and purpose to life. In contrast, today we live in a disenchanted, one-story world that denies the existence of the divine or the supernatural. In much of the West, the commonly shared habits, goals, and symbols of day-to-day life and the meaning commonly ascribed to it point us to the physical world around us and normally no further. Thus, as we inherit these habits, goals, and symbols from our culture, we consciously and subconsciously absorb (though mostly subconsciously) the drive to live for, long for, and learn of things on the first level.

And yet even within this one-story frame, some have reacted against the moral order of modernism, which seeks to offer meaning, significance, and morality without ultimate, transcendent meaning or an ultimate, transcendent God. Although some have found the disenchanted new moral order freeing, many others have found it uninspiring and feel it lacks "fullness."[10] These diverse attitudes have led to what Charles Taylor refers to as the "'nova' effect," which describes how, even within immanent frame, there has been a "multiplication of a greater and greater variety of different spiritual options."[11]

But even when religious activity is present, we still find ourselves in a *secular age*, an environment in which even the religious are strongly aware of the contestability of their beliefs. In this present age, it seems there is no position that cannot and should not be called into question from a variety of angles. In the next chapter, we will discuss more trends associated with the immanent frame, but for now it is enough to note that the contestability of beliefs in late modernism has made us more prone to doubt.

---

9. See Charles Taylor, "Afterword: *Apologia pro Libro suo*," in *Varieties of Secularism in a Secular Age*, ed. Michael Warner, Jonathan VanAntwerpen, and Craig Calhoun (Cambridge, MA: Harvard University Press, 2010), 307.

10. James K. A. Smith provides a helpful gloss for Taylor's usage of *fullness*: "A term meant to capture the human impulsion to find significance, meaning, and value—even if entirely within the immanent frame" (*How (Not) to Be Secular: Reading Charles Taylor* [Grand Rapids, Eerdmans, 2014,] 141).

11. Taylor, "Afterword: *Apologia pro Libro suo*," 306.

The Age of the Spinmeister

In addition to being characterized by the immanent frame, the current cultural context could also be described as "the age of the spinmeister." Many people, though they might not be able to fully articulate it, have been made skeptical and distrustful of any persuasive efforts because of what has been termed the "PR effect." The modern world has produced a professional industry of spinning news, press releases, commercials, and marketing campaigns that, on a regular basis, seek to change our perceptions. Though those in this industry may not intend to be devious or manipulative and may manage not to cross the line and tell outright lies, it can feel as if truth is not their primary concern. It seems that to them, persuading the general public into getting on board is more important than the truth—the end justifying the means. Facts are spun in order to convince us to buy a product—whether it be an idea, a worldview, a politician, or simply a pair of shoes. Hugh Heclo offers a list of the strategies that top public communication representatives use:

- Stay on a simple message (rather than dealing with complex realities).
- Appeal to emotions (rather than taking time to reason with the audience).
- "Frame" issues to steer people toward the desired conclusion (rather than informing them about the substance of any given issue).
- Project self-assurance (rather than admitting uncertainty or ignorance).
- Counterattack or change the subject (rather than trying to answer tough questions).
- Avoid self-criticism (rather than trying to correct your errors).
- Claim to have the whole answer (rather than admitting there is any independent expertise that is not on your side).
- Above all, talk to win (rather than to get at the truth of things).[12]

These techniques have become standard fare. This culture of spinning has deeply impacted the general mind-set of late moderns and has made us suspicious when anyone attempts to convince us of anything. "Once you realize you are the target of a sell-job," writes Heclo, "trust goes out the window. It's time to keep your hand on your wallet."[13] We intuitively sense that all "the rhetorical tricks, focus group-tested talking points, and slick strategies are a way of saying that [we] are not being taken seriously," and we can't help but respond with resentment and skepticism.[14] Though this visceral skepticism is pervasive, it may

---

12. Hugh Heclo, *On Thinking Institutionally* (Boulder, CO: Paradigm, 2008), 29.
13. Heclo, *On Thinking Institutionally*, 30.
14. Heclo, *On Thinking Institutionally*, 30

be especially acute among a younger generation strongly affected by the failed promises of spin culture—a generation that has become profoundly disillusioned. The cynical backlash against a culture of glibness is palpable.

Heclo elaborates on the effect that a culture of spin has had on the way we view persuasive efforts, observing a paradox: "the more professional and adept our leaders have become in plying the persuasive arts, the more distrustful their audience has become."[15] We find ourselves being skeptical when someone claiming authority tells us what we should think or believe. Most have discovered the hard way that if they don't keep their defenses up, they will fall prey to a sales job, only to have buyer's remorse set in. And when that happens one too many times, people begin to steel themselves so that they'll never be "had" again.

In a culture that, in its perpetual spinning to win over people's trust, ironically breeds *dis*trust, it can be hard for the unbeliever, when approached by a Christian, not to feel as though he is the target of a "Christian sales job." Some apologetic and evangelistic methods, especially when rigidly applied, give the nonbeliever a sneaking suspicion that even Christians are spinning, using the same modern sales techniques as everyone else. Though we trust this is not normally intentional, it is nonetheless the perception, and, truth be told, it is how Christians often approach persuasion. Christians, both in dealing with their own doubts and in trying to persuade skeptical friends, can end up just offering their own spin. Notice, for example, how eerily similar the list above sounds to the way many Christians approach apologetics: Project self-assurance and never admit uncertainty. Keep things as simple as possible and avoid nuance. Never admit weaknesses and always, *always* talk to win.

———

With these two features of contemporary culture—the immanent frame and the age of the spinmeister—in mind, we suggest that we as Christians need to do some deeper thinking about our posture toward other perspectives.

Option 1: A Spin. Some believers and nonbelievers hold their view of the world as what James K. A. Smith, summarizing Charles Taylor, refers to as a "spin": "an overconfident 'picture' within which we can't imagine it being otherwise."[16] And because those who adopt a spin see their perspective as simply "obvious" and don't understand how anyone could view things any other way, they tend to "smugly dismiss those who disagree" with them.[17] People so deeply absorb

---

15. Heclo, *On Thinking Institutionally*, 30.
16. Smith, *How (Not) to Be Secular*, 95.
17. Smith, *How (Not) to Be Secular*, 95.

their picture of or spin on the world as an underlying frame that, while their persuasive efforts may not be exactly the same as the manipulative, PR type of spin described above, which is consciously created, the final product can look similar.[18]

Holding and presenting your view of the world as a spin is a recipe for mutual caricature and unsympathetic listening. Spin makes entering into sustained mutual dialogue with those who hold different views difficult, if not impossible, because it inevitably leads to what Taylor refers to as "conversation-stoppers" (these tend to sound something like, "I have a three line argument which shows that your position is absurd or impossible or totally immoral").[19]

For example, I once heard a well-known apologist answer a question about suffering in a room full of university students with the prefatory remark that the problem of evil was an "easy one to handle," implying that nonbelievers were wrongheaded for even raising the issue. Of course, this is not to say that atheists don't offer their own conversation-stoppers, but our point is that for Christians and atheists alike, this kind of spin does more to close the door to authentic dialogue than it does to open it.

Option 2: A "Take." The second option is to recognize that our view of the world is a *take* and, while embracing a picture of reality and a certain way of inhabiting the world, to acknowledge both the contestability of our view and "the pull and tug" of alternative views.[20] Believers and unbelievers who inhabit the immanent frame in this way are willing to admit possible weaknesses of their own position, especially given the assumptions and plausibility structures of other "takes." When someone recognizes that there are different frameworks, which lead to different interpretations of both evidence and experiences, the conversations they have with those who hold views different from their own tend to be much more open and fruitful.

That said, all "takes" are not equal. Being willing to grant a certain degree of plausibility in other "takes" does not negate a Christian's ability to show the problematic aspects of those "takes" and demonstrate Christianity's deeper explanatory power. In the following chapters, you will learn a variety of ways the Christian "take" or worldview has the greatest explanatory power in response to certain key features of late modernism. In offering the Christian "take," however, we should also be aware that there are other "takes" that "make sense" to others, *given the larger framework they hold.*

---

18. See Taylor, *A Secular Age*, 555–57. This spin is produced by both believers and unbelievers; in *A Secular Age*, Taylor is most concerned to push back against the secular spin within the academy.

19. Taylor, "Afterword: Apologia pro Libro suo," 318. He notes, "This applies to both religious hard liners and atheist fundamentalists (e.g., the New Atheists)."

20. Smith, *How (Not) to Be Secular*, 94.

For example, in the next chapter we'll see that, to the Christian, the intuitive sense of morality, meaning, and beauty that humans have points to God. However, an atheist might explain this with evolutionary psychology, asserting that the human brain produces categories such as morality and beauty for the purpose of survival and reproduction. Or to offer one more example, a Christian sees the human desire for something beyond this life as evidence of the existence of another world, yet the non-Christian may simply see this desire as a case of "wish fulfillment." We believe other "takes" lack the explanatory power the Christian story has to offer, but given that we live in an era marked by pluralism, seeking to listen sympathetically and understand others who operate within different frameworks will lead to more open and fruitful interactions.

APOLOGETICS AT THE CROSS APPLIED: Tone and Contextualization

In this culture of spin, Christians have an opportunity to look radically different from most by refusing to spin as they seek to lead others to the gospel. It is certainly true that as apologists we seek to convince others, and there is a place for using technique in our persuasive efforts. However, as we have stressed throughout this book, our persuasion must first and foremost be informed by the cross. We will often startle others when, rather than taking our cues from our culture, we subvert the typical spin techniques that have become so commonplace. Compared to Hugh Heclo's abbreviated list of spin techniques, a cross-shaped approach to persuasion—what might be called an "apologetic PR"—would look quite different:

- Keep coming back to the cross (but be willing to deal with complex realities and questions).
- Never simply appeal to emotions in order to manipulate (but be sure to take time to understand the other person and deal with their questions in a way that treats them as holistic beings).
- Admit that you are looking at the world as a Christian (but communicate with them that you are willing to try to understand where they are coming from).
- Be humble and admit areas of personal weakness, uncertainty, or ignorance (while affirming that you have great confidence in your faith in Jesus for a variety of reasons).
- Be willing to discuss tough questions (rather than quickly counter-attacking or changing the subject)
- Be self-critical (rather than never admitting weaknesses).

- Admit limits in your knowledge (rather than acting as though you are an expert on every subject).
- Above all, speak with grace and truth for the good of the other person (rather than seeking simply to win).

This quick list provides a framework for our posture and tone in our communication and is therefore a good starting point, but we also need specific, practical strategies for engaging others within late modernism. How can we engage with different people's plausibility structures when they are alien to Christianity?

ENGAGING FROM THE INSIDE OUT

A Christian student recently asked me for help with a friend—let's call her Sarah—who was a self-described secular humanist. Whenever my student tried to approach Sarah about Christianity, she kept bringing up moral issues she had with Christianity, and eventually she even wrote out a reply that went something like this:

> Every week religious leaders are telling people they have to do such-and-such because God has commanded it. I think it's wrong to condemn anyone or seek to regulate their life like that—and especially not just because some supposed god or religion tells you to do so. I don't want to live that way; it doesn't even seem humane. Simply quoting a bunch of antiquated religious texts written by men over a long period of time isn't going to change my opinion. Of course, I don't think the Bible can be taken seriously, but that doesn't make me a relativist. In fact, I don't see us as that different. You validate your opinion and way of life by citing the Bible, and I validate mine by looking to my hopes and desires. If someone wants to become a priest or a prostitute or anything in between, though I *could* judge them, I don't. I just wish them the best and move on with my life. It has been fun chatting, but to be honest, I see Christianity as not only irrelevant but also dangerous because it dehumanizes people by suppressing their ability to make personal choices and find personal fulfillment in life.

How would you have responded? In particular, where would you have begun?
My student told me she was in the process of looking up ways she could respond. She wanted to demonstrate that the Bible is not filled with myths and errors. Her commitment to research these challenges and stress the Bible's historical reliability is to be applauded, and I commended her for it. However,

as she set off to find answers, we both agreed that Sarah could just as easily go online and find a list of reasons that the Bible can't be taken seriously.

We have seen this kind of interaction play out on a number of occasions, and we've noticed that while dealing with the details of historical issues is important and giving some quick points concerning the Bible's trustworthiness can help, it's not usually effective to start apologetic conversations with a drawn-out, detailed argument for the Bible's reliability. Often, when an apologist seeks to interact with someone who has assumed the "givens" of late modernism, he or she will need to begin by working with the other person's assumptions before they will even consider accepting the plausibility of the Bible or the traditional evidences for Christianity. Therefore, a different approach is needed.

The approach we suggest is what we've termed *inside out*—a frame of reference that the Christian can internalize and apply to a wide array of apologetic situations. In line with the others-centered approach we've been emphasizing, this approach begins with the apologist entering into the other person's own plausibility structures and engaging them within it. The goal of starting with the other person's assumptions is to create space so they can consider some of the problems with their own outlook and be willing to consider the plausibility of Christianity.

Notice how in the familiar "building block model" (represented in the graphic on the following page), apologetic conversations have a step-by-step feel to them. The apologist starts by establishing basic and universal logic and then proceeds to argue for general theism, present historical evidence for the Bible's reliability, and finally share the message of the gospel.

In contrast to the way the building block model places the gospel at the end of the interaction, the inside out model insists that the gospel and a robust Christian theology be at the center of apologetic interactions and woven into the dialogue throughout. Furthermore, this model suggests that apologists—instead of attempting to get unbelievers to build along with them based on a preconceived apologetic building plan or an assumed framework for rationality, which they may or may not share—focus on points where Christianity overlaps with the views of other people.

These two aspects of the inside out model allow a Christian's apologetic approach to be both gospel-centered and others-centered. While holding to a robust view of the gospel, the apologist places emphasis on understanding the other person's view in order to see where their framework has internal inconsistences and lacks the ability to cohere with human experience and history. In the graphic, the overlapping area represents common assumptions and connecting points that can be identified as things to affirm, while the area that does not overlap represents points at which the gospel will need to challenge the other person's views.

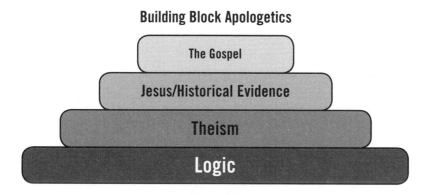

Building Block Apologetics

The Gospel

Jesus/Historical Evidence

Theism

Logic

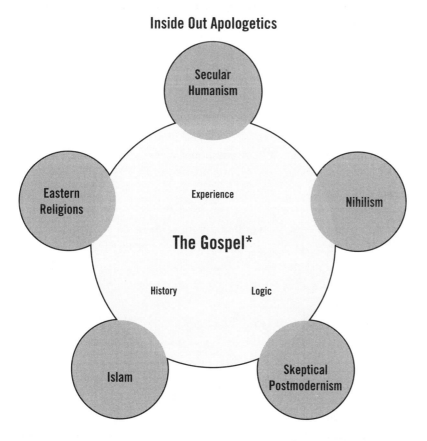

Inside Out Apologetics

Secular Humanism

Eastern Religions

Nihilism

Experience

The Gospel*

History   Logic

Islam

Skeptical Postmodernism

* The circle in the middle of the diagram represents Christianity with the gospel at the center as its core messsage. Or course, the Triune God—whose mission is expressed in the gospel—is at the center of all reality. However, we have placed the gospel at the center of this diagram because the Triune God reveals himself in the gospel, and it is in the gospel that we encounter him. For instance, the central proclamation in the New Testament, which Paul refers to as "of first importance" (1 Cor 15:3), is God's saving work in the life, death, and resurrection of Jesus Christ.

By placing the gospel at the center of apologetic conversations, the inside out approach understands logic, experience, and history in light of the gospel. Imagine these elements as not only floating around "the gospel" but also as entailments of Christianity that when viewed properly are part of the gospel's fabric and can extend out to bring someone to the core of the Christian message.

What we're offering in this chapter is not intended to become a rigid system or method to be followed slavishly; instead, we hope to provide some mental scaffolding to keep in mind as you engage unbelievers.

Inside

Here are two diagnostic questions for engaging inside a non-Christian "take":

1. What can we affirm and what do we need to challenge? The most beneficial approach is first to affirm the aspects of the other person's position that you find admirable and then to identify points that are *impractical* or *inconsistent*. We've already seen an example of this approach in Paul's speech in Athens, where Paul finds points of contact with the pagan culture and also challenges their perspective. To offer a few contemporary examples in the Western world, Christians can affirm:

- the fight for human rights
- the emphasis on appreciating diversity
- the virtue of serving the oppressed and marginalized in society

However, as we engage others, we should identify underlying assumptions we need to challenge. For example, in confronting Western culture, Christians would need to contrast

- the culture's sense of moral autonomy ("How dare anyone, even God, tell me what to do!") with moral dependence on God
- the culture's denial of divine accountability ("A loving Creator wouldn't judge his creatures") with the reality of God's divine judgment
- expressive individualism ("I look within myself to define myself") with finding identity in Christ and submitting to his lordship

2. Where Does It Lead? One way to help others see their blind spots is to trace out where their assumptions and beliefs will ultimately lead if they are applied consistently. Fallen cultures often contain assumptions that make Christianity seem implausible, yet those who hold these assumptions usually haven't worked them out in their head. Those assumptions are, after all, the very air they breathe. Because of this, by asking questions and discussing the implications of certain views, an apologist can expose those views as overly simplistic and unlivable.

For example, let's return to the case introduced above. Sarah objects to Christianity because she thinks it's wrong to try to "regulate anyone's life."

If I were to respond directly to her, I would affirm that religious leaders have at times abused their power, but I would also point out that this certainly doesn't apply just to religious leaders. The abuse of power is not simply a Christian issue; it is a human issue. Human history teaches us that all systems of belief, including the beliefs that make up secularism, are inclined to look down on those who disagree and to persecute them. However, though Christians are humans who are capable of abusing their power, Christianity is unique in that it has the resources to self-correct its adherents. After all, the founder of Christianity, whom all Christians are to imitate, willingly abdicated all his power (which he had every right to claim) and died on a cross. Far from persecuting his opponents, he forgave those who killed him. Jesus taught that *true* Christian leadership is about service, not lording power over others.

After admitting to Sarah that she makes a valid point, I would attempt to help her see the implications of her reasoning when it is applied consistently and taken to its logical end: "Of course power can be abused and regulations can be unwarranted, but don't you think we should regulate people's lives in *some* areas? What would a society be like that didn't regulate people's lives at all?" In response to this, she would, like most, admit that some regulation is necessary, so then my next question would be, "In that case, what should the source of these ethical norms be for an individual or a society?"

There are different ways to make the point, but the goal of the conversation would be to push her basic assumptions to their logical end, helping her see that "hopes" and "desires" are not a stable foundation for humans to find morality, value, or even meaning. You might, for instance, use the example of the two men from the end of last chapter (the Anglo-Saxon warrior and the twenty-first-century Manhattanite) and ask, "What if someone's hopes and desires are similar to those of the Anglo-Saxon warrior who has the impulse to kill anyone who disrespects him?"

Sympathetically listening to others and admitting when they have a point but then pushing their basic assumptions to their logical conclusions will help them see the problems and challenges within their own view. Creating uncertainty in the other person's view will create the space needed to discuss other options—namely, Christianity.

The point of starting from the inside of an unbeliever's perspective is to challenge the assumptions they hold in such a way that you don't cut off the conversation by wrongly assuming you share the same framework for reasoning. The goal is to enter their framework to challenge it on its own terms by helping them see that it is *inconsistent* and *unlivable* in order to lay the groundwork for them to take Christianity—which previously seemed strange to them because it was outside of their perspective—more seriously.

Outside

Even while working from the inside, one can already begin pointing to the outside—to Christianity and the gospel. The transition between moving from the inside to the outside of someone's view should feel fairly seamless, and in the course of the conversation, you will often go back and forth between the inside and the outside. For our purposes, however, it will be most helpful to treat the inside and outside as two distinct sides of the same coin.

The Gospel as Central to "Inside Out"

The gospel should not simply be the last thing offered at the end of an apologetic chain. As Lesslie Newbigin has put it, "The church's affirmation is that the story it tells, embodies, and enacts is the true story and that others are to be evaluated by reference to it."[21] The gospel, the Christian story, is central in evaluating what can be challenged and affirmed in other views. Moreover, cruciform persuasion requires that the gospel be *told*, *embodied*, and *enacted* throughout apologetic conversations. Thus, while we are providing some guidelines in this chapter for apologetic conversations, keep in mind that the gospel ought to be woven in and explained throughout.

Remember, the Christian framework, while overlapping in certain ways, is largely on the outside of the assumed framework of the unbeliever. Once you have created space by working inside an unbeliever's plausibility structures, you can then begin to show that the Christian "take" on things, which at first glance may have seemed strange and even repulsive to them, actually offers a more consistent, livable, and compelling view of life.

Here are two diagnostic questions for moving outside of a non-Christian "take" to Christianity.

1. Where do competing narratives borrow from Christian story? Having listened carefully to take inventory of what can be affirmed and what needs to be challenged in an unbeliever's view, we will be positioned to show how the Christian story includes vital resources that, though they may be present in the unbeliever's framework, are actually borrowed from Christianity, since their framework does not have anything to ground such resources.

Tim Keller explains an approach that serves well as a transition from what we are calling the *inside* of an unbeliever's assumed mental framework to the

---

21. Lesslie Newbigin, *Proper Confidence: Faith, Doubt and Certainty in Christian Discipleship* (Grand Rapids: Eerdmans, 1995), 76.

outside of their framework (i.e., to Christianity).[22] Keller suggests using what he refers to as "A" and "B" doctrines together to both speak into and challenge culture. "A" doctrines are Christian beliefs that are generally affirmed in a given culture. For example, "A" doctrines include those things in Western culture we listed above that Christians can affirm: the fight for human rights, the emphasis on being appreciative of diverse cultures, and the virtue in serving the oppressed and marginalized in society. When we see unbelievers in Western cultures affirming beliefs like these, we can essentially say, "Yes, as a Christian I affirm that too! In fact, the Scriptures have been saying that for centuries—even when the culture around it was saying something very different."

"B" doctrines are Christian beliefs that a particular culture finds difficult to accept, if not all together repulsive. These beliefs include things such as divine judgment ("A loving Creator wouldn't judge his creatures") and exclusivism ("Of course there isn't just one way to God").

Connecting an "A" doctrine to a "B" doctrine is an effective way to engage others who have assumed the narratives of the culture surrounding them. Keller uses an analogy of tying stones to logs in which he compares stones, which obviously sink in water, to beliefs that are difficult for a culture to accept, and logs, which float in water, to the beliefs of Christianity that a particular culture finds appealing or assumes to be true.[23] The stones that are difficult Christian beliefs can only be floated if they are tied to logs of biblical truth that are already floating. Keller refers to this concept as "sympathetic accusation": "the basic way to handle objections is to sincerely agree with your listeners' beliefs at some point, but then to question a second, mistaken belief on the basis of the first. It is to say: 'Since you believe *this*, why not believe *that*?' This forms an alliance between the Bible and one of the listeners' own beliefs, which can powerfully move people to accept other things the Bible says."[24]

Let's return to the example of my student's friend Sarah, who believes Christianity is irrelevant and dangerous. How could "A" and "B" doctrines be used in this conversation? Sarah both insists she is not a moral relativist and also implicitly assumes that life should have certain goals (e.g., freedom and fulfillment). Both of these ideas can be affirmed as "A" doctrines, because the Christian Scriptures also deny moral relativism and offer a clear vision of certain ends that should be pursued. Moreover, Christianity also speaks to the human desire for true freedom and fulfillment, though with a different conception

---

22. See Timothy Keller, *Center Church: Doing Balanced, Gospel-Centered Ministry in Your City* (Grand Rapids: Zondervan, 2012), 119–34.

23. Keller, *Center Church*, 124.

24. Timothy Keller, *Preaching: Communicating Faith in an Age of Skepticism* (New York: Viking, 2015), 115, 112.

than that of Sarah. On the other hand, the "B" doctrines that Sarah rejects are the absolute moral norms that Christianity provides, which she perceives as restrictive to human flourishing. According to her framework, Christianity is irrational and dehumanizing because it makes demands on people.

Now it's time to tie the "A" and "B" beliefs together. The connection can be made by asking some questions along these lines: "Since you believe in moral truth, why not believe in a God who provides the basis for moral truth? In fact, don't you need to believe in one to have the other? And if there is a higher truth and a higher being, wouldn't it make sense that discovering this being and his order will lead to true freedom and fulfillment—to living life the way it's meant to be lived?"

Later in the conversation, you might explain further: "In order to avoid falling into moral relativism, a belief we both deny, it seems we need something—or better yet, *someone*—who stands above our own subjective goals, desires, and beliefs to provide objective moral truths. And it would make sense, if there is a God who stands above all societies, that his objective truth would at times press up against certain subjective, temporal cultural sensibilities and that different cultures will therefore feel at times like his expectations are "suppressive." It would also be surprising if this God were not, in his design for living in his world, to ask us to follow him over following the culture. God's laws or "demands" can feel limiting, but he is making them in the same way that a good father provides structure and boundaries for his teen daughter. At first, the teen will probably resent the rules her father gives her, but as she gets older, she will realize why he did so: to enable her to lead a healthy, meaningful, and mature life."

2. How does Christianity better address our experiences, observations, and history? How does Christianity better "capture the rich texture of this life and history"?[25] Being able to answer this question in conversations and to connect human and cultural aspirations to Christianity is directly related to having a rich understanding of the gospel.

As we saw in chapter 6, the biblical authors used a myriad of images and metaphors from their cultural context when explaining the different dimensions and implications of the gospel. Because the gospel is multifaceted, it can be communicated not only with propositional statements but also with stories, analogies, and common experiences. The New Testament authors stress the importance of holding to the true gospel (e.g., Gal 1:8–9; Jude 3) and give us formulas that summarize the content of the gospel (e.g., 1 Cor 15:1–4), and yet they do not

---

25. Charles Taylor, *The Language Animal: The Full Shape of Human Linguistic Capacity* (Cambridge, MA: Harvard University Press, 2016), 219. This section is similar to what Taylor refers to as a "hermeneutical argument" (see pp. 216–21).

offer a *singular* formulaic approach. Instead, the New Testament demonstrates a controlled flexibility, calling Christians both to faithfully communicate the message of the gospel and tailor their presentation of that message to specific contexts. The gospel itself was originally articulated in certain languages and used imagery from certain cultures. Thus, to present the gospel faithfully means first to understand the Christian message within the context of the Bible and its native culture, and then to apply the message in a way that those in your current context can understand and relate to. This means that as Christians, we must work hard to understand the Bible and our present cultural location so that the gospel we present can be both true to the Bible and understandable to those to whom we are ministering.

After creating space by working inside of an unbeliever's plausibility structures, you will be in a better position to persuade them of the relevancy and truth of the Christian "take." At this point we must now ask, "What are some of the ways we can connect the human and cultural aspirations of late modernism to the gospel? In what way does the Christian story offer the greatest explanatory power for human experience? To model how these questions can be answered, we turn to the next chapter, where we cover some of the key features of late modernism in order to apply "inside out" and examine how Christianity offers a deeply livable, coherent, and satisfying view of reality.

Diagnostic Questions for Apologetic Interactions

Inside:

1. What in this view can be affirmed and what needs to be challenged?
2. Where does this view lead?
   - How is it inconsistent?
   - How is it unlivable?

Outside:

1. Where do competing narratives borrow from the Christian story?
2. How does Christianity better address our experiences, observations, and history?

CHAPTER ELEVEN

ENGAGING IN LATE MODERNISM

There is a generalized sense in our culture that with the eclipse of the transcendent, something may have been lost.

Charles Taylor, A Secular Age

A CONSTRUCTIVE ENGAGEMENT WITH LATE MODERNISM

This chapter surveys four significant aspects of late modernism that have particular relevance for apologetics: modern pluralism, the ethics of authenticity, religious lethargy, and the therapeutic turn. Within Western culture as a whole, there are many different subcultures, and the features presented in this chapter are not meant to be exhaustive or universal. Instead, our aim is to describe general trends in our current situation, so that we can model ways both to challenge and to affirm the most widespread aspects of the cultural aspirations of late modernism.

Learning to Engage within Late Modernism

Four Significant Features of Western Culture:

1. Modern pluralism
2. The ethics of authenticity
3. Religious lethargy
4. The therapeutic turn

This chapter sets out both opportunities and challenges posed by each feature and uses "inside out" to engage with those who have assumed these cultural "givens." In the engagement with the final three features, relevant "pressure points" are introduced in order to challenge their assumptions and offer the Christian story as a more consistent, livable, and intellectually satisfying vision of reality.

For a deeper look at our current cultural situation and the way it came into being, see Charles Taylor's book, *A Secular Age*.[1] We must warn you, however, that while we highly recommend Taylor's book, it is a massive tome that can be overwhelming to newcomers. Fortunately, there are more accessible interpretations of Taylor's work, most notably James K. A. Smith's *How (Not) to Be Secular*, which offers a more direct "translation" of Taylor's work, and Timothy Keller's *Making Sense of God* and *Preaching* (specifically chs. 4 and 5), which appropriate it more specifically for apologetic use. Reading either Taylor's work or one of these interpretations of it would be a good next step after reading this chapter.[2]

In this chapter, we'll pick up where chapter 10 ended, using the inside out approach to explore challenges and opportunities that exist within our current cultural context and to develop answers to the questions posed at the conclusion of the previous chapter: What are some of the ways we can connect the human and cultural aspirations of late modernism to the gospel? In what way does the Christian story offer the greatest explanatory power for human experience?

What Explains More?

Secularism has its own "takes" on the opportunities described in this chapter, but they are often reductionist. John Polkinghorne, former University of Cambridge professor of mathematical physics turned priest, emphasizes this point: "The theist and the atheist alike survey the same world of human experience, but offer incompatible interpretations of it. My claim would be that theism has a more profound and comprehensive understanding to offer than that afforded by atheism. Atheists are not stupid, but they explain less." In the next paragraph, he adds, "Although atheism might seem simpler conceptually, it treats beauty and morals and worship as some form of cultural or social brute facts, which accords ill with the seriousness with which these experiences touch us as persons."[3]

---

1. MODERN PLURALISM

There is a strong connection between the immanent frame and the cultural shifts that accompanied it and modern pluralism. While premodern cultures include conditions in which, as sociologist Peter Berger describes, "religion has, for the individual, the quality of objective certainty," the cultural shifts that

---

1. Charles Taylor, *A Secular Age* (Cambridge, MA: Harvard University Press, 2007).
2. James K. A. Smith, *How (Not) to Be Secular: Reading Charles Taylor* (Grand Rapids: Eerdmans, 2014); Timothy Keller, *Making Sense of God: An Invitation to the Skeptical* (New York: Viking, 2016); Timothy Keller, *Preaching: Communicating Faith in an Age of Skepticism* (New York: Viking, 2015).
3. John Polkinghorne, *The Faith of a Physicist: Reflections of a Bottom-Up Thinker* (Minneapolis: Fortress, 1996), 70.

accompanied the one-story immanent frame undermine this certainty and rob it "of its taken-for-granted status."[4]

Pluralism itself is nothing new. There have always been places where various cultures have intersected with each other. In ancient times, this would often happen at cities on trade routes. Even so, cross-cultural interactions were much more limited. With the advent of globalization and new technologies, the "world" seems to be in our backyards, at our fingertips, and on our screens.

Throughout most of human history, even where pluralism was found, there tended to be one dominant view, and minority communities learned to exist and operate within that overarching culture. Given these conditions, the insular quality of social life meant that most people did not have to deal seriously with the claims of other communities. Sociologist James Davison Hunter explains how this played out in America: "Even through the modern period, diversity existed within a dominant culture. In nineteenth-century America, Catholics and Jews had to learn how to survive in an overpoweringly Protestant culture, and through most of the twentieth century, Jews, secularists, Buddhists, Hindus, and Muslims have had to learn how to survive in a predominately Christian culture."[5]

Times have changed. In the West, this insulation has eroded; no longer in America or in the rest of the Western world does there exist one dominant religious culture that is given "overwhelming credibility" or is seen as being "beyond challenge."[6] And as a result, religious belief has become far more fragile.

Hunter notes that even if there is no one dominant, overarching system of beliefs in a culture, in some quarters certain groups will still have the upper hand—for example, in American universities, secularism reigns supreme. Even so, for a worldview to have the upper hand in select communities is far cry from it having a widespread dominance, à la Christianity in the past.

Modern pluralism is often acutely felt by the first-year university student who has just left the confines of an insulated Christian home. Students may find themselves having a crisis of faith when they realize, for example, that there are actually many atheists who don't have horns and pitchforks. In fact, many of them seem quite normal, friendly, and smart! The same could be said for what happens when a Christian student builds genuine relationships with other religious students, such as Hindus, Jews, and Muslims. For Christian students, many of whom are facing modern pluralism in a personal way for the first time, the diversity of the university setting can be a dizzying and confusing experience.

---

4. Peter Berger, *The Heretical Imperative: Contemporary Possibilities of Religious Affirmation* (Garden City, NJ: Doubleday, 1980), 24.

5. James Davison Hunter, *To Change the World: The Irony, Tragedy, and Possibility of Christianity in the Late Modern World* (New York: Oxford University Press, 2010), 201.

6. Hunter, *To Change the World*, 201.

Initially, Christian students may wonder why other students don't see how "obvious" the truth is and can be tempted to think that their own acceptance of Christianity proves their greater intelligence. However, in the university setting, modern pluralism quickly teaches them otherwise. Their peers are seeing the world differently, not because they are unintelligent, but because they are interpreting the same world with a different framework. They aren't necessarily ignoring basic logic, but they are arriving at different conclusions. In other words, modern pluralism does not simply point to the existence of a variety of worldviews; it also points to different (while overlapping) interpretive frameworks that support a variety of conclusions concerning fundamental issues of life and truth.

Opportunities

Modern pluralism can feel daunting. And yet, as Peter Berger reminds us, it's not all bad, because "it is better for social conditions to encourage us to decide upon faith than for us to live amid circumstances that 'give' us faith, making our religious identity akin to our hair color or our particular allergies rather than a personal quality that arises from our free assent."[7]

Because modern pluralism has weakened the conditions that support belief in Christianity, it has made it necessary for Christians to be more intentional with their faith than they were in the past, when Christianity was taken for granted (and in some cases was only held as a weakened form of "cultural Christianity"). In this way, modern pluralism presents not only a challenge to us as Christians, but also an opportunity to strengthen the church by intentionally focusing on her internal culture. The internal culture of the church, which comprises, for example, the way Christians conduct worship, maintain relationships with each other, choose leadership, determine the content of preaching, order their calendar, and teach their children, produces its own framework for living and thinking. Christian communities seeking to thoughtfully engage the diversity of the modern world should intentionally build their own countercultural plausibility structures. Once again, we see that a healthy doctrine of the church will not be far away from a healthy apologetic.

Furthermore, modern pluralism not only calls Christians to an internal intentionality, but also presents an opportunity for us as Christians to demonstrate *external* intentionality, engaging people within our own communities who hold a variety of belief systems and worldviews. Because of the globalization mentioned above, the world has come to the West, and rather than seeing this as a tragedy to be lamented, Western Christians should see it as an opportunity to take the gospel to the world by just crossing the street.

---

7. Peter L. Berger, "The Good of Religious Pluralism," *First Things*, April 2016, www.firstthings.com/article/2016/04/the-good-of-religious-pluralism.

One consequence of modern pluralism is that people are reluctant to commit to any one religious position, which has in turn created a tendency toward one of two positions: theological pluralism or a general religious skepticism.

Theological pluralism insists that all religious traditions—or at least all major religious traditions—describe the same reality and lead their adherents to the same ultimate destination. This relativizing of religious truth claims is expressed in the popular sentiment, "Of course there can't be just one way to God." Theological pluralism sees all major religions as different paths up one mountain: each way is different, but each offers a valid way to the heavens. What is important, according to theological pluralism, is not doctrine, but rather that people are tolerant of other religions, recognizing that we are all just taking different routes to the same place.

Inside. While we can certainly agree with theological pluralists in eschewing judgment on others *solely* because their cultural perspective is different from our own (i.e., ethnocentrism), we should be prepared to connect this shared belief (the disavowal of ethnocentrism) with the exclusivity of Christianity. This is another example of tying "A" and "B" beliefs together to challenge the assumptions that call Christianity into question.

At first glance, theological pluralism can sound humble and tolerant, but it's actually not. In saying they are against any one doctrine of salvation, theological pluralists are actually articulating a doctrine of salvation themselves. Claiming there are many paths to salvation contradicts how most of the actual adherents of Christianity, Judaism, and Islam (just to name three big traditions) understand their religion; thus, the theological pluralist is being *intolerant* by asserting that all such religions are wrong to claim exclusivity.

Most groups find it offensive when others gloss over the genuine distinctives of their beliefs. For instance, often theological pluralists describe a being or god at "the top of the mountain," which they articulate as some sort of all-loving divine spirit that is beyond our grasp. Those pluralists who go so far as to suggest this (not all do) are bumping up against even the major religious traditions. Buddhists, for one, would not articulate their religion in this way at all. As for us as Christians, while we agree that God is love, we would assert that he is also described as having many other important attributes.

Moreover, the position of the theological pluralist isn't particularly humble either. In essence, they are saying, "All these religious people may *think* they know the truth, but it is only *us*, the theological pluralists, who really understand. They can only see their one path up the mountain, while we, from the top, can see them all. We must correct their myopic viewpoints and demand that they be more inclusive and tolerant."

In addition to theological pluralism, modern pluralism can also lead to *religious skepticism*, which rejects all faiths as merely culturally conditioned human expressions and denies the truthfulness of any religion. The religious skeptic asserts that there are no ultimate religious truths; there are only regional opinions.[8]

We can agree that we are indeed historically conditioned, insofar as we are impacted by the cultural contexts we have lived in and currently live in. However, once the religious skeptic tries to assert that cultural context is the sole determining factor for what people ultimately believe, then religious skepticism becomes self-defeating. Religious skepticism itself has to be deemed as nothing but a conditioned response to culture and therefore as untrue. While our cultural context certainly does condition us in many ways, it does not have to be ultimately decisive in what we believe as individuals. Thus, while the skeptic might say, "The only reason you are a Christian is that you were born in South Georgia rather than Saudi Arabia," the Christian could just as easily respond—helping the skeptic take their thinking to its logical, consistent end—"Wouldn't that apply to you as well? Wouldn't the only reason you are a religious skeptic be that you were born in Minnesota rather than Morocco?"

Out. Christianity, while recognizing that cultural and social locations affect beliefs, upholds the dignity of each person by refusing to reduce them to a mere product of cultural conditioning. Moreover, Christianity acknowledges that different religions have beliefs that overlap, without ignoring the major differences between them or flattening them out to the lowest common denominator—which leaves very little, if anything, left.

From the outset, the gospel was proclaimed as both an *exclusive* all-*inclusive* message in that while Jesus is the only way to salvation, the salvation made possible through Jesus is extended to all people. The ultimate vision of the gospel and the culmination of the kingdom of God is a world where the beauty of the world's diversity assembles to form a cohesive society that is aimed at a common good (Rev 7:9). In line with the promises made throughout Scripture, the message of Jesus' death, deity, and resurrection both embraces and transcends human cultures. Larry Hurtado, a historian who specializes in the study of Christian origins, has stressed that one of the features that set apart Christianity from other religions in the ancient world was its "transethnic and translocal" quality, "addressing males and females of all social levels."[9] In other words, one

---

8. Granted, objections on the basis of pluralism can be more nuanced, especially in academic settings. For a response to pluralism as an objection to Christianity, see Alvin Plantinga, *Warranted Christian Belief* (Oxford: Oxford University Press, 2000), 437–57.

9. Larry W. Hurtado, *Destroyer of the gods: Early Christian Distinctiveness in the Roman World* (Waco, TX: Baylor University Press, 2016), 186.

of Christianity's unique features in its original ancient context was that while it denied that its God could be worshiped along with other gods, it attracted people from various regions, ethnicities, and races.

The exclusivity of the gospel might push up against certain assumptions of the modern West, but just as in the early church, the exclusive message of the gospel is proving to be remarkably inclusive. Today, Christianity has become the most geographically diverse religion in the world. Its growth in the non-Western world is incredible. More Christians attend church in China than in all of Europe. East Asia is projected to have 171.1 million Christians by 2020, which will be 10.5 percent of its population. Africa will be comprised of 630 million Christians by 2020, which amounts to 49.3 percent of its population.[10] Furthermore, while the hub of other major religions continues to be in the region in which they were founded, Christianity's geographical center has quite remarkably migrated throughout its history.[11] This migration further testifies to Christianity's unique transcultural message.

In sum, just like any group that gathers around a common interest or belief, Christianity is exclusive (even groups that gather around a belief in tolerance embrace a form of exclusivism), but Christianity has also proven to be remarkably inclusive in the way it embraces all kinds of people, no matter what culture, country, or socioeconomic background they may be from.

2. THE ETHICS OF AUTHENTICITY[12]

Robert Bellah and his coauthors describe a phenomenon that is widespread in Western culture, which they refer to as *expressive individualism*: the belief "that each person has a unique core of feeling and intuition that should unfold or be expressed if individuality is to be realized."[13] Charles Taylor, in describing expressive individualism as a basic assumption of the age of authenticity we live in, adds that this individuality must be lived out in opposition, "against surrendering to conformity with a model imposed on us from outside."[14] In other words, the most important thing you can do as an individual is throw off the shackles of exterior expectations and be "true to yourself." Accordingly, human

---

10. See Timothy Keller, *Making Sense of God: An Invitation to the Skeptical* (New York: Viking, 2016), 26.

11. See Andrew F. Walls, *The Missionary Movement in Christian History: Studies in the Transmission of Faith* (Maryknoll, NY: Orbis, 1996), 16–25.

12. This is an expression used in Charles Taylor, *The Ethics of Authenticity* (Cambridge, MA: Harvard University Press, 1991); see also his *A Secular Age*, 472–504.

13. Robert N. Bellah et al., *Habits of the Heart: Individualism and Commitment in American Life*, rev. ed. (Berkeley: University of California Press, 2008), 334.

14. Taylor, *A Secular Age*, 475.

flourishing occurs when we cast off external norms and look within ourselves to find and foster our authentic self.

One need only take a brief look at the message being sent by institutions, marketing companies, and entertainment mediums to see this trend toward expressive individualism, so it should come as no surprise to us. In everything from cartoons and movies to popular TV shows and graduation speeches, you will find the same basic message: "Follow your passion. Don't accept limits. Chart your own course. You have a responsibility to do great things because you are so great."[15] As columnist David Brooks observes, the gospel being preached in the culture is "the gospel of self-trust"[16]—and *gospel* is not too strong a word, for embedded in these clichés are assumptions about meaning, identity, and ethics.

A Challenge in the Culture and the Church

Gabe Lyons and David Kinnaman conducted research that revealed the following:

- 84 percent of Americans believe that "enjoying yourself is the highest goal of life"
- 86 percent indicate that to enjoy yourself, you must "pursue the things you desire most"
- 91 percent agree that "to find yourself, look within yourself"

But what about Christians? The church is not far behind:

- 66 percent of regular church attenders say that "enjoying yourself is the highest goal of life"
- 72 percent affirm that you should "pursue the things you desire most"
- 76 percent agree that "to find yourself, look within yourself"

These startling statistics are yet another indicator that a healthy apologetic must begin with healthy discipleship within the church.[17]

Self-authorizing morality, which holds personal choice as the highest good, is a natural extension of this self-oriented outlook on life. Personal freedom is seen as an end to itself. And once a culture makes individual choice and independence from external norms the ultimate good, traditional religion, with its overt call to submit to something beyond ourselves, is seen not only as boring and antiquated, but also as dangerous and oppressive.

---

15. David Brooks, *The Road to Character* (New York: Random House, 2016), 7.

16. Brooks, *Road to Character*, 7.

17. David Kinnaman and Gabe Lyons, *Good Faith: Being a Christian When Society Thinks You're Irrelevant and Extreme* (Grand Rapids: Baker, 2016), 57–58.

Self-Authorizing Morality

In his explanation of self-authorizing morality, Charles Taylor cites French philosopher Alain Renaut: "The man of humanism is the one who no longer receives his norms and laws either from the nature of things (Aristotle) nor from God, but who establishes them himself on the basis of his reason and will."[18]

Opportunities

We should be thankful we live in a culture where most of us have the freedom to choose in many important areas of our lives, such as who we will marry and what our occupation will be. Furthermore, the modern sense of identity and freedom we've been discussing is in some ways connected to the emergence of what is actually a biblical ideal: equality for all people—regardless of background, ethnicity, race, gender, or religion.[19] Nevertheless, freedom and autonomy become problematic when they are rooted in an unbiblical, individualistic conception of flourishing that teaches casting aside all external expectations—whether from religion, society, or others—and to look to personal desires and feelings to find meaning in life.

As we mentioned in our initial discussion of the inside out approach, one way to engage someone who adheres to this view is to help them carry the assumptions of their view to their logical end. For instance, we could point out that basing our identity and purpose solely on our internal feelings and desires is not only *unstable*, since feelings and desires often change, but actually *impossible* to do, since, as we saw in chapter 9, culture is always cultivating our desires and telling us how we should feel about and respond to our impulses. We cannot help but act according to the expectations and opinions of those around us. As Charles Taylor puts it, "No one acquires the languages needed for self-definition on their own."[20] We are always defining our personal identity and ethic in dialogue with our community. Thus, three themes we ought to explore as we connect with and critique expressive individualism and self-authorizing morality are identity, justice, and community.

Identity

Inside. Everyone finds themselves searching intensely for self-worth. As Jewish anthropologist Ernest Becker observes, there is a universal search for "cosmic significance."[21] None of us simply look "within ourselves" to find our "true self";

---

18. Quoted in Taylor, *A Secular Age*, 588.

19. Charles Taylor, *Sources of Self: The Making of the Modern Identity* (Cambridge, MA: Harvard University Press, 1989); Taylor, *A Secular Age*, 637, 745.

20. Taylor, *Ethics of Authenticity*, 33.

21. Ernest Becker, *The Denial of Death* (New York: Free Press, 1973), 3.

we all cannot help but look externally, to the culture and those around us, for affirmation that we are valuable and worthy. It is for this reason that the "hero" narratives our culture tells us—in everything from Disney movies to Fourth of July parades and football games—resonate so deeply with us: they provide deeply embedded, living pictures we strive to emulate in order to be validated.

Everyone, even the nonreligious, look to something or someone for identity, worth, significance, and happiness. Everyone has something or someone ultimate that, practically speaking, they worship as their god.[22] For some of us, our god, the thing in which we find our identity, is our intelligence. For others, it's being in a relationship or being attractive or successful or athletic. We are all building our identity on something. But life has a way of threatening or even robbing us of our sources of identity. And whenever that happens—whenever the thing, person, or symbol we deify is taken away—we feel as if we have been robbed of our true self. We are left without an identity; we feel faceless, nameless, and insignificant. In his well-known commencement address at Kenyon College, David Foster Wallace expressed this truth with great eloquence:

> In the day-to-day trenches of adult life, there is actually no such thing as atheism. There is no such thing as not worshipping. Everybody worships. The only choice we get is what to worship. And the compelling reason for maybe choosing some sort of god or spiritual-type thing to worship—be it JC or Allah, be it YHWH or the Wiccan Mother Goddess, or the Four Noble Truths, or some inviolable set of ethical principles—is that pretty much anything else you worship will eat you alive. If you worship money and things, if they are where you tap real meaning in life, then you will never have enough, never feel you have enough. It's the truth. Worship your body and beauty and sexual allure and you will always feel ugly. And when time and age start showing, you will die a million deaths before they finally grieve you. On one level, we all know this stuff already. It's been codified as myths, proverbs, clichés, epigrams, parables; the skeleton of every great story. The whole trick is keeping the truth up front in daily consciousness.
>
> Worship power, you will end up feeling weak and afraid, and you will need ever more power over others to numb you to your own fear. Worship your intellect, being seen as smart, you will end up feeling stupid, a fraud, always on the verge of being found out. But the insidious thing about these forms of worship is not that they're evil or sinful, it's that they're unconscious. They are default settings.

---

22. See Timothy Keller, *The Reason for God: Belief in an Age of Skepticism* (New York: Dutton, 2008), 163.

They're the kind of worship you just gradually slip into, day after day, getting more and more selective about what you see and how you measure value without ever being fully aware that that's what you're doing.[23]

You don't have to be religious to feel the effects of worshiping something that leaves you empty, something you were not made to worship.

Out. The moments of insecurity or despair that result from losing an object of worship—a universal part of the human experience—are opportunities to explore more deeply. The apologist, focusing specifically on the life and experience of the person they are talking to, can explain that at the root of their problem is idolatry. In the same way that pain warns us to pull our hand away from something that will burn us, the empty feeling we get when our "gods" fail us is God's way of saying, "Something is desperately wrong; you need to change course." Any time we build our lives on something other than God, that thing will eventually destroy us, because it will ultimately prove to be unstable. Whatever it is, no matter how good it may be, it was never meant to be what we love and worship above all else.

The good news of Christianity is that we are able to know and live in a right relationship with the one person who will always prove stable and, rather than destroying us, will sustain, love, and care for us: *the one true God.* Moreover, when we have a right relationship with God, we can live in a right relationship with the rest of the world. Jesus entered into the world to save us from the slavery of idolatry in order that we might know the one we were designed to love above all else as the source of all value and significance.

Christianity affirms the fundamental goodness of life—work, relationships, leisure, and sex, to name a few aspects—but recognizes that these good gifts become life-destroying when they are made ultimate. When these idols fall, we feel deep insecurity and angst. None of these false gods will ever deliver; they merely enslave us and control our lives. When we have them, we feel dissatisfied, and we want more. But when we don't have them, we bear a burden to try to get them, or we despair because we think they are unattainable.

Idolizing anything will destroy us, yet the answer is not to shun others and give up the things of the world altogether—after all, God commanded that we love others and accept all good gifts with thanksgiving as from him. Rather, the answer that Christianity provides is that we are to find joy, value, and significance in the one who is eternally secure, enabling us to enjoy the good gifts he has given us in this world without the heavy burden of investing our very selves in

23. David Foster Wallace, "Transcription of the Kenyon Commencement Address—May 21, 2005," http://web.ics.purdue.edu/~drkelly/DFWKenyonAddress2005.pdf.

what we know is ultimately fleeting. Christianity invites us to invest our whole selves in eternal and meaningful realities.

Justice

Inside. Despite the accusations of simple moral relativism often leveled against them, late moderns typically have a strong sense of the *wrongs* in this world, coupled with an impulse to do something about them. Social justice and human rights are in vogue, and rightly so. Countless organizations have been formed to help serve the poor, end sex trafficking, provide disaster relief, curtail racism, and cure diseases—just to name a few that are broadly agreed upon as moral issues. We as Christians should affirm unbelievers in their pursuit of these causes, which are grounded in two foundational beliefs for our modern morality: basic human dignity and universal benevolence. Human dignity and universal benevolence are also, however, the sticking point, because while Christians have strong reasons for affirming them, secular views do not have the resources to offer "thick" accounts for these moral beliefs. In particular, the late modern "turn to the self" lacks the ability to provide sufficient *grounding, motivation,* or *hope* for these modern ethical intuitions.[24]

Grounding? Basic human dignity and universal benevolence are far from trans-historical assumptions.[25] The standard assumption in ancient cultures was that different people groups were unequal. This is why, for example, such practices as slavery, infanticide, human sacrifice, and widow burning were accepted. The idea of basic human dignity was a later development rooted in a Christian framework that was for centuries the backbone of the Western tradition and has remained a central feature in modern morality. Beginning with the Enlightenment in the 1700s, late modernism has attempted to formally sever the connection with Christianity while, often unknowingly, living off of Christianity's moral heritage.[26]

The question we ought to ask, then, is, "If you deny Christianity [or theism altogether], what reasons do you have for believing in universal human dignity and rights?" Nature doesn't provide a basis for human dignity or give us a modern moral instruction book. Instead, what we observe in nature is that the strong eat the weak. It is for this reason that Tennyson described nature as "red

---

24. Expressive individualism and self-authorizing morality—which, after being combined with other developments, unnecessarily grew out of the originally Christian ideal of universal love and respect for others. Ironically, these developments in the age of authenticity have now turned on Christianity and serve as reasons that many find Christianity to be implausible. This is a key point narrated in the works of Charles Taylor.

25. See Christian Smith, "Does Naturalism Warrant a Moral Belief in Universal Benevolence and Human Rights?" in *The Believing Primate: Scientific, Philosophical, and Theological Reflections on the Origins of Religion*, ed. Jeffrey Schloss and Michael Murray (Oxford: Oxford University Press, 2011), 295–98.

26. See Nicholas Wolterstorff, *Justice: Rights and Wrongs* (Princeton, NJ: Princeton University Press, 2008); Taylor, *Sources of Self*.

in tooth and claw."[27] Observations from nature alone seem to lead us far away from modern conceptions of justice.[28]

Considering that Christianity is the historical origin for beliefs that are assumed in our modern conceptions of justice, here are some helpful questions to ask: Where do we get the sense of justice we have? Why do we strive to fix the world, to make it better? For women's rights? To serve the poor in distant countries? And why is our belief in universal benevolence superior to the belief of other cultures that they can, for example, enslave others and mistreat women? It seems that more than an assumed self-authorizing morality is needed to provide satisfying answers to such questions.

Motivation? Understanding and articulating the basis for their moral beliefs is not the only problem that secularists who feel the weight of the injustice in the world face. Though many may strongly sense that they should do something about injustice, it is one thing to have a general desire for justice, and it's a very different thing to actually labor self-sacrificially against injustice in ways that effect substantive change. Most people are simply more committed to their own personal welfare than to the welfare of others.

And why shouldn't they be? Expressive individualism can only provide shallow motivations to give selflessly of one's money, time, health, social standing, and even one's life for the good of others. After all, if we are to be "true to ourselves," why should I give of myself selflessly for the sake of others? And, given naturalism, if we are all just going to decompose in the ground and if all life will eventually cease with no one surviving to remember anything, why should we even care? Why not simply seek your personal happiness rather than put yourself through hardships for people you might not even know?

Hope? Even as we challenge the ability of other late modern frameworks to ground this modern quest for justice and find the motivation to carry it out, we can, as explained above, affirm both the intuitive desire many have to right wrongs and their efforts to do so. If we generously acknowledge unbelievers' desire for and efforts at attaining justice, they will be much more likely to have open, honest discussions with us. And one of the things that most people would concede is the strong sense they have that justice remains elusive. Though there are actions we can take to solve some problems, it seems there are many issues we will never be able to fix. Trying to see that justice is done can often feel like trying to plug multiple holes in a dam with your fingers; once you get one plugged, three more gaping holes open up. Once we begin to think about all the injustices in the world, it can become overwhelming; there seems to be no

---

27. Alfred Lord Tennyson, *In Memoriam A. H. H.* (London: Bankside, 1900), canto 56, p. 60.
28. In chapter 13, we will discuss how neither science nor culture is able to ground morality.

end in sight. And even beyond the present moment in time, if we accept that in the end, the world will simply cease to be, then our cosmic insignificance constantly casts a shadow over the best of our intentions: ultimately, justice will never be served. What will all of our efforts come to in the end?

Out. Christianity offers not only the grounding and motivation needed for us to seek justice, but also a reassuring hope that justice will be ultimately done. We have a sense of right and wrong because there is a God whose moral law stands above that of individual people or cultures. The message and pursuit of justice resonate with us because God has created us in his image and desires that we seek his righteousness and peace as a way of representing his very nature to the world. When God entered the world as a human in the person of Jesus Christ, the ethic he taught—which asks that we *love our neighbor and enemies*—was unique in the ancient world.

It was not, however, simply Jesus' teaching that was revolutionary. Jesus' followers also stood out because Jesus provided them with a deep motivation to serve others selflessly. Christians believed not only that God's very being ensured there is an unchanging standard of justice, but also that because of his deep love for his creation, God made it possible for all to be forgiven and set free from their own acts of injustice. God himself entered the world and lived as Jesus, a man without sin, enduring our suffering so he could empathize with our weaknesses. And most incredibly of all, he did this in order that he might absorb the violence of this world and take on himself the judgment we deserve. It is receiving this mercy and being freed from our own self-absorption that enables and motivates Christians to give of themselves freely for the sake of others.

Jesus' resurrection points us forward to his return, when he will usher in a new world and make all the wrongs right. In the end, justice will be satisfied. Yet because of his sacrifice, he is able to offer those who will humble themselves and turn to him the opportunity to be on the right side of justice. His sacrifice makes all our sacrifices meaningful; all of our strivings for true peace and all of our social causes will have eternal significance. Even in the darkest of times, this is an enduring vision of hope that can support the long-suffering pursuit of justice.

Community

Inside. Humans are relational beings. We laugh at jokes. We cry at loss. We celebrate success. We long to know and to be known. We all desire to belong to something bigger than ourselves, whether it's a family or some other group. Just ask yourself, *What are my best memories—the greatest moments of my life?* Invariably, the majority of people will realize that most of their fondest memories are shared with others.

Despite our longing for relationships and the joy we find in them, we all know firsthand that they are also the source of much heartache and turmoil. As the biblical scholar N. T. Wright puts it, "We all know we are made to live together, but we all find that doing so is more difficult than we had imagined."[29] Marriages that begin full of hope and promises too often end in bitter divorce. Families grow apart. Best friends turn against each other.

This longing for community and relationships is still very much alive in today's world. The emphasis on authenticity that pervades our culture may make it seem like a desire for community or relationships is subsiding, but "finding yourself" is typically just code for finding what new group you will join. Notice how when someone "expresses their individuality" with a certain style of music, automobile, or set of beliefs, there are normally an awful lot of other people expressing their "individuality" in the same way.

The problem is that even though people are still seeking out community and relationships (whether or not they admit it), shared hobbies or interests alone do not provide the support needed for communal flourishing. Moreover, expressive individualism corrodes interpersonal relationships, as it causes us to view neighbors, friends, and marriages as instruments for our own self-actualization. Thus, if they cease to serve our personal happiness, we quickly abandon them. If our ultimate purpose in life is self-fulfillment, it will be difficult to treat others as much more than commodities to get what we want.

Even apart from expressive individualism, it is human nature to want to get more than we give in our relationships, and expressive individualism exacerbates this tendency. One of the essential vices of a fallen human nature, pride, can make it very hard not to resent the success or even happiness of others. C. S. Lewis once remarked, "Pride is *essentially* competitive—is competitive by its very nature—while the other vices are competitive only, so to speak, by accident. Pride gets no pleasure out of having something, only out of having more of it than the next man."[30]

Imagine, for example, that a friend of yours has succeeded in life; she has done something wonderful and is being recognized for her accomplishment. You want to be happy for her. Instead, you hate her for it or, at the very least, resent her a little bit. All you can think is, *If I had just had a little more time, I could have done a better job, and it would have been* me *who was being recognized. If only they could have seen what I've done—what I'm capable of doing.* Human nature already makes it hard to celebrate others, but when your relationship with someone is built on self-interest, it's only that much worse. How can pride and selfishness be overcome, and what resources other than self-interest are needed for flourishing relationships?

---

29. N. T. Wright, *Simply Christian: Why Christianity Makes Sense* (New York: HarperCollins, 2006), 33.
30. C. S. Lewis, *Mere Christianity* (New York: Macmillan, 1960), 109, emphasis in original.

Out. Christianity teaches that we are to weep with those who weep and rejoice with those who rejoice (Rom 12:15). Everyone longs for a genuine community where people truly love and care for one another; the problem is, of course, that this sort of flourishing community isn't possible if everyone is looking to their own self-interest and ignoring the interests of others. The foundation of the church is a mutual identity in Christ, and as Christians we are therefore to see others and ourselves as children of the King, endowed with worth and value. We also know that because we exist to serve God and not ourselves, we are to "do nothing out of selfish ambition or vain conceit" and value others above ourselves (Phil 2:3). This turn away from ourselves—a strange idea in an era of authenticity and individualism—frees us to pursue the good of others and the good of the world. Christianity, in offering a vision for life and true friendship, has the resources to cultivate thriving relationships and flourishing communities.

Finally, this profound yearning for relationships also points to a mysterious and distinctly Christian view that stands behind the gospel: God himself has always existed as a relational being; he exists in three persons—Father, Son, and Holy Spirit. Relationality is not something God was lacking before he created angels or human beings; relationality has always been fundamental to the nature of God himself, and by extension, reality. God has eternally been a personal God relating in community.[31]

3. RELIGIOUS LETHARGY

Late moderns have absorbed a cultural narrative that no longer assumes a divinely ordered world in which there are God-given ways to live. As a result, instead of looking to God for significance or meaning in life, many have, as James K. A. Smith explains, "constructed webs of meaning that provide almost all the significance they need."[32] For this reason, in general, people do not have a sense of needing "some bit of information that is missing," nor are they holding their breath, waiting for someone—least of all a Christian—to come and answer all their questions.[33] They see life from a different framework than we do. It is not "nagging questions about God and the afterlife" that drive late moderns, but rather, as Smith explains, nonreligious longings, goals, and "quests for

---

31. See Gregory E. Ganssle, *Our Deepest Desires: How the Christian Story Fulfills Human Aspirations* (Downers Grove, IL: InterVarsity, 2017), 43–52.

32. Smith, *How (Not) to Be Secular*, vii.

33. Writing in a British context, Francis Spufford expresses a similar point in his own comical and poignant way. See his *Unapologetic: Why, Despite Everything, Christianity Can Still Make Surprising Emotional Sense* (San Francisco: HarperOne, 2012), 5.

significance," which fill their lives to such an extent that "there doesn't seem to be anything 'missing.'" And because of this, Christians "can't just come proclaiming the good news of a Jesus who fills their 'God-shaped hole.'"[34] Even if, on occasion, the late modern does begin to wonder if they *are* missing something, that there is a hole in their lives, they don't normally assume it is "God-shaped"; instead, they suspect what they are missing must be wealth, achievement, comfort, thriving relationships, or even something unknown they haven't yet encountered. This widespread apathy toward the bigger questions of life produces obvious challenges for Christians trying to engage others with the gospel.

Given that many people already find significance in the world they live in and don't feel, at least most of the time, that they're missing anything that Christianity offers, the important questions become:

- How should we give a defense when people don't even care and aren't asking any questions?
- What do we do when people aren't interested?
- How do we approach a culture when apathy and lethargy are an increasingly common stance toward traditional religions?

Opportunities

This apathy toward Christianity is obviously problematic, but it also presents an apologist with opportunities. Within the secular webs of meaning and value that late moderns construct for themselves, they will often feel vulnerable at certain points where, despite their seeming apathy, they will feel the "cross-pressures" of a life cut off from transcendence.[35] Even as—sometimes *especially* as—late moderns live in abundance and comfort, the sense that "somewhere there is a fullness or richness which transcends the ordinary" haunts them.[36] Below are four examples of pressure points that provide opportunities for Christians to engage those who claim religion is irrelevant.

The Everyday Stuff

Inside. In the simple, everyday experiences of life, a sense of purpose and meaning is impossible to escape. As atheist philosopher John Gray has written, "Other animals are born, seek mates, forage for food and die. That is all. But we humans–we think–are different."[37] Or perhaps more accurately, as humans,

---

34. Smith, *How (Not) to Be Secular*, vii.
35. See Taylor, *A Secular Age*, 594–617.
36. Taylor, *A Secular Age*, 677.
37. John Gray, *Straw Dogs: Thoughts on Humans and Other Animals* (London: Granta, 2002), 38.

we *sense* that we are different. It is not simply that we *want* our lives to have purpose and meaning; we actually have an instinct to live that way.

Some, who you'll read more about in the next chapter, will argue that since there is no reality beyond this physical world, we must create our own meaning in life. However, this idea not only lacks logical consistency, but also does not bear out experientially, for the webs of meaning we construct for ourselves are temporary and frail. In his book *Straw Dogs*, Gray forcefully argues that in a godless world, human life is without choice, consciousness, selfhood, or free will.[38] But if this is the case, then how are we really free to create our own meaning in life? Furthermore, if all that exists is matter, then even if you do something that is remembered a hundred or a thousand years from now, eventually the solar system will be destroyed, and even colossal achievements will not have a trace of significance. As another unbelieving philosopher, Thomas Nagel, has stated, in the end "it wouldn't matter if you had never existed."[39] But we don't live like that—we simply can't live out this belief consistently. What best accounts for this sense, which seems so difficult to shake, that there is purpose in life, and that even the normal stuff of life is meaningful?

Out. Christianity says that humans find a nihilistic life difficult, if not impossible, because we have been hard-wired by God to live with purpose and meaning. It is for this reason that even if people deny God and can't find a rational reason to live with purpose and meaning, they still work, marry, raise children, think, build, plan, and play as if there is a point to it all. Whatever people may say to the contrary, they can't escape the sense that their lives are more valuable and meaningful than slime mold. Even if our lives are aimed at the wrong goal, we still aim it at something.

The Christian story makes sense of these experiences and explains why humans, even those who deny God and have no explanation, live this way. The reason we intuitively aim our lives at certain ends and find meaning in our tasks is that we are made in the image of God. Sadly, because of sin, our inherent longing for purpose is thwarted, and no matter what we do, we know that when we die, it will all turn to dust—at least, we can at times be overcome by these feelings of despair. Yet at the heart of the Christian story is the claim that through the death and resurrection of his Son Jesus Christ, God has rescued us from sin and futility, giving our work eternal significance and fulfilling our longing for purpose. Moreover, in the person of Jesus Christ, we are given a model of how we are to live a life of purpose and meaning aimed at the true and eternal goal.

---

38. Gray, *Straw Dogs*.

39. Thomas Nagel, *What Does It All Mean? A Very Short Introduction to Philosophy* (New York: Oxford University Press, 1987), 96.

A Literary Example: The Everyday Stuff

Fyodor Dostoyevsky's character Ivan from the novel *The Brothers Karamazov* is best known for his invective against God in which he starkly lays out the seeming incompatibility of a good, all-powerful God with the existence of evil. And yet, throughout the novel, Ivan also finds that, despite his commitment to strong empiricism and his rejection of religion, he cannot help but be deeply moved by "irrational" things such as an intense desire to live:

> Do you know I've been sitting here thinking to myself: that if I didn't believe in life, if I lost faith in the woman I love, lost faith in the order of things, were convinced in fact that everything is a disorderly, damnable, and perhaps devil-ridden chaos, if I were struck by every horror of man's disillusionment— still I should want to live . . . I have a longing for life, and I go on living in spite of logic. Though I may not believe in the order of the universe, yet I love the sticky little leaves as they open in spring. I love the blue sky. I love some people, whom one loves you know sometimes without knowing why. I love some great deeds done by men, though I've long ceased perhaps to have faith in them . . . It's not a matter of intellect or logic, it's loving with one's inside, with one's stomach.[40]

Beauty

Inside. The sense of awe we feel when we hear and see beautiful or lovely things, which sometimes even bring us to tears, also has a way of challenging spiritual lethargy. We all know what it feels like to be deeply moved by a summer sunset, a masterful painting, a song that leaves us speechless, the sight of our children curled up in bed, or the smile of our spouse. Most people simply assume the category of beauty without considering where it comes from.

Some might deny beauty with their mind, but their heart won't let them off the hook so easily. Others might object that beauty is in the eye of the beholder, and to a certain extent, that might be true. But even if we cannot always agree on what exactly beauty looks like, that's not really the point: the category of beauty is still assumed.

If we are all simply an accident of nature, a chance collection of atoms, then what is beauty? Can we speak of the glorious sunset as beautiful? A lover as beautiful? One of Mozart's compositions as beautiful? The sight of a young boy compassionately helping his widowed neighbor cross the street as beautiful?

And if we say something is beautiful, say our children or our lover, what do we really mean by this? There are many ways to explain the category of beauty

---

40. Fyodor Dostoyevsky, *The Brothers Karamazov*, trans. Constance Garnett (New York: New American Library, 1957), 212–13.

intrinsic to humans, and even materialists have their own, but the question is: Which explanation is most powerful and convincing?

If you tell your fiancée you find her beautiful, do you mean you prefer her random conglomeration of atoms to other beings' random conglomeration of atoms, while admitting your preference for her appearance itself is a product of neurons firing in your body that you have little to no control over? Consistently embracing this perspective seems almost unthinkable to most humans: when we look at a gorgeous sunset or our child, or when we hear a breathtaking story, we intuitively assume a deeper and fuller significance than a purely secular framework provides.

Out. Christians believe that true beauty exists because God exists; all that is good, true, and beautiful is from God himself. God created the world for people to enjoy and delight in, and though the beauty in this world exists in a fallen state, marred by the effects of sin, it witnesses to himself, pointing us to his lovingkindness. Moreover, the fallen beauty we see in this world is but a shadow of what is to come; the beauty we see here, though it brings us joy, also makes us long for the coming day when beauty will be fully renewed to a perfect state.

A Cultural Example: Beauty

In their song "Somewhere Only We Know," the English rock band Keane expresses the bittersweet longing that beauty often evokes in people, no matter how religiously lethargic they may be. Remembering the sublime feeling that beautiful scenes in nature or moments in their past evoked in them, people will sometimes return to old places where they once experienced it, hoping to find it again. But they are almost always disappointed and deeply saddened when they realize the places from their past aren't what they once were. The song expresses how people desperately long to return to these places and re-experience these feelings because they sense something meaningful and perhaps even transcendent in them—something that cuts to their very purpose in life.

C. S. Lewis, in *The Weight of Glory*, explains that the reason beauty—whether we find it in nature or in moments from our past—promises us so much, yet is so fleeting, fills us with joy, and breaks our hearts, is that it points to a reality beyond itself:

> [Those things] in which we thought the beauty was located will betray us if we trust to them; it was not *in* them, it only came *through* them, and what came through them was longing . . . They are not the thing itself; they are only the scent of a flower we have not found, the echo of a tune we have not heard, news from a country we have never yet visited . . .
>
> We cannot mingle with the splendours we see. But all the leaves of the New Testament are rustling with the rumour that it will not always be so. Some day, God willing, we shall get *in*.[41]

---

41. C. S. Lewis, *The Weight of Glory and Other Addresses* (New York: Macmillan, 1949), 4–5, 13.

One of C. S. Lewis's central characters in his novel *Till We Have Faces* expresses this yearning that is felt in the midst of beauty: "It was when I was the happiest that I longed most . . . And because it was so beautiful, it set me longing, always longing. Somewhere else there must be more of it."[42]

The Christian explanation of beauty also provides a reason for Christians to create and admire beautiful things, such as music, plays, paintings, sculptures, novels, and movies.[43] Because beauty and design point beyond the creation to the ultimate creator of beauty, there is not simply an impulse to invest in and enjoy the beautiful, but also a higher reason to create. In a sense, creating and admiring beautiful things are ways for us as Christians to worship and steep ourselves in a facet of God's nature. While committed materialists may experience the same impulse to create as Christians, they cannot provide such a powerful justification and meaning for their work.

The Good Life

Inside. Even when someone sets out to construct their own web of meaning apart from God, they do so in hopes of finding fulfillment and happiness—of finding the good life. Despite the incredible diversity of cultures and, even more remarkably, different types of people in the world, doesn't everyone ultimately want the same basic things? Everyone wants a purpose. Everyone wants to know they matter. Everyone wants to be a part of something bigger than themselves. Everyone wants the good life. This cuts to the heart of humanity. We are always out for it, and even if we find it, we want more. Yet when we pursue happiness, we do so only to find that it is fleeting. Even if we manage to grab hold of happiness for a while, experience tells us it will one day slip through our fingers, disrupted by the trials and disappointments of life.

C. S. Lewis argues that every natural desire has an object within this world toward which it is aimed. We get hungry and thirsty, and we live in a world where there is food and water. We have sexual desires, and sex exists. Thus, when humans have a desire that "no natural happiness will satisfy,"[44] it should give us serious pause about the possibility of the existence of something beyond the natural that is made to fulfill that desire. As Lewis himself puts it, "If I find in myself a desire which no experience in this world can satisfy, the most probable explanation is that I was made for another world."[45]

---

42. C. S. Lewis, *Till We Have Faces: A Myth Retold* (New York: Harcourt, Brace and World, 1980), 74.
43. See Andy Crouch, *Culture Making: Recovering our Creative Calling* (Downers Grove, IL: InterVarsity, 2008).
44. Lewis, *Weight of Glory*, 6.
45. Lewis, *Mere Christianity*, 120.

Out. Everyone, especially at certain points in their life, feels that they want something, or someone, that is just out of their reach. To an unbeliever feeling this way, the Christian would respond, "You feel that way because the world and its ways are not what you were made for; you were made for something, *someone*, much greater. You were made for God, and therefore, to paraphrase Augustine, your heart will be restless until it rests in him."[46] Moreover, even though in this life the Christian will experience foretastes of the good life, their hope rests in another eternal world where their desires will be satisfied fully. Fellowship with Christ in the present offers a fuller experience of life, including hope in the midst of loss, joy in suffering, and the promise of a future, deeper satisfaction found in God's eternal love.

Death

Inside. A terror of death seems to haunt us all—so much so, according to cultural anthropologist Ernest Becker, that we try our best to ignore the reality of our own mortality.[47] But it is there, underlying everything. With every moment that passes, everything around us seems to be creeping toward decay. Death is a reality that there is no use denying. A popular secular sentiment is to dismiss death by saying that in death we merely cease to exist. In death there is no meaning, no life, and no hope, so the best thing we can do is block death out of our mind. While this might be easy for some to say, it is much more difficult, if not impossible, to maintain consistently.

> ### A Cultural Example: "After the Storm"
>
> The popular song "After the Storm" by the indie band Mumford and Sons reveals that despite the prevalence of religious lethargy in late modern culture, an underlying fear of death remains. The song, however, also points further to a powerful vision of a future hope that echoes the final scenes of the Christian story, a time when there will be no more sadness or fear.

Atheist philosopher Luc Ferry asserts that the question of death, and in particular our awareness of it, far from being a matter we can easily ignore or dismiss, is at the heart of our distinctiveness as humans: "As distinct from animals . . . a human being is the only creature who is aware of his limits.

---

46. Augustine of Hippo, *Confessions*, trans. Henry Chadwick (Oxford: Oxford University Press, 1991), 3.

47. See Becker, *The Denial of Death*.

He knows that he will die, and that his near ones, those he loves, will also die. Consequently he cannot prevent himself from thinking about this state of affairs, which is disturbing and absurd, almost unimaginable."[48]

When people really, truly consider what it means that they will die, they cannot help but be deeply disturbed by the question. Thus, by sympathetically getting someone to seriously consider what will happen to them after they die, an apologist can place an existential weight on their shoulders that is difficult for them to bear, let alone shrug off.

Out. In an age in which people assume they can create their own webs of meanings and significance in life, death serves as "God's dismantling tool."[49] If late moderns are forced to face the thought of death, it will sober, humble, and even confuse them. As Old Testament wisdom reminds us:

> It is better to go to a house of mourning
>   than to go to a house of feasting,
> for death is the destiny of everyone;
>   the living should take this to heart.[50]

Yet while death alerts us to important realities, according to Christians, the story doesn't end there. If Jesus rose from the dead, then we too, though we die, will be made alive in him (John 11:25–26; 1 Cor 15:12–28). Death has lost its sting, and life has new meaning. As Ferry explains, our greatest desire as human beings is "to be understood, to be loved, not to be alone, not to be separated from our loved ones—in short, not to die and not to have them die on us."[51] Christianity's response to this universal human desire not to die is that in Christ, death is not only *not* the end of life, love, and community, but the door to a deeper experience of all these things; for this reason, Christianity is something the unbeliever should at least *want* to be true. The beauty of the Christian story certainly doesn't prove it is true, but all the same, the fear of death and the Christian view of resurrection can awaken the spiritually lethargic to the relevancy of religion and the possibility of believing.[52]

---

48. Luc Ferry, *A Brief History of Thought: A Philosophical Guide to Living* (New York: HarperCollins, 2011), 2–3.

49. David Gibson uses this terminology in reference to death in his contribution to Kevin J. Vanhoozer and Owen Strachan, *The Pastor as Public Theologian: Reclaiming a Lost Vision* (Grand Rapids: Baker Academic, 2015), 131.

50. Ecclesiastes 7:2.

51. Ferry, *A Brief History of Thought*, 4.

52. We'll discuss the Christian view of salvation and the resurrection more in chapter 13.

4. THE THERAPEUTIC TURN

In the West, the sense of personal and universal brokenness was traditionally defined with a religious vocabulary, namely, *sin*. Now, however, as C. S. Lewis lamented in middle of the twentieth century, "a sense of sin is almost totally lacking," and the moral register has been traded for a therapeutic one.[53] While sin was once assumed to be the main human problem, sickness has become the prevailing description for our modern malaise.[54]

In 1966, Philip Rieff composed a seminal work, *The Triumph of the Therapeutic*, in which he foresees an age when the pursuit of feeling better will overshadow the quest for justice, forgiveness, or redemption. In this new cultural context, he asserts, the main core value of society will be happiness, and thus the religious person, who was "born to be saved," will be overshadowed by the psychological person, who is "born to be pleased."[55]

Rieff's main contentions have proven true. To most late moderns, the goal of life is to make yourself happy. This belief clearly impacts the assumptions our culture makes concerning what is wrong with the world. In this late modern era, the normal struggles and issues of life are seen as just that—completely normal. If someone feels overwhelming guilt or sadness, they don't suspect they need to make any fundamental change in their beliefs, and they certainly don't think they need to "repent" of anything. Our problem is not that we are sinful, selfish, or disobedient, but rather that our mind-set is skewed; the main issues we have are psychological, and we can work those out. We may need therapeutic fine-tuning every now and again or, in more serious situations, perhaps even professional help. And traditional religion, far from being a viable solution, is actually part of the problem because the external moral constraints it places on us push up against expressive individualism, prohibiting us and making us feel guilty, suggesting that it's not okay for us to just be ourselves—whatever we've decided "being yourself" is.

In our present cultural ethos, the therapeutic turn is related to a phenomenon that author David Brooks refers to as "the Big Me." Brooks explains this concept by reflecting on the humble ways in which the Allies celebrated their WWII victory in the days following V-J Day:

---

53. C. S. Lewis, *God in the Dock: Essays on Theology and Ethics* (Grand Rapids: Eerdmans, 1970), 95.

54. See Taylor, *A Secular Age*, 618–22.

55. Philip Rieff, *The Triumph of the Therapeutic: The Uses of Faith After Freud* (1966; repr., Chicago: University of Chicago Press, 1987), 25; see also Alasdair MacIntyre, *After Virtue*, 3rd ed. (Notre Dame, IN: University of Notre Dame Press, 2008), 30–31.

The people . . . had been part of one of the most historic victories ever known. But they didn't go around telling themselves how great they were. They didn't print up bumper stickers commemorating their own awesomeness. Their first instinct was to remind themselves they were not morally superior to anyone else. Their collective impulse was to warn themselves against pride and self-glorification. They intuitively resisted the natural human tendency toward excessive self-love.[56]

Compared with the current cultural ethos, Brooks's illustration serves to represent the shift that has occurred from a mind-set that, though self-assured, was also humble—"Nobody's better than me, but I'm not better than anyone else"—to a mind-set in which people find self-promotion intuitive: "Recognize my accomplishments, I'm pretty special."[57]

In contrast to the therapeutic turn (and the related "Big Me" ethos), a central idea of Christianity has always been that because of sin and the fall, which have marred both human nature and the natural world, humans will never be able to be perfectly happy in this life.[58] Yet in our late modern world, as Rieff predicted, even many in the church have succumbed to the cultural pull of the therapeutic turn.

For example, for his book *Soul Searching*, Christian Smith surveyed students thirteen to seventeen years old. He found that even though the majority of American teens are still religious and active in their churches, they are not only incredibly inarticulate about their faith, but they also see God as "something like a combination Divine Butler and Cosmic Therapist: he is always on call, takes care of any problems that arise, [and] professionally helps his people to feel better about themselves."[59]

Perhaps most alarming is that the majority of the young people interviewed in this study were unaware that they were practicing something different from historic Christianity. They assumed that the way they see God is the way Christians have always seen God. Yet what they adhere to is a hollowed-out version of Christianity that places self as the center rather than God. This ought to serve as a sobering reminder that apologetics has to be applied not only outside the church but even within its walls.

56. Brooks, *Road to Character*, 4.
57. Brooks, *Road to Character*, 5.
58. See Taylor, *A Secular Age*, 635.
59. Christian Smith with Melina Lundquist Denton, *Soul Searching: The Religious and Spiritual Lives of American Teenagers* (Oxford: Oxford University Press, 2005), 165.

Opportunities

A High View of Human Dignity

Inside. As we've already seen, late modernism places a premium on human dignity; it is one of the recurring "A" doctrines of Christianity that the culture affirms. At first glance, trading sin for sickness may seem to heighten human dignity because it removes the embarrassment and shame of knowing we have violated our Creator's laws and that our nature has been marred and broken. In reality, however, redefining our primary problem as sickness instead of sin actually degrades human dignity,[60] because, as Charles Taylor describes, we are now to view ourselves as simply "incapacitated," as helpless victims who need to be "manipulated into health."[61] Once the "B" doctrine of sin has been tied to a high view of human dignity in this way, it will make much better sense to the late modern.

The Banality of Mourning in a Therapeutic Age

Death serves, once again, as a pressure point for unbelievers who have embraced the therapeutic turn. The humanist philosopher Luc Ferry explains:

> Psychology, it is a well-known fact, has dethroned theology. Yet on the day of burial, at the foot of the grave and the coffin, a certain discomfort takes hold of us. What are we to say to the mother who has lost her daughter, to the grief-stricken father? We are dramatically confronted with the question of meaning or, rather, with its eclipse in a secularized world . . . Whatever comfort a few compassionate gestures may bring, however precious this is, it does not measure up to the question posed by an absence that we know well has become, in a strict sense of the word, meaningless. Whence the banalities one always hears. They do not, however, conceal that the king is naked . . . Without being completely useless, the crutches offered by psychoanalysis are only that: clever prostheses.[62]

Out. Instead of reducing humans to biological machines or to determined products of culture that can simply be reprogrammed, Christianity emphasizes human dignity in the way it views people as God's image bearers, affirms that they are able to make significant choices, and describes how God deemed them worthy to be redeemed for a meaningful life. However, at the same time, it is

---

60. This is not to discount the legitimacy of forms of psychiatry. The problem occurs with a reductionism, when sickness replaces the concept of sin.

61. Taylor, *A Secular Age*, 620.

62. Luc Ferry, *Man Made God: The Meaning of Life* (Chicago: University of Chicago Press, 2002), 3.

important that we recognize the reality of sickness—including mental illness—and the gains of modern medicine. Sickness itself is a result of sin entering the world, and part of the human vocation is to bring holistic healing to the world, which includes alleviating suffering and caring for the sick. This kind of care will often take the form of sacrifice on behalf of the caregiver. Christianity provides a thick motivation, and even a moral obligation, to make scientific discoveries and to care for the world, especially those who cannot care for themselves.

Sin as Idolatry

Inside. Late moderns often see their "sin" as something to giggle about—an outdated notion that the grown-up modern mind need not be afraid of. Even those willing to consider a belief in God tend to dismiss their own sin, because, after all, who doesn't make mistakes? And if there is a God, isn't it kind of his job to forgive? What kind of God would he be if he didn't? In a therapeutic culture that doesn't take everyday sins seriously, how should Christians enter into a conversation about it?

One familiar way to explain sin is by using the Old Testament law to demonstrate the need people have for forgiveness and reconciliation. The law has often been used as a mirror so that people can see how far they fall short of God's standard. This use of the law to reveal sin is biblical, and in some contexts, it still can prove quite effective in initial conversations. However, for many today, being presented with a divinely instituted law that "they must be accountable to, or else" will not fit within their current framework.

While breaking God's law is something that most late moderns can easily shrug off, what they cannot so easily shrug off is the existential weight they feel in the face of the pressures of what seems like limitless choices and possibilities—the pressure of being successful, having the latest products, finding fulfilling relationships, discovering themselves, and managing their image. Not only do they feel the pressure to perform; they also often feel the disappointment and despair when they don't measure up. And, as Charles Taylor notes, even when they do measure up, they are left discontent: "Even people who are very successful in the range of normal human flourishing (perhaps especially such people) can feel unease, perhaps remorse, some sense that their achievements are hollow."[63]

When in the nineteenth century the Frenchman Alexis de Tocqueville visited America, he observed that, despite America's prosperity, there was a "strange melancholy which oftentimes . . . haunt[ed] [its] inhabitants . . . in the midst of their abundance."[64] If only he could see us now. For those who have

---

63. Taylor, *A Secular Age*, 621.
64. Alexis de Tocqueville, *Democracy in America*, trans. George Lawrence (New York: Harper, 1988), 296.

embraced the therapeutic turn and the "Big Me" culture, the melancholy, the unrest, the sense of being haunted that de Tocqueville observed is all the more ubiquitous. The character Tyler Durden in the movie *Fight Club* captures this discontentment poignantly: "We have no Great War. No Great Depression. Our Great War is a spiritual war. Our Great Depression is our lives. We've all been raised on television to believe that one day we'd all be millionaires and movie gods and rock stars, but we won't. And we're slowly learning that fact. And we're very, very pissed off."[65]

Out. Despite the enormous prosperity of the West and the vast resources poured into the medical industry to help us "feel better," there is a restlessness and anxiety that characterize the modern world. It is often when someone is feeling the all too common existential weight of discontentment and sadness that there is an apologetic opening to introduce the concept of idolatry—one of the main ways both the Old and New Testaments describe sin.[66]

As we've already seen under our discussion of identity above, the human heart is inevitably driven by something that it worships and desires above all else, whether it's money, sex, power, fame, or success. Yet when these temporal things are made ultimate, disappointment or despair will eventually come. The late modern person knows what it's like to feel devastated at the loss of something they had placed all their hope in. Tim Keller puts it like this:

> The very things upon which these people were building all their happiness turned to dust in their hands *because* they had built all their happiness upon them. In each case, a good thing among many was turned into a supreme thing, so that its demands overrode all competing values. But counterfeit gods always disappoint, and often destructively so.[67]

Idolatry, of course, is not the only way the Bible speaks of sin. There are other angles to the doctrine of sin that people need to come to grips with. And as we will see in the next chapter, returning to explain how God's commandments fit within the Christian picture of a loving heavenly Father will be important. But explaining idolatry in relatable modern terms can often serve as a helpful way for an apologist to introduce the concept of sin to the late modern, so they can begin to see the fundamental human problem and the power of the gospel for restoration.

---

65. *Fight Club*, directed by David Fincher, screenplay by Jim Uhls, based on the novel by Chuck Palahniuk, distributed by 20th Century Fox, September 10, 1999.

66. See, for example, Exodus 20:3–4; 34:17; Psalms 78:58; 97:7; Galatians 5:20; Colossians 3:5; 1 Peter 4:3.

67. Timothy Keller, *Counterfeit Gods: The Empty Promises of Money, Sex, and Power, and the Only Hope That Matters* (New York: Viking, 2009), xvii.

LOOKING BACK AND AHEAD

This chapter has charted some initial apologetic trajectories that can be used to appeal to the intuitions and experiences of late moderns. Admittedly, many more themes of late modernism could have been discussed, and even the perspective we've given on the themes we've chosen to discuss can be challenged by competing cultural narratives at different points.

Also, keep in mind that we do not intend this chapter to force you into any rigid system—far from it. We hope that by charting these initial trajectories, rather than boxing you in, we have encouraged you to think creatively, to be flexible, and to personalize and contextualize what we have discussed to the unique apologetic situations you find yourself in.

Finally, Christians must remember that in any fallen culture, there will be aspects of Christianity that will seem crazy, foolish, or dangerous. We must remain true to the gospel, which challenges all human cultures at certain points. Working from the *inside* of other people's frameworks *out* can help them see how what may initially seem to be the "strange" message of the gospel makes sense of the world, fulfills our deepest longings, and is more consistent and livable than competing options. However, working *inside* of an unbeliever's framework and then *out* to Christianity will often include not just addressing personal aspirations or cultural plausibility structures, but also responding to very specific questions and critiques that people have toward Christianity. It is to these specific critiques that we turn in the following chapter.

CHAPTER TWELVE

DEALING WITH DEFEATERS

The riddles of God are more satisfying than the solutions of men.

G. K. Chesterton, "The Book of Job," in On Lying in Bed and Other Essays

People have serious issues with Christianity. Sometimes these are scathingly expressed as skeptical objections; other times they are more mildly expressed as earnest questions. In this chapter, we will group these questions and objections together as what we call *defeaters*. Though unbelievers you encounter will present you with many of the same defeaters—such as the problem of evil or the restrictive nature of Christian morality—keep in mind that everyone you talk to is a unique individual who has a unique perspective and a unique set of reasons for rejecting Christianity.

Because of this, our goal in this chapter is not to give you "a universal map" for answering each defeater so you can memorize and then mechanically recite it. As we discussed in chapter 5, you shouldn't just give everyone the same map; you will need to draw many different maps. Our goal, then, is that you—while keeping the inside out approach in mind as the broader backdrop—learn trajectories for responses that you can personalize when you are drawing a map to answer a particular set of challenges to Christianity.

In offering guidance for responding to these defeaters, we are not suggesting that we've provided some sort of exhaustive compendium. Instead, consider this chapter similar to a set of instructions for learning how to perform an athletic move in a sport. First, some basics must be established: "This is how you hold the bat. Stand this far from the plate. Pivot your hips like this. Watch the ball out of the pitcher's hand. Make sure you follow through." With too many instructions, you would likely become overwhelmed and maybe even feel paralyzed. With too little coaching, you wouldn't even know where to start. Thus, to best prepare you for everyday apologetic interactions, this chapter seeks to strike a middle ground, providing basic instructions and examples for dealing with defeaters while keeping technical jargon to a minimum.

Just as in sports, there is no substitute for real-life practice if you wish to develop as an apologist. In-game learning trains us to be flexible and adjust to the situation at hand. Just like balls thrown by a wild pitcher, questions and objections unbelievers have can be all over the place. We will need to know how to make adjustments when a curveball or changeup comes instead of a fastball. While you will likely feel awkward at first, as you engage more frequently with unbelievers, you'll become more confident, and making such adjustments will become intuitive and natural to you.

DEFEATER #1: "Christianity is too restrictive. It denies people the opportunity to flourish by following their heart."

A common view of Christianity is that it takes the fun out of life. Because it seems like Christianity continually tells us what we cannot do, many see God as nothing more than a cosmic killjoy. As we saw in chapter 3, this contempt for Christian morality isn't new. Even in its earliest days, Christianity was known for ethics that the surrounding culture found strange and even dangerous.[1] Since it's easy to understand why unbelievers have often seen Christianity as too restrictive, you might tactfully respond to this objection: "I can understand why you would see Christianity this way, but I wonder if you might hear me out, because while Christianity does include ethical norms that may seem strange, simply obeying a bunch of rules is not the heart of the Christian message."

Jesus himself taught that he came not to suppress people or steal their joy, but to free them from the shackles of the world, the flesh, and the devil so that they can truly flourish: "I have come that they may have life, and have it to the full" (John 10:10). At the same time, however, part of the reason people see Christianity as a straitjacket is that many in the late modern era have defined "flourishing" in a way that blinds them to the beauty of Christ's offer.

The Problem with Flourishing by "Just Following Your Heart"

It's helpful to bring out some of the cultural assumptions that lead to this objection. One such assumption is what we described in chapter 11 as "expressive individualism," the belief that everyone has within themselves an identity to be discovered—a "true self" just waiting to be actualized.[2] According to this belief, human flourishing occurs when we "follow our heart" and cast off external norms to find our authentic self.

---

1. See Larry W. Hurtado, *Destroyer of the gods: Early Christian Distinctiveness in the Roman World* (Waco, TX: Baylor University Press, 2016).

2. See Robert Bellah et al., *Habits of the Heart: Individualism and Commitment in American Life* (Berkeley: University of California Press, 1985), 333–34.

In your interactions with those who have embraced expressive individualism, there is no need to criticize everything associated with it. Even as we point out the problems with expressive individualism, we can affirm some of the cultural developments that have accompanied it, such as the freedom to choose a spouse or a career path. That kind of freedom has been unheard-of for most people throughout human history, and it is not something most of us would want to turn back the clock on. However, even though expressive individualism may be related to a number of positive developments, there are several reasons why it proves unstable as a basis for human flourishing.

1. Expressive individualism corrodes life-giving interpersonal relationships that require commitment and sacrifice. Families, friends, and marriages are viewed instrumentally and are quickly abandoned if they cease to serve as a means for self-actualization. There is little motivation to make a long-term commitment to anyone. If I feel my wife, kids, and other close friends are restricting my ability to pursue what my heart tells me, why should I continue to devote myself to them? I will put up with them only as long as the benefits they provide me outweigh my obligations to them. After all, if a relationship is confining, why not find new relationships that don't demand self-denial and sacrifice? If someone were to hold consistently to the tenets of expressive individualism, it's difficult to see how they wouldn't find themselves suffering from weak, malnourished relationships. Research from the social sciences seems to support this conclusion: though we late moderns are surrounded by others, we often "feel deeply, dangerously alone."[3]

Cultural Example: "Something's Missing"

As humanist philosopher Luc Ferry observes, despite the web of meanings late moderns create for themselves, they are deeply "frustrated" because they can't shake the feeling that they're not "on earth only to purchase automobiles or ever better stereo systems."[4] A glimpse of this longing for something beyond the payoff of cardboard consumerism and low-commitment relationships is expressed in a wide range of cultural mediums, but perhaps most familiarly in song. John Mayer's "Something's Missing" epitomizes this mysterious unease in the midst of abundance. After listing how he has obtained all the seemingly necessary elements of the contemporary vision of the good life, he admits something is still lacking in his life, though he doesn't know what it could be.

---

3. Sebastian Junger, *Tribe: On Homecoming and Belonging* (New York: Hachette, 2016), 18. Though religion is not in view, Junger offers a fascinating perspective and includes references to the scientific research.

4. Luc Ferry, *Man Made God: The Meaning of Life* (Chicago: University of Chicago Press, 2002), 8.

At this point in a conversation, however, someone might reply, "I don't live like that. I understand the pull of expressive individualism, but I do have relationships that are altruistic." This is significant. Many who have generally assumed expressive individualism do strive to live sacrificially in some of their most intimate relationships. Here is something else we can affirm and use as an opening to help respond to their initial objection to Christianity.

When people refuse to abandon important relationships in the name of personal freedom and instead value others more than their own self-actualization and autonomy, they seem to be admitting something parallel to the Bible's teaching, namely, that saying no to some desires is an important part of genuine flourishing. They are admitting that personal sacrifice is essential for deep, life-giving relationships. This concession opens the door for Jesus' teachings to be seen in a new light. When Jesus tells us we must die to live and gives us rules to live by, he is inviting us to a deeper, truer kind of flourishing.

2. Perhaps the most acute problem within this modern assumption—that people are to look within themselves to find their true self—is its impracticality. It is impossible to live out. We can't help but constantly look to those around us to learn what we should value and how we should legitimize our own significance. We are always defining our lives in dialogue with our community. One prominent example is the way we embrace and try to live out the "hero" narratives that our communities and traditions tell us. By ingraining such stories into us, and in countless other ways, the communities we live in teach us what to worship, what to seek and value above all else—whether it's money, beauty, power, intellect, or self. We all look to something or someone for our identity and sense of worth. This leads to a third problem with denying Christianity in the name of freedom.

3. Though expressive individualism may promise us freedom, it cannot deliver on that promise, because we all look to external sources for significance and affirmation, which enslave us. As Jesus taught, everyone has a master. If what a particular group of friends or your parents or a partner or your kids think of you is the most important thing to you, then you will build your life, your happiness, and your worth around them. Their responses to you will limit you and control your life. If they reject you, if they let you down, or if they are taken from you, your life will feel empty. And you know it. So you will do anything you can to avoid losing them.

Or consider other things—good things, but not ultimate things—that we build our lives around: careers, success, possessions, security. These "gods" will restrict us, consume our time, and wreak havoc on our emotions. If we make them ultimate, they will, in the end, not just let us down; they will destroy us.

> ### A Literary Example: Sin as Idolatry
>
> *The Pearl* by John Steinbeck is a novella about a poor pearl diver named Kino, who discovers a pearl of immeasurable value. Gradually, Kino becomes obsessed with the pearl, and it ruins his life: he is nearly killed; his hut is burned down; and worst of all, he hurts his wife for trying to destroy it. While Kino initially saw the pearl as a blessing he could sell to save his son's life, it ultimately becomes a curse—the reason that his son dies. Kino's greed and love of the pearl blind him to what really mattered to begin with: his love for his family. The story powerfully illustrates how something that is good as a means will transform into an evil that enslaves us when we make it an end to itself.

When Jesus promised his followers an abundant life, he wasn't telling them he would usher in a life of freedom from norms and submission. That is impossible. We all submit to and are enslaved by something. Jesus, however, can paradoxically promise true freedom (John 8:32–36) through submission, because he is the one person we were designed to submit to, the one person in whom submission results in true freedom—the freedom to become the people we were designed to be. To better understand this, we need only look at Jesus, the most free and satisfied human who has ever lived.

How Christianity Liberates

It is important to stress that Jesus' call to absolute allegiance goes much deeper than a list of rules. For many, the idea of absolute allegiance will sound restrictive and totally off-putting. But this is why the previous section is so important. Committing to something that restricts you—and even enslaves you—is unavoidable. Everyone is a slave to something. According to Jesus, the only way we can be free is by submitting to him: "For whoever wants to save their life will lose it, but whoever loses their life for me will find it" (Matt 16:25).

Consider what it costs to become an elite musician or athlete. Elite musicians and athletes have the freedom to play, create, and improvise in beautiful and exciting ways. However, in order to achieve this freedom, they must restrict themselves, giving up on just doing whatever they think or feel at any given moment. Carefully following the instructions and example of experts, musicians and athletes make countless sacrifices of their natural desires every day, whether it's giving up hours of time to practice or eating a certain diet. Awe-inspiring improvisation on the soccer field or the concert hall is only made possible by long hours of disciplined training. True freedom comes through suppression. We can see this is true in many areas of our life; it is also true in ultimate ways.

We don't give our children rules to suppress them; we give them rules so they can live well. In the same way, the Bible doesn't give ethical commandments to restrict people from flourishing—the very opposite is true. God, who is good, gives commandments because *they are the only way* to truly flourish. God's rules point us to a deeper wisdom that leads to a virtuous life. He teaches us how to become like the ultimate exemplar of human flourishing, namely, Jesus Christ.[5]

This brings us to perennial questions that transcend any one generation or culture: What is it like to be truest to our humanity? To flourish in life? To live in a way that leads to the "good life"? Christianity teaches that the answer to these questions is not an abstract system or a list of rules; it is a person. During his time on earth, Jesus presented a breathtaking picture of the ideal human. He combined power with humility. Innocence with courage. Truth with generosity. The vulnerable and brokenhearted were drawn to him because of his compassion. Those who hungered for truth flocked to him because he taught with an authority like no other. The corrupt leaders feared him because he could not be tamed. He stood for justice while offering forgiveness to all, even to those who killed him. Astonishingly, his own brother and Saul of Tarsus, both of whom were skeptical of his seemingly outlandish claims, came to worship him as the very embodiment of God.

The irony at the heart of expressive individualism is that all human beings are slaves to something. In Western culture, we tend to see ourselves as rugged individuals constantly forging our own way through life. We desperately grasp for complete freedom and self-determination, not realizing that we do so at the expense of our own humanity. In our quest for autonomy and self-determination, we fail to see the cosmic irony of our situation: we will never be able to escape our own finitude. Christianity teaches something that is counterintuitive to late modern assumptions: in order to save your life, in order to be truly free, you must lose your life for the sake of Christ. The apologetic goal in this sort of discussion is to lift Christ high, praying others will see that they will only ever find their true purpose and freedom if they seek it in Christ.

---

5. See Jonathan T. Pennington, *The Sermon on the Mount and Human Flourishing: A Theological Commentary* (Grand Rapids: Baker, 2017).

For Further Reading

Bellah, Robert et al. *Habits of the Heart: Individualism and Commitment in American Life.* Berkeley: University of California Press, 2008.

Lewis, C. S. "Membership." Pages 30–42 in *The Weight of Glory and Other Addresses.* New York: Macmillan, 1949.

_____. *Mere Christianity.* Pages 49–50, 92, 223–27. New York: HarperCollins, 1952.

Taylor, Charles. *The Ethics of Authenticity.* Cambridge, MA: Harvard University Press, 1991.

DEFEATER #2: "The Christian sexual ethic is dehumanizing, and Christians are homophobic."

Truth and Tone

The modern social imaginary has taught us, "Look inside yourself and be the true you." This has led, by extension, to the idea that if you find yourself attracted to someone of the same sex, then you should embrace that as a part of your identity in the same way you would embrace your race or ethnicity.

Unfortunately, in recent years Christians in general have had a bad track record, not only in responding well to issues of sexuality, but in living consistently themselves. Great wisdom and tact will be needed, both in how we respond to the issue publicly and in how we speak to individuals who have been deeply hurt by inflammatory rhetoric. At the same time, however, we must never forget that love and truth are inseparable, and that sacrificing one in the name of the other only undermines both.

Our Assumption and Some Basics

As you think about this issue and engage with those who are unsettled or even angry about the stance Christians take on it, keep in mind that we should be the first to admit that Christians—particularly when influenced by certain traditions and cultures—can and have misinterpreted the Bible. Nevertheless, there are a variety of reasons to give us confidence that God's creation ideal is for sex to be a uniting and potentially procreating act between a man and woman within the context of marriage.

A significant point often overlooked in street-level discussion is that both Jesus and Paul appeal to the creation order when discussing marriage. This is significant, because even though Jesus did not teach specifically on homosexuality in the gospels, by referencing the Genesis account when he answers the Pharisees' question about divorce, he rules out homosexuality (e.g., Matt 19:1–11). The same can be said of Paul, who references the creation account in direct relation to homosexuality (Rom 1:24–32). Jesus and Paul both assume that God's binary design of humans was intentional and that he instituted marriage as the union of man and woman.

Homosexual relationships go against God's design. In warning us against this type of relationship, God is not seeking to hurt us. He forbids homosexual relationships because he desires us to live according to his good design so that we can be free to flourish.

Crafting a Response

In some situations, you might explain how Matthew 19:1–12, Genesis 1–2, and even Romans 1:18–32 outline God's beautiful design for marriage and sex as being between a man and a woman, also adding that this has been universally taught by the church for nearly two thousand years.[6] Of course, someone could easily object that they don't believe in the Bible and don't care about the Christian tradition. "Fair enough," you might respond. "I explain this in hopes that you might try to be sympathetic to my position. Jesus is my Lord. I obey and follow him. He has told us the type of sexual relationships he created humans for, and he calls on his followers to trust and obey him, so that's what I aim to do. After all, if he is God, he knows what's best for me much better than I do."

1. The issue of authority. On many occasions, it can be prudent to respond to this objection by pointing to the authority of Jesus. You might start by asking, "Would you say the belief that Jesus rose from the dead is contingent on what he said about marriage? In other words, do you not believe in the resurrection because you don't like what Jesus said about sex?"

They will likely respond, "Well, no, that's not what I'm saying. I don't believe in Jesus' resurrection for other reasons."

This would allow you to discuss the resurrection of Jesus: "This is probably the root of many of our differences. I believe he did rise from the dead and that he is the Savior of the world, so I trust his teachings. Would you be open to talking more about this?"

---

6. In *Creation and Covenant*, Christopher C. Roberts writes, "After an initial patristic period in which Christian beliefs about sexual difference were fluctuating and diverse, a more or less rough consensus on sexual difference existed from the fourth to the twentieth centuries" (*Creation and Covenant: The Significance of Sexual Difference in the Moral Theology of Marriage* [New York: T&T Clark, 2007], 185–86).

On one hand, the potential strength of this is that it enables you to point to Jesus rather than to just focus on one kind of sin. On the other hand, we should not imagine that an unbeliever can somehow make a simple, "logical" decision about the resurrection completely detached from the moral and emotive factors involved in making up their mind about Jesus. As the atheist philosopher Thomas Nagel has admitted, he's not indifferent to religious questions: "I don't want there to be a God! I don't want the universe to be like that."[7] Nagel is expressing a fundamental issue that plagues discussions about God. As humans, we fear losing control. We are well aware of the implications of submitting to someone as Lord. Considering this, when we discuss Christian morality with an unbeliever, we should avoid papering over the question of whether Jesus' teaching is *good* in the false hope that we can persuade them with a strictly rational appeal. If we decide to focus first on reasons to accept Jesus' authority, we will likely need to circle back around to defend his vision for sexuality.

2. Dying to live as sexual beings. We live in a culture where sex is free and seemingly unbounded. Sex has been placed on such a high pedestal that to suggest what we are claiming about sexuality seems old-timey, prudish, and even irrational. In our culture, the mantra of many is "if it feels good, do it." But the Bible calls us to something higher and more sacred, and it gives us these guidelines to help mold us into a certain kind of person who will truly flourish.

Christians have long recognized that different sins have different consequences. And yet, the underlying heart issue of all sin is the same: It is us saying to God, "No, I'm going to do it my way." Every sin, from a little white lie to a ruthless murder, is rooted in a worship of self over God. We want to make our own rules. We want to follow our own way. We think we know best. It was this posture toward God that set the world wrong to begin with, resulting in the disordered and broken creation we now live in. It is this posture toward God that now separates us from him. The good news Jesus Christ brought is that God desires us to return home and reunite with him, restoring our relationship to what it was originally meant to be. God is not singularly against any one sin; he is against all things that stand against his creation order, his authority, our relationship with him, and his good plan for the world.

God's plan for human sexuality includes two options: either a lifelong committed marriage between a man and a woman or a life of singleness. Both options, just like any of the choices we make in life, mean saying yes to some things and no to other things. Both paths call for discipline and obedience. But according to Christianity, these are the only two ways to true joy and human

---

7. Thomas Nagel, *The Last Word* (Oxford: Oxford University Press, 1997), 130.

flourishing. Of course, this does not mean these two paths will always "feel right." At times, a married person's sexual instincts might tell them to sleep around. At times, a single person might feel so lonely that they deeply desire to use sex to find physical and emotional intimacy. Thankfully, even when we step off God's intended ways onto our own paths, grace remains, and redemption is available. When we turn to Jesus, we find forgiveness, not condemnation (1 John 1:9).

As we saw earlier, we cannot trust our own "feelings" and "urges," or even "the way we are wired," to lead us to the good life, a life where we know our Creator and live out our true meaning and purpose. Jesus calls us to say no to ourselves and yes to him, trusting that his way is better than ours. Even if following Jesus makes us feel like we are dying, in the end, it is actually the only way we can truly live.

For Further Reading

Allberry, Sam. *Is God Anti-Gay? And Other Questions about Homosexuality, the Bible and Same-Sex Attraction.* Rev. ed. Surrey, UK: Good Book Company, 2015.

Fortson, S. D., and Rollin G. Grams. *Unchanging Witness: The Consistent Christian Teaching on Homosexuality in Scripture and Tradition.* Nashville: B&H Academic, 2016.

Roberts, Christopher C. *Creation and Covenant: The Significance of Sexual Difference in the Moral Theology of Marriage.* New York: T&T Clark, 2007.

Sprinkle, Preston. *People to Be Loved: Why Homosexuality Is Not Just an Issue.* Grand Rapids: Zondervan, 2015.

Wilson, Todd. *Mere Sexuality: Rediscovering the Christian Vision of Sexuality.* Grand Rapids: Zondervan, 2017.

DEFEATER #3: "Christians are a bunch of hypocrites; this includes many of the individuals I meet today and the way the church has collectively mistreated people through history."

Remembering the Importance of Word and Deed

First of all, this objection is the very reason we should never disconnect apologetics from discipleship and a strong doctrine of the church. Consider, for example, what a negative impact the lethargic response of southern white Protestants to racial injustice had on their ability to witness persuasively to the same minority groups.[8] God intends for us, his church, to be an embodiment and foretaste of his kingdom, and we should be living out the gospel together in such a way that our lives form an apologetic. As we discussed in chapter 6, we must do apologetics in both word *and* deed.

What about the Moral Shortcomings of Individual Christians Today?

Three relevant points can be made regarding the failure of individual Christians to live up to Christianity's high standards of virtue.

1. Just because someone who claims to be a Christian does something bad doesn't mean Christianity is bad. As the secular philosopher John Gray has written, it isn't just religion that can go bad; any human activity—including science—has the potential for evil.[9] In the same way that it would be foolish to dismiss science because some scientists produce weapons of mass destruction and drugs used for torture, it would be foolish to dismiss Christianity just because some Christians do evil things. It must also be recognized that though genuine believers sometimes do evil things, there are pseudo-Christians—believers in name only—just like there are pseudo-scientists.

2. According to Christian theology, individual Christian growth takes place over time. Even when someone genuinely converts to the Christian faith, they do not immediately conform their life to the teachings and ways of Jesus. And like all Christians, though the new believer will mature over time, they will never reach perfection in this life.

3. Sometimes people convert to Christianity out of abusive or other unstable, dysfunctional situations. While they may change in a variety of positive ways, they still may look much less moral than someone else who has no particular religious beliefs but grew up in a wholesome and stable environment. The church is a hospital for the morally sick, which, ultimately, is all of us. As such, it wouldn't make sense for the church to admit only those who are perfectly well, because the entire purpose of a hospital is to bring healing to those who are sick or broken.

What about the Church's Past Failures in History?

Unfortunately, it isn't just individual Christians who have failed. Oftentimes, skeptics will point out certain glaring failures of the church, such as slavery and segregation, to justify their misgivings about the Christian faith. While the

---

8. See Russell Moore, "A White Church No More," *New York Times*, May 6, 2016, www.nytimes.com/2016/05/06/opinion/a-white-church-no-more.html.

9. See John Gray, "What Scares the New Atheists?" *Guardian*, March 3, 2015, www.theguardian.com/world/2015/mar/03/what-scares-the-new-atheists.

church truly did fail in addressing these issues, there are certain false narratives that have grown up around them. For this reason, when someone brings up the issue of the church's failures throughout history, we recommend taking a two-step approach in which you first admit past failures but then seek to correct and clarify the prevailing anti-Christian narrative. In the sections that follow, we will use this two-step method specifically to respond to criticism concerning slavery and segregation, but it could also be applied to other failures of the church.

Slavery

Admit faults. When seeking to understand what the Bible says concerning slavery, Christians have at different points throughout history allowed self-interest to cloud their interpretation. For example, in the nineteenth century, some southern Christians in the United States used the Bible to support race-based chattel slavery. Their brutality and the indignity to which they subjected fellow human beings are inexcusable.

Correct and clarify the prevailing anti-Christian narrative. First of all, the Bible does not develop or advocate a pro-slavery theology. The worst that can be said about slavery in the Bible is that in a historical and cultural context where slavery was the norm, the Israelites too had slaves—though their laws concerning treatment of slaves were much more humane than the laws of those in the world around them.[10] In actuality, though, what the Bible has to say concerning slavery is much, much better than simply commanding that slaves be treated humanely. Harry A. Hoffner Jr. observes that "the spirit of abolition" can be seen from the very beginning of the Bible, when God made man and woman in his own image—in doing so, assigned all people inherent worth and dignity. And this affirmation of human dignity only continued to be expressed in the laws God gave his people in Genesis through Leviticus: All that "remained [was] for discerning and compassionate souls to recognize and apply [its] implications."[11]

In other words, it is up to the church to work out the implications of God making all humans in his own image. It is up to the church to recognize that the institution of slavery is incompatible with the Christian faith. Unfortunately, the church at times has misinterpreted and misapplied the Bible before getting it right—particularly when self-interest supplants Christian principles. Slavery in the American South is an unfortunate case in point.

---

10. For more on slavery in the Bible, see Paul Copan, *Is God a Moral Monster? Making Sense of the Old Testament God* (Grand Rapids: Baker, 2011), 124–57.

11. Harry A. Hoffner Jr., "Slavery and Slave Laws in Ancient Hatti and Israel," in *Israel: Ancient Kingdom or Late Invention?* ed. Daniel I. Block (Nashville: B&H, 2008), 154–55.

The good news, however, is that in the end, Christian moral potency will overcome self-interest. It was Christian men and women who, realizing the implications of the "image of God" theology of the Bible, ultimately played a pivotal role in undermining and abolishing slavery. We see this illustrated in the untiring work of Thomas Clarkson (1760–1856) and William Wilberforce (1759–1833) in Great Britain and in the organized efforts of the Quakers in America. The movement to end slavery was led by Christians, who used arguments rooted both explicitly and implicitly in Scripture. Christian theology—in particular, the doctrine of the image of God—along with other cultural forces, finally put an end to slavery in Great Britain, France, America, Spain, and Latin America.[12]

Segregation

Admit faults. Because of weak biblical support for segregation, Christians often hid their prejudice behind political doctrines such as states' rights and the separation of church and state. Rather than lifting up the marginalized and working for racial equality, as is taught in the Scriptures, white Christians and white churches in the American South often took a passive stance toward discrimination. At times, they did even worse, actively supporting the Jim Crow laws to the detriment of their Christian witness. Again, fear and self-interest worked against clear-headed theological reflection and moral action.

Correct and clarify the prevailing anti-Christian narrative. As is apparent in the leadership of men and women such as Martin Luther King Jr., James Lawson, Fannie Lou Hamer, Fred Shuttlesworth, and Bob Moses, biblical revelation and the Christian faith were driving forces in the desegregation movement—especially the following four biblical dynamics.

1. The desegregation movement's approach was shaped by the Old Testament prophets' fiery preaching against the sinfulness of humanity and for the pursuit of social justice. Many black antisegregationist leaders had no faith in the liberal doctrine of natural progressive development. Many of them saw it as impractical and ineffective because, like James Lawson and C. S. Lewis, they believed the "normal course of human society was corrupting [and] sinful."[13] Change would only come if Christians actively and vigorously pushed back on societal prejudice and selfishness.

---

12. See Rodney Stark, *For the Glory of God: How Monotheism Led to Reformations, Science, Witch-Hunts, and the End of Slavery* (Princeton, NJ: Princeton University Press, 2003), 338–65.

13. David L. Chappell, *A Stone of Hope: Prophetic Religion and the Death of Jim Crow* (Chapel Hill: University of North Carolina Press, 2004), 69.

2. Those opposing segregation were motivated by a belief in God's active presence in the world. Black antisegregationist rallies, often permeated with a deep spirituality and belief in the miraculous power of God, had the feel of revival crusades. This is not to say that all antisegregationist leaders were Christians, but it is to say that most of them were driven by biblical revelation and Christian hope. This was not primarily a group of secular unbelievers. As historian David Chappell asserts, "It is hard to imagine masses of people lining up for years of excruciating risk against southern sheriffs, fire hoses, and attack dogs without some transcendent or millennial faith to sustain them."[14]

3. Perhaps most prominently of all, the nonviolent nature of the movement was shaped by the light and love ethos of the New Testament taught by Jesus in the gospels. Martin Luther King Jr. continually emphasized the importance of the Christian doctrine of love to the antisegregationist movement: "Our actions must be guided by the deepest principles of our Christian faith. Love must be our regulating ideal. Once again we must hear the words of Jesus echoing across the centuries: 'Love your enemies, bless them that curse you, and pray for them that despitefully use you.'"[15] The real change King brought about did not come through the exercise of violence and hate, but by the peace and love found in the teachings of Jesus.

4. A hope in the coming kingdom of God—where there will be neither Jew nor Gentile, neither slave nor free—motivated them to bring aspects of that kingdom into their present existence. As abolitionist leader James Lawson explained, Christians should desire to break down racial barriers because "the redeemed community of which [they are] already [citizens] recognizes no barriers dividing humanity."[16] One of the central goals of the Christian life is to manifest the future kingdom of God on earth as it is in heaven, and that includes seeking equality for all people in Christ.

Jesus, the ideal picture of humanity, is represented by imperfect disciples. We must not only help skeptics understand why Christians can make grave mistakes, but also explain to them the errors in the prevailing narratives about issues such as slavery and segregation. Christian theology, when correctly rooted in the teachings of Jesus and the rest of Scripture, offers powerful resources for good and stands as a corrective force against evil and injustice.

---

14. Chappell, *Stone of Hope*, 102.

15. Martin Luther King Jr., *Stride Toward Freedom: The Montgomery Story* (1958; repr., Boston: Beacon, 2010), 51.

16. Quoted in Chappell, *Stone of Hope*, 69.

For Further Reading

Chappell, David L. *A Stone of Hope: Prophetic Religion and the Death of Jim Crow.* Chapel Hill: University of North Carolina Press, 2004.

Copan, Paul. *Is God a Moral Monster? Making Sense of the Old Testament God.* Pages 124–57. Grand Rapids: Baker, 2011.

Hoffner, Harry A. Jr. "Slavery and Slave Laws in Ancient Hatti and Israel." Pages 154–55 in *Israel: Ancient Kingdom or Late Invention?* Edited by Daniel I. Block. Nashville: B&H, 2008.

Stark, Rodney. *For the Glory of God: How Monotheism Led to Reformations, Science, Witch-Hunts, and the End of Slavery.* Princeton, NJ: Princeton University Press, 2003.

DEFEATER #4: "Faith, in contrast to reason and science, is for people who believe things without any evidence. It is long past time that we move beyond old myths about the supernatural and the divine and seek to discover truth using reason and empirical observation."

Identify the "Coming-of-Age Narrative" That Lies Behind This Defeater

One of the "unchallenged axioms" many moderns subscribe to is the following narrative: Nonreligious people have had the courage to embrace the cold, hard facts that science has presented humankind with. They have chosen to let go of comforting, childish religious beliefs and have grown up, taking an adult stance on reality.[17] Though this might make for a powerful coming-of-age story, it is based on mistaken assumptions.[18]

Scientific Methods Are Not Based on Reason Alone

Is it really possible to adopt a theory for discovering truth that doesn't require faith? The initial problem with scientism is that the central claim it makes—that science is the only criteria for discovering truth—cannot be justified by science and therefore undermines itself. In this way, the view is ultimately incoherent.[19]

---

17. See Charles Taylor, *A Secular Age* (Cambridge, MA: Harvard University Press, 2007), 362–66, 560–93.

18. For an account of someone who once assumed this reductionistic story but then tells his own coming-of-age story—from childish scientism to growing into a mature faith in God, see Alister McGrath, *The Big Question: Why We Can't Stop Talking about Science, Faith, and God* (New York: St. Martins, 2015), 1–75.

19. See John C. Lennox, *God's Undertaker: Has Science Buried God?* (Oxford: Lion Hudson, 2009), 43.

A question to ask, then, in a conversation with someone who ascribes to scientism might be, "How can science prove that science is the only source of truth?"

Because modern science is unquestionably an important enterprise in grasping truth, we should be quick to affirm how thankful we are for it—for the countless discoveries and world-changing inventions it has made possible. What we must take issue with, however, is the claim that science is the only means by which to obtain truth. When you encounter a person who makes this claim, you can help them better understand your position by prompting them to reflect more deeply on the assumptions that modern science is necessarily predicated on.

It is likely that the person with this objection to Christianity has embraced what Charles Taylor refers to as a "'subtraction' story," the (false) narrative that secularism is the "neutral" position that is left over once all religious and supernatural beliefs have been canceled out.[20] The problem with this narrative is that secularism—in all its variations—actually has its own set of beliefs and values that cannot be proven and therefore requires a type of faith.[21] For example, two of the assumptions essential to modern science—the rationality of the universe and the reliability of basic cognitive faculties—cannot be proven by science. They must first be believed.

Often people assume that scientific methods only use basic logic and empirical facts to solve a problem, but they are mistaken. This allegedly neutral methodology cannot actually avoid faith and intuition.[22] One cannot *simply* observe significant facts and then form a hypothesis to solve a problem. After all, what makes a fact *significant*? How can one determine if a problem the "facts" are being used to solve is *worthwhile*? There is no scientific way to determine beforehand what problems are *worth* solving or which facts are *significant*. Faith has to be placed in intuition and personal experience or some other source beyond science in order to proceed.[23] Moreover, what are the rules for forming a hypothesis once the data has been examined? The history of science teaches us that accepted theories are not the straightforward result of the accumulation of facts.[24] Imagination, intuition, and historical circumstances are all involved in successful hypothesizing.

---

20. See Taylor, *A Secular Age*, 26–29.

21. See Stephen LeDrew, *The Evolution of Atheism: The Politics of a Modern Movement* (New York: Oxford University Press, 2016).

22. See Michael Polanyi, *Personal Knowledge: Towards a Post-Critical Philosophy* (Chicago: University of Chicago Press, 1962).

23. See Albert Einstein, *The World As I See It* (1984; repr., New York: Citadel, 2006), 125.

24. Thomas S. Kuhn was instrumental in challenging the assumption that scientific theorizing was the straightforward accumulation of facts (*The Structure of Scientific Revolutions*, 50th anniv. ed. [Chicago: University of Chicago Press, 2012]).

Scientism Undercuts Itself

Another problem with the secular view that some form of materialism is what is left after other sources of truth like religion are "subtracted" out is that it has a difficult time grounding and subsequently justifying our reasoning capabilities. How can materialists scientifically prove that they can trust their reasoning ability? What makes them so certain that their reasoning is directed toward truth? If the goal of evolution is survival, then why aren't human reasoning capacities directed toward simply surviving rather than discovering truth? These sorts of questions have led the well-known Christian philosopher Alvin Plantinga, along with many of his unbelieving peers, to a problem that plagues many atheists: taken together, naturalism and evolutionary theory are self-defeating.[25]

The scientific method(s) cannot account for much of reality.[26] While modern science has given us access to important knowledge about the world, the scientific method(s) cannot prove or even explain a wide range of knowledge and experience that nearly everyone would agree we are fully justified in taking to be true. The scientific method cannot, for example, account for logical and mathematical truths; it must simply assume them. It cannot prove many of basic beliefs we all take for granted, such as the idea that other minds exist and that our memories actually happened. It cannot account for beauty—aesthetics is outside of its purview. It cannot make ethical statements; one cannot, through scientific methods, determine if certain actions are morally wrong (see chapter 13). Consequently, science cannot account for justice, human rights, or good and evil. If we all sought to apply this absolutizing view of science consistently, we wouldn't be able to accept many important truths.

Moreover, if science proceeds by assuming only natural causes, then it cannot actually touch on the question of God. If someone proceeds in science on the basis of methodical naturalism, experiments can only seek to answer questions about this world; they cannot answer questions concerning things beyond the material world. The implication of this is that, within these limits, it is not just belief in God that requires a form of faith beyond the answers science can provide; disbelief in God does as well.

We've seen some of the internal shortcomings and inconsistencies of seeking to use science to attack religious belief. Part of the task of responding to this defeater is helping others see that we all assume truths that cannot be substantiated by "reason" and empirical evidence alone. In actuality, skeptics, just like

25. See Alvin Plantinga, *Where the Conflict Really Lies: Science, Religion, and Naturalism* (New York: Oxford University Press, 2011), 349; see our chapter 13 for further explanation of this point.

26. There are different forms of the scientific method. For a brief discussion, see Lennox, *God's Undertaker*, 32–35.

everyone else, believe what they do about the world for a variety of reasons, many of which are not "provable." The takeaway for responding to this defeater is this: *Unbelievers should not inconsistently demand a standard of proof for God that could never be applied to some of their most basic commitments.*

Science and Its Limits

"Scientific truth is characterized by its precision and the certainty of its predictions. But science achieves these admirable qualities at the cost of remaining on the level of secondary concerns, leaving ultimate and decisive questions untouched."[27]

Biblical faith is *not* believing in something without good reasons. This defeater also misrepresents Christianity. To believe in Christianity is not to have "blind faith"; there are many valid historical, rational, experiential, and societal reasons for the Christian faith. And in fact, as we explain in chapters 11 and 13, the Christian account of reality offers a more livable and wide-ranging explanation of reality than the accounts offered by secularism. The Christian framework was actually a key factor in providing the soil for modern science to grow in the first place. To initiate a conversation with an unbeliever about this, you might ask them, "What do you think was the framework or view of the world that made modern science possible?"

As part of the Christian framework, the following three beliefs were vital in the rise of modern science:

1. The doctrine of creation, by implying that there was a regularity and orderliness to the universe, led to a confidence that nature could be studied and understood.
2. The conviction that the investigation of nature would inspire a greater appreciation for God was an important motivation for the study of nature.
3. The doctrine of original sin led to a suspicion of pure reason and to the view that experimentation was necessary to gain knowledge about nature.[28]

---

27. Spanish philosopher José Ortega y Gasset, quoted in McGrath, *The Big Question*, 4.
28. McGrath, *The Big Question*, 37–38; see also Peter Harrison, *The Bible, Protestantism, and the Rise of Natural Science* (Cambridge: Cambridge University Press, 2001). For more on the third point, see Peter Harrison, *The Fall of Man and the Foundations of Science* (Cambridge: Cambridge University Press, 2009).

The Christian framework also gives us reason to expect that our cognitive faculties will match up with the world around us—whereas naturalism has no reason to expect such a fit. This is why Alvin Plantinga argues there is actually "deep concord between science and theistic belief."[29] As the historian Rodney Stark has shown, there are religious reasons why modern science emerged in Christian Europe and not in such sophisticated societies as China, ancient Greece, and Islamic nations.[30] For example, when the cosmos is viewed as "an emanation of the absolute spirit," as in some other religions, modern science is unable to get off the ground.[31] Among other factors, it was the Christian belief that the universe is contingent, formed by a personal and sovereign Creator who ordered the universe, that enabled science to mature. Thus, far from there being a deep conflict between science and faith, it was the Christian faith that provided, as Alister McGrath writes, the "conceptual framework, within which science could flourish."[32]

For Further Reading

Copan, Paul et al., eds. *Dictionary of Christianity and Science: The Definitive Reference for the Intersection of Christian Faith and Contemporary Science.* Grand Rapids: Zondervan, 2017.

Lennox, John C. *God's Undertaker: Has Science Buried God?* Oxford: Lion Hudson, 2009.

McGrath, Alister. *The Big Question: Why We Can't Stop Talking About Science, Faith, and God.* New York: St. Martin's, 2015.

Plantinga, Alvin. *Where the Conflict Really Lies: Science, Religion, and Naturalism.* New York: Oxford University Press, 2011.

DEFEATER #5: "I can't believe in God because there is so much evil and suffering in the world."

When responding to someone with this objection, the best place to start is often to ask them some thoughtful questions like, "Would you mind telling me more about why you find suffering and evil such an obstacle to believing in God?"

---

29. Plantinga, *Where the Conflict Really Lies*, 350.
30. See Stark, *For the Glory of God*, 150–57.
31. Lesslie Newbigin, *The Gospel in a Pluralistic Society* (Grand Rapids: Eerdmans, 1989), 20.
32. McGrath, *The Big Question*, 38. C. F. von Weizsäcker refers to modern science as "a legacy of Christianity" (*The Relevance of Science* [New York: Harper, 1964], 163).

or "Was there a particular time in your life when you remember coming to this conclusion?" Their responses will likely provide some clues into whether they are struggling more with the more abstract *logical problem of evil*, which is the perceived rational contradiction between the existence of suffering and a loving God, or the more concrete *experiential problem of evil*, which is related to how people understand and deal with bad things that happen in their own lives.

We will first address the experiential problem because, as theologian Henri Nouwen once commented, "For most people the most burning question is: how to make it another day, another week, another year."[33] Though we will address the logical and experiential problem of evil individually, we have found that the two are often intertwined, so in actual conversations, you will frequently ping back and forth between both.

The Experiential Problem

Suffering is not just a Christian problem; it is a human problem, perhaps *the* human problem. Suffering and death are experiences that cast a shadow over everyone's lives, no matter what their worldview.

It can be helpful to first start on the inside of the unbeliever's framework, with their distress over suffering, and then move outside of their framework by exploring the various explanations for how we should view suffering and what we should do in response to the wrongs in the world. This will provide them with a broader context and give you an opportunity to help them work toward Christianity.

A Range of Traditional Options

Contrasting the Christian vision with other views is a good way to make a case for how Christianity best explains common human experiences and provides the strongest resources for living in the midst of suffering.

The Evil as Illusion View

As a prime example of this view, Buddhism admits there is suffering in the world, but claims that evil is based on a broader illusion. The reason people suffer is that they have unfulfilled desires, so the solution is for them to subjugate all desire and, in doing so, achieve enlightenment. Only when we rid ourselves of desire and detach ourselves from the material world will we achieve self-transcendence and peace.

---

33. Henri J. M. Nouwen, *Love, Henri: Letters on the Spiritual Life* (New York: Convergent, 2016), 127.

Points to Affirm: Like Christianity, this view affirms that there is a point to suffering. We should expect it, learn from it, and be changed by it. Moreover, Christians recognize, somewhat similar to Buddhism, that the attachment to material things does often bring suffering.

Points to Challenge: Christianity does not teach that evil is an illusion or that we should seek to overcome suffering by detaching ourselves from the world around us. Instead, it teaches that evil is very real and that we should be deeply invested in this world, working to alleviate injustice and overcome evil—both of which are enemy intrusions into God's good creation.

The Fatalistic View

This view was common in ancient Greek and Roman cultures, and it is still prevalent in many forms today. A person cannot outrun fate, so they must endure whatever evil befalls them in a stoic sort of way. Stoic resolution in the face of suffering and death is the path to achieving a legacy of glory and honor.

Points to Affirm: Christians also believe that suffering is an inevitable part of life, that it has meaning, and that we should strive to face it nobly.

Points to Challenge: Christianity does not glorify suffering as something to seek out or to face with stoic indifference. Christians are encouraged to express honestly their grief, weaknesses, and hope in the face of pain and evil. Christianity offers a very different form of noble suffering.

The Moralistic Religious View

Whenever someone suffers, it is because they have committed a corresponding evil action. A person's lot in life is directly related to the actions they have taken in this or a previous life, and they receive exactly what they deserve. Thus, the way to avoid suffering is to do good.

Points to Affirm: Like the moralistic religious take, Christianity teaches that suffering has meaning and that it can have a refining effect on us. Furthermore, the Christian story affirms that, in general, the suffering in the world is rooted in evil rebellion against God.

Points to Challenge: Christianity does not teach that there is some sort of simple cause-and-effect relationship between sin and suffering or that suffering is equally handed out to everyone on the basis of their past deeds. Rather, the amount one suffers is not "deserved" or, on balance, "fair." This can be seen both in the life of Job and in the life of Jesus. The reasons we suffer, at least in the short run, are often mysterious.

The Cosmic Conflict View

This dualistic view sees the world as locked in a conflict between good and evil forces, neither of which is ultimately sovereign. Think of the celebrated *Star Wars* movies. The dark side—standing behind suffering and injustice—and the light side of the force—standing behind all that is good—are doing battle.

Points to Affirm: Christianity also affirms that there are real evil forces at work that cause both injustice and suffering. Humans should stand on the side of good and resist evil.

Points to Challenge: The Christian God gives humans real choices and responsibilities, but he is at the same time the ultimate sovereign, and his divine plan cannot be thwarted. God is more powerful than evil and will ultimately triumph over it. Also, Christianity, rather than seeing the universe in two black-and-white divisions, good and evil, recognizes that both good and evil cut through the heart of us all.

Secular Options

Secular views of suffering differ from the more traditional views sampled above.[34] All the traditional views claim that, in some way, suffering has real meaning—that it is something we should learn from, grow through, or even be transformed by. Most traditional views also add that this current life is not the end of the story. Current secular views, however, deny both of these points and posit that suffering is meaningless and there is no life after we die. So from a secular perspective, *if* there is such a thing as "meaning" or a "meaningful life," it can only be found in this life and is rooted in the happiness and fulfillment we create for ourselves.[35] Because suffering has no transcendent meaning or purpose, it should be avoided and eradicated at all costs. There are two general secular responses for how to live in the face of the common human problem of suffering: the *secular pessimistic take* and the *secular optimistic take*.

The Secular Pessimistic View

There is no meaning, no purpose, and no morality in the universe. God is dead. And so is meaning. One day we will all cease to exist. We are the accidental

---

34. For an important resource and a deeper look at how various worldviews understand suffering and evil, see Timothy Keller, *Walking with God through Pain and Suffering* (New York: Dutton, 2013).

35. Some will say that meaning in life is found in the utilitarian idea of serving the greater good. Accordingly, suffering might serve the "greater good." However, several problems exist with this view. It lacks the clear resources to motivate one to sacrifice personal happiness for the happiness of others. Moreover, the "greater good" still has no ultimate meaning. The significance of a selfless act will die with humanity. And "the greater good" or "happiness," as Alasdair MacIntyre observes, has various forms, and thus it is not a useful guide. A framework that provides a transcendent *telos* for humanity is needed to ground the "good" (see *After Virtue*, 3rd ed. [Notre Dame, IN: University of Notre Dame Press, 2008], 51–78).

by-product of a mechanistic universe that is generally hostile toward life. While no one in their right mind wants to suffer, at the end of the day, we must admit that we live in a cruel world where suffering is both meaningless and ultimately inescapable.

Points to Affirm: We suggest you admit this view has a certain unflinching consistency to it. Indeed, if the universe will eventually suffer heat death, in the end, nothing will be remembered, and our lives won't matter. You can also affirm the sober, experiential realism this view holds to: this world can be cruel, and human achievement will never be able to eliminate suffering or prevent future extinction.

Points to Challenge: This view is basically unlivable. We all automatically live as if there is meaning in the world. Even a hardened and pessimistic secularist like John Gray admits that although "other animals do not need a purpose in life," humans "cannot do without one."[36] Humans will assign meaning, purpose, and morality in the day-to-day trials of life; it is simply what we do.

The Secular Optimistic View

This view affirms that because there is no transcendent meaning in the world that we can discover, we are left to create our own meaning. The gospel of secular optimism is that we have been liberated from conforming to some external source of truth or meaning and are free to determine what is good and meaningful for ourselves. A representative of this position explains: "Secularists see a universe without apparent purpose and realize that we must forge our own purposes and ethics . . . But although the universe is purposeless, our lives aren't . . . We make our own purposes, and they're real."[37] Often, this take is accompanied by an idealism regarding humans' ability to overcome suffering. Rather than waiting for any kind deity to act on our behalf or placing our hope in an afterlife in which all will be made right, we must, as a "Humanist Manifesto" states, "save ourselves."[38]

Points to Affirm: It is important to avoid accusing a secular optimist of having no meaning in their life. If you did, they would likely scoff, "I have a caring relationship with my wife. I am raising my kids to be kind and moral people. I create jobs with my business, and I volunteer in several charity organizations. I sacrifice, and in some sense suffer, for all these things because each has great

---

36. John Gray, *Straw Dogs: Thoughts on Humans and Other Animals* (London: Granta, 2002), 199.

37. Jerry A. Coyne, "Ross Douthat Is on Another Erroneous Rampage against Secularism," *New Republic*, December 26, 2013, https://newrepublic.com/article/116047/ross-douthat-wrong-about-secularism -and-ethics; see Keller, *Making Sense of God*, 63.

38. "Humanist Manifesto II," American Humanist Association, 1973, https://americanhumanist.org/ what-is-humanism/manifesto2.

meaning and value." These are all commitments we should affirm rather than denigrate. Also, while some of the nonsecular views surveyed above have too often led to a passive resignation to evil, Christians can agree with optimistic secularists that humans should indeed work to combat the evils of the world.

Points to Challenge: First, this view lacks a cogent rationality. If we create our own webs of meaning and significance, what happens when we are all gone? If our meaning and significance will disappear with humanity's destruction, why do any of our efforts really matter in the long run? One popular response to these questions is that we should simply not ask them. We shouldn't think about them. Just live your life right now the best you can, and don't spend time thinking too deeply about the distant future. We would suggest, however, that if a view about the world encourages people not to think about certain inescapable aspects of life—namely, death and suffering—its rational merits should be called into question.

Second, this view is thin experientially. If meaning is assigned only within the confines of this life, then what happens when the sources of that meaning—family, career, friends—begin to go bad? What happens when, in the inevitability of life, the delicate filaments that compose the web of meaning we've constructed for ourselves are torn or disintegrate altogether? When this happens, our very concept of meaning and significance itself will be threatened, undermined, or destroyed.[39]

The Christian View

For Christians, suffering and death should be neither sought after nor avoided at all costs. Instead, living well requires us not to attempt to ignore the universal experiences of suffering and death, but rather to think deeply about them. Unlike the various forms of secularism, suffering is not only meaningful; it can teach us and transform us into something magnificent (2 Cor 4:17). As C. S. Lewis famously put it, for Christians, "God whispers to us in our pleasures, speaks in our conscience, but shouts in our pains."[40]

Christianity understands pain and suffering not as a sign that the world is meaningless and arbitrary, but rather that it is not the way it was originally intended to be. Because humans turned away from God, the giver of life, the result was a distorted creation and the invasion of death. Evil is not an illusion; it is very real. It cannot simply be defined by relative personal or cultural preference. Evil is anything that stands against God and his plan for creation.

---

39. See Keller, *Making Sense of God*, 74.
40. C. S. Lewis, *The Problem of Pain* (New York: Macmillan, 1962), 93.

The Christian message is that God, in the person of Jesus, is redeeming this fallen world and will one day usher in justice and eternal peace. While Christians can agree with secularists that we should fight for justice and peace, we must be sure to assert that these categories are not just a matter of our own cultural preferences. Christians have a much more stable basis for philanthropic causes than relativistic cultural ideals. In other words, while we can agree with our secular friends that we should fight to end things like sex trafficking and injustices against women, we ought to ask them, "How can these things be considered anything more than mere cultural preferences?" The justification Christianity provides for activism is far stronger, because it is based on the inherent worth of humans made in God's image, the divinely given vocational calling to care for creation, and the moral obligation all humans have to their Creator.

The Christian story also provides a powerful motivation, absent in secular views, for making sacrifices and enduring pain for the sake of justice and goodness. For in Christianity, justice and goodness have transcendent meaning; they matter to God and will matter for eternity.

In his poignant work *A Lament for a Son*, former Yale philosopher Nicholas Wolterstorff reflects on Jesus' words, "Blessed are those who mourn," and then asks, "Who then are the mourners?" He concludes that the mourners are "those who have caught a glimpse of God's new day, who ache with all their being for that day's coming, and who break out into tears when confronted with its absence . . . The mourners are aching visionaries."[41]

Secular visions of justice struggle to kindle such deep commitment to this world alongside such hope for the future. Consider, for example, the Stoics, who said that in facing life's challenges, we should steel ourselves and seek to empty ourselves of emotion: "Be calm. Disengage yourself. Neither laugh nor weep." Jesus, in stark contrast, tells us, "Be open to the wounds of the world. Mourn humanity's mourning, weep over humanity's mourning, be wounded by humanity's wounds, be in agony over humanity's agony. But do so in good cheer that a day of peace is coming."[42]

Luc Ferry refers to this as the "seductive promise" of Christianity—a promise the long-standing, impersonal pagan view of eternity was no match for.[43] Because Christians know they are saved by and into an eternal love, they can rest in the assurance that "the life of [their] loves will not come to an end with earthly death."[44]

---

41. Nicholas Wolterstorff, *A Lament for a Son* (Grand Rapids: Eerdmans, 1987), 85–86.

42. Wolterstorff, *Lament for a Son*, 86.

43. Luc Ferry, *Learning to Live: A User's Manual* (Edinburgh: Canongate, 2010), 86.

44. Ferry, *Learning to Live*, 87.

The Logical Problem

Despite the rich resources Christianity offers for responding to and living with suffering, those with a secular perspective will often object: "I don't care if Christianity helps deal with reality better than the other major worldviews. That doesn't mean it's true. The problem I have with Christianity is that I don't see how a good and all-powerful God could allow suffering and evil into the world. If God were good, knew about all the evil and suffering that goes on in the world, and could do something about it, then he would. If he allows suffering when he could do something about it, he is not really good, and if he allows suffering because he can't do anything about it, he is not really all-powerful. Christianity's conception of God has a major logical problem." In responding to this objection, we will need to point out how there are certain cultural assumptions bound within it that stack the deck against Christianity.

The Secular Problem of Good and Evil

Secularists have no clear basis from which to judge something as good or evil. The categories of good and evil are a problem for the skeptic. The false assumption that needs to be exposed is that one can just assume such categories. Christianity provides an obvious grounding for morality; nontheistic viewpoints do not. Secularists who try to argue for moral obligation (rather than just subjective moral feelings) have a steep uphill climb awaiting them (see ch. 13). For other critics, the argument is that Christianity simply does not make sense on its own terms. Thus, they try to avoid making a judgment about whether good and evil actually exist. And yet, experience and intuition teach us that we cannot actually live without making moral judgments. So in response to these two positions, we ought to ask, "Do you believe in good and evil? If so, what do you ground such categories in? And if you deny the reality of good and evil, is that denial livable?"

God's Infinite Knowledge and Wisdom

Christian theology acknowledges mystery. In this world, it's impossible to exhaust the reasons for an infinite God to allow suffering and evil. At this point, it is important to recall from previous chapters some of the cultural changes that occurred during and after the Enlightenment. Many in our current culture assume what Charles Taylor refers to as the "immanent frame," which gives them the sense that the universe they live in—and all the social and ethical orders in it—"can be fully explained in their own terms and don't need to be conceived as dependent on anything outside, on the 'supernatural' or the 'transcendent.'"[45] The modern self has a heightened view of what it can understand about the world through its own reason. While previous societies wrestled with the experiences and questions of suffering, this did not normally lead to disbelief in God until, as Taylor recounts, human confidence in our own ability to analyze and draw conclusions became dominant and our sense of mystery faded from the social imagination.[46]

It is exactly this confidence in our ability to understand the world comprehensively that the Bible challenges (e.g., Deut 29:29; book of Job; Rom 11:33–36). When we allow for a watered-down understanding of God and an enhanced view of ourselves, we are playing into the hands of those who base their objection to God on the existence of suffering. Part of responding to the logic of this objection is to help the person see the problem with their confidence in their own reasoning capabilities and to cast a grander vision of God. Your response might go something like this:

> "You are right to say Christianity teaches that God is both all-powerful and perfectly good, but your picture of the Christian God is too simplistic and does not correspond well with what Christians have long believed about him. According to the Bible, God has revealed himself so that he can be known personally, but he has not revealed himself exhaustively (take Deut 29:29, for example). We can know him, but because he is the Creator and we are his creatures, we have creaturely limits. He is infinite, and we are finite; we cannot see or understand all the reasons he has for what he does and what he allows. So while you are correct to say that God is omnipotent and good, it is important that you also include *his infinite knowledge and wisdom* as you consider the evil and suffering in the world."

In other words, this objection only stands if you accept the principle, "If God had a good reason for allowing evil, I would know what that reason is."[47] Yet this principle fails to be self-evident and contradicts the picture of the God in the Bible.

Two analogies. To help us better understand, we might compare our ability to see the reasons God allows evil and suffering with our ability to see no-see-ums (a small bug that is barely visible to the naked eye). If I claimed there was a giant dog in a tent and you opened it but could not see it, you would be right

---

45. Charles Taylor, "Afterword: *Apologia pro Libro suo*," in *Varieties of Secularism in a Secular Age*, ed. Michael Warner, Jonathan VanAntwerpen, and Craig Calhoun (Cambridge, MA: Harvard University Press, 2010), 307.

46. See Taylor, *A Secular Age*, 223, 306–7, 317–19.

47. C. Stephen Evans, *Faith Beyond Reason: A Kierkegaardian Account* (Grand Rapids: Eerdmans, 1998), 134.

to claim I was wrong. However, if I claimed there were no-see-ums in the tent, you wouldn't be able to know if they were there or not. Similarly, if God is the God presented by the Christian Scriptures, we, as philosopher Stephen John Wykstra has put it, have "good reasons to think that if there were God-purposed goods for sufferings . . . these would often be beyond our ken."[48]

We might also compare our ability to understand God with an infant's ability to fully understand its parent.[49] I (Josh) can remember when my wife and I took our young daughter in for her first vaccination shots. Had she been able to articulate her feelings, she would have likely questioned, "Why are these two people who have doted on and diligently cared for me allowing this stranger to cause me so much pain?" At that point in her maturity, the gap between our reasons for allowing her to experience pain and her capacity to understand was too great. As she grew up, there were many similar situations in which we asked her to trust our wisdom and judgment, even when she couldn't fully understand.

And yet, some might object to this: "But it's not just that there is evil in the world; it's the *sheer amount* of evil in the world that leads me to believe there can't be anything that justifies it." However, this objection does not negate our point, because it still makes the mistake of underestimating the majesty of God as he is presented in the Christian Scriptures. Even in the face of widespread suffering, it remains reasonable to trust in a God who has reasons for allowing it that are beyond our understanding.

The Cross as God's Response to Evil and Suffering

Others may object, "But the analogy of a parent and child breaks down. Over time, an ideal father would give his daughter more reason to trust him in the evident care he shows for her. That's not how it is with us and God. He doesn't show us that sort of evident care." However, this is exactly what Christianity claims that God *has* shown us and *does* show us. God publicly entered into the world in the person of his Son Jesus Christ and suffered with us and for us. He bears the marks of evil and pain. When looking at the cross, no believer can wonder, *Does God care?* He cared so much that he sent his Son to hang on a cross and die to make things right. The incarnation and death of God's Son—the centerpiece of the Christian story—give us reason to trust that God cares. It is when we look at the crucified Jesus that "we come to understand what it means that God is compassionate, that God is a God who suffers with us."[50]

---

48. See Stephen John Wykstra, "Rowe's Noseeum Arguments from Evil," in *The Evidential Argument from Evil*, ed. Daniel Howard-Snyder (Bloomington: Indiana University Press, 1996), 139.
49. See Wykstra, "Rowe's Noseeum Arguments," 139–42.
50. Nouwen, *Love, Henri*, 127.

A Literary Example: An Excerpt from "Jesus of the Scars"

"The other gods were strong; but Thou wast weak;
They rode, but Thou didst stumble to a throne;
But to our wounds only God's wounds can speak."[51]

For Further Reading

Keller, Timothy. *Walking with God through Pain and Suffering.* New York: Dutton, 2013.

Lewis, C. S. *The Problem of Pain.* New York: Macmillan, 1962.

Meister, Chad, and James K. Dew, eds. *God and the Problem of Evil: Five Views.* Downers Grove, IL: InterVarsity, 2017. For three Christian positions that are not mutually exclusive, see the chapters in this book by Philip Carey, William Lane Craig, and Stephen Wykstra.

Plantinga, Alvin. *God, Freedom, and Evil.* Rev. ed. Grand Rapids: Eerdmans, 1989.

Wolterstorff, Nicholas. *A Lament for a Son.* Grand Rapids: Eerdmans, 1987.

Wykstra, Stephen John. "Rowe's Noseeum Arguments from Evil." Pages 126–50 in *The Evidential Argument from Evil.* Edited by Daniel Howard-Snyder. Bloomington: Indiana University Press, 1996.

DEFEATER #6: "I can't believe in a God of judgment and wrath."

Reframing

Certain modern intuitions concerning justice and related beliefs about forgiveness offer connecting points for responding to this objection (think back to the "A" and "B" doctrines discussed in chapter 10). Forgiveness is related to judgment in that many late moderns assume forgiveness should be everyone's default position—especially any deity. One approach to this defeater, then, is to reframe a question about judgment—"How can God be so wrathful and full of judgment?"—with an opposite question about forgiveness: "Do you have an issue with a God who forgives?"[52]

---

51. Edward Shillito, "Jesus of the Scars," in *Masterpieces of Religious Verse*, ed. James Dalton Morrison (New York: Harper, 1958), 235. Public domain.

52. This basic question and the approach that follows, which confronts cultural intuitions about God's character, are skillfully on display as Timothy Keller recounts his discussion with a woman after a church service (see *The Reason for God: Belief in an Age of Skepticism* (New York: Dutton, 2008), 72.

This may seem like a strange question to ask, but its value lies in its ability to help others begin to consider the assumptions of their own cultural location. Other more traditional cultures have no problem with a God who judges; rather, they are offended by a God would forgive immoral people without them making amends. In other words, you may ask, "Could it be that your beliefs about judgment and forgiveness are bound up with local cultural assumptions that don't mesh with many other cultures or with who God really is?"

God's Anger and Love

With the anthropocentric turn in the West, judgment became a problem for God rather than a problem for the unrepentant.[53] The starting point is no longer our own moral failings or our inability to fully see judgment as God sees it; instead, the cultural assumption is that God, if he exists, is on the hook for judging us. We have been cultivated to think more positively about what we deserve and less about God's holiness and the true nature of his love.

The Anthropocentric Turn

Charles Taylor describes the anthropocentric turn by recounting four shifts in thought that occurred approximately around the turn of the seventeenth and eighteenth centuries. People began to believe that

1. God does not require that we obey him sacrificially for purposes greater than ourselves; the only thing we owe him is the achievement of our own good as humans.
2. Rather than needing to rely entirely on the grace of God, humans can "rise to the challenge" of carrying out the divine plan by using their own reason and exerting their own will.
3. Since God's purpose for us is to seek our own good, and we can discover the entirety of God's being and plan by examining nature and understanding its design, all of God's cards are, in a sense, on the table. There is no veil that humans cannot tear back, no mystery that we will not one day be able to explain.
4. Humankind is not so inherently sinful and broken and, as a result, so limited in our present condition that we need God to completely transform us in order for us to develop as human beings or do good in this world.[54]

Because God is holy, he stands against the corruption of his good creation. Because he is loving, he is not indifferent toward the corruption of the world

---

53. See Taylor, *A Secular Age*, 222–24, 260–65.
54. See Taylor, *A Secular Age*, 222–24.

he loves. God's judgment flows out of both his holiness and his love; it is part of his settled and active opposition against anything that opposes the good.[55]

We love our kids. We are deeply invested in their lives. So if one of them were to become a dreadful person, ruining their life and their family's future with reckless living and destructive behavior, we would not simply be indifferent. We would be angry. In this way, deep love is connected to the capacity for deep anger. Indifference toward destructive behavior in someone you claim to love would call into question the sincerity of your love. Of course, analogies have their limits. Human love is different from God's love. But this illustration can help a person struggling with God's wrath to begin reflecting on how, even in our own finite experiences, love is not the opposite of anger. The two are deeply connected.

Another perspective on condemnation in the New Testament is that God in judging is giving people over to what they want (Rom 1:18–32). In other words, God punishes people who want freedom from him by giving it to them. The apostle Paul paints a verbal picture of how, when detached from God's authority, people spiral deeper and deeper into their own narcissistic idolatry and destructive behavior. Like a drug addict who refuses help and continues to binge on the drug that is destroying them, our insistence on idolatry leads us to devastation. From this perspective, judgment is essentially God saying, "Okay, you can have what you want." While this is not the only perspective on God's judgment offered by the Bible, it can help a person begin to think more deeply about human culpability.

Forgiveness and Justice

Forgiveness is a popular sentiment in late modernism. Many people still long for and idealize worldwide peace and reconciliation. This longing is beautiful, and it's something we should affirm. Too often, however, it amounts to nothing more than a cheap sentiment—"Why can't we all just forgive each other and get along"—that lacks substance or realism. In a culture that promotes individualism, personal rights, and self-actualization, the sacrifice that forgiveness requires is difficult, if not altogether unbearable.

What worldview can give us the resources we need not just to cope with evil, but to live lives of peace and love toward others? Why would anyone actually forgive the corrupt cop who used fake evidence to get them arrested? Or the coworker who slanders them out of jealousy? Or the genocidal leader who

---

55. See Keller, *Reason for God*, 73. Keller cites Becky Pippert in her *Hope Has Its Reasons:* "Anger isn't the opposite of love. Hate is, and the final form of hate is indifference . . . God's wrath is not a cranky explosion, but his settled opposition to the cancer . . . which is eating out the insides of the human race he loves with his whole being."

murdered their people? On the other hand, can people even be held responsible as moral agents for such acts?

Not only do we instinctually sense that the actions described above are wrong, but we also recognize that they are difficult to forgive. And this is only intensified if we assume, as do many late moderns, that our lives are fundamentally about pursuing our own interests and comforts. What reason is there for me to forgive anyone? How would it benefit me? Besides, doesn't a strong sense of justice (which late moderns tend to have) dictate that I obtain justice for my grievances?

Christianity not only provides a substantive foundation for forgiveness, but also gives us the assurance that justice will be done in the end, which frees us up to live lives of peace. Theologian Miroslav Volf, a Croatian who experienced cruel violence in the Balkans, asserts that forgiveness is only possible because of God's justice. Volf explains:

> It takes the quiet suburban home for the birth of the thesis that human nonviolence corresponds to God's refusal to judge. In a scorched land, soaked in the blood of the innocent, [that thesis] will invariably die. And as one watches it die, one will do well to reflect about many other pleasant captivities of the liberal mind.[56]

Our hearts desperately want justice to be served. We want the guilty to be punished. We correctly desire for things to be made right. This is why Volf even goes so far as to assert that if God does not bring people to justice, if he does make a final end to evil, then he is not a God who is worthy of our worship.[57]

If, however, there is no God who will ultimately bring a final judgment, then why shouldn't we obtain justice for ourselves? In contrast, the Christian view offers two powerful reasons for us to forgive others:

1. A belief in divine vengeance serves as a restraint. We are not to seek vengeance, because it is God's prerogative, not ours. God will see that justice is done in the end.
2. A belief in human sinfulness calls us to recognize that we ourselves have done things that make us the guilty.

By trusting in God—who not only promises that justice will be served, but who secured forgiveness by suffering for us as a human—we are declared to be

---

56. Miroslav Volf, *Exclusion and Embrace: A Theological Exploration of Identity, Otherness, and Reconciliation* (Nashville: Abingdon, 1996), 304.

57. Volf, *Exclusion and Embrace*, 303.

no longer guilty and are also freed from the stranglehold of bitterness we feel toward those who have wronged us. We are able to offer true forgiveness as people who have experienced true forgiveness. Jesus not only taught his followers to love their enemies and pray from those who persecute them; he himself forgave his enemies as he hung on the cross for them. Christianity—by tying justice, judgment, and love together in a way that makes sense—offers forgiveness and gives reasons to forgive.

For Further Reading

Keller, Timothy. "How Can a Loving God Send People to Hell?" Pages 70–86 in *The Reason for God: Belief in an Age of Skepticism*. New York: Riverhead, 2008.
Volf, Miroslav. *Exclusion and Embrace: A Theological Exploration of Identity, Otherness, and Reconciliation*. Nashville: Abingdon, 1996.

DEFEATER #7: "The Bible is unreliable and cannot be taken seriously."

In giving a short response to this objection, it is best to focus on the New Testament gospels, since they provide the earliest accounts of Jesus' ministry. We recommend this approach, not because the reliability of the rest of the Bible cannot be defended, but rather for the following reasons:

1. Our intent is to give you succinct yet substantial answers to common objections.
2. Jesus is at the center of the Bible and the heart of the gospel story. Critics, well aware of the importance of Jesus to Christianity, often take aim at the gospel accounts.
3. Finally, these accounts of Jesus can be a strategic place to start, since Jesus, in a sense, vouched for the legitimacy of both the Old and New Testaments. He held the Hebrew Scriptures in high regard and personally commissioned the apostles, who were central in the formation of the other New Testament writings. If we trust Jesus as Lord, then we will certainly wish to agree with his high view of the rest of Scripture.

We also recommend using a positive tack rather than a defensive one. After listening carefully to the concerns of someone who is skeptical of the Bible's reliability, the following points provide an outline for a response.

The Gospel Writers Relied on Eyewitness Testimony and Careful Research.

In the early part of twentieth century, a group of scholars made critical mistakes that slanted many people's view of the gospels. These scholars believed the gospels to be folk literature, analogous to old German fairy tales. They asserted that stories of Jesus were passed down orally by way of anonymous community traditions, and that, over time, the stories took on a life of their own independent of the actual historical events they originated from. Though it was Jesus' disciples and other eyewitnesses to his ministry who communicated the original gospel traditions, when these eyewitnesses eventually died, the original traditions were altered.

This theory is roughly comparable to the telephone game. Someone starts out by telling a secret to one person. It is then passed down through a chain of participants until the last person repeats the secret out loud. The humorous part of the game is that the last person normally utters something that only vaguely resembles what was originally spoken. In the same way, by the time the gospel traditions were written down, they only vaguely resembled the original accounts of what actually happened.

A major problem with this theory is that many of the eyewitnesses to the events in Jesus' life were alive and active in the early church until well after the gospels were written. In *Jesus and the Eyewitnesses*, the New Testament scholar Richard Bauckham argues that these eyewitnesses would have functioned as authoritative sources for and guardians of the oral gospel tradition. It was common in oral societies for people to serve such a role. Returning to the telephone game analogy, it would be as if the person first telling the secret listened in each time the secret was passed on from person to person, making sure it was passed down correctly.

Skilled historians who lived in the period when the gospels were written relied as much as they could on eyewitness testimony. We see this in opening of Luke's gospel, where he purposefully appeals to eyewitness testimony and uses the historiographical language of the day (1:1–4). This points to the great care that was taken in the book's composition.[58]

A second-century pastor by the name of Papias also provides information concerning the eyewitness nature of the gospels. Papias identifies three generations of people: (1) the eyewitnesses themselves, (2) the elders who sat at their feet, and (3) the disciples of the elders. Papias writes that when he was younger, in the 80s at the latest, many members of the three generations were still alive, including the eyewitnesses. By that time, Mark had been completed,

---

58. See Richard Bauckham, *Jesus and the Eyewitnesses: The Gospels as Eyewitness Testimony*, 2nd ed. (Grand Rapids: Eerdmans, 2017), 1–11, 116–24.

and Matthew and Luke had either been written or were in the process of being written. This evidence suggests that the gospels were not simply oral traditions that were passed down and altered during the various stages of transmission; rather, they were oral history that had been guarded by eyewitness testimony.

In another important point, Bauckham argues that the names present within the gospels themselves are meant to assure the readers of their accuracy.[59] Throughout the gospels, figures are distinguished by use of their proper names; these people were meant to serve as living guarantors of the tradition.

A simple but important example that can be used to illustrate this point is found in Mark 15:21. Here Mark, in what is most likely the earliest gospel written, specifically names not only Simon of Cyrene, but also his two sons Alexander and Rufus. None of other gospels keep the names of the sons; they only mention Simon. It appears that Mark expects his readers to know both of these sons. But even so, why reference them by name? The best explanation is that Mark is referencing Simon's testimony by way of his sons, who were known figures in early Christianity.[60] Matthew and Luke, who wrote their gospels later, had no reason to include Alexander and Rufus's names, because they would no longer have been well-known. This suggests that Mark mentioned Simon's two sons in order to point out living eyewitnesses who could corroborate his account.

Consider also the identification of the primary witness at the beginning and the end of each gospel (sometimes called an "*inclusio* of eyewitness testimony"). In Mark's gospel, we can see quite clearly that his primary witness is Peter (Mark 1:16; 16:7)—and this corresponds with the early tradition that Mark was dependent on Peter's eyewitness experience.[61] Peter's name also occurs with remarkable frequency throughout Mark's gospel.

To summarize the major point in this section: the gospels were written too soon after the gospel events happened—eyewitnesses to Jesus' life were still alive and prominent in the church—to be myths.

The Gospels Are too Counterintuitive to Be a Hoax.
The Negative Portrayal of the Disciples

In the gospels, when Jesus tells his disciples that he will be killed, they don't understand. In fact, the gospels regularly portray the disciples as misunderstanding Jesus. As Jesus attempts to teach them humility and the importance of serving others, they argue over which of them is the greatest. Some of the

---

59. See Bauckham, *Jesus and the Eyewitnesses*, chs. 3–9.

60. See Bauckham, *Jesus and the Eyewitnesses*, 51–52.

61. Bauckham, *Jesus and the Eyewitnesses*, 124–27. A similar occurrence is found in the Gospel of John with the beloved disciple. See Bauckham, *Jesus and the Eyewitnesses*, 127–29.

disciples fall asleep when Jesus needs them most. At one point, Peter so misjudges Jesus' mission that Jesus refers to him as "Satan" (Matt 16:23).

This is an odd way to portray the leaders of a movement whose message you are promoting. Can you imagine a PR campaign for a movement intentionally portraying its own leadership as dim-witted and even "Satanic"? There does not seem to be any advantage to the authors writing the stories of the gospels like this—unless, of course, their goal was to be faithful to the way things actually happened. The gospels seem to prize veracity, even at the expense of the early church leaders' own reputations.

The Role of Women

In the first century, women were not allowed to testify in a court of law because it was believed that they could not give trustworthy testimony on important matters.[62] It is remarkable, then, that all the gospel traditions not only depict women as playing an important role in Jesus' ministry, but also as the first eyewitnesses to Jesus' resurrection.[63]

It would be counterintuitive to invent a story in this way. In the "myth" model for understanding gospel formation, it would have been easy to change the details of the story to fit with first century-norms, refashioning the accounts so that women were not featured so prominently, especially at the resurrection. However, this did not happen in any of the gospels. The prominent role of women in the gospels is best explained by the commitment of the early church to be faithful to the eyewitness accounts of Jesus' life.

The Differences Are Not Smoothed Out

The differences between the gospels are actually an apologetic for their veracity. If the gospel writers were colluding to deceive others, they would have sought to smooth out anything that could be perceived as conflicting. But this isn't what we find in the Gospels. While the basic story is the same across all four gospel accounts, the details often vary from one gospel to another. If they were making up a false story, wouldn't the early Christians, recognizing that such differences would fuel skeptics' questions, try to smooth them out?

Differences in precision in the gospel accounts point to the veracity of the events. Such differences are not the same as contradictions. There is a divergence between contradictions and legitimate diversity, which is what you would expect,

---

62. See Richard Bauckham, *Gospel Women: Studies of the Named Women in the Gospels* (Grand Rapids: Eerdmans, 2002), 268–77; see also N. T. Wright, *Resurrection of the Son of God* (Minneapolis: Fortress Press, 2003), 607.

63. Bauckham also argues that the variations in the lists of women in the Gospels further indicate each Evangelist's care in naming the women who served as eyewitnesses (*Jesus and the Eyewitnesses*, 51).

for instance, when each individual in a family recounts the events of a vacation they go on together. Though each family member would give many overlapping details (location, transportation, major occurrences), they would—provided they were not colluding—each tell the story of their vacation with legitimate differences in perspective, whether in the events they choose to share, how they summarize those events, or the order in which they arrange the events. We see and even expect this kind of legitimate diversity when people reliably recount historical events today, and it's also the sort of thing we find in the accounts of Jesus in the New Testament.[64]

For Further Reading

Bauckham, Richard. *Jesus and the Eyewitnesses: The Gospels as Eyewitness Testimony.* 2nd ed. Grand Rapids: Eerdmans, 2017.

Blomberg, Craig. *Can We Still Believe the Bible? An Evangelical Engagement with Contemporary Questions.* Grand Rapids: Brazos, 2014.

Kitchen, K. A. *On the Reliability of the Old Testament.* Grand Rapids: Eerdmans, 2003.

Köstenberger, Andreas J., Darrell L. Bock, and Josh D. Chatraw. *Truth in a Culture of Doubt: Engaging Skeptical Challenges to the Bible.* Nashville: B&H, 2014.

DEFEATER #8: "The Christian doctrine of the Trinity is confusing and illogical."

To many skeptics, the Trinity doesn't seem rational. How can three persons—the Father, the Son, and the Holy Spirit—each be fully God and yet there only be one God? To them, the Trinity, far from being a reason to believe in Christianity, is a reason not to believe in it, because it is so confusing and illogical.

Though the rationality of the Trinity might not work within the hard rationalistic framework of the Enlightenment, it is not illogical. A helpful example to consider is Alister McGrath's account of attempting to get his mind around things such as the wave-particle duality of quantum theory while still thinking within the old construct of classical Newtonian physics. Physicists with a classical Newtonian background find quantum theory counterintuitive, yet those who are used to working within quantum theory understand its rationality even at an

---

64. For a response to critiques on the reliability of the New Testament documents, see Andreas J. Köstenberger, Darrell L. Bock, and Josh D. Chatraw, *Truth in a Culture of Doubt: Engaging Skeptical Challenges of the Bible* (Nashville: B&H, 2014), 79–106.

intuitive level. In a similar way, the Christian Trinity will not appear rational if one presupposes the hard rationality of the Enlightenment, but within Christian theology, the Trinity makes sense and illuminates life.[65]

The doctrine of the Trinity grounds our understanding of love and relationships within the very being of God. A Trinitarian God is a personal, relational, and communal God; each person of the Trinity shares in the life of the other (John 16:12–14; 17:1, 20–23). A belief in this Trinitarian God, who created the world we all inhabit (John 1:1–3), "encourages an ethic of self-giving love [because] if we are going to live in accord with the shape of things, we need to adopt a stance of availability, of openness to others and willingness to enter when others open to us."[66] The very logic of the universe is love, grounded in the self-giving love of the Trinity.

The Trinity and its rationality actually illuminate our understanding of the world. In the words of C. S. Lewis, "I believe in Christianity as I believe that the Sun has risen, not only because I see it, but because by it I see everything else."[67] We might say that belief in the Trinity illuminates the world we live in. Most people intuitively recognize that what makes life worth living is loving relationships. Moreover, when many unbelievers imagine what God would be like if he existed, they tend to assume he is loving. These intuitions make best sense with the Christian picture of God as a personal being whose very essence is communal love.

This notion of eternal love as essential to God's being differentiates the Christian conception of him from the Muslim conception. Muslim theology emphasizes the absolute oneness of Allah—he does not exist in Trinity. In eternity past, before Allah created anything, he was entirely alone. Because love requires an object, and a relationship two persons, Allah could not have been a loving, relational being before he created the universe: he had no one with whom to relate. In order to be a loving being, Allah needed his creation. In contrast, the Christian God, because he has always existed in Trinity, has always been a loving, relational being. His love is not contingent on creation; he is an eternal communion of self-giving, deeply intimate love. The Christian God is eternally loving; Allah is not.[68]

It is not just other religions that the Christian conception of love contrasts with; it also differs substantially from the secular, materialist viewpoint. For if,

---

65. See McGrath, *The Big Question*, 198.

66. Peter J. Leithart, *Traces of the Trinity: Signs of God in Creation and Human Experience* (Grand Rapids: Brazos, 2015), 110.

67. C. S. Lewis, *The Weight of Glory and Other Addresses* (1949; repr., San Francisco: HarperOne, 2001), 140.

68. See Nabeel Qureshi, *No God but One: Allah or Jesus?* (Grand Rapids: Zondervan, 2016), 65–66.

as materialists assert, there is no God and we are simply the result of natural processes, then love is nothing more than chemicals in the brain. Love is just a chemical condition passed down from our ancestors to help us survive.

In advancing a Trinitarian conception of God, the Christian view of the world offers a much stronger basis for love than any other view: Love is an ultimate reality found in God himself. And because we are made "in the image of a selfless, loving God, [we are also] in our very nature . . . designed to be selfless and loving. When we are self-centered instead of selfless, we act against our very nature."[69] In our fallen, broken state, we find it difficult, if not impossible, to truly love others as we are designed to. But amazingly, Christ has made it possible for humankind to enter once again into the eternal reality of God's love. In extending God's love to us, he enables us to truly love others.[70] In a world created by the triune God, love is at the very center of reality. Trinitarian love is the logic of the universe.

For Further Reading

Leithart, Peter J. *Traces of the Trinity: Signs of God in Creation and Human Experience.* Grand Rapids: Brazos, 2015.

Qureshi, Nabeel. "*Tawhid* or the Trinity: Two Different Gods." Pages 47–72 in *No God but One: Allah or Jesus?* Grand Rapids: Zondervan, 2016.

Sanders, Fred. *The Deep Things of God: How the Trinity Changes Everything.* Wheaton, IL: Crossway, 2010.

MOVING BEYOND DEFEATERS

Of course, these eight defeaters are not the only challenges leveled against Christianity. Nevertheless, they are some of the most common objections, and they can be used as examples to help you think through interacting with other defeaters. Building on chapters 10 and 11, this chapter has equipped you with trajectories for responses that you can expand on and personalize as you interact with unbelievers. We now turn to the final chapter, where we will offer a model for making a positive case for Christianity.

---

69. Qureshi, *No God but One*, 71.

70. See Timothy Keller, *The Reason for God: Belief in an Age of Skepticism* (New York: Riverhead, 2008), 225–26.

CHAPTER THIRTEEN

MAKING A CASE

It is for this reason that the present age is better than Christendom. In the old Christendom, everyone was a Christian and hardly anyone thought twice about it. But in the present age the survivor of theory and consumption becomes the wayfarer in the desert, like St. Anthony; which is to say, open to signs.

Walker Percy, "Why Are You a Catholic?"
in Signposts in a Strange Land

A WIDENING OF THE APOLOGETIC ENTERPRISE

When I (Josh) was growing up in the southeastern part of the United States, there were two dominant religions: Baptist and football. It would take a visitor little time to realize which faith had captured my community's heart and elicited their deepest devotion.

Go to a SEC (Southeastern Conference) college campus on a Saturday in the fall, and you will witness devoted worshipers of all ages citing liturgy (cheers), singing praises (fight songs), and participating in ordinances (tailgates and other pregame rituals) that have been passed down through the generations. You need only view the reactions of the losing and winning teams' fans after the game to realize how many of them wrap up their identities in their team's success. I have witnessed highly educated and respected church leaders almost physically fight over a game. The hostility and resentment between different fan groups still amaze me. Idols are powerful forces; they appeal to us in profound ways and at multiple levels.[1]

My point is not that college football is evil—anything can become an idol. But if you spend a few weeks around this football culture as an outsider

---

1. This illustration is inspired by James K. A. Smith's *Desiring the Kingdom: Worship, Worldview, and Cultural Formation* (Grand Rapids: Baker Academic, 2009); see also Charles Taylor, *A Secular Age* (Cambridge, MA: Harvard University Press, 2007), 481–83.

or take a step back as a devoted fan, it may seem bizarre to you. Why are so many people so intensely devoted to a group of twenty-year-olds throwing a leather ball around?

College football followers would rarely think to make an appeal to the "skeptical" by simply listing player stats or reasons you should become a fan. Instead, they would tell hero stories of legendary players from yesteryear or perhaps some human interest stories about current players. They would explain the long-standing traditions associated with game day. Or they would just invite the unconvinced to a game. As the newcomer joins the faithful fans for a ritual-filled and boisterous pep rally the night before, the communal tailgate in the morning, and the sing-along with the band as game time nears, they start to feel a twinge of excitement. Then, after they're ushered into the stadium with an electric atmosphere of 90,000 fans hanging on every play, it isn't long before they find themselves high-fiving the random woman in front of them and hugging the stranger beside them. For most fans, it was these kinds of experiences that led to their conversion. True conversion is never simply an intellectual experience.

An important point emphasized in this book is that Christian persuasion should be *holistic*. Neither the responses to defeaters in the previous chapter nor any of the arguments for Christianity surveyed throughout should be abstracted from the genuine discipleship and worship of the church. The church is both a living apologetic appeal and the formative context out of which apologetic arguments are supported as plausible.

To use another analogy, imagine trying to convince someone to enlist in a war on behalf of a distant nation they are antagonistic toward. You approach them and say, "I have five airtight arguments for you to leave your current way of life—all the things you love—and join us in battle." They would probably say something like, "I don't care how good you think your arguments are; I have absolutely no interest in them!" It's not even plausible for them to imagine doing what you are asking of them, so they are not interested in hearing whatever supposed "rational" reasons you might be able to produce for taking such actions. Logic alone is incapable of inspiring us to risk our lives for a cause. In a similar way, people find Christianity implausible for a variety of reasons that we cannot adequately address by simply giving them what seems to some Christians to be "five airtight reasons."

As Christians living in the late modern era, we should not simply give an unbeliever logical arguments and then walk away, imagining we've done our apologetic job. For as philosopher Charles Taylor reminds us, "We are in fact all acting, thinking, and feeling out of backgrounds and frameworks which we do not fully understand."[2] As we have seen, it is these frameworks that we must learn to interact with, even when they are difficult for us to understand and—as is normally the case—have not been given much thought by the person we are trying to lead to the gospel.

In light of a holistic understanding of how humans decide and the importance of unarticulated frameworks, we have outlined a vision for a multidimensional approach to apologetics. Apologetics at the cross calls the church to (1) live out an apologetic that undermines misconceptions of Christianity and embodies a more compelling and beatific vision of life (chs. 6–8); (2) help others see the problems with their own backgrounds and frameworks that cause them to approach Christianity as implausible (chs. 9–11); and (3) offer intelligent responses to objections and reasons for committing to Christ (chs. 12–13).

Apologetics at the cross is not a narrowing of the apologetic task but a broadening of the enterprise, developing the multiple kinds of apologetic seeds within the Bible (chs. 1–2) and retrieving the insights from the rich sources within Christian tradition (chs. 3–5). With that in mind, this final chapter turns to the task of offering a survey of reasons why Christianity makes sense. In other words, as we discussed in chapter 5, we are offering examples of arguments that can be used when drawing apologetics maps for others. This survey is only an introduction to the arguments that have been detailed in more narrowly focused books. Pay attention to the "For Further Reading" after each major section in order to delve deeper into exploring forms of each argument in these other resources. Finally, the inside out model continues to serve as helpful mental scaffolding, both as a broader backdrop that this chapter fits into and as an approach that enables constructive interaction with competing explanations of our lives and the world around us.

SIGNPOSTS

Only shallow truths can be proven absolutely; the deepest answers of life are beyond absolute proof.[3] Thus, this chapter is not offering coercive "proofs" for God. Christianity cannot be proven in that sense, though it can be justified. It can and should be trusted. Instead of "proof," consider the following arguments to be signposts. Signs say or signal something, but it is possible to interpret them according to mistaken frameworks or to ignore them altogether. There are ways around signposts. But the question is, "What take on these signs provides the

---

2. Charles Taylor, *A Secular Age* (Cambridge, MA: Harvard University Press, 2007), 387.

3. See Alister McGrath, *The Big Question: Why We Can't Stop Talking About Science, Faith, and God* (New York: St. Martins, 2015), 170.

deepest, richest, and most coherent view of reality?" The questions posed in this section can be used to prompt others to consider the best way to interpret these signs.

Why Can We Make Sense of the Universe?

The world is something that we can understand. Not fully, but we *can* understand it. We are so accustomed to being able to comprehend aspects of the world around us that fundamental questions are quickly passed over: "What makes science and understanding in general possible? Why is it that the structures of the universe can be charted mathematically?" As theoretical physicist John Polkinghorne muses, "The universe might have been a disorderly chaos rather than an orderly cosmos. Or it might have had a rationality which was inaccessible to us."[4] Or as Oxford mathematician John Lennox explains, "It is very striking that the most abstract mathematical concepts that seem to be pure inventions of the human mind can turn out to be of vital importance for branches of science, with a vast range of practical applications."[5] What makes best sense of this "fit" between our minds and the universe?

> The eternal mystery of the world is its comprehensibility . . . The fact that it is comprehensible is a miracle.
>
> *Albert Einstein, "Physics and Reality"*

Some argue that the human mind is simply imposing this structure on the world; the structure is only illusory. Yet this fails to come to grips with the precise agreement between the scientific theories and both the observations and correct predictions made about the physical world.[6]

Others explain this fit as simply a cosmic coincidence. The correspondence between mathematics and the universe and the comprehensibility of natural laws has happened by chance. Many, however, find this "explanation" actually does little to explain.

Some see our cognitive ability to make sense of the world to be explained by our evolutionary drive to survive. Recall that the inside out method discussed in chapters 10 and 11 advocated the approach of seeing where a framework leads or, to put this slightly differently, seeing if a worldview can be consistent on its own terms. For those who have embraced naturalistic evolution, you can ask, "Does your view give us good reason to trust the powers that produce knowledge in us, to put our faith in the fit between our cognitive faculties and the world

---

4. John Polkinghorne, *Science and Creation: The Search for Understanding* (London: SPCK, 1988), 20.

5. John C. Lennox, *God's Undertaker: Has Science Buried God?* (Oxford: Lion Hudson, 2009), 61. For more on this, see Paul Davies, *The Mind of God* (London: Simon and Schuster, 1992), and the classic article by E. P. Wigner, "The Unreasonable Effectiveness of Mathematics in the Natural Sciences," *Communications in Pure and Applied Mathematics* 13, no. 1 (1960): 1–14.

6. See McGrath, *The Big Question*, 86–87.

around us?" In other words, for the sake of discussion, assume that our cognitive faculties are simply materials produced by natural forces. If this is true, do we have good reason to trust these faculties?

Various philosophers have argued that, in fact, if naturalism and evolution are both true, "our cognitive faculties would very likely not be reliable."[7] Even many prominent nonbelievers—such as Friedrich Nietzsche, Thomas Nagel, and John Gray—agree with theists on this point.[8]

Why the agreement between these believing and nonbelieving intellectuals? They are taking naturalistic evolution to its consistent end. Naturalistic evolution is concerned with the way we behave (i.e., survival and reproduction) rather than the truthfulness of our beliefs. From a naturalistic perspective, there is no reason to suppose content generated by neurological structures is true. As philosopher Alvin Plantinga puts it, "All that's required for survival and fitness is that the neurology cause adaptive behavior; this neurology also determines belief content, but whether or not that content is *true* makes no difference to fitness."[9] In other words, if naturalism and unguided evolution were both true, we would have no reason to trust that we are making any sense of the universe—which, of course, means that one's own claim to knowledge is undercut.

This fit between our minds and the world around us does not prove Christianity. However, the belief in God does make better sense than secular frameworks for understanding this phenomenon. Christianity has shown itself to be, in some sense, ahead of its time in providing the framework for explaining the intelligibility of the universe. Alister McGrath writes:

> God created the world with an ordered structure, which human beings are able to uncover by virtue of bearing the "image of God." That has been a settled conviction of the Christian faith since its earliest days, a thousand years before anyone started to do science seriously and systematically. Yet this intellectual framework fits what we now know—and *did not* know until the 1700s.[10]

---

7. Alvin Plantinga, *Where the Conflict Really Lies: Science, Religion, and Naturalism* (Oxford: Oxford University Press, 2011), 314. For earlier forms of this argument, see Arthur Balfour, *The Foundations of Belief* (New York: Longmans, 1895); C. S. Lewis, *Miracles*, rev. ed. (San Francisco: HarperOne, 2015); Richard Taylor, *Metaphysics*, 4th ed. (Upper Saddle River, NJ: Prentice Hall, 1991).

8. See Friedrich Nietzsche, *Nietzsche: Writings from the Late Notebooks*, ed. Rüdiger Bittner, trans. Kate Sturge (Cambridge: Cambridge University Press, 2003), 26; Thomas Nagel, *The View from Nowhere* (Oxford: Oxford University Press, 1989), 79; John Gray, *Straw Dogs: Thoughts on Humans and Other Animals* (London: Granta, 2002), 27.

9. Plantinga, *Where the Conflict Really Lies*, 327.

10. McGrath, *The Big Question*, 88.

For Further Reading Lennox, John, C. "Designer Universe?" Pages 57–75 in *God's Undertaker: Has Science Buried God?* Oxford: Lion Hudson, 2009. McGrath, Alister. "Inventing the Universe." Pages 77–99 in *The Big Question: Why We Can't Stop Talking About Science, Faith and God.* New York: St. Martin's, 2015.

Why Is It That the Universe Seems Fine-Tuned for Life?

Increasingly, there is a growing awareness that a great deal had to go right for life to occur. By analogy, imagine the universe being regulated by a complex system of dials, with each having to be at a surgically precise position for life to exist. These include the cosmological constant, the strong and electromagnetic forces, carbon production in stars, the proton/neutron difference, the weak force, and gravity. In these examples, the fine-tuning needed for conditions for life to occur range from 1 part in 10 to 1 part in 10^{53}.[11] If one were off, even in the slightest, human existence would not be possible.

The impression of design is overwhelming.
Paul Davies, The Cosmic Blueprint

With regard to fine-tuning, Alvin Plantinga modestly concludes, "On balance, the sensible conclusion seems to be that there is indeed an enormous amount of fine-tuning, although the precise amount isn't known, and it is possible to quarrel with many of the specific examples proposed."[12] While in general, the fine-tuning of the universe has become widely accepted, does it function as a signpost to a fine-tuner?

For scientists like Francis Collins, one of the world's leading geneticists and director of the National Institutes of Health, the answer is yes: "To get our universe, with all of its potential for complexities or any kind of potential for any kind of life-form, everything has to be precisely defined on this knife edge of improbability." Thus, he concludes, "You have to see the hands of a creator who set the parameters to be just so because the creator was interested in something a little more complicated than random particles."[13]

As an illustration, imagine ten of the highest percentage free throw shooters in the NBA each getting to take a free throw. With each attempt, none of them

---

11. See Plantinga, *Where the Conflict Really Lies*, 198.
12. Plantinga, *Where the Conflict Really Lies*, 198–99.
13. Francis Collins, "Reflections on the Current Tensions between Science and Faith," Christian Scholar's Conference, Pepperdine University (2011), quoted in Alan Lightman, "The Accidental Universe: Science's Crisis of Faith," *Harper's Magazine*, December 2011, https://harpers.org/archive/2011/12/the-accidental-universe/3.

even hit the rim. This, of course, could have been an amazing coincidence. Surely they have all at one time in their careers shot an air ball. And it is possible that it happens for all ten of them at the same event. Maybe they all had too much to drink right before arriving at the gym, or some other explanation could defend this as an unplanned coincidence. Most, however, would find this occurrence suspicious and assume this was something they had planned.

Others remain skeptical of analogies like these, explaining that the fine-tuning argument proves nothing. Again, it depends on what one means here by "prove." We suggest that you can agree this does not "prove" God in the hard sense of the term. It could be, as some argue, that there are zillions of universes, and it just so happens that our universe was the one that happened to be finely tuned for life. Then again, the theory of multiple universes is only conjecture. As MIT physicist Alan Lightman has noted, "We have no conceivable way of observing these other universes and cannot prove their existence."[14]

But for argument's sake, given the chance that there are zillions of universes out there, it could be that all the "cosmic dials" would happen to land on the right numbers for life in some universe. In other words, the odds for a single individual entering the lottery and winning are not good, but some individual normally ends up winning. Indeed, if one accepts by faith that zillions of universes exist, it is possible to avoid the fine-tuning of the universe as a pointer to theism.

While not rationally coercive, something about the fine-tuning of the universe is still difficult for many to shake off so easily. Plantinga gives insight into why this is the case by imagining we are in the Wild West:

> I'm playing poker, and every time I deal, I get four aces and a wild card. The third time this happens, Tex jumps up, knocks over the table, draws his sixgun, and accuses me of cheating. My reply: ". . . have you considered the following? Possibly there is an infinite succession of universes, so that for any possible distribution of possible poker hands, there is a universe in which the possibility is realized; we just happen to find ourselves in one where someone like me always deals himself only aces and wild cards without ever cheating . . ." Tex probably won't be satisfied; this multi-game hypothesis, even if true, is irrelevant.[15]

Why would the multi-game hypothesis be irrelevant? Plantinga continues, "No doubt *someone* in one of those enormously many poker games deals himself all the aces and a wild card without cheating; but the probability that

---

14. Lightman, "The Accidental Universe," https://harpers.org/archive/2011/12/the-accidental-universe/6.
15. Plantinga, *Where the Conflict Really Lies*, 213–14.

I (as opposed to someone or other) am honestly dealing in that magnificently self-serving way is very low . . . It is vastly more likely that I am cheating; how can we blame Tex for opening fire?" It is analogous for those arguing in this way against the fine-tuning argument: "The fact, if it is a fact, that there are enormously many universes has no bearing on the probability (on atheism) that *this* universe is fine-tuned for life; that remains very low."[16]

So, while not rationally coercive, the fine-tuning of the universe remains as a signpost for a fine-tuner and fits well with the Christian belief in God as the Creator.

For Further Reading

Collins, Robin. "A Scientific Argument for the Existence of God: The Fine-Tuning Design Argument." Pages 47–75 in *Reason for the Hope Within.* Edited by Michael J. Murray. Grand Rapids: Eerdmans, 1999.

_____ . "The Teleological Argument: An Exploration of the Fine-Tuning of the Universe." Pages 202–81 in *The Blackwell Companion to Natural Theology.* Edited by William Lane Craig and J. P. Moreland. New York: Wiley, 2009.

Craig, Willian Lane. "Design and the Anthropic Fine-Tuning of the Universe." Pages 155–77 in *God and Design: The Teleological Argument and Modern Science.* Edited by Neil Manson. London: Routledge, 2003.

White, Roger. "Fine Turning and Multiple Universes." *Nous* 34, no. 2 (2000): 260–76.

What Makes Best Sense of the Consensus That the Universe Had a Beginning?

The question of whether the universe had a beginning or if it has existed eternally has been debated throughout history. Aristotle, for instance, believed in the eternality of the universe, while Christians and Jews have long believed that the universe has been created.

For a lengthy portion of time, the belief in the eternality of the universe became the dominant scientific position in the West until the study of such things as the redshift in light from faraway galaxies, cosmic microwave background, and thermodynamics pushed the consensus the other way. Currently, most scientists agree that the universe had a beginning.

> The more we get to know about our universe, the more the hypothesis that there is a Creator God, who designed the universe for a purpose, gains in credibility as the best explanation of why we are here.
>
> *John Lennox,* God's Undertaker

---

16. Plantinga, *Where the Conflict Really Lies*, 214, emphasis in original.

Those who disagree with this consensus sometimes argue for an "infinite regress" of causes, with no beginning. But this is not something that any type of scientific study has ever shown. It seems to be a theory posited to get around the conclusion that the universe had an origin. But, ironically, this theory still points us to another realm outside of what we can observe in nature to try to explain the universe. Experience in this world points us to the conclusion that everything that begins to exist has a cause. Since the universe began to exist, the universe had a cause.

Who Made God?

The question sometimes posed in response to the point in this section, "Well, then, who made God?" misunderstands the point. Everything that begins to exist has a cause, but God never began to exist. God has always been eternally existing outside of space and time.

Does this consensus that the universe had a beginning lead to the affirmation of divine causation? Not for everyone. Some have speculated that the universe was created in a quantum vacuum. But this really only takes us back to a form of our initial question. For if this is the case, where did this quantum vacuum—a kind of universe-making machine—come from? Likewise, some will say that the laws of physics created the universe. But again, where did the laws come from? Laws of physics do not create.

Again, to be clear, neither this nor any of the other points made so far in this chapter demonstrate the personal, holy God of Christianity. Yet the current scientific evidence does fit well with the claim Christians have long made: the universe had a beginning and a cause because it was created by God.

For Further Reading

Craig, William Lane, and James D. Sinclair. "The Kalam Cosmological Argument." Pages 101–201 in *The Blackwell Companion to Natural Theology.* Edited by William Lane Craig and J. P. Moreland. New York: Wiley, 2009.

Lennox, John C., "Designer Universe?" Pages 57–75 in *God's Undertaker: Has Science Buried God?* Oxford: Lion Hudson, 2009.

How Can Moral Realism Be Grounded?
Morality as Irresistible

Even if one refuses to assent intellectually to moral realism—denying that morality exists independently of our perception or feelings—people find moral judgments to be irresistible in practice. We cannot help but assume moral realism. The French secular-humanist philosopher Luc Ferry makes this point by asking his readers to consider, for example, their gut reaction to the extreme violence the Bosnian Serb armed forces used against the Bosnian Muslims in the 1995 Srebrenica massacre: "Before the slaughter, they amused themselves by terrifying their victims, shooting them in the legs, making them run before mowing them down, cutting off their ears, torturing and then murdering them."[17]

> I have yet to meet anyone, materialist or otherwise, who was able to dispense with value judgements.
>
> *Luc Ferry,* Learning to Live

You might ask the unbeliever, "If there is no objective standard of morality, why do we so viscerally feel that *this is wicked?* Is this only a feeling? Or is it actually *wicked?*"

To Ferry, that such actions are wicked is self-evident because those men, like all other human beings, had the choice to act differently than they did. If they were wild animals, he would not bring a moral judgment against them, but as men, they clearly had a choice and can therefore be condemned for their actions.[18]

Of course, as Ferry stresses, many materialists will argue that all value judgments are illusory and determined by cultural conditioning. The problem with this idea, however, as Ferry explains, is that no human alive, short of the sociopathic, can do away with value judgments altogether. Even materialists "starting with Marx and Nietzsche . . . have never been able to refrain from passing continuous moral judgement on all and sundry, which their whole philosophy might be expected to discourage them from doing."[19] The underlying reason materialists pass these moral judgments, of course, is that though they may deny it in theory, they cannot help but believe humans have the ability to make choices for which they should be held accountable.

This fundamental inconsistency is why the materialist's position is unsustainable. It's simply not livable. It crumbles the minute the philosopher walks out of his study and into the real world. Ferry, recognizing this reality in himself, admits that he "cannot invent . . . the imperatives of the moral life" and that

---

17. Luc Ferry, *A Brief History of Thought: A Philosophical Guide to Living* (New York: HarperCollins, 2011), 228.
18. Ferry, *Brief History of Thought*, 228–29.
19. Ferry, *Brief History of Thought*, 229.

truth, beauty, justice, and love seem to "impose themselves on [him] as if they [came] from elsewhere."[20]

How might we ground this morality "from elsewhere"? Humans are moral beings. Even if we deny real morality with our minds, we live as moral beings, inevitably making ethical judgments. How might this morality that we all seem to affirm in practice, if not also in theory, be grounded?

Grounding Morality in Culture?

Some have argued that morality is completely dependent on cultural attitudes and assumptions. In other words, we judge as "good" or "bad" based on our social location. What is viewed as "good" in one culture is viewed as "bad" in another. While dialoguing, you can agree with this last statement; cultures often view things differently. But the question is not whether cultures differ, but rather, "Is there any way to judge some cultural view or individual behavior as right or better and the opposite as wrong or inferior?" If someone answers positively, then they have admitted there is something that transcends culture and determines morality. If we say, for instance, that it is better for cultures to allow women to have the same rights as men, then we are admitting there is something that stands above culture.

If they answer negatively and claim there is nothing that stands above culture, then some more questions are necessary. As C. S. Lewis famously pointed out, what, then, can we conclude about Nazi Germany?[21] Is our condemnation of the Holocaust or our advocacy of human rights just a reflection of our cultural bias? And if someone goes so far as to answer, "Yes, we have no right to call a cultural practice evil," then you should ask how they can make a moral judgment that someone does not have the right to call a cultural practice evil. Moreover, they will not be able to sustain this position in practice. In other words, grounding morality in relative cultural norms collapses in on itself and is unlivable.

Grounding Morality in Science?

Attempts have been made to claim that neuroscience and naturalistic evolutionary theories can explain morality. How might you respond to this? You can affirm that science is helpful in *describing* physically certain aspects of morality. Science can help us as we explore the questions of morality, but quite a bit is riding on what is meant by *explain* and *morality*. The term *morality* is used to mean at least three different things in these discussions.

---

20. Ferry, *Brief History of Thought*, 236–37.
21. See C. S. Lewis, *Mere Christianity* (New York: Macmillan, 1960), 25.

1. Morality is used to mean the realm of right and wrong. Morality in this sense prescribes something; there is an obligation. This is sometimes called "real" or "authoritative" morality.
2. Morality is used to mean the social rules and practices of a given society at a purely descriptive level. In this sense, the morality of a culture is described, but it is not evaluated on the basis of what is "really" right or wrong.
3. Morality is used to mean something that is more practical or instrumental. In this meaning, something is being prescribed; there is a "do this, don't do this" sense, but it is not a moral obligation in the same sense of the first type of morality. Instead, it is more instrumental: "If you want to score a goal, you should shoot." In other words, the "should" is directed at achieving a purpose, but it does not say whether the purpose is "really" good or bad.[22]

Distinguishing these three definitions helps us avoid talking past each other in a conversation. Empirically based scientific studies can address the second two types of morality but are unable to address adequately the first category—"real morality." However, sometimes attempts at explanations will end up, as James Davison Hunter and Paul Nedelisky point out, looking like a shell game. The claim is made that "real" morality is being addressed, but then "through a sleight of hand," one of the other forms of morality are put "into play in ways that conflate the meanings of the terms."[23] In other words, various secular sciences can describe a goal within a society or even how best to achieve a certain goal, but they cannot provide what goal one ought to pursue. This is why the atheist philosopher Thomas Nagel admits that "from a Darwinian perspective our impressions of value, if constructed realistically, are completely groundless." And if true for basic values, Nagel adds that "it is also true for the entire elaborate structure of value and morality that is built up from them by practical reflection and cultural development."[24]

Science does not provide moral obligation. For instance, the goal of life, according to Darwinian science, is survival, which is often a bloody affair. Most recognize that the violence within nature is not a model for how society should operate. We don't judge bears to be *wicked* for slaughtering their prey, but as Luc Ferry's example reminded us, we do hold humans morally accountable for such acts.

---

22. See James Davison Hunter and Paul Nedelisky, "Where the New Science of Morality Goes Wrong," *Hedgehog Review* 18, no. 3 (Fall 2016): 48–62, www.iasc-culture.org/THR/THR_article_2016_Fall_HunterNedelisky.php.

23. Hunter and Nedelisky, "Where the New Science of Morality Goes Wrong," 56.

24. Thomas Nagel, *Mind and Cosmos: Why the Materialist Neo-Darwinian Conception of Nature Is Almost Certainly False* (New York: Oxford University Press, 2012), 109.

Once the claim that science can provide morality is exposed as a shell game, it becomes clear that moral theorists have largely abandoned the possibility of empirically demonstrating "real" morality, which is related to things like value, duty, and rights.

Despite the inability of science to explain adequately morality in its fullest sense, atheist philosopher Thomas Nagel can't shake the belief that "good" and "bad" are more than individual personal preferences. For Nagel, that pain is really bad and pleasure is really good "is just how they glaringly seem to me, however hard I try to imagine the contrary, and I suspect the same is true of most people."[25]

Grounding Morality in God

In search for answers to our deepest questions, like those concerning morality and the meaning of life, moving beyond science and culture is necessary. The philosopher Alasdair MacIntyre has argued that we must have an understanding of what something is designed for in order for moral evaluations to be considered factual statements.[26] For example, what do we mean when we consider a watch to be "good"? A positive evaluation relies on an understanding of the purpose of a watch. If we think a watch is designed to serve as a weapon, we will evaluate the watch differently than if we understand the watch to be made for telling time. Understanding an object's purpose is essential for knowing whether it is "good" or "bad." In making ethical evaluations, the same is true. Understanding the purpose for which humans were created is essential for moral realism.[27]

Looking to a transcendent, personal, and good agent beyond this world as the one who has designed the world and gives ultimate meaning to our lives is the simplest and most coherent explanation for the full range of moral truth. Once again, while this argument could be used in support of other forms of theism, the human need for value, moral obligation, and purpose in life fits seamlessly within the Christian story of reality.

---

25. Nagel, *Mind and Cosmos*, 110. For a strong argument against the ability of naturalism to ground certain moral categories, which are now almost universally assumed in the Western world, see Christian Smith, "Does Naturalism Warrant a Moral Belief in Universal Benevolence and Human Rights?" in *The Believing Primate: Scientific, Philosophical, and Theological Reflections on the Origins of Religion*, ed. Jeffrey Schloss and Michael Murray (Oxford: Oxford University Press, 2011), 292–317.

26. See Alasdair MacIntyre, *After Virtue*, 3rd ed. (Notre Dame: University of Notre Dame Press, 2007), 55–60.

27. MacIntyre uses an analogy of a hypothetical culture that loses a coherent framework for science while still retaining scientific terminology, which serves to illustrate the current cultural situation in which moral language has been retained without a larger teleological framework. In the absence of such a framework, the moral language ceases to be coherent (see MacIntyre, *After Virtue*, 1–5).

Considering the Possibilities for Morality

Philosophers David Baggett and Jerry Walls describe the way one might humbly ask someone to consider the possibilities for moral grounding.

> Take a look at this world and see what you can do by way of explaining morality and its distinctive features, and don't be surprised if you find that you can make some progress. But then, remind yourself of the fuller range of moral facts in need of explanation—values and duties to be sure, but also moral freedom, knowledge, responsibility, moral regrets, shame, forgiveness, the prescriptive power and rational authority of morality, the desire for the congruence of happiness and holiness, the needed resources for moral transformation, human dignity and equality and worth—and ask yourself this question: What better explains this full range of moral facts? This world alone? Or the conjunction of this world and its Creator, who made us in his image, created us for a purpose, invested us with the capacity for empathy and rationality and moral apprehension?[28]

For Further Reading

Hunter, James Davison and Paul Nedelisky. "Where the New Science of Morality Goes Wrong." *Hedgehog Review* 18, no. 2 (Fall 2016): 48–62.

Keller, Timothy. "Problem of Morals." Pages 176–92 in *Making Sense of God: An Invitation to the Skeptical.* New York: Viking, 2016.

MacIntyre, Alasdair C. *After Virtue: A Study in Moral Theory.* 3rd ed. Notre Dame, IN: University of Notre Dame Press, 2007.

Skeel, David. "Justice." Pages 109–36 in *True Paradox: How Christianity Makes Sense of Our Complex World.* Downers Grove, IL: InterVarsity, 2014.

Smith, Christian. "Does Naturalism Warrant a Moral Belief in Universal Benevolence and Human Rights?" Pages 292–317 in *The Believing Primate: Scientific, Philosophical, and Theological Reflections on the Origins of Religion.* Edited by Jeffrey Schloss and Michael Murray. Oxford: Oxford University Press, 2011.

What Is the Best Explanation for the Numerous Eyewitness Accounts of Miracles?

Countless people throughout history and across the world testify to the reality of miracles. Many of these eyewitnesses to miracles are well educated,

---

28. David Baggett and Jerry L. Walls, *God and Cosmos: Moral Truth and Human Meaning* (New York: Oxford University Press, 2016), 77.

reputable, and even, in many cases, once skeptical of miracles.[29] Yet many people deny that these accounts of miracles could have happened. How, then, do we account for these phenomena? What is the best explanation for this multitude of eyewitness accounts of miracles?

Some would say the best explanation is that miracles cannot happen, so they do not happen. As we saw in chapter 4, the influential eighteenth-century Scottish skeptic David Hume claimed that one could never be confident in the actual occurrence of a miracle because a miracle would violate the laws of nature. He argues, "A miracle is a violation of the laws of nature; and as a firm and unalterable experience has established these laws, the proof against a miracle, from the very nature of the fact, is as entire as any argument from experience can possibly be imagined."[30] Any alleged miracle is not to be believed, since it defies the most obvious and universal observations regarding the laws of nature. A major problem with Hume's argument is its circularity. Hume argues deductively excluding a priori any evidence for miracles. Thus, he employs one set of observed experiences (natural laws) to disallow other attested experiences (miracles).[31]

> The miracles in fact are a retelling in small letters of the very same story which is written across the whole world in letters too large for some of us to see.
>
> C. S. Lewis, "Miracles," in God in the Dock

Others would simply assert that since supernatural occurrences cannot be proven empirically, that is, they are not repeatable and testable, they cannot be accepted as true. Theoretically, even if a miracle happened, it could not be believed since it could not be scientifically confirmed. (Of course, we'd want to reply, as we have already seen in chapter 12, that science is only one limited way to confirm truth.)

For those who are skeptical of miracles, it seems that any naturalistic explanation for apparently miraculous occurrences is more credible than a supernatural one. How do the skeptical explain the innumerable testimonies of miracles in so many different locations and eras? There are several proposed explanations. One explanation is *fraud*. People are simply lying. For whatever reason—perhaps fame, power, or money—they make up stories about miracles. A second explanation

---

29. Richard L. Purtill defines a miracle as "an event (1) brought about by the power of God that is (2) a temporary (3) exception (4) to the ordinary course of nature (5) for the purpose of showing that God has acted in history" ("Defining Miracles," in *In Defense of Miracles: A Comprehensive Case for God's Action in History*, ed. R. Douglas Geivett and Gary Habermas [Downers Grove, IL: InterVarsity, 1997], 72). For well-documented and carefully researched accounts of miracles, see Craig S. Keener, *Miracles: The Credibility of the New Testament Accounts*, vols. 1–2 (Grand Rapids: Baker Academic, 2011).

30. David Hume, "Of Miracles," in *In Defense of Miracles*, 33.

31. See Keener, *Miracles*, 161–62.

is *hallucinations*. People under great stresses and mental pressures sometimes think they actually see things that in reality are not truly there. A third involves *psychosomatic healings*. The mind has an incredible power to convince itself of illnesses and healings. Sometimes mental factors cause a person to perceive that they have been miraculously healed. A fourth explanation is *wish fulfillment*. People simply deeply desire to experience a miracle. They want to live in a world in which God invades the natural and normal processes of life to work a fantastic deliverance or provision for them or their loved ones. Belief in miracles gives them hope in a difficult world.

Are the above the best explanations for miracles? Some of the points are indeed valid: (1) Miracles are not normal events. If they were normal, no one would consider the event a miracle. (2) Miracles by nature are not repeatable. They cannot be placed in a test tube, so to speak, and proven empirically. (3) Fraud, hallucinations, psychosomatic healings, and wish fulfillment no doubt account for some so-called miracles. Not every claimed miracle is actually a miracle.

Yet these naturalistic explanations do not adequately account for the incalculable number of miracles. One might explain away some miracles, but surely there must be a better explanation for the myriads of eyewitness testimony to a massive number of miracles. The powerful personal experiences and testimonies of reliable witnesses are not so easily explained away. A better take on these supernatural occurrences is that many of them are pointers to a reality beyond this world. Surely natural laws encompass what normally happens, but we go too far when we insist it cannot be otherwise. The laws of nature are not actually laws at all. The laws of nature are not unbreakable rules; rather, natural laws are what normally happens.

Both natural laws and divine miracles have a common source, namely, the Creator. When God works the supernatural, he does so by infusing something new within nature so that he signals his presence in the world. C. S. Lewis writes, "The divine art of miracle is not an art of suspending the pattern to which events conform but of feeding new events into that pattern."[32] Once the miraculous act occurs, the laws of nature, after assimilating the supernatural event into their natural processes, resume functioning normally. Thus, through a miracle, the Creator of nature signals his transcendent, supernatural power and his caring presence within the natural world.

---

32. C. S. Lewis, *Miracles: A Preliminary Study* (New York: Macmillan, 1947), 72.

Signposts and the "Immanent Frame"

Recall Charles Taylor's explanation of the "immanent frame," in which people are no longer inclined to see nature as pointing to transcendence (see chapter 10). If the plausibility of natural arguments for Christianity "is shaped by cultural pressures and imaginative constructions which ultimately transcend the rational arguments which underlie it,"[33] as Taylor's work suggests, then how do these signposts in this chapter function within the apologetic tools you have learned so far? Alister McGrath offers an answer in light of Taylor's work that parallels the meta-argument of chapters 11–13 in this book: "The best way of engaging a closed reading of the 'immanent frame' would thus seem to be to provide an imaginatively compelling alternative, which is seen to have rational plausibility."[34] He then adds:

> We need to break the "spell" of a closed world system, and open up alternative readings of our world— and perhaps that is best done, not by rational argument, but by capturing the cultural imagination with a richer and deeper vision of reality—in short, a "re-imagined nature" . . . This re-orientation will not arise from the cold certainties of closed logical argument, but from the open imaginative embrace of a luminous and compelling vision of truth, beauty, and goodness which stands at the heart of the Christian faith.

McGrath is not discounting reason (see his statement concerning "rational plausibility"). His point is that we do not need less than reason; we need more than reason.

For Further Reading

Craig, William Lane. "The Problem of Miracles." Pages 247–83 in *Reasonable Faith: Christian Truth and Apologetics.* Wheaton, IL: Crossway, 2008.

Keener, Craig S. *Miracles: The Credibility of the New Testament Accounts.* 2 vols. Grand Rapids: Baker Academic, 2011.

Lennox, John C. "Are Miracles Pure Fantasy?" Pages 165–84 in *Gunning for God: Why the New Atheists are Missing the Target.* Oxford: Lion Hudson, 2011.

Lewis, C. S. *Miracles: A Preliminary Study.* New York: Macmillan, 1947.

THE GREATEST STORY EVER TOLD

So far in this chapter, we have traced how observations and experiences can point to a transcendent reality beyond our universe, which is, of course, assumed

---

33. Alister E. McGrath, *Re-Imagining Nature: The Promise of a Christian Natural Theology* (West Sussex, UK: Wiley Blackwell, 2017), 143.

34. McGrath, *Re-imagining Nature*, 143.

within the Christian worldview. Each of the questions and explanations that followed can assist in opening the door to consider the distinctive aspects of the Christian story.

As we explored in chapter 8, stories "provide a vital framework for experiencing the world," and they "provide a means by which views of the world may be challenged."[35] They have a way to get under our skin. The deep questions of life—such as (1) Who are we? (2) What is the problem with the world, and what is its solution? and (3) Where are we going?—are not simply answered with isolated statements or logical syllogisms, but with stories that seep into our bones and powerfully shape our daily lives.[36]

The Christian story, told and embraced in life-changing ways in incredible numbers over the past two thousand years, has provided powerful answers to these universal questions, which even nonbelievers have noted. For the French philosopher Luc Ferry, the Christian story is extraordinarily profound and "not easy to resist."[37] Yet he says its problem is that it is "too good to be true."[38] For the British writer Julian Barnes, the potency of Christianity can be attributed to the beauty of the gospel story, even though it is a "beautiful lie," a "supreme fiction."[39] The following sections survey how you might tell this story, not as a lie, but as the true answer to life's universal questions.

Who Are We?

We are made by God in his image in the world God created for us, which means we have inherent value, meaning, and purpose. We were designed to live in right relationship to God, devoted to him and enjoying and stewarding his good gift of creation.

Despite the fairly obvious observation that natural abilities differ among humans, the Christian story affirms that we all have equal dignity as God's image bearers. We are not ultimately determined by biology or culture; the choices and purpose that humans instinctively assume are not illusions. Our Creator is not an impersonal force residing within the structure of the universe, like the *logos* of Greek philosophy, but instead a God who is both personal and separate from his creation. The climax of history is God entering into creation as a man, the God-Man, both affirming the goodness of creation and displaying his personal love for creation.

---

35. N. T. Wright, *The New Testament and the People of God* (Minneapolis: Fortress, 1992), 39.

36. These questions are inspired by Wright's four worldview questions. See *New Testament and the People of God*, 123.

37. Ferry, *Brief History of Thought*, 77.

38. Ferry, *Brief History of Thought*, 11

39. Julian Barnes, *Nothing to Be Frightened Of* (2008; repr., New York: Vintage, 2009), 53, 58.

Jesus himself is also the picture of the human ideal. As the faithful one, he loves the creation and the Father perfectly. He combines authority with compassion, and justice with mercy. He displays the freedom found in obedience. In short, he is the fulfillment and example of what humans were to be. He did what we fail to do, which leads us to the problem.

What Is the Problem with the World, and What Is Its Solution?

An almost universal intuition exists among people that something has gone wrong. Things are not as they should be. Some have suggested that religion itself is the problem. For example, John Lennon's song "Imagine" famously asks us to imagine a world with no religion, with the result being people living in peace. On several accounts, however, this fails to correspond with what can be observed about the world.

First, sociologists have increasingly emphasized that religion is not going away. The simplified secularization theories—suggesting that with the increase of modernization, religion would cease to exist—have been shown to be basically wrong.[40] Moreover, fascinating demographic work has been done by secular scholars who have predicted that the current trajectory will continue forward with the worldwide growth of conservative religions.[41]

Second, attempts to banish religion have often turned bloody.[42] The violence against religion in recent history has been featured in the French Revolution, in the Spanish Civil War, in the Soviet Union, and in China. These projects not only were ultimately unsuccessful in eradicating religion, but "peace" does not appear to be an apt description of the attempts to eliminate religion or the term normally associated with the names of such figures as Stalin and Pol Pot.

Yet in the cultural idea that Lennon gives expression to, there is something we can affirm. Religions—and, we would also add, any type of ideology—are prone to produce enmity and, given certain conditions, even violence. If one group believes themselves to be morally superior or more advanced, it seems nearly impossible for them not to look down on others and resent them for perceived defects. We have noted in the previous chapter that Christians themselves have not been immune to such failures. But even in an era that lauds tolerance and

---

40. See, for example, Peter Berger, who admits that a straightforward decline of religious belief, which he and other sociologists predicted, has not happened (*The Many Altars of Modernity: Toward a Paradigm for Religion in a Pluralist Age* [Berlin: De Gruyter, 2014]); see also Rodney Stark, *The Triumph of Faith: Why the World Is More Religious Than Ever* (Wilmington, DE: ISI, 2015).

41. See, for example, Eric Kaufmann, *Shall the Religious Inherit the Earth? Demography and Politics in the Twenty-First Century* (London: Profile Books, 2011).

42. See John Lennox's chapter "Is Atheism Poisonous?" in *Gunning for God: Why the New Atheists Are Missing the Target* (Oxford: Lion House, 2011), 83–95.

diversity, we hear much about being "on the wrong side of history" or the "evils of intolerance." As becomes clear upon reflection, these are judgmental expressions that exclude those who don't believe in secular progress. Exclusion, enmity, and feelings of superiority seem almost unavoidable. So we do have a problem. The deep-seated animosity toward others—which in too many cases produces wars, genocides, and destruction on earth—signals that something has gone terribly wrong. What is the solution?

The Christian claim is that the heart of the solution is not a series of abstract beliefs or an ideology, but rather a person. Jesus told his disciples to put away their swords. He taught, "Blessed are the peacemakers" (Matt 5:9). He charged his listeners to turn the other cheek. He called on his followers not to simply love those who love them but to love their enemies as well. Jesus willingly went to the cross to save the world and then prayed that those who were killing him would be forgiven. In other words, at the very heart of the Christian message is sacrifice and love for the stranger, for those who are different, for enemies. The core of the Christian story is not just a message, but a person who undermines the human inclination toward coercion and condescension.

However, the problem is not *simply* that we treat others poorly. The issue is actually much deeper; we have rebelled against our Creator. The result is a disordered creation. Our fundamental problem is vertical, which results in the horizontal issues we see all around us. Cut off from God, we are ill-equipped for our purpose and calling as image bearers. Jesus came to save us from our own self-absorption and impending judgment by restoring us to God. He came not only to show us how to flourish as humans, but also to *enable us* to live truly meaningful lives. And these meaningful lives are lives characterized by mercy and grace. Pride, which so often accompanies deep convictions and if unchecked can scornfully look down on others, is undercut the more people understand that they were in this dire position, only to be saved by the mercy of God.

In summary, the solution is that God, as a loving Father, has acted. He has not sat on the sidelines, simply to condemn creation or leave it to spiral into death and misery. God has entered into the world, in the person of Jesus, to absorb the cost of rebellion and to destroy evil to make this world right. His Spirit resides in those who turn from their self-absorption and pledge allegiance to their rightful Lord, in order to live eternally in right relation to God and the creation he is redeeming.

Where Are We Going?

The Christian story offers the answer to the inescapable problem of a universal desire, which Luc Ferry describes as the issue that all humans are attempting to come to terms with: to "be understood, to be loved, not to be alone, not to be separated from our loved ones—in short, not to die and not to have them die on us."[43] He recounts Edgar Allen Poe's poem "The Raven," and the bird's famous line, "Nevermore," as a powerful illustration of the existential terror that death brings. "Poe is suggesting that death means *everything that is unrepeatable*. Death is, *in the midst of life*, that which will not return; that which belongs irreversibly to time past, which we have no hope of ever recovering."[44]

Death casts a shadow over all of life. Death is seen in every idyllic experience of our childhood that we can never get back. Death is every mistake we have made that can never be reversed. Death is every friend, child, or loved one we have buried. We never get to go back. They are gone. Death is the future. It is our inevitable fate. Utter silent darkness. Cut off from all we love. All we hold dear. The finality of love and relationships is what makes death so intolerable.

The belief that death ushers in an impersonal existence absent of consciousness or the belief that death is just nothingness provides little to no solace. In contrast, in Christianity the darkness is ultimately banished. Instead, the believer is offered eternal relationships with God and others in mutual love. The resurrection promises that the loves in this world, the things we love in right relation to God, are not only meaningful; they will exist forever. Death cannot touch such love. Jesus' resurrection points us forward to God's redemption of both the world and individuals, real human beings—body, face, voice, personality. This non-ending is a fully embodied eternal salvation. Love will not end at death. God will undo death. He will reverse what seems irreversible.

But is it too good to be true? As Julian Barnes admits, the gospel is a beautiful story. But is it a lie? Ferry concedes, "Amongst the available doctrines of salvation, nothing can compete with Christianity—provided, that is, that you are a believer."[45] Later he adds, "Were it to be true I would . . . certainly be a taker."[46] One of our jobs as apologists is to ask the question, "But what if it *is* true?" One of our goals would then be for the unbeliever to respond, "It would be nice if that story were true, but too bad there are no good reasons to believe it is." An appreciation of the beauty of the story can be a first step to belief in the veracity of the story. Awakening the imagination can lead to an openness to the reasons to believe.

What are some of the reasons for believing this story? This chapter started out by surveying some of the signposts that point beyond contemporary secular

43. Ferry, *Brief History of Thought*, 4.
44. Ferry, *Brief History of Thought*, 5, emphasis in original.
45. Ferry, *Brief History of Thought*, 261.
46. Ferry, *Brief History of Thought*, 263.

narratives, with the purpose of opening doors for the gospel. Keeping the sign-posts from the opening section of this chapter in mind, we now turn to some historical signposts from the climax of the Christian narrative to provide a model to persuade others that it is both a beautiful and a *true* story.

For Further Reading

Vanhoozer, Kevin J. *The Drama of Doctrine: A Canonical-Linguistic Approach to Christian Theology.* Louisville: Westminster John Knox, 2005.

Wax, Trevin. "The Gospel Story." Pages 23–42 in *Counterfeit Gospels: Rediscovering the Good News in a World of False Hope.* Chicago: Moody, 2011.

Wright, N. T. *Simply Christian: Why Christianity Makes Sense.* San Francisco: HarperOne, 2006.

JESUS' DEATH AND RESURRECTION

When discussing any event in ancient history, 100 percent proof is not on the table for anyone. That is just not how historical evidence for the ancient world works. And do not forget, there is no such thing as a neutral observer, especially when approaching a question with such high-stakes implications. We should avoid portraying ourselves as unbiased or calling on unbelievers to be impartial. We can, however, seek to be fair, and we can ask the unbeliever to try to approach the Christian claim with as much fairness as possible.

The Story of Jesus' Resurrection Would Have Been Too Counterintuitive to Simply Be Made Up
An Unexpected Death

Due to the wide attestation, almost all New Testament scholars today agree that Jesus died at the hands of the Romans by crucifixion.[47] In contrast, Jewish scholars before Jesus arrived did not seem to have been expecting the true Messiah to die on a cross. This is why it would have been strange to first-century ears to hear the disciples continue to proclaim that Jesus was the messianic King after he was shamefully crucified. This death was reserved for the most

---

47. Numerous Christian and non-Christian sources record the death of Jesus. See Tacitus, *Annals of Imperial Rome* 15.44 (AD 115); Flavius Josephus, *Antiquity of the Jews* 18.3 (AD 93); Mara bar Serapion in a letter to his son (likely late first century AD); possibly the Babylonian Talmud, Sanhedrin 43a (circa second century AD); Mark, Matthew, Luke-Acts, John, 1 Corinthians.

despised criminals. No Jews in their right minds would have imagined that the long-awaited Jewish King would die on a cross, not even Jesus' own disciples.

The disciples' repeated failure to understand Jesus' statements concerning his death was because they apparently, along with other first-century Jews, believed that Jesus would do the normal things expected of the coming Messiah—serve as a national deliverer, perhaps engage in military victory, and set up a visible kingdom on earth—not die a dishonorable death on a cross. Since they didn't see his death coming, this of course meant they didn't see the resurrection coming either.

A Counterintuitive Claim: Resurrection

The work of scholars such as N. T. Wright has shown that the resurrection of Jesus was an unpopular notion with first-century Jews and Greeks—not the sort of thing one would make up in an attempt to start a movement. The dominant non-Jewish view was that bodily resurrection was impossible and unwanted. They believed the soul was good, and the physical body was bad.

Many Jews, on the other hand, looked forward to a future bodily resurrection; however, this resurrection was a corporate resurrection of *all the righteous*, not just one particular person.[48] What is more, this future resurrection was thought to occur along with the renewal of the entire world. It was not thought of as a single individual in the middle of history while the problems of the world continued to unfold.

Here is the key: The disciples simply would not have made up the story of Jesus' resurrection, because people were not expecting the Messiah first to be killed and then to rise from the dead. Neither Jews nor Greeks would have been naturally open to the idea.[49] Moreover, we know from history that Jesus was not the first would-be Messiah to gather a following, only to be executed. Nevertheless, as N. T. Wright observes:

> In not one single case do we hear the slightest mention of the disappointed followers claiming that their hero had been raised from the dead. They knew better. "Resurrection" was not a private event. It involved human bodies. There would have to be an empty tomb somewhere. A Jewish revolutionary whose leader had been executed by the authorities, and who

---

48. The examples of Lazarus being resuscitated from the dead and Herod Antipas thinking Jesus was John the Baptist "raised from the dead" are different from Jesus' resurrection. Jesus did not rise again only to one day grow old and die again. Instead, the claim was that Jesus was resurrected to an eternal glorified body.

49. For an extensive work on the Jewish and non-Jewish worldview concerning resurrection, see N. T. Wright, *The Resurrection of the Son of God* (Minneapolis: Fortress, 2003).

managed to escape arrest himself, had two options: give up the revolution or find another leader . . . Claiming that the original leader was alive again was simply not an option.

Unless, of course, he was.[50]

Counterintuitive Witnesses

It is also odd for a first-century context that in each of the four gospels, women were presented as the first eyewitnesses to the risen Jesus. At this time, women were not believed to give trustworthy testimony on important matters, which is why they were not allowed to testify in a court of law.[51] How would the public respond to an unpopular doctrine being propagated by people who did not culturally count as witnesses? It surely would not have helped. It would be counterintuitive to invent a story in this way, with the hope of it catching on, unless, of course, the various reports were all in agreement with this culturally uncomfortable detail because it was the way it actually happened.

More Than Five Hundred People Saw the Resurrected Jesus, and Some of Them Were Skeptical Prior to What They Witnessed
Multiple Appearances

Peter, James, Paul, and at one time more than five hundred people claimed to have seen the resurrected Jesus. Paul writes in 1 Corinthians 15 that the appearance to five hundred was just one of many times people saw Jesus and that many of these witnesses were still alive, which meant Paul's claim could have easily been invalidated if these witnesses weren't really around.

While it has been argued that Jesus' followers were in such a state of grief that they hallucinated, this does not explain why so many people at different times had the same hallucination. As projections of the mind, hallucinations are singular and subjective events. Regarding mass hallucinations—in which people in a group hallucinate the same image—modern psychologists have provided little scientific evidence to substantiate such occurrences.[52] Nor does grief explain why Paul, a committed Jewish leader who was persecuting Christians and clearly not grieving, would have hallucinated. Nor does the hallucination theory explain why the body was not produced by the authorities, who had the power and motive to extract the body to end this new movement.

---

50. N. T. Wright, *Who Was Jesus?* (Grand Rapids: Eerdmans, 1993), 63.

51. See Richard Bauckham, *Gospel Women: Studies of the Named Women in the Gospels* (Grand Rapids: Eerdmans, 2002), 268–77; cf. Wright, *Resurrection of the Son of God*, 607.

52. For modern research on hallucinations, see André Aleman and Frank Larøi, *Hallucinations: The Science of Idiosyncratic Perception* (Washington, DC: American Psychological Association, 2008).

Unlikely Disciples

Paul, the persecutor of the church, who was suddenly changed. Paul was an active persecutor of the church, and from his own testimony (and from Luke's in Acts) he claims to have had an encounter with the risen Jesus. Instantaneously, Paul went from an active persecutor to a bold proclaimer of the gospel. Paul was so convinced he had experienced the risen Jesus that for the rest of his life, he suffered both spiritually and physically for the sake of the gospel.

James the brother of Jesus—the skeptic turned believer. From the gospels we learn that Jesus' brother James was unbelieving during the time of Jesus' ministry (Mark 3:21, 31; 6:3–4; John 7:5). However, following Jesus' death and resurrection, James is reported as being not only a believer but a prominent Christian leader in Jerusalem. In 1 Corinthians 15:3–8, the early creedal passage, Jesus is said to have appeared to his brother James. We also know from Acts 15 and Galatians 1 that James became a leader of the church of Jerusalem. Furthermore, James not only became a believer and a leader, but he also, according to Josephus and other sources, became a martyr for the faith.

No Body Was Produced

If the resurrection claim had been made up, it would have been counterintuitive for the story to have begun in Jerusalem, as it did. The locale where Jesus died and was buried would have been the easiest place to disprove the claim of resurrection. All the Jewish or Roman authorities had to do was produce the body.

Some have sought to explain the inability to produce the corpse by arguing that Roman policy didn't allow the crucified to be buried, and thus Jesus' body was likely eaten by animals or discarded after death. In other words, there was no body left to produce. In some parts of the Roman Empire, and especially during wartime, the bodies of those executed were indeed regularly left on their crosses to rot or to be eaten by animals. But if this was normally how the Romans treated the Jews in and around Jerusalem, it seems the authorities would have offered an obvious reply to the Christian claim of an empty tomb: "*Of course* there is no body in the tomb because *he was never allowed to be buried*! Everyone knows that the standard operating procedure is to not allow the crucified to be buried." If it was a common practice at that time in Jerusalem, this would have been the obvious response to the claim of resurrection and an empty tomb.[53] Yet this is not how the authorities or Christian critics responded, apparently because it was common knowledge that the Romans normally allowed the Jews

---

53. For more on this discussion, see Craig A. Evans, "Getting the Burial Traditions and Evidences Right," in *How God Became Jesus: The Real Origin of Belief in Divine Nature—A Response to Bart D. Ehrman*, ed. Michael F. Bird (Grand Rapids: Zondervan, 2014), 74–75.

around Jerusalem to bury their dead. Instead, the story was circulated that the body had been stolen, which makes sense as a response if the body was actually missing from the tomb.

The Early Disciples Would Have Had Little to Gain and Much to Lose by Advocating for an Unpopular Story, So What Was Their Motive?
Dying for Your Own Lie?

If the disciples made up such a claim, why would they carry the deception so far? The apostles and early Christians were persecuted for their beliefs. Stephen was stoned (Acts 6–8); Herod Agrippa killed James the brother of John (Acts 12:1–2; supported by Josephus, *Antiquities* 20.200); and Nero sponsored the first statewide persecution in the early 60s (see Tacitus, *Annals* 15.37–41). Paul recounts how he experienced extreme persecution (2 Cor 6:4–9), and most scholars accept the tradition that he was martyred in the 60s (1 Clement 5:5–7; Eusebius, *Historia ecclesiastica* 2.25.5–8). According to Acts 5:17–42, Peter and John were sent to prison and flogged. John 21:18–19 implies that it was well-known by the time John's gospel was written that Peter died as a martyr.[54] It is difficult to see why Jesus' earliest followers would have been willing to endure such persecution if they knew themselves to be suffering for a hoax they invented. Thus, Gary Habermas emphasizes the long-standing and still incisive historical point:

> Virtually no one, friend or foe, believer or critic, denies that it was their convictions that they had seen the resurrected Jesus that caused the disciples' radical transformations. They were willing to die *specifically for their resurrection belief.* Down through the centuries many have been willing to give their lives for political or religious causes. But the crucial difference here is that while many have died for their *convictions*, Jesus' disciples were in the right place to know the truth or falsity of the event for which they were willing to die.[55]

A Radical Transformation

To offer a historical explanation for these events surrounding the origins of Christianity, one must be able to explain, as Craig Blomberg writes, "how a small band of defeated followers of Jesus were transformed almost overnight into

---

54. Eckhard J. Schnabel documents some of the persecution the early Christians experienced (*Early Christian Mission* [Downers Grove, IL: InterVarsity, 2004], 2:1533–38).

55. Gary R. Habermas, "The Resurrection Appearances of Jesus," in *Evidence for God: 50 Arguments for Faith from the Bible, History, Philosophy, and Science*, ed. William A. Dembski and Michael R. Licona (Grand Rapids: Baker, 2010), 174–75, emphasis in original.

bold witnesses, risking death by proclaiming his bodily resurrection before many of the same people who fifty days earlier had participated in his crucifixion."[56] Remember, a prominent alternative narrative is that the early disciples had to make up the idea of a raised Jesus. But where would this novel idea have arisen from? There was no precedent in Judaism for a raised Messiah. For those who believed in resurrection, it was something that happens for all the faithful at the end of history rather than for a single man in the middle of history. Thus, there was no clear context to formulate this idea. Unless, of course, an actual event generated it.

WORSHIPING A MAN: A Jewish Paradigm Shift That Happened Too Fast

The worship of a crucified and resurrected Messiah was scandalous in the first-century world and calls for an explanation. To Jews, it was blasphemy to worship a human. And as New Testament scholar Michael Bird has explained, "To Greeks, worshiping a man recently raised from the dead was like doing obeisance to the first zombie you met in a zombie apocalypse."[57]

While there could possibly be occasional exceptions in the Jewish community, devout first-century Jews—such as the very first disciples—were strict monotheists. In other words, they only worshiped one God, the Creator of all things.[58] These were not pagans who worshiped many gods. And they were not Jews who had radically departed from one of the most central verses in the Hebrew Scriptures: "The LORD our God, the LORD is one" (Deut 6:4). And yet, quite remarkably, they worshiped Jesus!

And it is important to note, Jesus was not worshiped as some kind of special angel. Angels do not create. This was a function of God in the Hebrew Scriptures. But it is clear that in some of the earliest biblical texts we have, Jesus *does* create (e.g., 1 Cor 8:4–6; Col 1:15–20). Angels are not to be worshiped (Rev 19:10; 22:8–9), yet Jesus was worshiped in the early church because his followers viewed him as sharing in the divine identity with God the Father (e.g., Heb 1; Rev 1:4–5).[59]

This devotion began almost immediately rather than growing over a long, gradual process. The historian Larry Hurtado emphasizes the point that the early disciples "define and reverence Jesus with reference to the one God" and explains

---

56. Craig L. Blomberg, "Jesus of Nazareth: How Historians Can Know Him and Why It Matters," Gospel Coalition, http://thinkingmatters.org.nz/wp-content/uploads/2011/07/JESUS-OF-NAZARETH.pdf.

57. Michael F. Bird, "Of Gods, Angels, and Men," in *How God Became Jesus*, 26–27.

58. See Deuteronomy 6:4; Isaiah 45:5–7; 2 Maccabees 1:24–25; Romans 11:36; 1 Corinthians 8:4–6.

59. See Richard Bauckham, *Jesus and the God of Israel:* God Crucified *and Other Studies on the New Testament's Christology of Divine Identity* (Grand Rapids: Eerdmans, 2008).

further that "we see the powerful effect of Jewish monotheism, combining with a strong impetus to reverence Jesus in unprecedented ways."[60]

How did such a dramatic paradigm shift happen so fast? What motivated this almost immediate shift? Such shifts in thinking normally come in gradual stages, but the evidence suggests that these conservative Jewish disciples made the shift rapidly. You should not make the mistake of thinking it was only one thing that caused the almost immediate shift. The reflection on the claims and actions of Jesus together with a close rereading of the Hebrew Scriptures were part of the impetus behind this shift. But their rereading of the Scriptures, their reevaluating of their previous understanding of Jesus' teaching, and—most importantly—their worship of Jesus is difficult to imagine without a dramatic paradigm shifting *event*. So while unbelievers will offer various theories to counter the historical evidence surrounding the question of Christian origins, once combined, the strands of history weave together to present a powerful case for the resurrection.

For Further Reading

Bird, Michael F., ed. *How God Became Jesus: The Real Origins of Belief in Jesus' Divine Nature—A Response to Bart D. Ehrman.* Grand Rapids: Zondervan, 2014.

Habermas, Gary R., and Michael R. Licona. *The Case for the Resurrection of Jesus.* Grand Rapids: Kregel, 2004.

Hurtado, Larry. *Lord Jesus Christ: Devotion to Jesus in Earliest Christianity.* Grand Rapids: Eerdmans, 2003.

Licona, Michael R. *The Resurrection of Jesus: A New Historiographical Approach.* Downers Grove, IL: InterVarsity, 2010.

Wright, N. T. *The Resurrection of the Son of God.* Minneapolis: Fortress, 2003.

CONCLUSION

I (Josh) once asked one of my students why he was so enthusiastic about apologetics. He immediately replied, "I want to crush atheists at their own intellectual game!" I asked, "Should that be the goal of *Christian* apologetics?" His smile suggested I had made my point. This short exchange stimulated my thinking beyond what we talked about in class that day. What does it mean to do *Christian* apologetics? Answering this question has been the aim of this book.

---

60. Larry Hurtado, *Lord Jesus Christ: Devotion to Jesus in Earliest Christianity* (Grand Rapids: Eerdmans, 2003), 151–52; see Bird, "Of Gods, Angels, and Men," 30.

Apologetics should start with the conviction that "Christian [apologetics] must arise from the gospel of Jesus Christ. Otherwise it could not be *Christian* [apologetics]."[61] The gospel is both the goal and the lens through which the apologetic task is approached. The gospel spurs us on to put others before ourselves; hence, the importance of an others-centered and holistic apologetic approach. This book has not presented every possible apologetic argument or question, but has rather introduced guiding emphases and modeled an approach that is flexible enough to adapt to any situation. As a survey book, this volume's purpose is to get you in the game. Now it's time for you to put your training into practice.

While apologetics should be contextual, it should also be formed out of the right context. A healthy church remains central to a healthy apologetic. Cruciform lives, functioning as apologetic portraits to the world around us, are not ultimately or primarily cultivated by attending weekend conferences, watching your favorite apologist on the internet, or even reading books like this. These are helps, but the church remains central to the formation of an apologist of the cross. The wisdom of the cross, so central in drawing the right apologetic map for the right situation, grows within the rich soil of God's people singing, reading, feasting, praying, and confessing around God's Word.

---

61. Oliver O'Donovan, *Resurrection and Moral Order: An Outline for Evangelical Ethics*, 2nd ed. (Grand Rapids: Eerdmans, 1994), 11, emphasis in original. Again we are appropriating this quote. Where we have bracketed *apologetics*, O'Donovan has the word *ethics*.

SCRIPTURE INDEX

SUBJECT INDEX

Abelard, Peter, 77
age of the spinmeister, 209
Agrippa, 193
Allberry, Sam, 260
Allison, Dale C. Jr., 113
analogy, 88–89
Anselm, 76
anthropocentric turn, 280
Aleman, André, 313
apocalypse, 56, 58, 60
apocalyptic, 20, 55–58
apologetic of glory, 16, 146–47, 162,
apologia, 15
Aquinas, Thomas, 77–79, 84, 88,
    100, 128
archbishop of Canterbury, 76
Arianism, 64
Aristotle, 82, 230, 297
Athens, 67, 72, 189–90, 216
Athenian, 58, 135, 162, 191–92
Augustine of Hippo, 64, 70–71,
    76–77, 84–87, 95, 100, 174,
    176–77, 243

Baggett, David, 303
Baker, Deanne-Peter, 128, 157
Balthasar, Hans Urs von, 100–101

Bahnsen, Greg, 119
Barnes, Julian, 307, 310
Barth, Karl, 99–101
basic logic, 111, 183–85, 225, 266
Bauckham, Richard, 39, 113,
    284–87, 313, 316
beauty, 240–42
Becker, Ernest, 230, 243
Bellah, Robert, 228, 252, 257
Bellarmine, Robert, 83
Berger, Peter, 156, 223–25, 308
Bettenson, Henry, 70
Bird, Michael, 314, 316–17
Bishop of Lyons, 64
Blomberg, Craig, 144, 287, 315–16
Bock, Darrell L., 21, 42, 43, 58,
    124, 144, 189, 287
Boethius, 74–75
Brooks, David, 167, 229, 245, 246
Brown, Peter, 145
Brown, Raymond E., 40
Bruce, F. F., 190
Brunner, Emil, 99
Brunner, Emil, 99
Butler, Joseph, 87–88, 92

Caecilius, 70